The Presidency and Domestic Policy

This book systematically examines the first terms of every president from FDR to Joe Biden and assesses the leadership style and policy agenda of each. Success in bringing about policy change is shown to hinge on the leadership style and skill in managing a variety of institutional and public relationships. Presidents are evaluated based on the level of opportunity they faced. The third edition of this timely book adds chapters on Donald Trump and Joe Biden and focuses on the significant domestic policy challenges of their respective times. For students of presidential history, leadership, and public policy, *The Presidency and Domestic Policy* provides unique insights into contemporary presidential leadership in a highly partisan age.

Michael A. Genovese received a Ph.D. from the University of Southern California in 1979. He holds the Loyola Chair of Leadership Studies and is Professor of Political Science, Director of the Institute for Leadership Studies, and President of the Global Policy Institute at Loyola Marymount University. He has been Fellow at Queens College, Oxford University. Professor Genovese has written over 50 books, numerous articles, and book chapters and has won over a dozen teaching awards, including the American Political Science Association's Distinguished Teaching Award.

Todd L. Belt received a Ph.D. from the University of Southern California in 2003. He is Professor and Director of the Political Management Master's Program in the Graduate School of Political Management at The George Washington University. Belt is the co-author of four books and has published over a dozen chapters in edited scholarly books and over two dozen articles appearing in academic journals. He was awarded the John W. Kluge Fellowship in Digital Studies at the Library of Congress and has held visiting positions at Wellesley College and Kyungpook University in Daegu, South Korea. He is the recipient of two teaching awards.

William W. Lammers (late) received a Ph.D. from the University of Minnesota in 1966. He was Professor of Political Science at the University of Southern California. He wrote several books on the presidency and was a noted authority on presidential politics and federal policies toward the aging.

The Presidency and Domestic Policy
Comparing Leadership Styles, FDR to Biden

Third Edition

Michael A. Genovese, Todd L. Belt, and William W. Lammers

NEW YORK AND LONDON

Designed cover image: "Details of the Resolute Desk are seen Friday, July 16, 2021, in the Oval Office of the White House. (Official White House Photo by Adam Schultz)". Wikimedia.org

Third edition published 2024
by Routledge
605 Third Avenue, New York, NY 10158

and by Routledge
4 Park Square, Milton Park, Abingdon, Oxon, OX14 4RN

Routledge is an imprint of the Taylor & Francis Group, an informa business

© 2024 Michael A. Genovese, Todd L. Belt, and William W. Lammers

The right of Michael A. Genovese, Todd L. Belt, and William W. Lammers to be identified as authors of this work has been asserted in accordance with sections 77 and 78 of the Copyright, Designs and Patents Act 1988.

All rights reserved. No part of this book may be reprinted or reproduced or utilised in any form or by any electronic, mechanical, or other means, now known or hereafter invented, including photocopying and recording, or in any information storage or retrieval system, without permission in writing from the publishers.

Trademark notice: Product or corporate names may be trademarks or registered trademarks and are used only for identification and explanation without intent to infringe.

First edition published by Paradigm Publishers, 2014
Second edition published by Routledge, 2016

ISBN: 978-1-032-72849-0 (hbk)
ISBN: 978-0-367-50874-6 (pbk)
ISBN: 978-1-003-42668-4 (ebk)

DOI: 10.4324/9781003426684

Typeset in Sabon
by Deanta Global Publishing Services, Chennai, India

This book is dedicated to:

Gabriela (from Michael)

and

Christine (from Todd)

Contents

Preface		*ix*
New to the Third Edition		*xi*
Acknowledgments		*xiii*

1	Strategies for Assessing Presidents	1

PART I
The High-Opportunity Presidents 25

2	Franklin D. Roosevelt: Artful Leadership during Hard Times	27
3	Lyndon B. Johnson: Legislative Leadership and a Credibility Gap	49
4	Ronald Reagan: One Big Year	69
5	George W. Bush: A Resolute Decider with a Co-President	90

PART II
The Moderate-Opportunity Presidents 111

6	Harry S. Truman: A Broker with Beliefs	113
7	Dwight D. Eisenhower: A Skilled Centrist	131
8	John F. Kennedy: A Quest for Heroic Leadership	150

viii *Contents*

9 Barack Obama: A Negotiator without a Partner   170

10 Donald Trump: Outsider, Disruptor, Norm-Buster,
    Dissembler   190

PART III
The Low-Opportunity Presidents   **215**

11 Richard Nixon: An Activist with an Enemies List   217

12 Jimmy Carter: An Outsider's Pursuit of "Trustee"
    Leadership   237

13 George H. W. Bush: A Reluctant Guardian   256

14 Bill Clinton: A Perpetual Campaigner under Siege   274

15 Joe Biden: Cleaning the Augean Stables   294

PART IV
Conclusion   **315**

16 Opportunity, Challenges, and Skill: Comparing the
    Presidents   317

    Index   *349*

Preface

In recent years, the job of promoting the general welfare of the republic's citizens has become increasingly difficult. Partisan polarization, in Congress and among the public, ramped up during the Clinton administration, further escalated during George W. Bush's two terms, reached staggering levels during Obama's time in office, and resulted in a type of open warfare during the Trump and Biden presidencies. How can a president lead in such an environment? Much depends upon the circumstances of the time, but also on the skill of the president.

Presidents of the United States are fascinating and widely varying individuals. Each brings to the White House a unique set of personal characteristics, policy preferences, and leadership style. And having attained the office, each governs in a distinct way. Presidents achieve varying degrees of success, and in some instances, they profoundly shape domestic policy. As a result of their efforts, achievements, and actions in office, their reputations vary from public admiration to disgrace.

But just how important are the differences among presidents, and just how much have individual presidents shaped policy? It is easy to overemphasize differences among presidents in the development of domestic policy. Constraints arising from weak electoral mandates, a weak economy, and the public mood for change have precluded some presidents from achieving landmark policy victories. For other presidents, the limits of a highly institutionalized office have restricted their choices of action. And then there is Congress, whose role in developing and shaping policy can be extensive and creative, in spite of the specific goals of the president.

Any understanding of presidential leadership and the formation of domestic policy thus must begin with a closer look at both individual leadership roles and the circumstances that shape opportunities for success. For that reason, the chapters in this book devoted to presidents who have served since 1933 combine a perspective on the individual president as well as a description of the circumstances under which each sought to make his mark. In this way, we hope to be sensitive to the unique qualities each

x *Preface*

president brought to the task of governing while controlling for the level of opportunity each faced. This perspective permits final comparisons of the strong and weak performers, consideration of the strategies that have worked under varying conditions, and an assessment of possible future leadership roles.

New to the Third Edition

The third edition of this book appears at the beginning of Joe Biden's first term. Biden attained office promising a return to normalcy from the exceptionally unique (if not chaotic) Trump presidency. For better or worse, Trump expanded our vision of what encompasses domestic policy, and his presidency caused a number of policy issues to move to the fore of the public agenda. Thus, the new edition of this book arrives at an auspicious time and includes the following attributes:

- Two new chapters, one on President Donald Trump and one on President Joe Biden.
- Updated tables, figures, and references throughout.
- Revised theoretical orientation, examination of each president, and conclusion that incorporates new material such as:
  ○ The increasing emphasis on judicial politics and appointments as a means of policymaking.
  ○ The politics and administrative repercussions of using "acting" heads of executive departments.
  ○ The use of social media as a tool of public, administrative, and congressional leadership.
  ○ The continuing relevance and increased salience of trade, immigration, and the environment as domestic policies.
  ○ The increasing use of administrative strategies to overcome partisan gridlock.
  ○ The growing ideological polarization of Congress, the public, and the media.
  ○ The politics of government shutdowns and increasing the debt ceiling.
  ○ Governing in an age of hyper-partisanship.
- A re-examination of the performance of prior presidents in light of the successes and failures of Presidents Donald Trump and Joe Biden.

xii *New to the Third Edition*

- A re-examination of presidents based on the long-term ramifications of their policies (such as crime policy and financial services reform under President Clinton).
- Updated bibliographic references.

We are honored to continue the legacy of William W. Lammers with this new edition.

Acknowledgments

Many people assisted in the completion of this work. The University of Southern California, Loyola Marymount University, the George Washington University, Wellesley College, and the University of Hawai'i at Hilo provided institutional support of great help. The expert research assistance by Katie McGrath, Brianna Brins, Dominique Easter-Green, Jennifer Trujillo, and Jordan "Kea" Calpito was indispensable. Helpful clerical assistance was provided by MacKenzie Burr and Clyde Ebanez. Finally, Jennifer Knerr, Leanne Hinves, and Jacqueline Dorsey at Routledge gave outstanding editorial support. To all of you, many thanks.

1 Strategies for Assessing Presidents

Presidents come to office promising great things, and citizens rightly expect results. Barack Obama rode a tide of hope into office with his promises of change. But his efforts were soon thwarted by unified Republican opposition in Congress. Donald Trump promised to "Make America great again," but his domestic agenda got side-tracked as he was unable to secure buy-in from his Republican majority in Congress. Democrats took over the House of Representatives after the 2018 midterm elections and Trump's agenda continued to go nowhere.

Despite formidable obstacles, citizens hold presidents responsible for a great many things beyond what they promise, including the health of the economy, the quality of the natural environment, and even world peace. And like Obama and Trump, all occupants of the White House face a number of roadblocks that inhibit their behavior and make governing a difficult art.[1] Given the public's high expectations and their own limited political resources, presidents must develop complex strategies to bridge this expectation–resource gap. If they fail to do so, they run the risk of political failure, voter disapproval, and electoral defeat. But presidents are not helpless. A wide range of options and opportunities are available to a politically astute, power-wise leader.[2]

In this book, we evaluate the styles and strategies presidents employ in their efforts to govern successfully. In doing so, it examines four dimensions of presidential activity—approaches to advisory processes and decision-making, administrative strategies, public leadership, and congressional leadership. All modern presidents (Franklin Roosevelt to Joe Biden)[3] are analyzed in the context of their respective domestic policy agendas. The book also looks at how different opportunity levels (high, moderate, and low) have affected presidential leadership and assesses how each president faced these varying circumstances.

For the purpose of our analysis, the level of opportunity is measured by extrinsic factors such as public demand, pro- or anti-government sentiments, issue ripeness, available resources, competing issues, and the

DOI: 10.4324/9781003426684-1

2 *Strategies for Assessing Presidents*

strength of the president's party in Congress. Factors more centered on the presidency itself are the size of a president's election victory, the issues over which the presidential contest was fought, and the president's popularity. Opportunity levels set reasonable expectations—that is, high-opportunity presidents should achieve more than low-opportunity presidents. What determines whether presidents achieve the political results their opportunity levels permit? *Skill.*

When presidents are categorized by opportunity level, it is easier to determine who the more skillful presidents are. We can also isolate which strategies and tactics employed to achieve their goals were the most successful. There is, however, one difficulty with this approach: although some objective indicators of presidential opportunity are available, ultimately the categorization is somewhat subjective.

If the level of opportunity establishes a possible range of presidential performances, the leadership style employed by presidents helps determine the public face and interactions they present to the people, Congress, and other political actors. Presidents display tremendous differences in their leadership styles. Some seek to emulate the aggressive style of President Franklin Roosevelt; others choose less assertive approaches. Leadership styles encompass *strategic choices*. Some presidents have sought to "hit the ground running"; others have been characterized as "hitting the ground stumbling" or even "marching in place."[4] In their public leadership, some presidents have sought to "go public" to build support for legislation.[5] Bill Clinton's enthusiasm for Theodore Roosevelt's use of the presidency as a "bully pulpit" to elicit public support for his programs led him to take to the road as president in a continuation, as it were, of his election campaign. Other presidents have sought less visible means, such as negotiations with congressional leaders, to achieve their goals. In another strategic choice, presidents frequently engage in policy shifts in the third year of their terms to reshuffle personnel and reshape the direction of their administration—as well as their re-election prospects.

In choosing a leadership style, presidents are influenced by a variety of factors, including their own personalities and prior career experiences. Many presidents rely on their historical favorites for views of how the president should lead. Some presidents have deliberately chosen a leadership style that contrasts with that of their predecessors. John Kennedy, for example, sought more assertive public leadership than that provided by Dwight Eisenhower. Carter strove to do away with the trappings of the "imperial presidency" and be a "man of the people." Reagan's short answer was to be the mirror image of Carter as he pursued a more optimistic persona and a more focused approach to his first-year agenda. George H. W. Bush showed an aversion to Reagan's limited attention to detail, and Clinton sought to have a more robust domestic agenda than his predecessor. Obama promised to have the most open and transparent administration in history, eschewing the secrecy of his predecessor and placing himself at the center of the decision-making process. The combination of presidential wishes to be different and the public's tendency to seek leaders who compensate for the problems of their predecessors has contributed to sharp swings in leadership styles from president to president.

The readily observed differences in leadership styles have not produced agreement among political scientists on how much these differences affect public policy.[6] Those who believe individual skill has a limited impact on policy outcomes have emphasized the extent to which presidential actions are shaped by other factors. These include the opportunities produced by power relationships in Congress, economic conditions, and levels of public support for new policy initiatives, among other things. And of course, a president's ability to make use of opportunity is predicated on the ability to accurately perceive the nature of the opportunity.[7]

In view of the uncertainty surrounding the impact of individual presidents on policy, it is time to take a harder look at the ways in which leadership styles and strategies have actually shaped policy outcomes. Far too often, passage of major legislation has been attributed to presidential leadership when it actually may have had little influence. During Franklin Roosevelt's years in the White House, for example, he frequently received credit for congressionally driven achievements.

While no two presidents serve under identical circumstances, a comparative approach can offer valuable insight into the extent to which leadership can make a difference. Such an approach requires assessing presidents' leadership styles and the strategies they pursued, as well as how well they were able to meet challenges and use opportunities effectively. The differences revealed can then be used to examine the impact of leadership styles on policy. The next section sets the stage for these analyses by describing the key concepts of leadership style, challenges and opportunities, and policy legacies.

Leadership Styles

In 1960, presidential scholar Richard Neustadt published a seminal study of presidential leadership.[8] The wide audience for the ideas he developed in Presidential Power included presidents themselves. Moreover, John Kennedy and several of his successors sought Neustadt's personal advice in organizing their presidencies. The lasting interest in Neustadt's ideas stems from his perspective of looking at presidential leadership from the vantage point of the presidents.

Neustadt's analysis was grounded in the view that the creation of Congress and the presidency as separate institutions with shared and overlapping powers usually makes it difficult for presidents to succeed with new policy initiatives. The leadership style prescribed by Neustadt

4 Strategies for Assessing Presidents

was closely modeled on the one used by Franklin Roosevelt. It called for presidents to pay careful attention to the manner in which their actions would affect their professional reputation, public prestige, and possible subsequent options. By shrewdly considering those factors in their leadership efforts, presidents would be better able to bargain effectively within the Washington community. Such presidents were powerful because they cared about and cultivated power, because they were attuned to what it took to have an impact on their political environment, and because they were well informed about that environment.[9]

More recent studies of presidential leadership have built on interpretations of leadership styles that Neustadt instigated. One found that recent presidents have used their public roles to put pressure on Congress rather than rely on their own bargaining roles within the Washington community.[10] Other studies have revealed that presidents display a broader range of leadership styles than the one envisioned by Neustadt, with his emphasis on FDR's approach. Greenstein's 1982 reassessment of Eisenhower, for example, paints a portrait of a president who employed a "hidden hand" leadership style. He engaged in few public quarrels on political issues, preferring instead to operate more actively and skillfully behind the scenes. This method largely escaped the notice of the public (and most political commentators) during his eight years in office.[11]

Other analysts, following up on Greenstein's work, have further explored the broad diversity in leadership styles. Some found that President Carter had a very distinct leadership style as he sought to provide "trustee" leadership by promoting measures he judged to be in the long-run public interest—such as a comprehensive energy package rather than proposals molded to short-run political calculations. In dealing with that orientation, Carter's congressional aides periodically wondered whether they would ever receive an easy issue to promote. Assessments of Reagan's leadership have often explored his "Teflon"-like ability to not have the negative fallout from some of the controversies that emerged from his administration stick to him. George W. Bush employed a more unilateral, "full speed ahead" approach, while Obama's cool style and nonconfrontational approach sometimes seemed out of place in the hyper-partisan sniping of Washington politics. Donald Trump's eschewal of long-standing norms of behavior and procedure caused scholars to re-think the role of these norms as guiding principles for executive leadership.[12] Presidents clearly have been choosing a variety of ways to govern, and therefore to lead.[13]

Leadership styles have four specific dimensions: approaches to advisory processes and decision-making, administrative strategies, public leadership, and congressional leadership. These dimensions are examined in the sections that follow.

Strategies for Assessing Presidents   5

Approaches to Advisory Processes and Decision-Making

No president stands alone in the decision-making process. Though the constitution does not require an advisory body to the president, George Washington saw the necessity of one midway into his first term and modeled his on the war councils he held during the Revolutionary War.[14] Today presidents recruit and organize their staff and conduct decision-making in strikingly different ways. They often fill their cabinets and staff with an eye toward coalition building and acquiring the specialized skills and expertise they consider important. Some presidents organize their staff around strong chiefs of staff (for example, George H. W. Bush) or around a limited or even no chief of staff role (such as Carter).

Administrative and management issues loom large in tales of presidential success or failure. Whether Iran–Contra or Watergate, nearly all presidential blunders can be traced to managerial problems. While a sound decision-making process does not guarantee a good decision, advisers and managers who ask the right questions and challenge group assumptions can help to produce useful and varied information to facilitate presidential decision-making.[15]

Administrative Strategies

Presidents' administrative goals and strategies for achieving them have a prominent place in their overall leadership style. President Carter, for example, was intensely committed to civil service reform; President Clinton endeavored, in an effort led by Vice President Al Gore, to "reinvent government"; President Obama worked to increase transparency and openness; and President Trump was dead-set on reversing Obama's policies. Such strategies may be important over time in shaping the capacity of the federal government to carry out various policies. For short-term political purposes, however, they are not likely to generate significant electoral benefits, as voters more often focus on the broad policies rather than the possible increases in administrative efficiencies.

A president's administrative strategies also can affect policies in many ways. For example, a president may use executive orders to interpret or carry out provisions of a law—a tactic pursued more recently by presidents facing high levels of polarization in Congress.[16] Presidents may also make use of signing statements to influence the execution of legislation and make decisions affecting the manner in which appropriated funds are actually spent. And of course, a president's appointment process can shape administrative rulemaking and judicial action. While these appointments may reflect a president's electoral and other considerations,[17] the ramifications on policy can be profound and lasting.[18]

6 Strategies for Assessing Presidents

Public Leadership

The public role of the president is an enormously important dimension of presidential leadership. Indeed, the White House often resembles a public relations firm. During the early years of the Reagan presidency, some one hundred White House staffers were involved in various aspects of listening to and communicating with the public.[19] Strategies are developed for enhancing the president's personal popularity, enlisting support for policy initiatives, defending the president against attack from political foes, and devising bully pulpit appeals that seek to modify public attitudes and actions.[20] President Trump took this role into his own hands—both figuratively and literally, through his prodigious use of Twitter.

Although public leadership strategies are not directly linked to shifts in public opinion,[21] they can help raise the profile of policy issues in the news media.[22] Popularity can make a difference as well in negotiating with Congress.[23] In 1981, for example, Reagan's popularity was a consideration as the conservative "boll weevil" Democrats from the South began lining up in support of his economic program. Overall, popular presidents have tended to propose programs that are broader than the programs of less popular presidents.[24] Their success rates may not be higher than those of unpopular presidents, but that may stem from their more ambitious proposals.[25]

Other reasons exist for presidents to actively cultivate their popularity. High popularity also can discourage primary challengers as a president seeks reelection.[26] While a good deal of presidential approval (at least until Obama) has been highly correlated with perceptions of the economy and may be unresponsive to persuasive efforts,[27] failing to cultivate public leadership cedes ground to the president's opposition and their countervailing messages.[28]

Congressional Leadership

Presidents have problems dealing with Congress for many reasons. Members have their own re-election concerns over which presidents usually have little influence. On specific votes, members are likely to be guided by personal beliefs, perceptions of constituency preferences, lobbying by segments of their core constituencies, and campaign fund-raising opportunities.

A persistent theme in studies of presidential relationships with Congress has been the difficulties presidents encounter when trying to change the voting positions of representatives and senators.[29] In summarizing this scholarship, George Edwards III noted, "In most instances, presidents exercise their skills at the margins, not at the core, of coalition building."[30] Matthew Kerbel found, however, that presidents could make a difference

Strategies for Assessing Presidents 7

if they exercised a measure of flexibility in their personal dealings with members of Congress and established an effective organizational capacity for handling those relationships. Nevertheless, the thrust of his analysis is that this power "is difficult to exercise from the Oval Office."[31] Given existing constraints, Congress watchers are likely to see the more effective presidents appealing for votes on only a few key issues and at points during committee votes rather than during floor proceedings.

Presidents can choose from a variety of strategies in attempting to influence legislative outcomes. Although agenda setting is shared with Congress, it can be an important strategy. Tactics for agenda setting include advocating an issue in an electoral campaign, giving prominent emphasis to an issue in the annual State of the Union address, making speeches to groups with a stake in a particular agenda item, mentioning the item in press conferences, and symbolically labeling top priorities in the first message sent to Congress. One of the more unusual instances of agenda setting occurred in the early days of the Clinton administration. The president's selection of First Lady Hillary Rodham Clinton to preside over the development of a major health care program signaled members of Congress as well as key interest groups that health policy would be an important issue in the new administration.

Presidents often have their best chances of influencing legislation if they act at the very beginning of their first year in office—known as the "honeymoon."[32] By moving rapidly, presidents can capitalize on their post-election popularity and act before opposed members of Congress, interest groups, and affected agencies have a chance to mobilize. In the second year Congress often is caught up in reelection concerns, which may reduce opportunities for presidential success. After the midterm elections, presidents generally are confronted with additional constraints if their party suffers the usual midterm losses of congressional seats. Since 1932 the party in the White House has lost an average of 28 House seats; in 1938, 1994, and 2010 the Democrats lost over 50 House seats.[33] Recently there have been two aberrations—when Democrats picked up five seats in 1998 due to public consternation over the impeachment of President Clinton and when Republicans gained eight seats in 2002 due to post-9/11 national security concerns. Because of the greater opportunities offered by a fast-start strategy, Paul Light argued that presidents should not seek to develop ideal proposals, but instead should proceed quickly with existing policy ideas and campaign pledges.[34]

Other aspects of skill and timing are essential to a president's success with Congress. Presidents must know when to employ their veto power, or use the threat of using it in their negotiations with Congress.[35] Presidents must also know when to take a public position, when to engage in shaping how an issue is defined, and when to signal compromise in order to

8 Strategies for Assessing Presidents

maximize the likelihood of success with Congress.[36] It is a delicate dance that requires a great deal of attention and prowess.

Challenges and Opportunities

Some presidents face greater challenges than others in both the international and domestic arenas. Presidents Harry Truman, Richard Nixon, and Barack Obama began terms as the nation was waging unpopular wars—in Korea in 1953, in Vietnam in 1969, and in Iraq and Afghanistan in 2009. While certainly important in their own right, foreign policy challenges constrain the amount of time that the administration has to devote to the president's domestic agenda.

Policy challenges may often create opportunities because of a widespread desire for action. In 1981, public frustration over slow economic growth and high inflation created widespread sympathy for trying something new—in this instance, Reagan's supply-side tax cuts. In 2001, demands for a forceful response to the 9/11 attacks empowered President George W. Bush to impose his will on the policy arena. The COVID-19 pandemic that began in 2020 permitted Joe Biden to pass a tremendously large rescue package just after assuming office. Public frustration with existing conditions does not mean, however, that policies will address voter concerns or that presidents will be able to build political support behind their policy preferences. Clinton, for example, found it extremely difficult to convert voter desires for reform of the health care system into support for one specific approach.

Political opportunity may fluctuate during a president's term in office, occasionally dramatically so. George W. Bush, for example, went from a low- to a high-opportunity president as a result of the 9/11 attacks against the United States. Lyndon Johnson went from a high- to a low-opportunity president as a result of increased opposition to his policies in Vietnam.

The opportunities a president faces for addressing major policy challenges are shaped by many factors, among them the public mood, the level of public support, the legislative setting, the availability of promising issues, economic and budgetary considerations, and foreign policy influences. These factors and those that often restrict opportunities for second-term presidents are described in this section, along with the reasons why opportunities may have declined for more recent presidents.

Public Mood

The public periodically displays a strong desire for government action, heightening presidential opportunity. President Kennedy, who was interested in these cycles, talked with historian and staff aide Arthur Schlesinger Jr. about their underlying patterns.[37] Over time, as problems grow and existing government action is seen as insufficient, public sentiment builds for reform. At such times presidents can claim a mandate for change that often moves Congress to act. Bumps in public demand for government action occurred following the 9/11 terrorist attacks, during the 2008 recession and housing and financial crises, and during the outbreak of the COVID-19 pandemic in 2020. But demand for government action can quickly fall if government actions fail to satisfy the public or if officials betray the public's trust.

Levels of public trust in government can have an enormous impact on a president's level of opportunity.[38] During the 1960s, presidents seeking to establish new programs were dealing with an electorate that, by today's standards, had a far higher degree of trust in the federal government. From the vantage point of the far more cynical 1990s, the 1960s appears to have been a stunningly different period: over 60 percent of the public agreed with the view that one can trust the government in Washington to do the right thing all of the time or most of the time, whereas when Bill Clinton entered the White House in 1993, the portion of the population with a similar view had fallen to only 22 percent. This figure rebounded to mid-50s levels immediately after the 9/11 terrorist attacks but then fell to an all-time low of 15 percent midway into Obama's first term (see Figure 1.1). At the beginning of Obama's second term, trust in government was still low, at about 26 percent. Trust in government picked up during the COVID-19 pandemic but still remained historically low. With the exception of the brief uptick after 9/11, low levels of trust in government are the norm for recent presidents and are a significant impediment to building support for policy proposals.

Figure 1.1 Trust in Government.

Source: Data from https://www.pewresearch.org/politics/2021/05/17/public-trust-in-government-1958-2021/

10 *Strategies for Assessing Presidents*

Public Support

Differences in levels of public support are yet another factor in the opportunities open to presidents (see Table 1.1). Elections can produce several advantages. For example, a large winning margin can give presidents the opportunity to argue that they received a "mandate" for their policies and to claim that they pulled legislators into office on their "coattails." Leading students of voting behavior discredit the view that large segments of the electorate produce a mandate by understanding a president's policy goals and voting on that basis.[39] Nevertheless, in 1981 Reagan, who had campaigned hard on his economic program and won by 10 percent, plausibly asserted the existence of a mandate and gained an initial advantage with Congress.[40]

Elections may have significant repercussions on a president's level of opportunity, especially in the extent to which the party a president defeats becomes discredited in the eyes of the voters. Discredited opposition parties worked to the advantage of Roosevelt in 1933, Johnson in 1965, and Reagan in 1981.[41] A discredited party serves as a weak opposition, thereby allowing the president more political latitude.

And of course, presidential popularity, often measured as job approval, is a critical factor in a president's opportunity level. Popular presidents carry the will of the people, and opponents are loathe to attract their ire. Most presidents suffer a decline in popularity over the first term in office, making policymaking more difficult as time goes on. In recent years, greater political polarization has led to relatively low and stable levels of popularity (especially notable for Trump and Biden).

The Legislative Setting

The size of the president's party in Congress is perhaps the most important indicator of the opportunities available to presidents to shape policy (see Table 1.2), but ideological orientations within the party may work against the president. For Democratic presidents, at least until the 1980s, conservative voting tendencies among southern Democrats frequently derailed new domestic policy initiatives and negated any advantages produced by the size of the party's delegation in Congress.

Although control of Congress by the president's party can be an advantage to the White House on some issues, David Mayhew found that some policy opportunities also may arise when presidents form coalitions with members of a Congress controlled by the opposition party (known as divided government). In 1996, for example, Republicans in Congress and a Democratic president concluded that each had a better chance in the fall elections if Congress enacted and the president signed major legislation, rather than face voter dissatisfaction with continued stalemate. Thus,

Table 1.1 Public Support Dimension of Presidential Opportunity Levels, 1932–2022

	Percent Winning Margin in First-Term Election (rank)		Percent of Total Vote in First-Term Election (rank)		Percent Popularity by Year, First-Term (rank)				Average (rank)	
					1	2	3	4		
Roosevelt	17.8	(2)	57.4	(2)						
Truman	–		–		79[b]	41	58	45	55.8	(5)
Eisenhower	10.5	(3)	54.9	(3)	68	65	71	72	69.1	(2)
Kennedy	0.2	(11)	49.7	(9)	76	71	62	74[c]	69.5	(1)
Johnson	22.6	(1)	61.1	(1)	65	50	43	42	54.8	(6)
Nixon	0.7	(10)	43.4	(12)	59	55	47	56	54.2	(7)
Carter	2.1	(9)	50.1	(8)	61	44	36	39	45.3	(11)
Reagan	9.7	(4)	50.7	(7)	56	43	44	55	49.4	(8)
G. H. W. Bush	7.8	(5)	53.4	(4)	63	66	72	39	59.9	(4)
Clinton	5.6	(7)	43.0	(13)	48	46	47	55	48.9	(10)
G. W. Bush	- 0.5	(12)	47.9	(10)	67	71	60	50	61.8	(3)
Obama	7.2	(6)	52.9	(5)	57	47	44	48	49.1	(9)
Trump	-2.1	(13)	46.1	(11)	38	40	42	44	41.1	(13)
Biden	4.4	(8)	51.3	(6)	49	41	–	–	45.1	(12)

Source: The American Presidency Project, www.presidency.ucsb.edu.

Notes: Presidential popularity is Gallup job approval; Truman's first year is from Roosevelt's death forward; Kennedy's average includes first three years until death; Johnson's average includes Kennedy's fourth year; Biden year two is through July.

Table 1.2 Congressional Dimensions of Presidential First-Term Opportunity Levels, 1932–2022

	Size of President's Party in Congress				Level of Surge/ Decline in President's Party				Midterm Election Change in President's Party			
	House		Senate		House		Senate		House		Senate	
Roosevelt (D)	313D-117R	(1)	59D-36R		+97	(1)	+12		+9	(1)	+9	
Truman (D)	244D-189R	(7)	57D-38R		+20	(6)	-1		-45	(11)	-12	
Eisenhower (R)	221R-213D	(9.5)	49R-47D		+22	(4)	+2		-18	(8)	-1	
Kennedy (D)	264D-173R	(4)	64D-36R		-21	(14)	-2		-4	(3)	+3	
Johnson (D)	295D-140R	(2)	68D-32R		+37	(2)	+2		-47	(12)	-4	
Nixon (R)	192R-243D	(12.5)	43R-57D		+5	(7)	+5		-12	(6)	+2	
Carter (D)	292D-143R	(3)	61D-38R		+1	(8)	0		-15	(7)	-3	
Reagan (R)	192R-243D	(12.5)	53R-46D		+34	(3)	+12		-26	(9)	+1	
G. H. W. Bush (R)	175R-260D	(14)	45R-55D		-2	(9.5)	-1		-8	(4)	-1	
Clinton (D)	258D-176R	(5)	57D-43R		-9	(12)	0		-52	(13)	-8	
G. W. Bush (R)	221R-212D	(9.5)	50R-50D		-2	(9.5)	-4		+8	(2)	+2	
Obama (D)	257D-178R	(6)	59D-41R		+21	(5)	+8		-63	(14)	-6	
Trump (R)	241R-194D	(8)	51R-49D		-6	(11)	-2		-40	(10)	+2	
Biden (D)	222D-213R	(11)	50D-50R		-13	(13)	+3		-9	(5)	+1	

Sources: Office of the Clerk of the US House of Representatives, http://history.house.gov/Institution/Party-Divisions/Party-Divisions/, https://history.house.gov/Institution/Election-Statistics/Election-Statistics/; Office of the Clerk of the US Senate, http://www.senate.gov/pagelayout/history/one_item_and_teasers/partydiv.htm; The Presidency Project, https://www.presidency.ucsb.edu/node/332343.

Note: Size of president's party based on time of president's inauguration, surge and decline based on congressional composition immediately prior to election, figures for Eisenhower include one Independent in Republican conference, and figures for Obama, Trump, and Biden include Independents caucusing with Democrats.

surprisingly, Mayhew's study of the period 1946–1990 revealed that the amount of major legislation passed with divided government was comparable to the results obtained when one party controlled both branches of government.[42] But this trend may not last as Congress—and, in particular, its leadership—becomes more polarized along party lines.

Related to the strength of a president's party in Congress is the length of the president's coattails on election to office for the first time.[43] Newly elected Republican president Ronald Reagan enjoyed an increase of 34 seats in the House and a Republican recapture of the Senate by adding 12 new Republican members. By contrast, Democrat John Kennedy's election produced no gain in the Senate and a loss of 21 seats in the House. When members of the president's party sense that presidential coattails may have helped expand the size of their party's vote, greater voting support for the president's policies may be forthcoming. Irrespective of the balance of power at the beginning, a president must still move quickly before the (almost inevitable) loss of House and Senate seats in the midterm election during the president's first term.

A president's success in the legislative arena also owes something to Congress's organizational characteristics and the policy preferences and political skills of those in powerful leadership positions.[44] In the two decades after World War II, southerners' dominance of congressional committees was a major issue. In fact, when Kennedy moved into the Oval Office in 1961, 10 of the top 15 committee chairmen were from the South and in most instances were decidedly conservative. The political skills of party leaders and the Speaker of the House also can make an important difference. For example, Kennedy's opportunities were reduced in early 1962 when the death of House Speaker Sam Rayburn (D-TX) brought to power John McCormack (D-MA), a less skilled Speaker. Additionally, when John Boehner (R-OH) became Speaker of the House with the Republican takeover in 2010, Obama's opportunities were severely limited by Boehner's implementation of the "Hastert Rule" (named after former Speaker Dennis Hastert)—that no legislation would be introduced in the House unless it enjoyed the support of a majority of the majority party.

Congressional leadership cannot stray too far from the public will, especially against a popular incumbent president. Newt Gingrich (R-GA), the Speaker of the House of the 104th Congress (1995–1997), attempted to capitalize on Republican gains in the 1994 midterm elections and pass the legislative proposals contained in the Republicans' "Contract with America." For a time, Gingrich succeeded in blocking President Clinton's agenda. But by 1996, Gingrich's stunning fall in popularity and a widespread public perception that House Republicans had strayed too far to the right gave Clinton considerable opportunity for centrist strategies.

14 Strategies for Assessing Presidents

Promising Issues

John Kingdon, who applies the label "windows of opportunity" to promising issues, has identified situations favorable to government action on a given issue.[45] According to Kingdon, a window of opportunity exists when three influences converge: recognition that a problem needing a solution exists, the availability of a policy proposal around which support can be built, and the presence of a "political stream" of forces able to instigate change, such as a popular president with considerable support in Congress.

The bank bailouts of 2008 illustrate this pattern—the stream of political forces was aligned at the right time to ensure quick policy action. Key to this was problem awareness by policymakers and the public. The reverse is also true—Kingdon argues that sometimes social and economic conditions that might seem to warrant a high level of attention by presidents, members of Congress, and the press may actually generate little comment and problem awareness.[46] This tendency to overlook problems is most likely to occur when no acceptable solution seems to be available. The deafening silence in the face of mounting budget deficits at points during the 1980s and the postponement until after the 1988 election of any attempt to cap the surging costs of the savings and loan debacle illustrate this tendency.

Economic Conditions and Budget Deficits

Economic conditions and budget deficits also play a key role in shaping a president's level of opportunity. In 1997, the strong economy was central to Clinton's ability to negotiate a balanced budget proposal with Republicans. In 2000, with the federal budget running a surplus, presidential candidates George W. Bush and Al Gore were able to offer contrasting policy visions for the nation. Bush campaigned on a platform of tax cuts, while Gore promised to put the surplus into an "iron clad lock-box" in order to shore up projected deficits in Social Security as the Baby Boomers retired. Once Bush prevailed, the surplus helped him push his promised tax cuts through Congress.

Deficits impact presidential opportunity as well. Periodically, large deficits and the concern they generate have given presidents an opportunity to promote deficit-reduction packages. More frequently, however, deficits have reduced opportunities for presidents to establish new programs. In 1993, Clinton found it necessary to move away from new spending initiatives.

The economic collapse of 2008 forced President George W. Bush and later President Obama to confront a possible global depression. Each poured money into the financial system in the hopes of averting tragedy. This, coupled with soaring budget deficits, made other high-priced domestic reforms unlikely, especially given congressional intransigence at repealing George W. Bush's tax cuts. Deficits were also a center-point of Senator Joe Manchin's (D-WV) effective opposition (in a 50-50 Senate) to Joe Biden's "Build Back Better" policy agenda, resulting in a significantly reduced package of policy initiatives.

Foreign Policy Influences

The demands of foreign policy, especially those involving the deployment of US troops to trouble spots, often have strong yet unpredictable impacts on opportunities for domestic action. The success with which George H. W. Bush executed the 1990–1991 Persian Gulf War produced a surge in popularity that seemed to give him some additional basis for promoting domestic policy initiatives. His son's opportunity expanded even more dramatically with the 9/11 attacks and, at least at first, the deployment of troops to Afghanistan and Iraq. Clinton's first term saw quite a different outcome despite his desire to be primarily a domestic president. In October 1993, 18 American soldiers were killed in Somalia, and in a chilling scene viewed worldwide on television. Suddenly, strategies for effecting the withdrawal of American forces replaced Clinton's domestic policies at the top of his agenda.

Foreign entanglements, then, may generate public support but may weaken a president's opportunities for domestic policy initiatives. Other important examples include the impact of the Vietnam War on Lyndon Johnson's Great Society programs and Jimmy Carter's attempt to free US embassy personnel taken hostage in Iran in 1979. President Obama was aware of this potential and moved as quickly as circumstances would allow to wrap up his predecessor's unpopular war in Iraq.

The Second Term

Presidents generally have less opportunity for effective leadership in their second term. Limitations begin with their typical reelection efforts. Sometimes presidents have won landslide victories, but their campaigns revolved around slogans like "Four More Years" or "Reelect the President" rather than efforts to develop support for new initiatives. The departure of staff and cabinet may be a problem as well. A president's key aides, weary after four years of very long hours and tempted by financially lucrative opportunities, may leave the administration. In dealing with Congress, presidents can anticipate a decline in their party's strength in the midterm elections during their sixth year in office. A president's lame-duck status is yet another reason a member of Congress would doubt that there are advantages in being "on the president's team."

16 *Strategies for Assessing Presidents*

Declining Opportunities

Since the mid-1970s, many new groups have organized for and against the agenda promoted by the Christian right. On the left, many new groups have sprung forth to champion immigration, racial, and environmental concerns, among others. The internet has helped these groups organize, spread their message, and fundraise. Most recently, changes to campaign finance law and the explosion in political campaign spending have greatly influenced the political field of play. The result of these converging forces of technology, interest group mobilization, and ideological and geographical sorting has led to hyper-partisanship, both among elected leaders and the public.[47] The confluence of hyper-partisanship and the increasing power of other actors have weakened the president's hand in appealing directly to members of Congress across the partisan aisle. Presidents have even found it difficult to persuade members of their own party as strong partisans call for policies that reflect ideological purity rather than compromise. Consequently, the amount of significant legislation emanating from Congress has declined as partisanship has increased.[48]

As polarization increases, the ramifications of policies have become discussed in extreme terms and the policy process described as a battleground requiring absolute victory. This has resulted in a concurring demonization of the other side. The politics of personal attacks didn't start recently, of course, but its current manifestation of attacking others for short-term gain and public notoriety emanates from Newt Gingrich's rise to Speaker of the House.[49] The president finds him-/herself increasingly dealing with individuals interested in publicly burnishing their credentials with ideological supporters rather than crafting good public policy. All of this is to the detriment of a president's ability to secure compromise and to advance policy.

Categorizing and Comparing Presidents

The four modern presidents who enjoyed the greatest opportunities to shape domestic policy were Franklin Roosevelt, Lyndon Johnson, Ronald Reagan, and George W. Bush (see Table 1.3). Unlike FDR, whose administration ushered in a dramatic change in party control of government, Johnson represented a continuation of Democratic Party control. Yet he was aided by a tremendous backlog of "unfinished business" in the form of legislative proposals that were moving forward in Congress. While George W. Bush entered office as a low-opportunity president, his opportunity level soared following the 9/11 attacks as his popularity climbed over 90 percent and he faced a compliant Congress. Reagan's opportunities were somewhat fewer than those of FDR, LBJ, and George W. Bush, but he had more than any of the other post-1932 presidents. Presidents with moderate opportunity

Strategies for Assessing Presidents 17

Table 1.3 Influences and Limitations Affecting Presidential Opportunities, 1933–2022

	Helpful Influences	*Limitations*
Roosevelt		

1933–1937	Intense public desire for action
	Discredited opponent and party
	Decisive election victory in 1932
	High level of popularity
	Potential for a major party
	  coalition
	Large congressional majorities
	Many promising issues
		No general solution to economic
		  problems available
		Conflicts over policy options in
		  specific areas
		Budget deficit over half of total
		  spending in 1932

1937–1941	Landslide reelection win	Formation of conservative coalition in 1937 Congressional losses in 1938 Few promising issues
1941–1945	Strong reelection win	Wartime issues predominate
Truman		

1945–1949	Majority Party President
	Economic growth and budget
	  surpluses
		Not elected, succeeded to the
		  presidency
		Unflattering comparisons to FDR
		  and low popularity
		Strength of southern Democrats
		  in Congress and a divided
		  coalition

1949–1953	Surprise election victory	Focus on Korean War
Eisenhower		
1953–1957	Decisive election victory High popularity	Minority party president Democratic party strength in Congress Few promising issues
1957–1961	Decisive reelection victory Some new proposals emerging	Two recessions and budget deficit problems Midterm election losses
Kennedy		

1961–1963	Majority party president
	High popularity
	
	Some promising issues
		Narrow election victory
		No surge in congressional
		  elections
		Southern Democratic strength in
		  Congress
		Chairs of key committees hostile

Johnson		
1963–1965	Two "first years" Activist public mood High level of trust in government	Decline in popularity High midterm loss of House seats

(Continued)

18   *Strategies for Assessing Presidents*

Table 1.3 (Continued)

	Helpful Influences	Limitations
1965–1969	Landslide reelection victory	Agenda shift to race riots, the Vietnam War
	Majority party president	
	Large congressional majorities, 1965–1966	
	Many very promising issues	
	Strong economy	
Nixon		
1969–1973	Activist era	Minority party president
	Discredited opponent and party	Weak election victory
	Some promising issues	Democratic strength in Congress
	Fairly strong initial popularity	
1973–1974	Landslide reelection win	Watergate quickly engulfed his presidency
	Still an activist era	
Ford		
1974–1977	None	Not elected, succeeded to the presidency
		Low popularity after Nixon pardon
		Weak economic performance
Carter		
1977–1981	Majority party president	Weak election victory
	Large congressional majorities	Divided Democratic Party majorities in Congress
	Some promising issues	Large deficit
		No easy solutions to inflation, unemployment, and the energy crisis
Reagan		
1981–1985	Public desire for new economic policies	Little public support for spending cuts
	Decisive victory and mandate	Democratic control of the House, 1983–1985
	Discredited opponent and party	
	congressional surge, control of Senate	
	Relatively low deficit	
1985–1989	Landslide reelection win	Distractions of Iran–Contra Scandal
	Sustained popularity	Return of Senate to Democratic control
		Few promising issues

(Continued)

Strategies for Assessing Presidents   19

Table 1.3 (Continued)

	Helpful Influences	Limitations
George H. W. Bush		
1989–1993	Close to majority party status High popularity, first 30 months	Unflattering comparisons to Reagan Modest election victory Democratic majorities in Congress Large deficit Few promising issues
Clinton		
1993–1997	Democratic Party strength in Congress, 1993–1994 Some promising issues Moderate but steady economic growth	Weak majority party status Public lack of trust in government Low popularity, first 24 months Republican control of Congress, 1995–1996 Large initial deficit
1997–2001	Strong Economy Fairly high popularity No midterm election loss in Congress	Modest reelection win Few promising issues Monica Lewinsky scandal and impeachment
George W. Bush		
2001–2005	Budget Surplus 9/11 Terrorist attacks boost popularity and create peace with Congress Public support for governmental action Midterm election gains in Congress	Not popularly elected Low initial popularity, first 8 months Agenda shift to War on Terror, Iraq and Afghanistan
2005–2009	Urgency of financial meltdown	Narrow reelection victory Unpopular war in Iraq drags on Faltering economy in last year Budget deficits Midterm loss of control of Congress
Obama		
2009–2013	Public mood for government action Moderate electoral surge in Congress	Budget deficits Unpopular wars diverting attention from domestic policy Bipartisan polarization in Congress Midterm election loss of House Few promising issues

(Continued)

20 *Strategies for Assessing Presidents*

Table 1.3 (Continued)

	Helpful Influences	Limitations
2013–2017	Moderate reelection victory	Slow economic recovery Intransigent Congress Midterm loss of Senate Foreign crises in Afghanistan, Syria, and Ukraine, ISIS
Donald Trump		
2017–2021	Strong economy "Disruptor" election Federal Court Appointments	No popular vote mandate Low popularity Midterm loss of House Ukraine scandal and impeachment COVID-19 pandemic
Joe Biden		
2021–2022	Public mood for government action COVID-19 Vaccines	No coattails, slim House margin 50-50 Senate Election denial Lingering COVID-19 pandemic Worldwide economic disruption Inflation

levels were Harry Truman, Dwight Eisenhower, John Kennedy, Barack Obama, and Donald Trump. The low-opportunity presidents were Richard Nixon, Jimmy Carter, George H. W. Bush, Bill Clinton, and Joe Biden.

The rest of this book is devoted to assessing and then comparing the performances of these presidents. It evaluates their relative levels of political opportunity, the scope of the strategies they pursued, and the skill with which the strategies were exercised. The categorization of presidents by opportunity level (high, moderate, and low) allows a fairer comparison of their skills based on their performances within an opportunity level. Is it fair to expect George H. W. Bush or Nixon or Carter or Clinton to achieve as much as FDR or LBJ? The individual assessments in the chapters provide a basis for overall comparisons in the final chapter.

The chapters that follow examine the actions and strategies adopted by presidents through the lenses of opportunity and skill. These assessments will reveal the level of presidential leadership exerted on the measures that have done the most to shape domestic policy since 1933. Our evaluations in Chapters 2–15 begin with Franklin Roosevelt because he was the first "modern" president and because of the continuing interest in his leadership and the wide range of strategies he employed.[50] Each chapter includes a brief summary of personal characteristics and policy goals

Strategies for Assessing Presidents   21

before turning to leadership styles and achievements.[51] All discussions of policy focus on domestic issues since they provide especially fertile ground for examining the impact of leadership styles and strategies. As presidents' legacies are largely created during their first four years in office, and because not all presidents get a second term, the analysis is limited to first terms. President Gerald Ford is not included in this study, because he occupied the presidency under unique circumstances for a very short time and was fulfilling part of Nixon's second term. The final chapter develops comparative assessments and addresses prospects for future presidential leadership.

Notes

1 Michael A. Genovese, *The Presidential Dilemma: Revisiting Democratic Leadership in the American System*, 3rd ed. (New York: Routledge, 2017), ch. 2.
2 See Michael A. Genovese, *Memo to a New President: The Art and Science of Presidential Leadership* (New York: Oxford University Press, 2008).
3 See Shirley Anne Warshaw, *The Domestic Presidency: Policy Making in the White House* (Boston: Allyn and Bacon, 1997); and Paul C. Light, *The President's Agenda: Domestic Policy Choice from Kennedy to Clinton*, 3rd ed. (Baltimore: Johns Hopkins University Press, 1999).
4 James P. Pfiffner, *The Strategic Presidency: Hitting the Ground Running*, 2nd rev. ed. (Lawrence: University Press of Kansas, 1996).
5 See Samuel Kernell, *Going Public: New Strategies of Presidential Leadership*, 4th ed. (Washington, DC: CQ Press, 2006); and George C. Edwards III, *On Deaf Ears: The Limits of the Bully Pulpit* (New Haven, CT: Yale University Press, 2003).
6 Robert J. Spitzer, *The Presidency and Public Policy: The Four Arenas of Presidential Power* (Tuscaloosa: University of Alabama Press, 1983).
7 Lara N. Brown, "Mistaking the Moment and Misperceiving the Opportunity: The Leadership Failings of Presidents George W. Bush and Barack Obama," in *The Quest for Leadership: Thomas E. Cronin and His Influence on Presidential Studies and Political Science*, ed. Michael A. Genovese (Amherst, NY: Cambria Press, 2015), 93–130.
8 Richard E. Neustadt, *Presidential Power* (New York: Wiley, 1960). For an extension of his views, see Richard E. Neustadt, *Presidential Power and the Modern Presidents: The Politics of Leadership from Roosevelt to Reagan* (New York: Free Press, 1990).
9 Fred I. Greenstein, *Leadership in the Modern Presidency* (Cambridge, MA: Harvard University Press, 1988), 312. For a contemporary critique of Neustadt, see Thomas E. Cronin, Michael A. Genovese, and Meena Bose, *The Paradoxes of the American Presidency*, 4th ed. (New York: Oxford University Press, 2017), ch. 4.
10 Kernell, *Going Public*.
11 Fred I. Greenstein, *The Hidden-Hand Presidency: Eisenhower as Leader* (Baltimore, MD: Johns Hopkins University Press, 1994).
12 Julia Azari, "The Trump Presidency Thrives on Norms," *Mischiefs of Faction*, May 8, 2020, https://www.mischiefsoffaction.com/post/the-trump-presidency -thrives-on-norms.

22   *Strategies for Assessing Presidents*

13 See Bert A. Rockman, *The Leadership Question: The Presidency and the American System* (New York: Praeger, 1984); and Genovese, *Presidential Dilemma*.
14 Lindsay M. Chervinsky, *The Cabinet: George Washington and the Creation of an American Institution* (Cambridge, MA: Belknap Press, 2022).
15 See Richard P. Nathan, *The Administrative Presidency* (New York: Wiley, 1983); Robert F. Durant, *The Administrative Presidency Revisited* (Albany: State University of New York Press, 1992); and James P. Pfiffner, ed., *The Managerial Presidency*, 2nd ed. (College Station: Texas A&M University Press, 1999).
16 Jason S. Byers, Jamie L. Carson, and Ryan D. Williamson, "Policymaking by the Executive: Examining the Fate of Presidential Agenda Items," *Congress & the Presidency* 47, no. 1 (2020): 1–31.
17 Jon Rogowski and Tyler Simko, "Presidential Patronage and Executive Branch Appointments, 1925–1959," *Presidential Studies Quarterly* 52, no. 1 (2022): 38–59.
18 Christopher Piper, "Going for Goals: Presidential Appointments and Agency Goal Change," *Presidential Studies Quarterly* 52, no. 1 (2022): 140–167.
19 William Muir, *The Bully-Pulpit: The Presidential Leadership of Ronald Reagan* (San Francisco: ICS Press, 1992), 21.
20 See Martha Joynt Kumar, *Managing the President's Message: The White House Communications Operation* (Baltimore: Johns Hopkins University Press, 2007).
21 Edwards III, *On Deaf Ears*.
22 Matthew Eshbaugh-Soha and Ronald J. McGauvran, "Presidential Leadership, the News Media, and Income Inequality," *Political Research Quarterly* 71, no. 1 (2018): 157–171.
23 Andrew W. Barrett and Matthew Eshbaugh-Soha, "Presidential Success on the Substance of Legislation," *Political Research Quarterly* 60, no. 1 (2007): 100–112.
24 Richard A. Brody, *Assessing the President: The Media, Elite Opinion, and Public Support* (Stanford, CA: Stanford University Press, 1991).
25 For a perspective suggesting popularity has only a marginal impact on presidential success, see George C. Edwards III, *At the Margins: Presidential Leadership of Congress* (New Haven, CT: Yale University Press, 1989); and Paul Brace and Barbara Hinckley, *Follow the Leader: Opinion Polls and the Modern Presidents* (New York: Basic Books, 1992).
26 Brody, *Assessing the President*.
27 Raphael Small and Roobert Eisinger, "Whither Presidential Approval?" *Presidential Studies Quarterly* 50, no. 4 (2020): 845–863; and Kathleen Donovan, Paul M. Kellstedt, Ellen M. Key, and Matthew J. Lebo, "Motivated Reasoning, Public Opinion, and Presidential Approval," *Political Behavior* 42, no. 4 (2020): 1201–121.
28 Todd L. Belt, "Leading the Public/Following the Public: Leadership in a Democratic Context," in *The Quest for Leadership*, ed. Michael A. Genovese (Amherst, NY: Cambria Press, 2015), 149–170.
29 The limitations of presidential skills compared with the impacts of a legislator's party and ideology are stressed in Jon R. Bond and Richard Fleisher, *The President in the Legislative Arena* (Chicago: University of Chicago Press, 1990). For similar case study conclusions, see Matthew R. Kerbel, *Beyond Persuasion: Organizational Efficiency and Presidential Power* (Albany: State University of New York Press, 1991).
30 Edwards, *At the Margins*, ch. 11.
31 Kerbel, *Beyond Persuasion*, 153.
32 See Light, *The President's Agenda*, ch. 9; Pfiffner, *The Strategic Presidency*, ch. 1; and Matthew N. Beckmann and Joseph Godfrey, "The Policy Opportunities

in Presidential Honeymoons," *Political Research Quarterly* 60, no. 2 (2007): 250–262.

33 Data source: The American Presidency Project, "Seats in Congress Gained/Lost by the President's Party in Mid-Term Elections" (Santa Barbara, CA: University of California), https://www.presidency.ucsb.edu/node/332343.

34 Light, *The President's Agenda*.

35 Samuel H. Kernell, *Veto Rhetoric: A Leadership Strategy for Divided Government* (Washington, DC: CQ Press, 2023). See also Richard S. Conley, "George Bush and the 102nd Congress: The Impact of Public and 'Private' Veto Threats on Policy Outcomes," *Presidential Studies Quarterly* 33, no. 4 (2003): 730–750; Rebecca E. Deem and Laura W. Arnold, "Veto Threats as a Policy Tool: When to Threaten?" *Political Science Quarterly* 32, no. 1 (2002): 30–45; Mark Kelso, "The President as Legislative Leader: The Use of Veto Power in Environmental Policy Making," *Congress & the Presidency* 46, no. 1 (2019): 135–158; James Pfiffner and Roger H. Davidson, *Understanding the Presidency* (New York: Longman, 1997); Robert Spitzer, "The Disingenuous Presidency: Reagan's Veto and the 'Make-My-Day' President," *Congress & the Presidency* 21, no. 1 (1994): 1–10; John T. Woolley, "Institutions, the Election Cycle and the Presidential Veto," *American Journal of Political Science* 35, no. 2 (1991): 279–304.

36 See Bryan W. Marshall and Brandon C. Prins, "Strategic Position Taking and Presidential Influence in Congress," *Legislative Studies Quarterly* 32, no. 2 (2007): 257–284; Kimberly Maslin-Wicks, "Two Types of Presidential Influence in Congress," *Presidential Studies Quarterly* 28, no. 1 (1998): 108–126; Amber Melissa McKay and Brian Webb, "Presidential Position-Taking, Presidential Success, and Interest Group Activity," *Congress & the Presidency* 46, no. 1 (2019): 89–108; Branddon Rottinghaus and Isaiah Johnson, "Presidential 'Pitches' and White House Pressure: Interpersonal Presidential Persuasion in a Shared Lawmaking Environment," *Presidential Studies Quarterly* 51, no. 4 (2021): 839–859.

37 Arthur M. Schlesinger Jr., *The Cycles of American History* (Boston, MA: Mariner, 1999).

38 For a discussion and formulation of how presidential approval and public trust in government can be translated into leverage for the president, see Daniel E. Ponder, *Presidential Leverage: Presidents, Approval, and the American State* (Palo Alto, CA: Stanford University Press, 2018), ch 2.

39 On the inability of presidents to literally create a mandate, see Edwards, *At the Margins*, ch. 8.

40 For a discussion of how the politics of presidential mandate claims have changed over the years, see Julia R. Azari, *Delivering the People's Message: The Changing Politics of the Presidential Mandate* (Ithaca, NY: Cornell University Press, 2014).

41 Stephen Skowronek, *The Politics Presidents Make: Leadership from John Adams to Bill Clinton* (Boston, MA: Belknap, 1997).

42 David R. Mayhew, *Divided We Govern: Party Control, Lawmaking, and Investigations, 1946–2002* (New Haven, CT: Yale University Press, 1991), ch. 7.

43 The importance of surge as an aspect of a president's opportunity level is discussed in Charles O. Jones, "Campaigning to Govern: The Clinton Style," in *The Clinton Presidency: First Appraisal*, ed. Colin Campbell and Bert A. Rockman (Chatham, NJ: Chatham House, 1995), ch. 1.

44 For a summary of legislative characteristics and their implications for presidential influence, see Roger Davidson, "The Presidency and Presidential Time," in

24 Strategies for Assessing Presidents

Rivals for Power: Presidential-Congressional Relations, ed. James A. Thurber, 2nd ed. (Washington, DC: CQ Press, 1996), ch. 2.

45 John W. Kingdon, *Agendas, Alternatives, and Public Policies*, updated 2nd ed. (New York: Longman, 2010).

46 Kingdon, *Agendas, Alternatives, and Public Policies*.

47 See Alan I. Abramowitz, *The Great Alignment: Race, Party Transformation, and the Rise of Donald Trump* (New Haven, CT: Yale University Press, 2018); Morris P. Fiorina, *Unstable Majorities: Polarization, Party Sorting & Political Stalemate* (Stanford, CA: Hoover Institution Press, 2017); Stanley B. Greenberg, *The Two Americas: Our Current Political Deadlock and How to Break It* (New York: Thomas Dunne, 2005); Matt Grossman and David A. Hopkins, *Asymmetric Politics: Ideological Republicans and Group Interest Democrats* (New York: Oxford University Press, 2016); Nolan McCarty, *Polarization: What Everyone Needs to Know* (New York: Oxford University Press, 2019); Lilliana Mason, *Uncivil Agreement: How Politics Became Our Identity* (Chicago: University of Chicago Press, 2018).

48 McCarty, *Polarization: What Everyone Needs to Know*.

49 See Julian E. Zelizer, *Burning Down the House: Newt Gingrich and the Rise of the New Republican Party* (New York: Penguin, 2021).

50 Numerous sources were used in assessing each president, including works by various administration officials, journalists, and academic writers; historical background discussions for each time period; studies of process relationships; case study analyses of particular policy enactments and the policy evolution of several administrations; public opinion polls; interpretations of presidential success votes in *Congressional Quarterly Weekly Report* and *Congressional Quarterly Almanac*; and the *Public Papers of the Presidents*. Archival research was undertaken at the Kennedy, Johnson, Carter, and Reagan presidential libraries and at the Nixon Presidential Materials Project. Materials examined at these libraries included staff aides' papers on domestic policy, legislative liaison, and public liaison, along with oral histories and exit interviews.

51 For a widely read interpretation of how leadership styles are formed based on presidential character, see James David Barber, *The Presidential Character: Predicting Performance in the White House*, 5th ed. (New York: Routledge, 2019). Additionally, recent scholarship suggests that a president's character is largely unchanging and predictive of success in the White House; see Lara M. Brown, *Amateur Hour: Presidential Character and the Question of Leadership* (New York: Routledge, 2021).

Part I

The High-Opportunity Presidents

2 Franklin D. Roosevelt
Artful Leadership during Hard Times

The Franklin Roosevelt presidency (served 1933–1945), regarded as one of the greatest in US history, raises central issues in the study of presidential leadership. Debate continues about Roosevelt's style of leadership, scope of power, and legacy. His policies broke new ground. In fact, the economic regulatory policies enacted during his tenure were largely intact until the 1990s, and the Social Security system he helped create mushroomed in the decades after its birth. Roosevelt's leadership style, although emulated by some presidents, has had its critics as well. Important questions have emerged about the extent to which FDR dominated Congress, the sources of his rhetorical successes, and how well he actually used the extraordinary opportunities available to him during his first years in office.

Personal Characteristics

Franklin Delano Roosevelt (1882–1945) was a unique president in at least one particular way. Thanks to a willing press, only a tiny portion of the public realized that their buoyant, optimistic president was confined to a wheelchair, the result of polio he contracted at the age of 39. Roosevelt was born in 1882 into an upper-class family descended from English and Dutch ancestors who arrived in New York in the 17th century. Theodore Roosevelt, whose presidential leadership (1901–1909) impressed Franklin as a young man, was a distant cousin, as well as the uncle of Franklin's wife, Eleanor.[1]

Franklin's boyhood was typical for those raised in a prominent New York family—life on a large family estate, a summer home, and European travel. He was schooled until age 14 by tutors at Hyde Park, the family estate located on the Hudson River about 80 miles north of New York City. Franklin spent his high school years at Groton, an exclusive preparatory school, and then attended Harvard University and Columbia Law School. At Harvard, he pursued some demanding courses but showed only moderate interest. Greater energy was devoted to his role as editor of the

DOI: 10.4324/9781003426684-3

28 *The High-Opportunity Presidents*

Harvard Crimson, the university newspaper. He performed satisfactorily while in law school, but again, without keen interest.

Career Path

As a restless young attorney, Franklin told several of his colleagues that he intended to pursue a career path modeled on that of his cousin Theodore. Remarkably, he did. He was elected to the New York Senate in 1910 at the age of 29, and three years later he entered the Wilson administration as assistant secretary of the Navy. He gained important administrative experience during his tenure there, and his responsibilities surged during World War I. In those years, he had an opportunity to study Wilson's approach to presidential leadership, how the federal bureaucracy operated, and some of the difficulties a department could have in its relationship with Congress. In 1920, the Democratic Party nominated Roosevelt as its vice presidential candidate, but he and his running mate, Ohio governor James Cox, went down in a convincing defeat.

In August 1921 Roosevelt's life changed dramatically just as he was returning to legal practice. While vacationing at the family summer home at Campobello Island, he was stricken with polio. Despite intense rehabilitation, Franklin permanently lost the use of his legs. It was only with great effort that he could maneuver himself a short distance with the use of a cane and a strong grip on the arm of a son or Secret Service agent.

After 1921, Roosevelt pursued recovery in the soothing waters of Warm Springs, Georgia, while continuing his keen interest in politics. His wife, Eleanor, encouraged his political interests by inviting prominent guests to engage him in policy issues. In 1928, Roosevelt took a gamble and won. He had debated holding off on a run for the governorship of New York but decided to enter the race anyway and won by only 25,000 votes. As governor of New York from 1929 to 1933, Roosevelt displayed some of the skills he would use later in the White House. His emerging leadership style included frequent press conferences, major radio addresses, efforts to pressure legislators through press releases, and assertive legislative leadership.

As governor, Roosevelt promoted programs such as tax relief for farmers and cheaper electric power. In 1930, as the Depression worsened, he was successful in establishing a limited old-age pension for those who met a means test. After winning reelection by a landslide in 1930, he established a state emergency relief program and an unemployment insurance program. The State Unemployment Relief Act gained considerable national attention because New York was the first state to establish such a plan.

Mounting voter frustration with the magnitude of the nation's economic collapse and President Herbert Hoover's sagging popularity sparked interest in the 1932 race for the presidency. The Democratic Party and others viewed Roosevelt's reelection effort in 1930 as a test of his potential in a presidential race, and his 700,000-vote victory only heightened their interest. But because a two-thirds majority of the party's delegates to the national convention was required to achieve nomination, he succeeded in capturing the top spot only after a tense struggle.

In the general election, Roosevelt had a tremendous advantage as the nation was seeking relief from its economic collapse. The downward spiral had begun with the crash of the stock market in October 1929. A spree of trading had caused stocks to lose 80 percent of their value. A rise in unemployment followed, with an ominous surge to 16.5 percent in 1931 and 25 percent in 1932. Adding to the nation's woes, 4,600 banks failed. During his campaign, Roosevelt emphasized themes more than specific programs since the opposition was already discredited. When the final results were in, Roosevelt had trounced Hoover in the popular vote, 57 percent to 40 percent. In an overwhelming electoral college win, he carried all states south and west of Pennsylvania. In the process, he forged a coalition that included southern Democrats (a traditional source of strength for the Democratic Party), northern urban Democrats, and farm belt Democrats, who showed stronger-than-usual support.

What Manner of Man?

Roosevelt was a complex man—in fact, more so than many people realized.[2] Frances Perkins, his longtime associate who served as labor secretary for his entire presidency, concluded in her memoirs that Roosevelt "was the most complicated person I have ever known."[3] Bruce Miroff reached a similar conclusion after reviewing Roosevelt's writings.[4]

In the spring of 1932, newspaper columnist Walter Lippmann wrote that Roosevelt was "a pleasant man who, without any important qualifications for office, would very much like to be president."[5] That observation revealed a frequently expressed concern that Roosevelt did not possess the convictions and assertiveness needed to serve as an effective president during difficult times. Years later, historian Garry Wills asserted that Lippmann's assessment of Roosevelt did not recognize the manner in which his confinement to a wheelchair had affected him. Roosevelt did not dramatically change his views on policy issues after his paralysis. What did change markedly was the resolve Roosevelt showed in his commitment to leadership.

Despite Roosevelt's complexities, some particular qualities stand out. For example, he had a tremendous desire to be at the center of any activity, including informal White House staff gatherings for cocktails at the end of most workdays and periodic poker parties with a few top associates. Roosevelt impressed people with his enthusiasm, optimism, and energy, prompting observations years later that his "radiant self-assurance was perhaps his greatest political asset."[6] His optimism was backed by hard

30 *The High-Opportunity Presidents*

work. In his eagerness to both maintain firm control of his White House and keep policy experiments moving, he frequently put in 14-hour days that rivaled the work habits of most of his successors.[7]

Roosevelt impressed many observers with his self-confidence, his genuine friendliness, and his desire to put visitors at ease. He was extremely skilled at persuading people to adopt his preferred position. In fact, visitors, including legislators, often would enter the Oval Office with one point of view and leave eager to promote a different course of action.

But FDR could be quite devious and display a ruthless political savvy. Schlesinger wrote that he liked to operate by "manipulating uncertainty," and applied it to his own staff, though not in a vengeful way.[8] Although Roosevelt was reluctant to fire people, he was quite willing to ease aides from prominent roles when their usefulness declined. On a daily basis, his coy and often indirect handling of people caused uncertainty and anxiety among those around him.

In his approach to knowledge, Roosevelt's interests were broad but shallow. He read some histories and biographies but nothing more complex. He was far more interested in talking to people and reading newspapers than examining lengthy reports. The eminent retired Supreme Court Justice Oliver Wendell Holmes perhaps echoed the view held by many when, after visiting Roosevelt, he offered this assessment: "A second-class intellect. But a first-class temperament!"[9]

Policy Views

Anyone searching for Roosevelt's major policy views must keep in mind his background.[10] His parents had been Democrats, but of the conservative Grover Cleveland variety. His ties were more to rural Hyde Park than to urban New York City.[11] Reflecting views common in the turn-of-the-century Progressive era, he was at first skeptical of labor unions. He also developed a strong and lasting interest in conservation. Roosevelt's experiences as governor of New York added strong interests in regulation of the utility industry and pension assistance for the elderly.

When he took office, Roosevelt had not yet devised any general approaches to reviving the economy. After all, the times were uncertain and the doctrine of "liberalism," as his policies would later be labeled, was still undeveloped. Roosevelt biographer James MacGregor Burns concluded that "probably the most persistent policy interest Roosevelt had was in the conservation of human and natural resources."[12]

Challenges and Opportunities

The public demand for action on Roosevelt's inauguration day was rivaled only by Lincoln's in 1861.[13] Humorist Will Rogers opined: "The

Franklin D. Roosevelt 31

whole country is with him just so he does something. If he burned down the Capitol we would cheer and say 'well, at least we got a fire started, anyhow.'"[14]

Four Immediate Challenges

Four immediate challenges faced Roosevelt and the nation as he assumed office.[15] The most urgent was mounting bank failures. A third of the nation's banks had already closed their doors, causing nine million people to lose their savings and prompting panicked customers to withdraw their funds to prevent a similar tragedy. Since even the most conservatively run banks did not have cash reserves to handle such a demand, governors in many states had resorted to declaring bank holidays.

The agricultural economy was a second wrenching problem. Farmers, unable to sell their produce at a profit, were therefore unable to meet their mortgage payments. In some instances, bank officials trying to instigate foreclosure proceedings faced unruly crowds and feared for their lives.

The lack of economic growth and high unemployment constituted a third difficult problem. The economy continued to function far below capacity, and unemployment levels hovered around 25 percent—or higher in some manufacturing areas such as Detroit and Chicago. Among African Americans, unemployment exceeded 50 percent in some parts of the country.

The fourth immediate challenge was providing relief for the destitute. Both private and state relief agencies had been overwhelmed by rising costs and had proven inadequate to the task. As a result, an estimated two million of the nation's citizens were homeless in "Hoovervilles."

Fortunately for Roosevelt, few foreign policy challenges appeared on the immediate horizon during his first term to compete with his determination to take action on the domestic front. During Roosevelt's first term, the American public lived largely apart from the realities of international relations.[16]

Roosevelt possessed both impressive advantages and sobering limitations throughout his first four years in office. Given the now-established patterns of honeymoons with the voters and rallying tendencies during a crisis, he undoubtedly enjoyed soaring popularity during his first months in office. By 1935, however, Roosevelt was confronting the typical third-year slump as his popularity sank to only 50.5 percent.[17] Despite unemployment levels of over 20 percent, only 9 percent of respondents found the relief and recovery effort too small. Of the rest, 31 percent judged it to be about right, and 60 percent termed it too great.[18]

Although Roosevelt had achieved a solid victory in the 1932 election, he realized he headed a party that had little success attaining the White House. Only Democrats Grover Cleveland and Woodrow Wilson

32 *The High-Opportunity Presidents*

(the result of a three-way race) had been elected to the presidency since the Civil War. Moreover, FDR had received a smaller percentage of votes than Republicans Calvin Coolidge in 1924 and Herbert Hoover in 1928. Roosevelt, then, faced the need to build a coalition broad enough to prevent the anti-Hoover voters of 1932 from returning to support a Republican candidate in 1936.

When he entered office in 1933, Roosevelt had large majorities of 313–117 (not counting independents) in the House and 59–36 in the Senate. Indeed, an unprecedented 97 Democrats were added to the House. Gains in the midterm election of 1934 drove those numbers up even higher: 322 in the House and 69 in the Senate. Congress was not without problems, however, since large majorities often divide into factions that can be unruly.

At first, southerners were quite supportive of FDR's programs because of the desperate poverty in their region. Yet over time, more than 100 southern Democrats found allies among Republicans who shared some of their underlying suspicions about "too much government." Roosevelt was fortunate in having generally able party leaders, but some potentially hostile southern Democrats were the chairmen of key committees.[19]

Economic Problems and Solutions

Roosevelt gathered a wide array of broad approaches to promoting economic recovery from Congress as well as the states, but little agreement existed on any one approach. The Depression was worldwide, and its causes were difficult to correct. They ranged from a global system of tariffs to a decade-long problem in the United States of agricultural overproduction and lack of consumer demand caused by highly uneven patterns of income distribution.[20] In view of this situation, some policymakers promoted nationalization of specific economic sectors, while others wanted to break up large corporations, and still others wanted to see the government develop a more comprehensive planning role. Because prices had been declining in general and even more sharply for agricultural commodities, some members of Congress pushed for policies to create inflation.[21]

Relief efforts and structural reforms such as new regulatory provisions could help, but less was known about how to revive an economy mired in high unemployment and underuse of the nation's manufacturing capacity.[22] Different monetary policies might have helped, but they were not understood at the time.[23]

Later in FDR's tenure, during World War II, the nation found that massive federal deficits, when combined with price and wage controls to prevent inflation, could provide the "jump-start" that had been advocated by British economist John Maynard Keynes. His writings impressively challenged earlier economic concepts, as he argued that debts could increase aggregate demand in two ways: first, by putting greater purchasing power in the hands of the consumer through lower taxes and, second, through direct government purchases of goods and services, producing a "multiplier" effect that would create additional new jobs.

Use of Keynesian economics faced two formidable barriers, however. First, Keynes's ideas were only beginning to gain circulation as Roosevelt took office. The second barrier was Congress itself. Even had the justifications for deficit spending been accepted, Congress, alarmed at the already high deficit spending on relief efforts, was unlikely to favor going further down that path.

Roosevelt's first-term challenge was to seize the opportunities created by the strong voices for change. But he needed to avoid moving too boldly when doing so would lead to the defeat of measures that could command majority support in Congress. FDR would have to strike a delicate balance, recognizing when to move, when to retreat, and when to wait.

The Court

In devising strategies, Roosevelt only had to look as far as the judicial branch of government to see a potential source of hostility. The makeup of the Supreme Court reflected the Republicans' prior dominance of national politics. From 1933 to 1936, the Court blocked FDR's New Deal legislation by declaring laws unconstitutional, often by a narrow 5–4 vote. Roosevelt's programs were breaking new ground, and the Court was reluctant to give judicial sanction to an expanded role for the federal government. In the spring of 1935, the president held a spirited press conference in which he accused the Court of having a "horse and buggy mentality."

Roosevelt contributed to his own problems in early 1937 after his reelection landslide. He made a rare political miscalculation in seeking to expand the size of, or "pack," the Supreme Court. The measure was defeated, however, when Republican and southern Democratic members of Congress formed a coalition.

Leadership Style

Roosevelt had a very clear leadership orientation: he wanted to be at the center of action in his presidency while exercising strong leadership. He never thought of the possibility of undertaking his responsibilities in any other way. He loved politics, craved the limelight, and was totally comfortable in the vortex of power.

Advisory Process and Approach to Decision-Making

In recruiting his cabinet, FDR paid considerable attention to the traditional issues of geographic region and ideology. The selection of Cordell Hull to

34 *The High-Opportunity Presidents*

fill the position of secretary of state brought a southerner and advocate of lower tariffs to the cabinet. A leading conservative voice was provided by Henry Morgenthau, an FDR neighbor from New York, who served as secretary of the Treasury. Henry Wallace, an agriculture expert from Iowa, filled the important secretary of agriculture post. Labor Secretary Frances Perkins, the first female cabinet member, was initially opposed by labor. Harold Ickes, who had been involved with Progressive-era reforms in Chicago, was the often rather cautious head of the Department of the Interior.[24] Staff operations in the Roosevelt White House differed dramatically from the large operations that have become standard in more recent presidencies.[25] It consisted of only a few official positions; key roles were filled by people with formal appointments in various departments, including long-time confidants and campaign advisers.

First Lady Eleanor Roosevelt was concerned that she would end up being confined to the traditional role of White House hostess. During FDR's first term, she promoted relief programs, in particular the National Youth Administration, and often served as "ombudsperson" for people having difficulty with a particular domestic program. In 1941, she became the Assistant Director of the Office of Civilian Defense but was forced to leave in 1942 after being unable to reconcile her vision of using the office to take on broader issues of social inequities, which caused her to clash with Director Fiorello LaGuardia.[26] Eleanor traveled extensively, acting as the eyes and ears of the president. There is no evidence that she modified her husband's views on policies, but the responses to her public actions helped FDR gauge public opinion.[27]

FDR preferred to control the access that advisers had to him by using a personal secretary (Missy LeHand) rather than working through a chief of staff.[28] Senior staff characterized him in that role as "dominant, dramatic at times, animated, attentive, and friendly."[29] In his quest for new policy ideas, the president emphasized competition rather than formal processes. At some points, more than one group would work on a given proposal. This method produced useful competition among advocates of different views, but it also produced bruised egos and considerable confusion.

Two patterns were apparent in Roosevelt's decision-making process. First, he was intensely concerned with the status of public opinion on various issues. According to Garry Wills, he had a strong desire not to get too far out in front.[30] Second, in making decisions about his legislative program, he engaged in extensive pre-submission consultation, particularly on which issues should go on his "must" list.

Administrative Strategies

Roosevelt's administrative strategies were an integral part of his presidency, saying once, "A cabinet member may get along without much administrative ability, but a President can't."[31] One strategy was the use of competitive appointments to elicit different kinds of information. For example, he appointed both George Peek, a favorite of farmers, and Rexford Tugwell, his left-leaning brain trust confidant, to advise him on agriculture policy. By placing people in competitive situations, Roosevelt hoped to gain more information as they contested for his favor.

His second strategy was to establish new agencies. Indeed, a record-setting 60 opened their doors during FDR's first two years in office. Roosevelt took this step because he (1) felt the existing departments had enough to do, (2) believed new agencies could give a new program full attention, (3) anticipated it would be easier to terminate a program run by appointees at new agencies than a program run by an existing agency with entrenched interests, (4) hoped to attract talented people to the new agencies, and (5) saw the new agencies as a way to ensure that administrators with sympathies toward him and the Democratic Party would be in charge.[32]

More fundamentally, for Roosevelt, administrative action was an essential tool in shaping policy implementation. Thus, he often sought broad legislative enactments that would provide considerable administrative discretion. Roosevelt's desire to experiment with policies through administrative action rather than tight legislative formulation is best illustrated by his relief and job policies. Several broad bills passed in 1933 provided the basis for shaping a wide variety of programs that included the Civilian Conservation Corps, the Public Works Administration, and the Federal Emergency Relief Administration (FERA). Roosevelt used the broad authority granted him by FERA to experiment with a variety of approaches. In its first year (1933–1934), the program concentrated on getting money to the destitute quickly. Roosevelt did not like the cost or the notion of a public dole, however, and created the Works Progress Administration (WPA) to quickly push work projects.

Administrative adaptation was central to Roosevelt's approach. This style gave him the substantial flexibility he sought and fit quite well with his personality and the relatively small-scale operations of the federal government in the 1930s. That being said, confusion did sometimes occur, and his style ultimately intensified questions about the proper division of control between the president and Congress over administrative agencies.

Public Leadership

Roosevelt's public role was a central component of his leadership efforts. In keeping with both his personality and his recognition that public attitudes were extremely important, he developed an optimistic persona—an obvious strategy for any president trying to lead a country during a difficult economic period. His speaking skills and buoyant optimism, expressed quite intensely in the opening days of his administration, showed results.

36 *The High-Opportunity Presidents*

In fact, top aide Raymond Moley believed it "was the confidence of the public rather than any specific reforms that led to the recovery which followed."[33]

Roosevelt's "fireside chats" were central to his confidence-building efforts. These talks, usually given on Sunday nights, sometimes were heard by almost half of the nation's population. Generally less than a half hour in length, they emphasized themes rather than specific factual information.

President Roosevelt also communicated with the public through the nation's newspapers. In fact, he held more press conferences than any of his successors. Roosevelt displayed a knack for simplifying complex policies and ideas,[34] but his approach was also notable. In contrast to today's large, televised conferences, FDR invited about two dozen reporters into the Oval Office, usually on Tuesdays and Fridays. Members of the press corps were flattered to be in the inner sanctum, where, aides hoped, they would be less apt to notice or comment on the president's wheelchair. He seemed to genuinely enjoy the banter, as well as the pursuit of angles that would make good stories. Using this mechanism, the president could promote favorable personal coverage and help steer publicity toward issues he was promoting in Congress. Despite Roosevelt's skills, he could only shape newspaper coverage to a degree. By late 1934, his unusually lengthy honeymoon with the press corps had begun to fade.

Congressional Leadership

Roosevelt allocated a good deal of time dealing with Congress, sometimes spending three to four hours on legislative matters in a given day. He worked very closely with party leaders in both houses and used other legislators to track votes. Of the unusually extensive range of legislative strategies and tactics favored by Roosevelt, the most far-reaching was to hold Congress in session throughout the spring of 1933 after the banking crisis was resolved. This tactic was part of an agenda-setting strategy that included careful attention to a presidential "must" list. To secure quick action, Roosevelt promoted bills that had many different components to enhance their congressional support.

Roosevelt showed considerable flexibility in the coalitions he sought to create. During 1933 and 1934, Roosevelt pursued a centrist coalition strategy without any particular effort to push to the left. His "all class" coalition policies included not only relief and reform measures but also a sharp reduction in veterans' benefits and adoption of the national ethics codes for business favored by the US Chamber of Commerce. In 1935, as he moved somewhat to the left, he spoke of a "tender sadness" as he looked back on his failed hope that "the leaders of finance and big business would learn something."[35] Even taking Roosevelt's third-year shift into account, Arthur Schlesinger characterized Roosevelt's coalitions as centrist, pointing out that "Roosevelt was opposed about as often on the left as on the right."[36]

Other strategies and tactics were aimed directly at members of Congress. For example, the White House would try to force action when a bill appeared to be stalled in committee, woo the support of various committee chairs, harness the parliamentary skills of several members of Congress from the South, encourage individual legislators to develop proposals on their own, and show a frequent willingness to compromise.

Legislative Enactments

The special session of Congress that extended from March 9 to June 16, 1933, and was known as the "First Hundred Days" produced a sweeping set of legislative responses to the problems created by the Depression (see Table 2.1). Lawmakers passed landmark legislation in each of Roosevelt's first three years in office and again in 1938. One broad area of response was economic regulation, used extensively to address problems in key sectors such as agriculture, labor relations, banking, and stock market operations. Relief policies and the development of the landmark Social Security Act of 1935 were a second broad area of response.

Economy Act and Veterans' Benefits

Passage of the Economy Act in 1933 and the fight over veterans' benefits were evidence of Roosevelt's efforts to build an "all class" coalition that included conservative support. The employment- and salary-cutting

Table 2.1 Legislative Enactments during FDR's "First Hundred Days," 1933

Date	Legislation
March 9	Emergency Banking Act
March 10	Reconstruction Finance Corporation (expanded)
March 20	Economy Act
March 22	"Beer Act"
April 5	Civilian Conservation Corps
May 12	Agricultural Adjustment Act
	Emergency Mortgage Act
	Federal Emergency Relief Act
May 18	Tennessee Valley Authority
May 27	Securities Act
June 13	Home Owners Loan Act
June 16	National Industrial Recovery Act
	Railroad Coordination Act
	Banking Act

38   *The High-Opportunity Presidents*

provisions of the Economy Act, which Roosevelt had advocated in his campaign, gave the president the authority to make major reductions in the number of government employees and the amounts of salaries. Projected salary cuts were in the 15 percent range, with projected savings of $100 million.

Veterans' benefits were hard to ignore if spending was to be cut because they constituted almost a quarter of the federal budget.[37] Roosevelt gained passage of the bill easily in the House, but he began to face resistance in the Senate. To aid his cause, he forcefully promoted the notion that he would take the blame from the veterans' lobby.

But Roosevelt's early victory did not end the controversy. A group of veterans gathered in Washington to press their demands, and some observers feared violence or a sad repeat of the Bonus Army showdown of 1932.[38] Roosevelt sought early relief jobs for the veterans, and Eleanor Roosevelt visited them several times to boost morale. Ultimately, the group left quietly. By the end of the special session, however, Congress had begun to worry about the next congressional election and forced Roosevelt to restore $100 million in cuts. Nevertheless, expenditures on veterans' benefits dropped more than 40 percent between fiscal 1932 and 1934.

Agricultural Adjustment Act

Roosevelt spent much of 1933 pursuing new policies for agriculture. Although modifications were required in the wake of Supreme Court decisions, the landmark legislation that eventually emerged created an enduring system of assistance for some specific crops, such as wheat and cotton. Once again, the president enlisted multiple legislative strategies.

Despite the widespread desire for action, differences of opinion among agricultural interests posed major problems.[39] The plan Roosevelt proposed and Congress ultimately adopted called for a new Agricultural Adjustment Agency (AAA) to pay farmers for taking cropland and livestock out of production, with a processing tax financing the program. While reduced production was central to the legislation, the bill also allowed experimentation with a wide variety of other approaches, including overseas dumping.

Given the decade-long deadlock on agricultural policy, Roosevelt realized that only by exerting strong leadership would he see an agricultural bill pass in the special session. The scope of the bill clearly helped ensure its passage since various groups could see some possibility that their preferred approach would be used.

Regulation of Financial Institutions

Efforts to regulate financial institutions produced the one instance of Congress "rubber stamping" a presidential policy in 1933, but there were repeated instances of significant congressional contributions. Passage of the Emergency Banking Act early in the "First Hundred Days" session of Congress found Roosevelt quickly borrowing ideas for legislation from departing Hoover administration officials who agreed to stay on to help draft the new measure. The legislation Roosevelt presented surprised some observers because of its conservative nature. The bill validated the actions the president had already taken, gave him complete control over the movement of gold, penalized hoarding, and authorized the issue of new Federal Reserve bank notes. It arranged for the reopening of banks with liquid assets and reorganized the rest.

Congress greeted this proposal with readiness for immediate action. With the bank holiday already in place, lawmakers knew they would have to act quickly to maintain public confidence. As a result, the House passed the bill, sight unseen, with a unanimous shout after only 38 minutes of debate. Some senators protested that the legislation would give too much power to the large banks, but the Senate acted quickly after limited debate, and the bill passed by a margin of 73–7. The legislation was approved for Roosevelt's signature on the same day it was received on Capitol Hill.

Roosevelt also introduced other significant changes to the banking system. These included modifying the role of the Federal Reserve system, prohibiting banks from selling securities, and creating the Federal Deposit Insurance Corporation. While the president played a small role in promoting this initial legislation, he played a bigger role in a second landmark banking measure passed in 1935. Roosevelt encouraged Marriner Eccles, recently appointed chairman of the Federal Reserve Board, to develop the new banking bill. In the Senate, Carter Glass (D-VA) substantially modified Eccles's proposals. Roosevelt contributed to those negotiations by designating certain provisions "must" legislation. The final provisions substantially expanded the authority of the Federal Reserve Board.[40]

The passage of securities industry regulations in 1933 and 1934 further exemplified the joint efforts of Roosevelt and Congress to achieve changes in regulatory policy. Once again, Roosevelt's proposal was based on plans solicited from various participants. When passed, the Securities Act of 1933 was an important first step toward transforming the nation's securities markets. By 1934 Roosevelt had realized that more changes were needed. In February the president asked Congress for legislation to regulate the New York Stock Exchange. Roosevelt designed a bill more comprehensive than the one being considered by Congress. This development produced an indignant response from financiers, with some talking of moving their operations to Canada. Public hostility toward the investment community was fueled in part by large investors "selling short" to profit from a decline in stock prices after an increase in the spring of 1933. The new legislation, the Securities Exchange Act, created the Securities and Exchange Commission and gave that agency substantial regulatory

40   *The High-Opportunity Presidents*

authority. Roosevelt selected Joseph P. Kennedy, a major financial contributor to his 1932 campaign and a shrewd operator within the business world, to head the new agency.

Labor Policies

Policies addressing the nation's labor movement and working conditions, like many other policies, did not unfold smoothly. Toward the end of the "First Hundred Days" Roosevelt became alarmed when he learned that serious support had developed in the Senate for a 30-hour workweek. To counteract this development, the president quickly proposed the National Industrial Recovery Act (NIRA), which was, in most respects, a movement to the right. It allowed the creation of pricing agreements for various sectors of the economy, called for fair competition codes for industry, barred child labor, fixed minimum wages, and recognized the right of collective bargaining by labor.

The Supreme Court had ruled that some provisions of the NIRA were unconstitutional.[41] While clearly desiring some protections for labor, Roosevelt nevertheless continued to resist an explicit endorsement of Senator Robert Wagner's bill, known as the National Labor Relations Act. Roosevelt continued to be coy and indecisive in various meetings with Senator Wagner and labor leaders as the bill proceeded through committee hearings. Roosevelt ultimately accepted key provisions of the proposed legislation, including the establishment of a separate labor relations board (which he had initially resisted). Ultimately, the same newspapers that had reported the president's early wavering on the bill gave him far too much credit for this landmark legislation.[42]

Roosevelt was far more supportive of the federal minimum wage program established by the Fair Labor Standards Act.[43] He had been a proponent of minimum wage provisions in the industry codes negotiated under the NIRA and became an even stronger proponent when the Supreme Court eliminated those provisions. Considerable legislative maneuvering was required for two reasons. First, labor leaders opposed a measure they believed would undercut their ability to attract members. Secondly, conflicts arose over questions such as whether to impose a lower minimum wage for the southern states. The legislation finally passed in 1938 called for a minimum wage of 25 cents per hour. All increases in the federal minimum wage since 1938 have been achieved by amending the original legislation.

Relief, Welfare, and Social Security

Attempts to deal with the human suffering caused by the Depression generated substantial legislation in Roosevelt's first term. FDR proposed and achieved the passage of three relief and social welfare measures in 1933.

These established both the federal role in citizens' well-being and the basis for considerable experimentation.

The signing of the Social Security Act on August 14, 1935, brought into being a measure that Walter Lippmann described as "the most comprehensive program of reform ever achieved in this country in any administration."[44] Like the NIRA and the AAA, the act contained multiple components. These included (1) retirement benefits for citizens over the age of 65 who contributed to the Social Security fund through payroll deductions; (2) unemployment compensation shared by both the federal and state governments; and (3) means-tested, jointly operated welfare assistance for the needy in the categories of aged, blind, disabled, and dependent mothers and children. The Aid to Families with Dependent Children (AFDC) program built on the programs already adopted by all states (except South Carolina and Georgia) that extended at least meager aid to widows with children.[45]

Despite the large majorities in Congress, Roosevelt recognized that conflicting pressures would make passage of a comprehensive measure difficult. Conservatives were skeptical of these programs in general, and many southerners (who packed the Ways and Means committee) feared that New Deal measures might disrupt the supply of cheap labor in their states. Other interests wanted a larger package than what the president felt the federal government could afford.

Roosevelt and key aides worked diligently to develop the proposed legislation.[46] In seizing the initiative from Congress in 1934, he established the Committee on Economic Security (CES). Committee staff members were drawn from states known for their political innovations and experimentation. With an eye toward southern states, Roosevelt also convened an advisory council chaired by a representative of that region.

The CES debated a state role in Social Security, but that approach was judged to be administratively unfeasible. The states did, however, have a major role in all other programs, including AFDC and unemployment compensation. This role stemmed from a respect, shared by FDR, for state governments as policy innovators. It was also due to the federal government's limited capacity for administering these programs and a desire not to run afoul of the Supreme Court.

While exploring different funding mechanisms, Roosevelt sought a solution that would deter politicians from tampering with it in the future. He explained:

> We put those payroll contributions there so as to give the contributors a legal, moral, and political right to collect their pensions and unemployment benefits... with those taxes in there, no damn politician can ever scrap my social security program.[47]

42 *The High-Opportunity Presidents*

Yet Roosevelt was concerned about future costs, and this led to a last-minute scaling back of the proposal. Congress passed Roosevelt's Social Security measure only after a variety of maneuvers by the White House.

Other Significant Legislation

Three other landmark measures were enacted during Roosevelt's years in the White House. In 1934, Congress created the Federal Communications Commission (FCC), which assumed responsibility for regulating the radio broadcasting industry. A second landmark measure was the 1934 National Housing Act.

In 1933, Congress had indicated its willingness to act in the housing area by passing provisions to protect both farmers and urban dwellers from foreclosure. It was eager to act again in 1934. Roosevelt proposed establishing a federal housing agency that would guarantee home mortgages made by savings and loan institutions. In addition, a mandatory system of building inspection would protect consumers. In assessing the scope of the National Housing Act, housing policy expert Joseph L. Arnold pronounced it a landmark enactment.[48] The act proved easy to promote because it would generate employment in the home construction industry as well as direct housing assistance. The real estate lobby, which had opposed some of Roosevelt's policies, also endorsed this legislation.

The third landmark measure was the 1944 GI Bill of Rights. This measure provided war veterans with educational assistance, from secondary schooling to college, and housing assistance. This uniquely successful domestic policy both aided veterans and relieved a potential labor surplus by steering significant numbers of World War II veterans to colleges rather than having them flood the labor market.

Two other measures passed in Roosevelt's first term—one creating the Tennessee Valley Authority (TVA) and the other increasing taxes—help underscore the manner in which the president and Congress were contributing to major policy enactments. The establishment of the TVA in 1933 was an important example of the collaboration characteristic of the first hundred days of Roosevelt's term. Shortly before his inauguration, Roosevelt and Senator George Norris, an Independent Republican from Nebraska and a leading progressive, visited the Muscle Shoals site on the Tennessee River, which was being considered as the location for a major hydroelectric power plant. FDR encouraged Senator Norris to pursue a program larger than the one proposed in his earlier bill vetoed by Hoover. Encouraged, Norris proceeded to draft a very comprehensive legislative proposal that FDR supported.

Roosevelt and Congress

President Roosevelt's strategies in dealing with Congress included getting off to an extraordinarily fast start in 1933, designing legislation that appealed to multiple interests, agenda setting with his "must" list, assembling centrist coalitions in 1933–1934 followed by a shift to the left in 1935, and exerting public leadership in order to sustain general support for his presidency and his legislative initiatives. Interestingly, the Roosevelt White House made few efforts to sell specific legislative measures to the public. Attempts to persuade individual legislators were reserved more often for committee votes than for final floor votes.

Yet Congress also made immense contributions. In 1933, for example, it moved ahead with the Banking Act despite Roosevelt's reluctance, and he was forced into proposing the NIRA because of his fears that a 30-hour workweek bill would pass. Some fundamental legislation, including the landmark National Labor Relations Act (also known as the Wagner Act), was enacted without any direct presidential support. Congress was not a rubber stamp, and as historian Alberto Romasco concluded: "the nature of the early New Deal was decisively influenced by the ongoing cooperation, rivalry, and spirit of bargaining and compromise which characterized the relationship between Roosevelt and ... the 73rd Congress."[49]

According to George Edwards III, the president's predominant role in policymaking is that of a facilitator rather than a director of policy change.[50] This view fits the Roosevelt case. In the process of trying new policies, Roosevelt created an environment in his relationships with Congress in which not only his personal staff but also agency heads, legislative specialists in Congress, state officials, and interest group leaders all had important influences in shaping far-reaching changes in domestic policy.

An Assessment

One forceful assessment of the New Deal was Roosevelt's landslide victory in the 1936 election. In gaining reelection, he engineered an enduring "inclusive coalition," brought together through his first-term policy achievements and his public leadership. The strength of that coalition was apparent not only in Roosevelt's 1940 and 1944 election victories but also in President Harry Truman's ability to achieve his come-from-behind victory in 1948.

A fundamental expansion of economic regulation was at the heart of New Deal domestic policy. Roosevelt may not have always been the dominant figure, but he usually was a significant contributor. Roosevelt's agriculture policies, beginning with the broad Agricultural Adjustment Act of 1933, became the basis for subsequent controls.

44 *The High-Opportunity Presidents*

The expanded regulation of financial institutions that took effect in the early Roosevelt years produced landmark changes in the banking system, including the establishment of deposit insurance. Americans quickly accepted the regulation of financial institutions, and mortgage protection became an extremely popular vehicle for expanding home ownership.

The establishment of the National Labor Relations Board and the provisions of the Wagner Act led to the rapid unionization of basic industries during the late 1930s and a far stronger labor movement after World War II. Union membership increased from some 3 million in 1936 to over 8 million in 1941 and 14 million by 1945.

The longest-lasting legacy of the New Deal was the Social Security Act. Each of its components, with the exception of the controversial AFDC program, still exists today. Over the years, Social Security became the one area of social spending in which American policy efforts rivaled those of the more generous social welfare states.

The slow pace of Roosevelt's efforts to assist African Americans was a missed opportunity. About 20 lynchings per year occurred in the early 1930s before falling to about two per year at the end of the decade.[51] The House could muster support for legislation, but the Senate was hampered by the likelihood of a southern filibuster. In the face of continuing tragedies, Roosevelt agreed in 1934 to meet with NAACP leader Walter White. The president explained to White that

> southerners, by reason of the seniority rule in Congress, are chairmen or occupy strategic positions on most of the Senate and House Committees. If I come out for the anti-lynching bill, they will block every bill I ask to keep America from collapsing. I just can't take that risk.[52]

Roosevelt continued to publicly denounce the lynchings and ultimately indicated his willingness to support an antilynching bill. But he declined to place such a bill in his category of "must" legislation, and efforts to pass legislation were unsuccessful.[53]

Using administrative strategies, the Roosevelt White House apparently succeeded in reducing discrimination and extending some aid to African Americans, and disparities declined somewhat.[54] Only reluctantly did he finally yield to pressure to establish the Federal Employment Practices Commission in 1941.

The biggest disappointment for Roosevelt and the nation was the modest economic improvement during the 1930s. While the economy did grow significantly, unemployment remained a problem. The gross domestic product increased from $58.3 billion in 1933 to $82.5 billion in 1936 and $100.5 billion in 1940, but the unemployment figures never dropped

Franklin D. Roosevelt   45

below 14 percent before World War II, and the averages for Roosevelt's first and second terms were 22.8 percent and 18 percent. Some critics point to Roosevelt's hostility to business and financial leaders as contributing to the slow recovery.[55]

Roosevelt often has been criticized for not developing a clear philosophy to guide the policies of the New Deal. But given the tremendous lack of agreement on specific policies among policy advocates and members of Congress, this charge warrants considerable skepticism. Efforts to pursue a single philosophical course of strong governmental action would have raised profound questions about the degree of influence a president should be able to assert.

In shaping New Deal policy responses, Roosevelt showed numerous skills. He sought ideas from a wide variety of sources, pursued active and ongoing congressional leadership with an impressive range of strategies, parlayed his fireside chats into an effective communications device, and often molded final policy impacts through the use of administrative strategies. However, FDR's level of influence in his legislative leadership had negative consequences as various members of Congress grew to resent his level of control.

In his decision-making process and administrative strategies, Roosevelt's effort to "manipulate uncertainty" has continued to draw criticism. At points, this strategy created confusion and resentment. For some, Truman's very forthright approach was seen as a welcome change from Roosevelt's sometimes overly elaborate maneuvering. The vast expansion of the federal government in recent decades has rendered this leadership style far less feasible today.

Ultimately, assessments of Roosevelt's performance often come back to the importance of his public roles, and his ability to reassure the public was the real strength of the New Deal.[56] Bruce Miroff more broadly concluded, "Although Roosevelt could not vanquish the Great Depression, his administration relieved the worst of mass distress, while restoring confidence in the power of democracy to meet both the material and moral needs of its citizens."[57]

How well did FDR play the hand dealt him? Overall, very well. He was a high-opportunity/high-achievement president who cast a giant shadow over all who followed him into the White House.

Notes

1 The discussion of Roosevelt's early experiences is drawn in part from Frank Freidel, *Franklin D. Roosevelt: A Rendezvous with Destiny* (Boston: Little, Brown, 1990).
2 Arthur M. Schlesinger Jr., *The Age of Roosevelt* (Boston: Houghton Mifflin, 1958), ch. 35.

46 *The High-Opportunity Presidents*

3 Frances Perkins, *The Roosevelt I Knew* (New York: Viking Press, 1946), 3.
4 Bruce Miroff, *Icons of Democracy: American Leaders as Heroes, Aristocrats, Dissenters, and Democrats* (New York: Basic Books, 1993), 235.
5 Quoted in ibid., 10.
6 Miroff, *Icons of Democracy*, 236.
7 A. J. Wann, *The President as Chief Administrator* (Washington, DC: Public Affairs Press, 1968).
8 Schlesinger, *Age of Roosevelt*, 554.
9 James MacGregor Burns, *Roosevelt: The Lion and the Fox* (New York: Harvest/ HBJ, 1984), 157.
10 See H. W. Brands, *Traitor to His Class: The Privileged Life and Radical Presidency of Franklin Delano Roosevelt* (New York: Doubleday, 2008).
11 See Robert Dallek, *Franklin D. Roosevelt: A Political Life* (New York: Penguin, 2018), ch. 1.
12 Burns, *Roosevelt*, 237.
13 Freidel, *Franklin D. Roosevelt*, 92.
14 Arthur M. Schlesinger Jr., *The Coming of the New Deal: 1933–1935*, Mariner Books ed. (New York: Houghton Mifflin, 2003), 13.
15 William Leuchtenberg, *Franklin D. Roosevelt and the New Deal* (New York: Harper and Row, 1963); and Richard S. Kirkendall, *The United States, 1929–1945: Years of Crisis and Change* (New York: McGraw-Hill, 1974).
16 Robert H. Ferrell, *American Diplomacy: The Twentieth Century* (New York: Norton, 1988), 185.
17 Kenneth S. Davis, *FDR: The New Deal Years, 1933–1937* (New York: Random House, 1995), 571.
18 George Gallup, *Gallup Poll Monthly Report, 1935–1971* (New York: Random House, 1972), 1.
19 Dennis W. Johnson, *American Public Policy: Federal Domestic Policy Achievements and Failures, 1901 to 2022* (New York: Routledge, 2023), 110.
20 For representative discussions, see Robert B. Carson, *What Economists Know: An Economic Policy Primer for the 1990s and Beyond* (New York: St. Martin's Press, 1990), chs. 3 and 5; and Kirkendall, *United States, 1929–1945*.
21 For a recent review of options that were considered, see Colin Gordon, *New Deals: Business, Labor, and Politics in America, 1920–1935* (New York: Cambridge University Press, 1994), ch. 1.
22 For a review of economic knowledge at the time, see Carson, *What Economists Know*, ch. 3.
23 Herbert Stein, *Presidential Economics: The Making of Economic Policy from Roosevelt to Reagan and Beyond* (Washington, DC: American Enterprise Institute, 1988).
24 For a detailed description of FRD's top advisors, see Derek Leebaert, *Unlikely Heroes: Franklin Roosevelt, His Four Lieutenants, and the World They Made* (New York: St. Martin's Press, 2023).
25 This discussion of Roosevelt's staff structure draws in part from Charles E. Walcott and Karen M. Hult, *Governing the White House: From Hoover through LBJ* (Lawrence: University Press of Kansas, 1995).
26 Matthew Dallek, *Defenseless Under the Night: The Roosevelt Years and the Origins of Homeland Security* (New York: Oxford University Press, 2016).
27 Joan Hoff-Wilson and Marjorie Lightman, eds., *Without Precedent: The Life and Career of Eleanor Roosevelt* (Bloomington: Indiana University Press, 1984).

Franklin D. Roosevelt 47

28 Kathryn Smith, *The Gatekeeper: Missy LeHand, FDR, and the Untold Story of the Partnership That Defined a Presidency* (New York: Atria Books, 2016).
29 Patricia D. Witherspoon, *Within These Walls: A Study of Communication between Presidents and Their Senior Staff* (New York: Praeger, 1991), 14.
30 Garry Wills, "What Makes a Good Leader," in *Understanding the Presidency*, ed. James P. Pfiffner and Roger H. Davidson (New York: Longman, 1997), 440–444.
31 Wann, *President as Chief Administrator*, 11.
32 Ibid.
33 Raymond Moley, *After Seven Years* (New York: Harper, 1939).
34 See Roger Daniels, *Franklin D. Roosevelt: Road to the New Deal, 1882–1939* (Champaign, IL: University of Illinois Press, 2015).
35 Ibid., 512.
36 Schlesinger, *Age of Roosevelt*, 555.
37 Ibid., 239.
38 Martin L. Fausold, *The Presidency of Herbert C. Hoover* (Lawrence: University Press of Kansas, 1985), 201–203.
39 On agricultural politics, see Alberto U. Romasco, *The Politics of Recovery: Roosevelt's New Deal* (New York: Oxford University Press, 1983); and Rexford Tugwell, *Roosevelt's Revolution: The First Year—A Personal Perspective* (New York: Macmillan, 1977).
40 Sidney Hyman, *Marriner S. Eccles: Private Entrepreneur and Public Servant* (Palo Alto, CA: Stanford University Graduate School of Business, 1976), 181–189.
41 *Schechter Poultry Corporation v. United States*, 295 U.S. 495 (1935).
42 Lawrence H. Chamberlain, *The President, Congress and Legislation* (New York: AMS Press, 1967), 175.
43 Willis J. Nordlund, *The Quest for a Living Wage: The History of the Federal Minimum Wage Program* (Westport, CT: Greenwood Press, 1997), ch. 3.
44 Quoted in Davis, *FDR*, 523.
45 Walter I. Trattner, *From Poor Law to Welfare State: A History of Social Welfare in America*, 4th ed. (New York: Free Press, 1989), 202.
46 Sources used for this case include J. Altmeyer, *The Formative Years of Social Security* (Madison: University of Wisconsin Press, 1968); Perkins, *The Roosevelt I Knew*; Edwin L. Witte, *The Development of the Social Security Act* (Madison: University of Wisconsin Press, 1963); Henry J. Pratt, *Gray Lobby* (Chicago: University of Chicago Press, 1976); Jill Quadagno, *The Transformation of Old Age Security: Class and Politics in the American Welfare State* (Chicago: University of Chicago Press, 1988); and John H. Williamson and Fred C. Pampel, *Old-Age Security in Comparative Perspective* (New York: Oxford University Press, 1993).
47 Freidel, *Franklin D. Roosevelt*, 150.
48 Joseph L. Arnold, "Housing and Resettlement," in *Franklin Roosevelt: His Life and Times, an Encyclopedic View*, ed. Otis L. Graham Jr. and Meghan Robinson Wander (New York: G. K. Hall, 1985), 187.
49 Romasco, *Politics of Recovery*, 27.
50 George C. Edwards III, *At the Margins: Presidential Leadership of Congress* (New Haven, CT: Yale University Press, 1989), 223.
51 Freidel, *Franklin D. Roosevelt*, 83.
52 Quoted in Davis, *FDR*, 484.
53 Leuchtenberg, *Franklin D. Roosevelt and the New Deal*, 186.

48 *The High-Opportunity Presidents*

54 Bruce J. Schulman, *From Cotton Belt to Sunbelt: Federal Policy, Economic Development, and the Transformation of the South, 1938–1980* (New York: Oxford University Press, 1991).
55 Alonzo H. Hambry, *Man of Destiny: FDR and the Making of the American Century* (New York: Basic Books, 2015).
56 Garry Wills, "What Is a Political Leader?" *Atlantic*, April 1994, 79.
57 Miroff, *Icons of Democracy*, 233.

3 Lyndon B. Johnson
Legislative Leadership and a Credibility Gap

On March 31, 1968, Lyndon Johnson (served 1963–1969) stunned a nation weary of the Vietnam War and urban unrest with this nationally televised announcement: "I shall not seek—nor will I accept—the nomination of my party for another term in this great office of all the people."[1] He only went public with his decision after Senator Eugene McCarthy (D-MN) made a surprisingly strong showing in the March 1968 New Hampshire primary. Just four years earlier, Johnson had been widely praised as a masterful legislative leader and one of the truly great presidents of the twentieth century. In fact, 1964–1965 had produced by far the biggest outpouring of new legislation since FDR's first term. Then things fell apart. Johnson went from high-opportunity/high-achievement president to political villain in a few short years. Lady Bird Johnson pronounced her husband's White House years as "the best of times, the worst of times." Johnson's leadership skills—and the limitations he faced—were an essential part of the story of this eventful period.

Personal Characteristics

The lanky, 6'5" Lyndon Baines Johnson (1908–1973) was a product of both Texas and Washington. He was raised in the Texas hill country west of Austin by a mother with high ambitions for her son and a father with a populist political orientation and a career that included ranching, real estate, state lawmaking, and service in a low-paying state job. After Johnson graduated from high school, he spent a year in California and then attended Southwest Texas State Teachers College rather than the more prestigious University of Texas at Austin. In college, he was an indifferent student but spent long hours talking with one of his political science professors. He also enjoyed campus politics and became an influential figure while an aide in the president's office, observing the state legislature in nearby Austin. Lyndon was a young man in a hurry as well—he graduated in only two and a half years. Before pursuing a life in politics, he became

DOI: 10.4324/9781003426684-4

50 The High-Opportunity Presidents

the only president after Herbert Hoover to teach in a secondary school, first at a poor rural school composed largely of Hispanic students and later in Houston. In these early years, Johnson was highly active in local politics. He got his start in national politics by gaining a congressional staff position after working on a local campaign.[2]

Career Path

Johnson had more extensive political experience in Washington than any other post-Hoover president. With the exception of the two years he spent as the Texas administrator for President Franklin Roosevelt's National Youth Administration, he held various positions on Capitol Hill, from that of a staff aide beginning in late 1931, to Senate majority leader from 1955 to 1961, to vice-president until 1963. Johnson showed not only intense ambition but also considerable skill in seeking out mentors who could teach him the art of politics and help him advance his career. These included Sam Rayburn (D-TX), who served as Speaker of the House on and off between 1940 and 1961; Senator Richard Russell (D-GA), the acknowledged dean of the southern senators; and to some degree President Roosevelt himself.

When his local member of Congress died in 1937, Johnson campaigned aggressively—talking himself to exhaustion, but won the coveted House seat. LBJ was viewed as a "comer" by Roosevelt, and through the influence of both fellow Texan Rayburn and Roosevelt, he gained important committee assignments. Frustrated with the seniority system in the House, he sought a Senate seat unsuccessfully, narrowly losing in a special election in 1941. He was luckier in 1948, winning by a narrow margin and earning the facetious nickname "Landslide Lyndon."

In the 1930s LBJ had been a staunch New Dealer on economic issues. But in the 1940s he began to vote more conservatively as both Texas and the nation became less supportive of the New Deal agenda. Among other things, he went along with popular sentiment in Texas and voted for the 1947 Taft-Hartley Labor Act and against federal civil rights actions such as antilynching laws.

Johnson's Senate career reached a new high in 1953 when he became its minority leader. Two years later he was selected as majority leader. LBJ built the position into one of greater influence and has been generally regarded as one of the modern Senate's most effective party leaders. The techniques he used as majority leader resembled those he would use so effectively as president. For example, he prided himself on an extensive information system that included detailed knowledge of what the Republicans were doing. Occasionally, he engineered vote trades by arranging aid for a given senator's state. He built loyalty among junior members with good committee assignments, and he was a master at manipulating legislative procedures.[3]

Lyndon B. Johnson   51

LBJ's move to the presidency actually began with his belated bid for the party's nomination in 1960, but he was no match for the strong primary performance by Senator John Kennedy (D-MA). After Kennedy put Johnson on the ticket in order to shore up support in the South, LBJ campaigned diligently in the fall election. As vice president, Johnson was not part of Kennedy's inner circle. Nor did Kennedy use Johnson in a major way in dealing with the Senate, believing it would produce resentment.

What Manner of Man?

Johnson's drive for power was intense and rooted in personal insecurity. He had virtually no hobbies other than politics and the pursuit of business deals. His energy seemed boundless, yet at points he drove himself to the point of exhaustion. During his first weeks in the presidency, for example, he seldom slept more than three or four hours a night. His long-standing routine was to begin work around seven, take a nap around four, and then continue working well into the evening. Sixteen- to 18-hour days were not uncommon.

Johnson's insecurities have been traced to early childhood experiences. His mother, a descendant of a prominent Texas family, sought to compensate for her own downward social mobility with her hopes for Lyndon.[4] Apparently, her high aspirations, coupled with little expression of parental love, shaped both his insecurities and his intense desire to succeed. Johnson also harbored many resentments. His targets included those whom he viewed as receiving a better education than he had, including the "Harvard crowd" surrounding Kennedy, but also the press corps he blamed for focusing on his failings. His frequent mood swings led some writers to conclude that he suffered from aspects of a manic-depressive personality.[5] Although Johnson had not attended a prestigious college and had little interest in books, his intelligence was apparent as he soaked up knowledge quickly.

Johnson's relationships with other individuals were complex. He thoroughly enjoyed the process of manipulation and was extremely effective in one-on-one situations, combining his legendary arm-twisting with carefully reasoned arguments. He would often augment his cajoling with vulgarity. Johnson could also be cruel, such as when he forced Vice President Hubert Humphrey to shoot a deer on the LBJ Ranch specifically because he knew Humphrey would hate to do it. Yet he often seemed to view staff as "family" and could, on occasion, be quite caring when they faced difficulties. Loyal staff aides learned to ignore his tirades. Top aide Joseph Califano captured his many dimensions when he wrote,

The LBJ I worked with was brave and brutal, compassionate and cruel, incredibly intelligent and infuriatingly insensitive, with a

52   The High-Opportunity Presidents

shrewd and uncanny instinct for the jugular of his allies and adversaries. He could be altruistic and petty, caring and crude, generous and petulant, bluntly honest and calculatingly devious—all within the same few minutes.[6]

Policy Views

Johnson, who found political ideologies too inflexible, was not a typical liberal. He seemed to have a love affair with economic growth and had little interest in redistributive policies that would aid the poor by increasing taxes on the wealthy. These ideas came together in 1964 as he promoted his War on Poverty along with a major tax cut.[7] He also viewed labor unions skeptically, viewing strikes as a waste of resources. His close ties with the business community—and his own investment successes—generated sympathy for its concerns.

LBJ did, however, support many liberal causes. Born into a family that periodically suffered economic difficulties in one of the nation's poorer states, Johnson identified with the view that government efforts could help people help themselves, and he showed genuine concern for the impoverished. In one poignant moment during his White House years, he cried as he viewed the Depression-era poverty depicted in the movie *The Grapes of Wrath*. As a teacher early in life, Johnson believed in the importance of education. His domestic agenda was rooted in his view that "government could directly or indirectly alleviate any distress."[8] Thus, his vision of his "Great Society" programs, while partially motivated by a desire for personal greatness, was also rooted in strong personal beliefs.

Johnson changed his views on racial issues dramatically over the course of his career. Early on, his voting record on racial issues paralleled that of other southern members of Congress. But by the mid-1950s, as he began thinking of a possible presidential bid, he began moderating his views. By 1962 he was advocating stronger steps than Kennedy wanted to take, and he increasingly saw civil rights issues in moral terms. His evolution was influenced partly by personal events—such as when an African American staff aide had difficulty finding "colored only" accommodations when driving back to Texas.

Challenges and Opportunities

Johnson faced both extensive opportunities and daunting challenges. In his first two years, he enjoyed a greater opportunity to achieve major domestic policy change than any post-Hoover president except Roosevelt. LBJ's opportunity was enhanced by a national sense that the components of Kennedy's domestic program that had not yet been passed should be enacted to honor the former president.

Johnson also benefited from having, in effect, two first years in office. In 1964, the first-year honeymoon effect enhanced his personal popularity, and with his landslide election win the same year, he was able to credibly argue that he now had a mandate for the domestic programs he had been promoting. In addition, because he had an opportunity (which he capitalized on handsomely) to work on new proposals throughout 1964, he was able to move his program in Congress more quickly in 1965 than a president who had not enjoyed the additional time. In turn, the surge of Democratic strength in Congress not only suggested the existence of a mandate but, in more practical terms, provided a group of new Democratic members of Congress who were in large part strongly committed to the president's expansive policy agenda.

Two other factors also contributed to Johnson's high-opportunity level. First, the lengthy list of programs that had been drawing increased support over the preceding five to ten years represented excellent "windows of opportunity" in that there was substantial agreement on the need for action and in some instances considerable agreement on the appropriate policy design.[9] Second, Johnson was aided by the general social and political activism stirring in American society by 1964.

The economic forces that Johnson faced in the mid-1960s were the exact opposite of those Roosevelt faced in 1933. Rather than confronting a depression that would cause an apprehensive nation to look to the government for new policies, Johnson assumed office at a time when economic conditions had seldom been better. Economic growth between 1963 and 1966 produced a three-year peacetime growth record of 6 percent in both 1965 and 1966.

In contrast to his early years, Johnson saw an unprecedented decline in his opportunities in his last three years. In Congress the Democrats lost 47 seats in the 1966 midterm elections. But this loss was only one indication of the changes in public attitudes. One fundamental source of Johnson's eroding opportunities was the dramatic shift in racial conflicts from the southern states to the cities of the North. This shift began with rioting in Harlem in 1964 and burst dramatically into the national spotlight with the Watts riots in Los Angeles in August 1965. Johnson faced a difficult dilemma since actions proposed to address urban problems could be construed as rewarding rioters.

Johnson hoped to avoid having the conflict in Vietnam disrupt his pursuit of Great Society programs. He did this by sidestepping debate and, at first, carrying out the military buildup in ways that caused as little disruption as possible to American society. Over time, resistance to Johnson's Vietnam policies mounted, and his two uniquely successful years dealing with Congress on domestic policy were followed by a presidency in increasing disarray.

54 The High-Opportunity Presidents

Leadership Style

Johnson sought to model his leadership on that of his friend, FDR. He often spoke of Roosevelt as "a second Daddy to me" and "a book to be studied, restudied, and reread."[10] Any president, in LBJ's view, needed to be the central figure in a political system in which Congress was reactive. Whereas Truman and Eisenhower had concerns about Roosevelt's assertiveness with Congress, Johnson strongly believed that decisive leadership was essential and that Roosevelt's performance was the one to emulate. He also strongly subscribed to the view that the president should speak for all individuals and interests.

Advisory Process and Approach to Decision-Making

As an accidental president, Johnson faced the same task Harry Truman had confronted in 1945—cabinet and staff members would have to be changed. But this would have to be done gradually and while maintaining a public perception of continuity between the two presidencies. By virtually all accounts, Johnson handled the initial transition very well with his emphasis on reassurance and continuity.

Inevitably, key personnel did begin to change. Some wished to leave, and others bowed to Johnson's preferences for replacement. The heart of Johnson's advisory process was at the staff level, where he modeled his system in part on FDR's staff operations.[11] At various times, several different people fulfilled aspects of the chief of staff role, but Johnson was very much in charge of overall operations. Johnson recruited some prominent Texans to surround himself, such as his own longtime aides Bill Moyers and Henry McPherson, both of whom had served in the Kennedy administration. Johnson surrounded himself with advisors who knew there was limited time for a president to act and that Johnson's broad domestic policy initiatives would need to be pushed with great speed.[12]

With his staff in place, Johnson launched an unusually broad search for domestic policy ideas.[13] In July 1964, the president created a system of outside task forces that would seek ideas from a broad range of experts. These groups were to operate in secret and avoid weighing either budgetary concerns or political feasibility as they worked to develop the best possible proposals in each policy area. At the beginning, each task force was made up of about a dozen individuals, some drawn from outside government. About half were chosen for their academic credentials; the other slots were divided among business, labor, and other interest groups. Interagency task forces took on new importance as well. Presidential commissions also were established on occasion, such as the Kerner Commission on Civil Disorders in the wake of rioting in Detroit in 1967. In all, a total of 145 task forces were convened during Johnson's five years in office.

The proposals that came out of these task forces were met by Johnson's considerable attention to issues of political feasibility. He phoned committee chairs frequently and read the opinion polls avidly. He also provided ample access for various interest groups of all persuasions as final proposals were being developed.

Because Johnson was a firm subscriber to the view that his popularity and clout would decline over time, he sought to move new proposals quickly. Moreover, because he believed that "consensus" could be achieved with programs that had some gains for virtually all Americans, he emphasized a broad range of new initiatives. Johnson's search for ideas and the results that emerged have sometimes been criticized for a lack of new direction. Many of LBJ's proposals already had been considered in Congress and were not highly innovative,[14] although these proposals enjoyed a degree of fine-tuning by Johnson in order to secure passage. Johnson did not come to power under the same conditions enjoyed by Roosevelt and Reagan—that is, as representatives of parties that had been out of power and as candidates oriented toward new approaches. Rather, Johnson was the head of a party that had been struggling to pass its existing agenda for some time.[15]

Administrative Strategies

Johnson did not consistently engage in administrative issues—he had neither the time nor the interest. However, he did encourage members of his staff to deal with policy implementation. The few formal reorganization proposals that came to light rarely commanded his attention.[16] Although Johnson periodically would become engaged with the bureaucracy on a highly specific issue, his primary goal was to pass legislation.

Not surprisingly, LBJ's administrative style created problems. The rapid emergence of new programs for states and urban areas led to considerable confusion. Many thought there was insufficient follow-through in the implementation of civil rights legislation. In his desire to move rapidly to wage a war on poverty, Johnson also sought to implement a system of community participation, which some critics found unwieldy and ineffective. By the end of the Johnson administration, it had become clear that administrative issues required greater attention.

Public Leadership

Johnson was neither well prepared nor well equipped to deal with public leadership. His years in the Senate had not provided the skills he needed to make effective public addresses. As for the media, he had become accustomed to dealing with the often-cooperative Texas press, so he was ill-prepared for sparring with the more adversarial White House press corps.

56 The High-Opportunity Presidents

He could be highly persuasive in small groups, but his speaking style before large audiences included exaggerations and promises more befitting a speech at a local courthouse than a national address. In contrast to Kennedy, who was at ease dealing with television, Johnson continually experimented but frequently was dissatisfied with his results. On television, he simply lacked the personal warmth and appeal of a Kennedy or an Eisenhower.

With the aid of skilled speechwriters, and when speaking from the heart on some domestic topics, Johnson could be rather effective. His 1964 State of the Union address generally received a favorable assessment. A commencement address delivered at the University of Michigan the same year, and commonly known as the "Great Society" speech, was one of his more well-received efforts. An oft-quoted line is: "The Great Society ... demands an end to poverty and racial injustice, to which we are totally committed."[17] His early statements on civil rights also drew generally favorable reviews.

Public speaking became more difficult for Johnson as he dealt with the problems of conflict over the Vietnam War and urban unrest. On the problem of urban unrest, he was torn between the desire to express concern for the injustices contributing to it and the desire to avoid the appearance of being unresponsive to calls for strong measures to prevent further rioting. He often resorted to recitations of economic progress and the scope of new programs, but they did little to alleviate the growing concern about the state of the nation.

Johnson's tendency toward deception also undermined his credibility. Lies about small matters, such as whether any of his relatives died in the Alamo, left many reporters and members of the public wondering whether he was trustworthy on larger issues. His tendency to make bold claims for his new policies, including labeling his poverty effort a "war," often produced skepticism when the policies produced less-than-advertised results. Various statements about Vietnam, starting with his 1964 campaign pledge to avoid American involvement, contributed as well to what many labeled his "credibility gap."

LBJ also found it hard to deal with the media in part because of his desire to manipulate the press. Formal press conferences were held somewhat sporadically and took on a combative quality as Johnson's popularity fell. In one of his more vulgar comments, Johnson responded to a reporter, "Why do you come and ask me, the leader of the Western World, a chicken-shit question like that?"[18]

Difficulties in relating to the public and the press were reflected in Johnson's popularity ratings. He was intensely interested in polling results and often would attribute a decline in approval ratings to various policies such as those on civil rights or Vietnam. Yet, he also contributed to his own problems with the persona he had created. He could not realistically present himself to a skeptical press as anything other than a Washington insider. Moreover, his poor press relations reduced his chances for positive personal stories.

Congressional Leadership

Legislative leadership was a central dimension of Johnson's view of his presidency. He continued many of the practices he had used as majority leader, including carefully reading the *Congressional Record*, zealously pursuing information, paying careful attention to coalition possibilities, and pushing hard to get key votes. While vote trades were considered periodically, the president also liked to use his extensive information about issues to push the merits of various proposals.

In the course of his attempts to persuade members of Congress, the president spent more time dealing with committee chairs than with rank-and-file members. Just as in his Senate days, Johnson went about gaining the support of individual legislators in many different ways—specific trades, appeals to the public interest, or a carefully developed personal appeal.

On occasion, Johnson would use public addresses to help spur passage of his legislation, but this was rare. More often, his primary role was playing the "inside game" of dealing with key committee chairs. In rallying public support, he felt more comfortable with efforts to mobilize interest groups and opinion leaders than with public addresses. Although the White House had no formal public liaison office, staffers promoted interest group activity heavily. They also called on opinion leaders, including key business figures, to solicit public endorsement of various legislative measures.

Johnson was also committed to a fast start. As he said after he retired, "You've got to give it all you can that first year. Doesn't matter what kind of majority you come in with. You've got just one year when they treat you right, and before they start worrying about themselves."[19] At the outset of his administration, he seemed to think often of Roosevelt's legislative performance in his first two years in office and to pursue legislation with an eye toward rivaling—if not surpassing—FDR's accomplishments.

Legislative Enactments

During Johnson's five years in the White House, the nation witnessed the most extensive outpouring of domestic legislation since Roosevelt's first term. Three landmark bills were enacted in 1964, followed by three more in 1965. Journalists wrote that Johnson had enacted the remaining components of the New Deal agenda in only 18 months. The pace slowed after 1965, but Congress continued to pass major legislation, including a

58   The High-Opportunity Presidents

landmark housing measure in 1968. Johnson's leadership was a key factor in several of these developments.

1964: A Remarkable Beginning

Johnson very definitely hit the ground running in 1964. In 1963, during his first weeks in office, he had provided the nation with the reassurance it needed, followed by a strong State of the Union address in January 1964 calling for swift enactment of stalled measures and a new War on Poverty. The 88th Congress (1963–1965), which had given President Kennedy considerable difficulty, responded to Johnson's leadership and the rising mood of activism in the country with not only three landmark measures but also several major policies, including one targeting urban mass transit and one targeting the environment. To achieve passage of the War on Poverty program, a substantial tax cut, and the Civil Rights Act of 1964, Johnson applied different styles of presidential leadership.

Economic Opportunity Act

Johnson exhibited his broadest range of influential skills when he pushed the Economic Opportunity Act of 1964. This measure was promoted as the president's War on Poverty, but ultimately other Great Society programs would be more central in the effort to reduce poverty. The push began on Johnson's first day in the White House. President Kennedy had asked Walter Heller, chairman of the Council of Economic Advisers, to develop a poverty proposal for 1964 but had given him little specific guidance. Johnson gave Heller strong encouragement with the comment, "That's my kind of program. It will really help people."[20] A frenzied planning process ensued, with various agencies trying to promote their programs among the many ideas being considered. Kennedy's brother-in-law, Sargent Shriver, took over development of the final proposal and later became head of the new Office of Economic Opportunity. The proposal emphasized creating job opportunities and services in poor areas rather than supporting incomes. One important idea was local participation in the design of needed services. As finally passed, the Economic Opportunity Act called for the establishment of Community Action Programs, which would determine the need for a variety of local services. The act included a Job Corps program to provide job training to youths. A volunteer program, Volunteers in Service to America (VISTA), was envisioned, along with a legal services program for the poor, neighborhood health centers, and a preschool program called Head Start.

Passage of this legislation was a testament to Johnson's political skills.[21] After encouraging a bold planning process, he discussed the measure in his State of the Union address and referred frequently to the War on Poverty in his daily remarks. He also highlighted the submission of his program to Congress in March with a special one-hour television interview carried by all three networks. Finally, virtually all segments of American society received calls and letters in a campaign to garner expressions of support. The administration enlisted not just antipoverty volunteers and minorities but also prominent educators such as university presidents, heads of various religious organizations, corporate and labor leaders, and state and local officials. In April, Johnson, sensing a tough fight in Congress, decided to pursue public support more directly by using his first trip as president—to Appalachia—to dramatize the nation's poverty problem. He also called legislators whose support was uncertain. When the bill passed in the House by a larger-than-expected margin of 226–184, veteran observers were amazed. House Majority Leader Carl Albert (D-OK) reportedly told the president, "I really can't figure out... how in the world we ever got this through."[22]

Tax-Cut Legislation

Johnson used very different tactics to promote passage of the tax cut President Kennedy had proposed in 1963.[23] Kennedy had called for reductions in every tax bracket, with total reductions of $11 billion for individuals and $2.6 billion for corporations. After difficulties and amendments, the measure had passed in the House before Kennedy's death, so Johnson pushed for its passage by the Senate.

Over lunch with Senator Harry Byrd (D-VA), Johnson struck a deal in which Byrd promised rapid action on the legislation and the new president promised to cut the size of the proposed deficit in his new budget to half of the $10 billion originally planned by Kennedy. With his typical delight in secrecy and surprise, LBJ then gave the press the impression that it would be impossible to keep the new budget under $100 billion even as he was hard at work producing a lower figure. He kept his side of the agreement with a proposal that cut Kennedy's proposed deficit by almost $5 billion. Commenting later on his efforts to achieve the reduction, Johnson said, "I worked as hard on that budget as I have ever worked on anything."[24] The size of the proposed tax cut was reduced slightly as well. In so doing, he had sent a message that deficits would be watched closely, thereby garnering support for his tax cut from the more conservative members of Congress. In the end, then, approval of the tax cut came easily, and Johnson was able to sign this landmark measure on February 26, 1964.

Civil Rights Act

During the last six months of his life, Kennedy had responded to the often-violent civil rights demonstrations with new urgency. He submitted a specific legislative proposal that, among other things, sought to end

60 *The High-Opportunity Presidents*

discrimination in public accommodations such as restaurants, hotels, and transportation. Other provisions called for strengthening voters' rights. At the time of his death, Kennedy's measure had made progress in the House, but it faced an uncertain future.

Johnson took over leadership of the civil rights bill with considerable intensity and a very distinct strategy. Public support for the bill had increased in the wake of Kennedy's assassination, and Johnson was also spurred by the public activism that was emerging. In the House, supporters of the bill overcame southern resistance, and the Civil Rights Act passed on February 10 by a vote of 290–130. It then faced deliberation in the Senate.

Johnson's strategies were informed by his keen knowledge of the Senate. One key step was to indicate to Senator Richard Russell (D-GA), leader of the southern contingent, that he would not accept a significant compromise on the proposed legislation. Sensing that he was better off working behind the scenes, Johnson dealt closely with Senator Hubert Humphrey (D-MN) on legislative strategies. Since the support of Republicans was necessary to break a filibuster, Humphrey was instructed to work closely with the Republican Senate Minority Leader Everett Dirksen (R-IL). Johnson also had several conversations with Dirksen about the issue. As the filibuster began, Humphrey successfully orchestrated an effort by supporters of the legislation to gradually wear down the southern Democrats. Dirksen then brought additional Republicans into the supporters' camp, and the filibuster was broken.

The historic Civil Rights Act of 1964 owed its passage to many factors. Civil rights protests, rather than presidential leadership, had put the issue on the public's front burner by the spring of 1963. Growing public support also was a factor, especially among whites outside the South. President Kennedy's actions beginning in June 1963 and the actions of key legislators such as Senators Humphrey and Dirksen made a significant contribution as well. Finally, President Johnson contributed to the act's passage by refusing to bargain with the southerners and by encouraging the legislative strategies that ultimately produced the necessary Republican votes. After his decisive win in 1964 and the addition of 37 Democrats to the House, the scene was set for another highly prolific period of congressional action.

The 89th Congress: A Flood of New Legislation

The 89th Congress (1965–1967) produced an extraordinary flow of legislation, including three landmark measures in 1965—Medicare, federal aid to education, and the Voting Rights Act. It also saw a steady pace of major enactments, including an innovative Model Cities program in 1966 and several significant environmental measures. President Johnson did have some failures, however. One was home rule for the District of Columbia, and another was a labor-endorsed measure that would have eliminated state right-to-work laws. Nevertheless, Johnson enlisted a variety of strategies in promoting an unusually successful legislative agenda.

Medicare

By 1965, the time for enacting health insurance for the elderly had arrived.[25] There was strong public support, and Johnson had made Medicare a major issue in the 1964 campaign. The remaining stumbling block appeared to be the resistance of congressional committee chairs. Johnson and the chairman of the House Ways and Means Committee, Wilbur Mills (D-AR), ultimately became the key figures as Congress debated a broader plan of health coverage than was originally envisioned.

Johnson contributed to the passage of Medicare in several ways. First, he used a combination of the findings of an advisory panel; staff work by Undersecretary of Health, Education, and Welfare Wilbur Cohen; and the contributions of Nelson Cruikshank, representing the AFL-CIO, to expand the original legislation. At this juncture, a fateful decision was made: Johnson's planners decided not to incur the wrath of the American Medical Association (AMA) over fee structures. Second, Johnson gave the bill added importance by touting it in his State of the Union address and then having it symbolically designated the first bill to be considered by both houses of the new Congress. Third, in a classic display of his ability to manipulate an individual legislator, LBJ confronted Senator Byrd on his reluctance to report out the bill by inviting him to the White House and, to Byrd's surprise, arranging for television cameras to be present as he left. The startled senator, when asked on camera about the bill, indicated somewhat reluctantly that his committee would report it out. Finally, once the legislation had been passed, Johnson shrewdly promoted the program with a group of AMA leaders, thereby helping to achieve smooth implementation of the new measure.

Federal Aid to Education

Before 1965, federal aid to education (elementary and secondary) had been debated often but never enacted. In 1965, however, both changing conditions and presidential strategies contributed to swift passage. The most important condition that changed was southern resistance to the legislation. Southerners, who had wanted aid for segregated schools, saw their bargaining position crumble with passage of the Civil Rights Act of 1964. Additionally, the lobbying groups that had been fighting over the issue for years seemed more willing to compromise.

62 *The High-Opportunity Presidents*

President Johnson made education a top priority in the fall campaign, and he wanted to act quickly in 1965 before opposition could form.[26] He began by appointing, without announcement, a presidential task force, headed by John Gardner, president of the Carnegie Corporation. The task force proved to be one of Johnson's most successful. It met in secret and consulted behind the scenes with key groups such as the monsignors of the Catholic Church, Jewish organizations, southern leaders, and the various education lobbies. Thus, through selective intervention without publicity, the executive branch was able to foster a climate of learning and accommodation between the proponents and the opponents of general aid to education.[27]

Voting Rights Act

In 1965, pressures for legislation on voting rights mounted when it became apparent that the voting rights provisions contained in the 1964 Civil Rights Act could not be easily implemented in areas of staunch resistance. The issue was dramatized in March when the Reverend Martin Luther King Jr. led protests in Selma, Alabama. African Americans were still being denied the right to vote, and other aspects of segregation were still being practiced despite the provisions of the 1964 Civil Rights Act. Marches and protests brought the expected rough handling and jailings. Johnson federalized the Alabama National Guard to keep order, and television coverage helped intensify nationwide support for additional legislation.

The Johnson administration, which had been considering additional voting rights legislation before the Selma protests, decided to act. The key provision of the new legislation was a trigger mechanism that would use low minority voter registration according to a "coverage formula" as a basis for federal intervention (this provision was struck down by the Supreme Court in 2013). Once the bill had been drafted, Johnson met with the leaders of both parties to discuss the next steps. They encouraged the president to make a national address, which he did—but from Capitol Hill. In that appeal for support, he placed the issue in historic terms as he said in part, "I speak tonight for the dignity of man and the destiny of democracy... so it was at Lexington and Concord. So it was a century ago at Appomattox. So it was last week in Selma, Alabama."[28] The public found it one of the most moving and eloquent speeches of his career.[29]

Environmental Measures and Model Cities

Environmental measures also began to emerge from Congress. In October 1965, with strong leadership from Senator Edmund Muskie (D-ME), Congress set auto emission standards for automobiles. The Johnson administration was more directly involved in passage the same year of

Lyndon B. Johnson 63

the Highway Beautification Act, a cause actively promoted by Lady Bird Johnson.

The Model Cities legislation passed in 1966 had emerged from one of the 1965 task forces.[30] It was developed as a complement to the Community Action Programs Johnson had instigated as part of the War on Poverty and was to be the showpiece of the new Department of Housing and Urban Development. The stated goal of the legislation was to improve the quality of urban life by providing federal block grants that would cover 80 percent of the costs of projects such as low- and moderate-income housing, health care, crime prevention, and even recreation. Any city could vie for inclusion in the program, but only 60 to 70 would be chosen.

Johnson found it difficult to promote passage of this legislation in a Congress that was increasingly reflecting voter unease about the direction of his programs. Some opponents of the bill openly argued that it simply rewarded protesters who were burning down the nation's cities. In the face of resistance, industry, labor, civil rights, and religious groups undertook a massive lobbying campaign. Johnson and several top aides, together with future Housing and Urban Development Secretary Robert Weaver (the nation's first African American cabinet member), sought legislative support. In the House, Johnson was able to hold together most of his northern Democratic supporters, and the measure passed by a majority of 178–141. Senate passage came more easily, and another Great Society experiment was launched.

The 90th Congress: Johnson Keeps Trying

From one Congress to the next, Johnson never stopped trying to promote his domestic agenda. During his last two years in office, he faced a sharply reduced Democratic majority in the House with the loss of 47 seats in the midterm election and growing national frustration over urban rioting and the war in Vietnam. Yet, task forces kept turning out new proposals, and Johnson kept seeking various opportunities for additional legislative action. Successes, however, became more elusive as the president found his window of opportunity closing. Some environmental and consumer measures were passed, in part because of strong pressure within Congress, and an administration proposal for increases in Social Security benefits also passed.

The biggest events of the last two years of Johnson's presidency were the passage of the Civil Rights Act of 1968 (targeting housing discrimination) and the belated effort to raise taxes. The Senate had killed a housing discrimination bill in 1966 with a filibuster, and another bill was buried in committee in 1967. A similar fate was predicted in 1968 when legislation was introduced for a third time. The situation, however, had

64   The High-Opportunity Presidents

changed. The tireless advocacy by the NAACP helped. Senator Dirksen then switched his position, which was critical to break a filibuster, and the measure passed.

House action occurred in the midst of the widespread urban rioting that followed the April 1968 assassination of Reverend Martin Luther King Jr., and sections of the nation's capital erupted in flames. Members of the House, looking at an election in the fall, were highly sensitive to public opposition. Johnson urged members of the House Judiciary Committee to act on the legislation. With some members concluding that a dramatic step would be helpful, and amid strong lobbying by many different groups, the committee reported out the Senate bill intact, and it went to the House floor. The full House passed the legislation within 24 hours.

Johnson and Congress

It is not easy to determine just how much credit Johnson deserves for the legislative outpouring that occurred during his years in the White House. Some statistical studies of a large group of measures have had little success in isolating a significant influence stemming from presidential skill. Jon Bond and Richard Fleisher, for example, concluded that Johnson won about 5.5 percent more often than might be expected from the nature of the underlying coalition strength in the House, but about 3.2 percent less often in the Senate.[31] Mark Peterson found that Johnson facilitated the large amount of legislation that emerged by not squandering his opportunities.[32]

Favorable circumstances also helped Johnson enormously. His legislative skills would not have produced a comparable outpouring of legislation had he held office in 1961. Yet, he made significant contributions to passage of some landmark measures, including his uncompromising stance on the 1964 Civil Rights bill and the very president-centered process that led to enactment of the War on Poverty. Strategies and tactics, in short, can make a difference. Johnson made the most of his opportunities and served as a facilitator during a period of strongly desired action on both ends of Pennsylvania Avenue.

The realignment of the political parties in the late 1960s added to the conservative embrace of big government and a big presidency. The FDR coalition of the 1930s–1940s brought unlikely allies together—liberal northern Democrats with conservative southern Democrats—united behind the personality and policies of Roosevelt. After LBJ's Great Society programs were enacted, these groups drifted apart, and the conservative South realigned with the Republican party. Johnson was well aware that this would be the case as he commented on civil rights legislation: "We just delivered the South to the Republican party for a long time to come."[33]

An Assessment

The Johnson years produced fundamental changes in American life. The most far-reaching change was in the social status of African Americans. The Civil Rights Act of 1964 ended segregation in public facilities such as restaurants and transportation systems, legally at least, and the Voting Rights Act of 1965 dramatically increased the availability of the right to vote. In Selma, Alabama, over 50 percent of African Americans were registered to vote four years after the protests had begun. Increases in some areas of Mississippi were even more dramatic. While not producing as dramatic a change, the Open Housing Act of 1968 offered African Americans greater home-buying opportunities.

Another fundamental social change was the expansion of access to health care for the elderly and segments of the poor, combined with changes in the organization of the health care system. By addressing a very real health insurance need for the elderly, Medicare proved to be highly popular. Unfortunately, the program, which initially paid all "usual and customary fees" coupled with the costs of expanded longevity, became increasingly expensive.

The federal aid to education program paid out significant funds initially, but the compromise formula used to achieve passage reduced the amount of targeting possible. As funding declined, the federal government once again had a very small role by the 1990s, and both authority and funding responsibilities shifted to the states. The Johnson-era environmental policies had some initial impacts, but stronger efforts were more feasible during the Nixon years when interest in environmental issues soared.

Johnson's economic policy legacies were mixed. Growth was substantial, and unemployment was low. But as Johnson attempted to fund both guns (Vietnam) and butter (the Great Society), the burden on the economy caused a downturn in a variety of economic indicators.

Many assessments of Johnson's War on Poverty have concluded that "poverty won." But this is a misleading interpretation of a complex set of relationships. If one looks simply at the portion of the population living below the poverty line, a dramatic improvement occurred—from 20 percent in 1963 to 12 percent in 1968. This decline in poverty was the result in part of the tight labor market during those years, which has been variously attributed to the growth created by the tax cut and the additional military spending incurred by the onset of the Vietnam War. The decline in poverty among the elderly can be traced in part to the impact of Medicare beginning in 1966. Later, when Medicare assistance for health costs was combined with the substantial rise in Social Security benefits in the 1970s, the number of the elderly in poverty declined significantly.

The performance of other programs included in Johnson's War on Poverty is more debatable. Their potential impact was muted in part by the military spending ramping up in 1966 that prevented Johnson from increasing outlays for his most effective programs, and they received only modest resources. Food stamps and the earned income tax credit, while not receiving much public attention during Johnson's time in office, assumed higher profiles in later years. In addition, Head Start showed positive results and found lasting interest and support.

Although ambivalent about the measure at first, Johnson can be credited for being the driving force behind the passage of the Immigration and Nationality Act of 1965, securing key compromises on the way to passage. The law removed prior quotas that tilted heavily against would-be immigrants from Asia and Africa. Instead, a new preference framework was introduced, with family ties as the highest priority. The law profoundly changed the nation's demographic landscape.[34]

Overall, Johnson's performance in office revealed both impressive talent and glaring weaknesses. On the plus side, Johnson often built coalitions that were, according to one legislative aide, designed to be razor thin to get the most in a legislative package. His intense interest in seizing opportunities was evident not only during the good times of 1964–1965 but also in 1968, when he successfully seized the opportunity to pursue open housing legislation. Moreover, Johnson's use of his task forces to generate legislative proposals was, arguably, one of the more successful presidential efforts of that type.

When Johnson's performance is measured in terms of his ability to use his high-opportunity level in 1964–1965, he warrants high marks. In terms of getting the most from situations, a recent assessment by former senator Eugene McCarthy seems most perceptive: "Johnson could get what there was in a situation, but not more."[35] In many cases, Johnson's strategy was to "get laws on the books" that, if initially imperfect, could be tweaked later.[36]

On the negative side, Johnson played an often inept public role, especially when trying to help the country move beyond his "politics of the best possible coalition." Between his initial staunch espousing of the case for civil rights and his strong speech on voting rights in 1965, he was at points quite effective. But when faced with the difficult issues arising from urban riots, his persona as a legislative bargainer and the sense that he was not entirely trustworthy reduced his effectiveness. In many ways, he simply failed to satisfy a nation that desired both a sense of direction and a measure of reassurance about its domestic policies.

Several conclusions about Johnson's leadership stand out. He was a president who cared deeply about the programs he was promoting, and he had impressive political skills, which he used to move his legislative agenda. Yet his strategy of seeking to pursue "something for everyone" was a painfully inadequate vision for a nation going through a period of rapid social change.

Notes

1 Lyndon Baines Johnson, *The Vantage Point: Perspectives of the Presidency, 1963–1969* (New York: Holt, Rinehart and Winston, 1971), 429.
2 On Johnson's background, see in particular Robert Dallek, *Lone Star Rising: Lyndon Johnson and His Times, 1908–1960* (New York: Oxford University Press, 1991); and Paul Conklin, *Big Daddy from the Pedernales: Lyndon B. Johnson* (Boston: Twayne Publishers, 1986).
3 Rowland Evans and Robert Novak, *Lyndon Baines Johnson: The Exercise of Power* (New York: New American Library, 1966).
4 James David Barber, *The Presidential Character: Predicting Performance in the White House* (Englewood Cliffs, NJ: Prentice Hall, 1972); and Doris Kearns Goodwin, *Lyndon Johnson and the American Dream* (New York: Harper and Row, 1976).
5 John R. Bumgarner, *The Health of the Presidents: The 41 United States Presidents through 1993 from a Physician's Point of View* (Jefferson, NC: McFarland & Co., 1994).
6 Joseph A. Califano, *The Triumph and Tragedy of Lyndon Johnson: The White House Years* (New York: Simon and Schuster, 2015), 10.
7 See Nancy Beck Young, *Two Suns of the Southwest: Lyndon Johnson, Barry Goldwater, and the 1964 Battle between Liberalism and Conservatism* (Lawrence, KS: University Press of Kansas, 2019).
8 Conklin, *Big Daddy from the Pedernales*, 193.
9 James L. Sundquist, *Politics and Policy: The Eisenhower, Kennedy, and Johnson Years* (Washington, DC: Brookings Institution, 1968).
10 Stephen Hess, *Organizing the Presidency*, rev. ed. (Washington, DC: Brookings Institution, 1988), 94.
11 Ibid., ch. 7.
12 Joshua Zeitz, *Building the Great Society: Inside Lyndon Johnson's White House* (New York: Viking, 2018).
13 Charles E. Walcott and Karen M. Hult, *Governing the White House: From Hoover through LBJ* (Lawrence: University Press of Kansas, 1995), 152–153.
14 Mark A. Peterson, *Legislating Together: The White House and Capitol Hill from Eisenhower to Reagan* (Cambridge, MA: Harvard University Press, 1990).
15 This major distinction between Johnson's circumstances and those of Roosevelt and Reagan is drawn from Stephen Skowronek, *The Politics Presidents Make* (Cambridge, MA: Harvard University Press, 1993).
16 Marlan Blissett, "Untangling the Mess: The Administrative Legacy of Lyndon Johnson," in *Lyndon Baines Johnson and the Uses of Power*, ed. Bernard J. Firestone and Robert C. Vogt (Westport, CT: Greenwood Press, 1988), ch. 4.
17 Irving Bernstein, *Guns or Butter: The Presidency of Lyndon Johnson* (New York: Oxford University Press, 1996), 132.
18 Dennis D. Riley and Bryan E. Brophy-Baermann, *Bureaucracy and the Policy Process: Keeping the Promises* (Lanham, MD: Rowman & Littlefield, 2006), 140.
19 Quoted in Hess, *Organizing the Presidency*, 22.
20 Steven F. Hayward, *The Age of Reagan: The Fall of the Old Liberal Order, 1964–1980* (New York: Three Rivers Press, 2001), 12.
21 Barbara Kellerman, *The Political Presidency: The Practice of Leadership* (New York: Oxford University Press, 1984), ch. 7.
22 Quoted in the *Herald Journal*, October 20, 1971, 3.

68 *The High-Opportunity Presidents*

23 Phillip M. Simpson, "Lyndon B. Johnson and the 1964–1968 Revenue Acts," in *Lyndon Baines Johnson and the Uses of Power*, ed. Bernard J. Firestone and Robert C. Vogt (Westport, CT: Greenwood Press, 1988), ch. 13.

24 Johnson, *Vantage Point*, 36.

25 Sheri I. David, *With Dignity: The Search for Medicare and Medicaid* (Westport, CT: Greenwood Press, 1995); and Theodore R. Marmor, *The Politics of Medicare* (New York: Aldine Publishing, 1973).

26 Bernstein, *Guns or Butter*, ch. 7.

27 Michael R. Reople and Lance W. Bardsley, "Strategies for Governance: Domestic Policy Making in the Johnson Administration," in *Lyndon Baines Johnson and the Uses of Power*, ed. Bernard J. Firestone and Robert C. Vogt (Westport, CT: Greenwood Press, 1988), 21.

28 Johnson, *Vantage Point*, 165.

29 Conklin, *Big Daddy from the Pedernales*, 216.

30 Bernstein, *Guns or Butter*, ch. 18.

31 Jon R. Bond and Richard Fleisher, *The President in the Legislative Arena* (Chicago: University of Chicago Press, 1990), 206.

32 Peterson, *Legislating Together*, 244–246.

33 Bill Moyers, "Second Thoughts: Reflections on the Great Society," *New Perspectives Quarterly* 4, Winter (1987): 13–15.

34 Daniel Tichenor, "*The Historical Presidency*: Lyndon Johnson's Ambivalent Reform: The Immigration and Nationality Act of 1965," *Presidential Studies Quarterly* 46, no. 3 (2016): 691–705.

35 Eugene McCarthy, remarks at a meeting of the Town Hall of Los Angeles, June 14, 1995.

36 Norman J. Glickman, Laurence E. Lynn Jr., and Robert H. Wilson, "Understanding Lyndon Johnson's Neglected Legacies," in *LBJ's Neglected Legacy: How Lyndon Johnson Reshaped Domestic Policy and Government*, ed. Norman J. Glickman, Laurence E. Lynn Jr., and Robert H. Wilson (Austin, TX: University of Texas Press, 2015), 8.

4 Ronald Reagan
One Big Year

Ronald Reagan (served 1981–1989) swept into the White House more committed to changing domestic policy than any president since Lyndon Johnson. The actor-turned-politician was a high-opportunity president with a clear agenda, but debates continue about how much change he actually accomplished and what leadership style his presidency really embodied. Granted, the landmark economic legislation passed in 1981 was a tribute to Reagan's effective "going public" and fast-start strategies. Many aspects of his media strategies still draw praise. Even the "Teflon factor"—Reagan's ability to sustain personal support even in the face of adverse developments—has generated considerable interest. But just how much did this high-opportunity president achieve?

Personal Characteristics

Ronald Wilson Reagan (1911–2004) was the only president since 1932 to have changed his party identification (in his case, from Democrat to Republican). He also was the nation's oldest president up to that point at the time of his election. Eisenhower was 70 when he left the presidency; Reagan celebrated his 70th birthday during his first weeks in office. And Reagan was the nation's only divorced president up to that time.

"Dutch," as he was sometimes known, grew up in small towns in northern Illinois. His father, Jack, who suffered from bouts of alcoholism, persistently changed sales jobs. Jack Reagan was an avid Democrat and was pleased at one point to acquire a minor job with one of Roosevelt's New Deal agencies. Ronald attended Eureka College, a nearby small church-related school. He enjoyed drama, football, and his involvement with student government while completing his economics major.

DOI: 10.4324/9781003426684-5

70 *The High-Opportunity Presidents*

Career Path

Reagan followed an unusual career path to the presidency. After graduating from college in 1932, he went into broadcasting in Des Moines, Iowa, where he reported "live" (working from a teletype delay) baseball games being played 300 miles away in Chicago. In 1937 Reagan accompanied the Chicago Cubs on a spring training trip to Los Angeles. There, a studio screen test sparked the beginning of an acting career. On the payroll of Warner Brothers Studio, Reagan often played the "all-American boy." In 1940 he married Jane Wyman, a well-known actress. Two years later he entered the US Army Air Corps and was assigned to making training films in nearby Culver City, California.[1]

From 1947 to 1952, Reagan served as president of the Screen Actors Guild, a labor union representing actors. During that time, many feared that communists had infiltrated the movie industry, and aggressive hearings by the House Committee on Un-American Activities produced heated controversies among Guild members. Reagan also participated in several Democratic Party electoral campaigns, including that of staunch liberal Helen Gahagan Douglas, who lost the 1950 California Senate race to Richard Nixon. With his acting career waning, Reagan divorced Wyman in 1948 and four years later married another actress, Nancy Davis. In 1957, Reagan accepted an offer from General Electric to lecture its employees and host a weekly TV program. In writing his own speeches, and at points in listening to his new arch-conservative father-in-law, Reagan began to change his political philosophy. In 1962, he formally switched to the Republican Party, and in 1964 delivered a nationally televised speech in support of Republican presidential nominee Barry Goldwater. The speech was so well received that Reagan—and others—began to realize he might have a career in politics.

In 1966 Reagan ran a strong campaign and had the advantage of running against an unpopular incumbent seeking a third term, and further benefitted from a growing Republican tide to win election as governor of California. In his eight years in office he developed a distinct leadership style.[2] He encouraged his staff to prepare brief "mini-memos," and he delegated responsibility extensively. He used public addresses effectively to support his favorite causes and to gain leverage with the legislature. Despite his rhetoric of limited government, he actually presided over a period of considerable expansion in state government. He possessed a shrewd ability to go along with various new or larger programs while maintaining the public's perception that he opposed government expansion. Often, people seemed to conclude that he was at least trying to constrain government operations.

After leaving the governor's office, Reagan made an unsuccessful bid for the Republican presidential nomination in 1976. Reagan performed well in the primaries against incumbent Gerald Ford and did especially well in the South and with conservatives. In the 1980 race for the Republican presidential nomination, Reagan was the best-known conservative in a field that included former House member and Central Intelligence Agency director George H. W. Bush, Senators Robert Dole (KS) and Howard Baker (TN), and Representative John Anderson (IL). After a strong showing by George H. W. Bush in Iowa, Reagan's win in New Hampshire helped gain momentum for his nomination victory.

The fall election between Reagan and incumbent Jimmy Carter was closer than Reagan's ten-point margin would suggest. The lead changed hands several times, with the decisive shift occurring in the last days before the election and in the wake of a televised debate in which Reagan was able to shake the image of a candidate whose extreme views would be dangerous. He was aided as well by the ongoing hostage crisis in Iran, the energy crisis, a weak US economy suffering from high levels of both inflation and unemployment, and Carter's lack of popularity.

What Manner of Man?

Ronald Reagan was known for his confidence and optimism. An avid storyteller, he was very fond of happy endings. And there was no doubt in his mind that America's story could continue to be one of unbounded success. His optimism was especially evident during the economic difficulties of 1982. Staff aide Peggy Noonan found this trait part of a long-standing desire to cheer people up, possibly stemming from his early experiences in a family with an alcoholic father.[3]

Reagan also possessed a good sense of humor—and an ability to use it effectively. During a 1984 presidential debate with his Democratic challenger, Walter Mondale, he helped diffuse the age issue by commenting that he would not raise the question of Mondale's youth and inexperience. Self-deprecation often came to his rescue as well. In the wake of newspaper stories suggesting that he occasionally dozed off at meetings, he commented about putting a chair in the cabinet room with a sign saying "Ronald Reagan Slept Here."[4] Reagan's humor often helped to deflect personal criticism and to convey the image of a president who was not overly impressed with himself. While Reagan's modesty made him likable, he had few close friends.[5] A variety of staff memoirs frequently pointed to a president who was friendly only up to a point.

While often somewhat distant, Reagan was rarely vindictive. His cheerfulness and modesty, however, masked greater ambition than many realized, as he had discussed the possibility of running for Congress as early as the 1940s. Journalist and veteran Reagan watcher Lou Cannon concluded that many observers underestimated him because they failed to see beyond

72 *The High-Opportunity Presidents*

his genial demeanor. This caused many to miss Reagan's hard, self-protective core of drive and ambition.[6]

During his political career, Reagan sought and used information in unusual ways. He liked to glean information and insights in person rather than in writing. He also possessed an ability to read audiences, an advantage developed through his many years of experience as an actor and public speaker. As early as his 1966 race for governor, he seemed to be ahead of the polls in determining which ideas could be promoted most effectively.

Reagan often used the information he had gathered in the stories he enjoyed telling—even if they were not true. For example, he repeatedly referred to a "welfare mother" in Chicago who was ripping off the system even though his secretary of health and human services had declared the case bogus three times. On environmental policy, he asserted that there were as many trees in the country as at the time of the American Revolution (the US Park Service stated that the correct figure was approximately 30 percent).

Policy Views

According to Fred Greenstein, "Reagan ... was startlingly uninformed about and inattentive to the specific content of policy—a president who appears to have been more dependent on his aides for detailing direction than any president since Harding."[7] Major policy plans would be handed to him and often accepted without question. But for those issues important to him, such as the best ways to present his economic policy ideas, he was interested in at least a moderate degree of detail.

Tax cuts were a cornerstone of Reagan's policy views.[8] During the course of the 1980 campaign, he advocated "supply-side" economics (later termed "Reaganomics"), which envisioned tax reduction as a spur to economic growth and ultimately greater tax revenue. Lower tax rates also were viewed as an incentive for people to work more.

Another central Reagan objective was fewer government regulations. His concerns often reflected his opposition to the social regulations of the Great Society more than the industry-specific regulatory policies that characterized the New Deal. Many members of the nation's business community loudly criticized the expansion of government regulation into areas such as environmental and consumer protection, and Reagan was highly sympathetic to that view.

Cuts in domestic spending were another Reagan goal, but virtually no specific targets were suggested. Instead, he spoke generally of eliminating "waste, fraud, and abuse," often accompanied by anecdotes from his California experiences. He spoke of greater roles for the states rather than the federal government in determining policy. He even mused about the possibility of changing Social Security into a voluntary system, but he realized this was not feasible.

Another policy goal was increased spending on defense. The president felt strongly that America's military posture had been allowed to deteriorate under Jimmy Carter's leadership. Thus, when "deficit hawks" such as Office of Management and Budget Director David Stockman looked for ways to reduce the deficit, Reagan would often point out that funding for the military was a separate category and was "off limits."

Surprisingly, the oft-touted goal of balancing the budget came last on Reagan's policy list. At first, he promised a balanced budget by 1983, but deficits mounted nevertheless. Even as the administration sought choices among policy goals, Reagan insisted that defense spending and tax reductions take priority.

Challenges and Opportunities

The economic challenge Reagan faced was formidable. Since 1973 the US economy had been characterized by high levels of unemployment, lower productivity, and high inflation. With inflation levels over 10 percent in both 1979 and 1980, coupled with another increase in unemployment, Americans sensed that something new needed to be tried.

Momentum was the key to Reagan's opportunities at the outset of his administration. The election did not create a mandate, but it did create an opportunity.[9] In a three-way race with low turnout, Reagan had actually received the support of little more than a quarter of the eligible electorate. Nevertheless, his final election surge to a ten-point win, along with Republican success in capturing control of the Senate and a gain of 34 seats in the House, was shocking. Speaker Thomas "Tip" O'Neill (D-MA) proclaimed that he would not use procedural steps to stand in Reagan's way. The president's initial popularity ratings were not especially high but were boosted in April by the March 31 near-fatal attempt on Reagan's life. The event raised his public support by over 10 percent into the high-50 percent range, where it stayed for the coming months.

Among the promising issues, tax-cut measures were popular with the public and in Congress, and a proposal similar to Reagan's three-year tax cut had made considerable progress in 1978. Democrats also were interested in some degree of tax reduction. To members of Congress on both sides of the aisle, Reagan made a strong case for his supply-side approach, even though few prominent economists favored the idea. However, the sense of economic disarray had created a strong desire to try a new approach.

Public support for other Reagan measures varied and tended to drop off after his first year. Both voters and members of Congress were fairly skeptical about the merits of deregulatory policies, and environmental

74   *The High-Opportunity Presidents*

regulations were quite popular at the time. At first, the public supported an increase in defense spending, but that support declined markedly after 1983. Domestic spending cuts were popular in the abstract, but not for popular programs like Social Security. Unfortunately for Reagan, there were no easy spending reduction targets that could generate the savings he hoped to achieve.

Leadership Style

Reagan's orientation to presidential leadership was somewhat unusual. Despite abandoning his earlier commitments to most of FDR's domestic policies, he admired Roosevelt's rhetorical skills and, like FDR, placed great emphasis on the importance of reassuring the electorate. In Reagan's view, a president's proper role was that of preacher, and he was skeptical of a more activist role for the nation's leader. Much of Reagan's leadership orientation had developed over the course of his career, especially during his years as governor of California. The president and his staff cultivated the media at the outset, recruited seasoned Washington figures for several key staff positions, and established a limited and focused first-year agenda.

Advisory Process and Approach to Decision-Making

Reagan's cabinet, which he selected quickly and with limited personal involvement, tilted toward elderly businessmen with establishment ties. It included one woman, Jeane Kirkpatrick, Ambassador to the United Nations, and one African American, Samuel Pierce, Secretary of Housing and Urban Development. Donald Regan, Secretary of the Treasury, brought to his office a background in the securities industry. James Watt, Secretary of the Interior, was noted for his harsh criticism of many environmental regulations.

The configuration of the top staff positions had a major impact on Reagan's accomplishments. He decided on a "troika"—in which James Baker served as chief of staff, Edwin Meese as special counselor to the president, and Michael Deaver as special assistant to the president for special events. Top staff aides in areas such as legislative liaison and press relations reported to Baker, while Meese chaired a series of cabinet councils. Baker's role was central as Reagan pursued a fast start in 1981. Michael Deaver was responsible for planning all special events and had a major media role. Through the Office of Planning and Evaluation (OPE), Reagan instituted an effort to coordinate policy with poll results.

Meese coordinated a group of what was at first seven cabinet councils (later two) composed of four to six department heads who had overlapping policy areas. At their meetings, the councils reviewed policy and developed options. During Reagan's first term, more than 500 such meetings were held, more than half devoted to economic affairs. Adding to their prestige, Reagan often attended.[10] The gatherings produced some important ideas, and cabinet officers were given a sense of involvement, but at points, these councils engaged in a rather routine shuffling of proposals. Until abandoned in the second term, these meetings enhanced the contributions of cabinet members to the administration to an extent greater than most other presidencies.[11]

At the beginning of his second term, Reagan sent James Baker to head the Treasury Department, and its former secretary, Donald Regan, replaced Baker as chief of staff. Regan's autocratic leadership style quickly drew wide criticism, and many Washington observers were relieved when Regan was fired after the Iran–Contra scandal and replaced by veteran legislator Howard Baker, a Tennessee Republican. Nancy Reagan was a driving force in that shift, as she openly despised Regan and felt he was not doing enough to protect the president's reputation.[12]

Reagan's role in the decision-making process was limited. He often presided passively at the larger meetings and then made decisions as he interacted with a few advisers and responded to formal recommendations. On occasion, he made decisions without thoroughly reviewing his options. In early 1981, for example, he quickly endorsed a proposal for reducing Social Security benefits for those retiring before age 65. After Reagan's troubles with Social Security in 1981, James Baker strove to avoid any policy moves that would jeopardize political support by checking the political feasibility of an action with polling.

Reagan's decision-making approach had both strengths and limitations. Colin Campbell concluded in 1986 that the troika arrangement in the first term successfully brought a range of policy options to the president and seemed to meet his needs quite well.[13] During the momentum of the first year, he was able to produce 223 proposals—a performance rivaling that of the generally more action-oriented first-year Democratic administrations.[14] The level of promotion declined markedly, however, after the first year.

Administrative Strategies

Reagan's administrative strategies were dramatically demonstrated in August 1981 as he responded to a strike by the nation's 11,500 air traffic controllers. The Professional Air Traffic Controllers Organization had supported Reagan in the 1980 election and did not anticipate that its strike would lead to drastic action. The president, however, summarily dismissed the controllers who did not immediately return to work and replaced them with controllers from the military. Similarly, the National Labor Relations Board encouraged management to take a hard line on strikes during the Reagan years.

76 The High-Opportunity Presidents

The Reagan administration pursued a variety of administrative strategies in its attempts to control the federal bureaucracy and achieve its policy goals. In the civil rights area, the biggest, most systematic push was against affirmative action.[15] In particular, the president's appointments to the Civil Rights Division of the Justice Department reflected a skepticism toward existing affirmative action policies. The selection of judicial nominees was often made along the policy interests of the Christian right, becoming one of Reagan's most important legacies. Because he found relatively young, ideologically committed conservatives to fill court openings, Reagan's followers shaped the law for many subsequent years.

Another Reagan strategy consisted of using personnel selection to accomplish desired policy objectives. From the beginning, appointments at the subcabinet and agency levels were controlled more extensively than those for several earlier administrations. Reagan hoped to shape lower-level action by establishing clear goals.[16] The recruitment of upper-level staff was biased toward candidates with conservative credentials, especially individuals opposed to the regulatory actions of the agencies they would head.

Most assessments of Reagan's administration have judged its accomplishments as modest. Economist Peter J. Boettke concluded,

> The Reagan presidency surely promised more than it delivered in terms of regulatory relief. Despite the rhetoric, the Reagan administration did little to turn back the role of the state in economic activity. For those who believe in the efficacy of the free market and the ideals of limited government, the Reagan years represent merely frustration and missed opportunities—the embodiment of the triumph of politics over principle.[17]

Public Leadership

President Reagan was at home in front of television cameras. According to Mary Stuckey,

> His rhetoric was short, sharp, and thematic. His delivery was designed specifically for television and was full of word pictures designed to complement the visuals of television. His style is best characterized as conversational, even chatty. In keeping with the apparent intimacy of the television medium, Reagan spoke to the electorate in a friendly, informal fashion, reducing the formal distance between himself and his audience.[18]

These results did not occur by chance. During his earliest days in the White House, Reagan tried to cultivate members of the Washington press corps.

Staff members were encouraged, however, to limit their own availability to the press, especially on issues of political strategies and when difficult questions might be involved.[19] Press conferences were used infrequently, techniques such as gestures to whirling helicopter blades or to his partially deaf ear were used when Reagan did not want to answer a difficult question. Under the guiding influence of Michael Deaver, the White House developed a "theme for the day" in media coverage. Deaver emphasized not the technical aspects of stories but the "visuals" and paid careful attention to physical details such as where the president might best stand in different situations.

The administration's emphasis on domestic policy during its first two years at the expense of attention to some key foreign policy issues was unique. Reagan gave no fewer than five major speeches dealing with the economy in 1981 and another three in 1982. Later, speeches on domestic matters virtually disappeared—none were made during the final two years of the first term, and only three were given during the entire second term.

The Reagan White House frequently used the bully pulpit as the president sought to expand on his general views of America and what actions might be appropriate for its citizens. He sought to promote three broad themes: (1) a free society that rests not on competition between individuals but on the development of voluntary associations and the art of teaming up; (2) the imperfect quality of human nature; and (3) personal responsibility.[20] While he did not use moralistic themes more than other presidents, Reagan's economic policies were discussed in moralistic terms to an unusual degree.[21] William Muir believes Reagan's use of the bully pulpit had a very significant impact: "To the American public he restored a common sense view of human nature, human goodness, and human society. He renewed public confidence in America's private and public institutions, not the least the American presidency."[22]

Congressional Leadership

In organizing his legislative liaison operations, Reagan recruited an experienced and able group of aides.[23] They included veteran lobbyist Max Friedersdorf and Kenneth Duberstein, who was responsible for the difficult task of mobilizing support for Reagan's 1981 economic package in the House. Chief of Staff James Baker, as head of a legislative strategy group (LSG), also had an extremely important role in congressional relations, especially in 1981. The LSG met almost daily and was responsible for many strategic decisions as well as coordinating both legislative and public support–building efforts.

Reagan was willing to personally lobby members of Congress. In 1981 he met no fewer than 69 times with various groups of members. He had considerable confidence in his own persuasive abilities and undertook a

78　The High-Opportunity Presidents

direct lobbying role with enthusiasm. That enthusiasm did not cover a wide range of issues, however, and his legislative liaison aides preferred to focus closely on the president's personal agenda. As a result, after 1981 the task of promoting policies in Congress fell increasingly to his legislative liaison staff.

Legislative Enactments

Ronald Reagan began his presidency with a fairly clear and fixed set of priorities. He was determined to focus attention on economic issues and push for enactment of a select few big-ticket items. This strategy helped him achieve some significant early victories.

1981: The Big Year

Reagan produced two important measures during his first year in office. The Economic Recovery Tax Act provided multiple changes in the nation's tax policies, including reduced tax rates on individuals and corporations of 5 percent the first year and 10 percent each of the next two years. In addition, the bill indexed taxes to correct "bracket creep" (when inflation forces taxpayers into higher tax brackets). Other key changes included a reduction from 70 percent to 50 percent on investment earnings, tax advantages for businesses, and a reduction in the federal inheritance tax to allow estates of up to $600,000 to be inherited tax-free. On the spending side, the Omnibus Budget Reconciliation Act of 1981 (OBRA 81) reduced existing spending levels by approximately $37 billion and projected future cuts for a three-year total of $130.6 billion.

Reagan used multiple strategies and expended considerable energy to achieve these legislative successes.[24] At several key points he successfully went public to place pressure on reluctant members of Congress. His first foray occurred when he addressed a joint session of Congress a month after his assassination attempt. A second dramatic effort occurred two days before the House vote on tax cuts due to insufficient votes to ensure passage. After a persuasive appeal, the president urged Americans to contact their senators and representatives and tell them this was "an unequaled opportunity to help return America to prosperity and make government again the servant of the people." Speaker O'Neill described the speech as "devastating." In view of the swift and overwhelming public response, Democrats became reluctant to oppose the legislation and resistance crumbled.[25]

Once in office, Reagan adopted a fast-start strategy and immediately began creating his proposals. David Stockman worked around the clock seeking budget cuts, and some cabinet members were barely able to locate their desks before being lobbied to accept the cuts Stockman was proposing. To help achieve speed and to reduce likely congressional resistance, Stockman decided to simply earmark some $75 billion for "unspecified" future cuts.

Developing the tax-cut proposal was a difficult process in part because of the uncertainty about economic assumptions. The fundamental problem was that Reagan was proposing to simultaneously wring inflation out of the economy and provide the framework for strong economic growth. Unfortunately, for anyone setting monetary policy, these goals are contradictory: fighting inflation and promoting growth require, respectively, restrictive and expansionary money-supply policies. The pressure on policymakers to agree on some kind of economic projection was intense. In the compromise that ensued, a "rosy scenario" was adopted to defer difficult decisions.

In seeking votes, Reagan dealt with individual members extensively. In the House he especially targeted the "boll weevil" Democrats, a group of southern Democrats who were sympathetic to many of his objectives. The president usually adopted a soft sell since both he and his plan were highly popular in most of the boll weevils' districts. In other instances, the White House undertook classic deal making for votes.

Reagan strategists had intended passage of OBRA 81 and its spending cuts to justify the tax-cut portion of the president's package. Some policymakers, including Republicans, were skeptical of the scope and nature of the spending cuts. Some voices of the business community, including the *Wall Street Journal*, expressed concern as well.

In the face of such skepticism, the tax cuts proved to be as difficult to pass as the spending cuts. The legislation was plagued by several major changes and intense bidding wars for supporters, who were lured by modifications of tax reductions to aid their specific interests. The Republican efforts to gain support proved difficult not only because of Democratic resistance but also because many Republicans worried that the bill might lead to increasingly large federal deficits.

In the Senate, Reagan sought and received help from several legislative leaders for passage of his tax-reduction package. He had met with Senate Majority Leader Howard Baker several times before inauguration day, and Baker continued to work with both Reagan and his LSG in the days leading up to the vote on the tax-cut legislation. Privately, Baker had misgivings about the economic package but worked effectively in garnering Republican support. The chairmen of various Senate committees played along and had influential roles.

The tax bill that finally emerged from the Senate was considerably different from the one Reagan had proposed. The president and his aides clearly supported two of the changes, which they had been reluctant to propose because of likely political attacks. The first, the introduction of tax indexing, passed easily and contributed significantly to the large deficits

80 The High-Opportunity Presidents

in Reagan's second term. The second change was the reduction, from 70 percent to 50 percent, in the tax on investment income in the top marginal tax brackets. The changes viewed with greater concern were the tax advantages inserted for businesses. David Stockman quickly labeled the amended legislation a "Christmas Tree" bill for lobbyists. The costs of these measures alarmed Stockman, who said he "did not really know what all those numbers added up to."[26] As the bargaining continued, enough votes were gathered for passage of the bill by the Republican-controlled Senate.

The tax-cut legislation also met obstacles in the House. The Democrats, recognizing that some form of tax cut would pass in 1981, tried to craft an alternative to the proposal. Adopting the same strategy he had used for passage of the spending cuts, Reagan pried enough southern Democrats away from their party to gain passage of his own. His "inside" efforts included a weekend stay at Camp David for 15 wavering Democratic members of Congress, 12 of whom ultimately voted for the tax cuts. Then, in a more dramatic "outside" gesture, he went public two days before the vote with great effectiveness.

Reagan's triumphant signing of the new legislation in August 1981 constituted the high-water mark in terms of both his influence and Congressional support for his economic policies. During his August vacation, a sharp drop in the stock market was attributed to investors' nervousness about deficits and the likelihood of inflation. In response, Reagan strategists devised a modest plan for further spending reductions and some tax changes, but members of Congress had little enthusiasm for restarting this debate and approved only $4 billion of the $13 billion in reductions that Reagan had requested.

Policy Responses: 1982–1989

After a successful first year in which he hit the ground running and achieved several key legislative victories, Reagan's relations with Congress began to sour. Power began to shift to Congress as Senate Republicans attained control of the agenda. Reagan's second term was marked by passage of a landmark tax bill and continuing budgetary conflicts with a headstrong legislature. At points, the president's large requests for increases in defense spending were labeled "DOA"—dead on arrival—when his budgets were delivered to Congress.

Responses to the Recession

In the economic downturn of late 1981 through 1982, unemployment surged to almost 10 percent. The government was clearly taming inflation, but economic uncertainty was widespread. In this context, several important measures emerged from Congress. The president had been highly critical of the Comprehensive Employment Training Act (CETA), passed during the Carter administration, because of its cost and partial use of public sector jobs. The president wanted a new program that relied more heavily on the private sector. Two key enactments were the Joint Training Partnership Act (JTPA) and a bill calling for new transportation spending, largely to provide jobs. Passage of JTPA came only after considerable lobbying by the Reagan administration. On Capitol Hill, successful compromises emerged with the efforts of an unlikely pair of senators—Republican Dan Quayle of Indiana and Democrat Edward Kennedy of Massachusetts.

Reforming the Federal Tax System

The debate surrounding the passage of tax cuts in 1981 was only the first of many tax policy debates held during the Reagan years. The combination of Reagan's cuts and loss of tax revenue as the nation slid into a recession produced unprecedented peacetime deficits, with 1982 projected to be over $100 billion and future figures far larger. In 1982, Congress, worried about the mounting deficits, passed the Tax Equity and Fiscal Responsibility Act. The heart of the measure was a tax increase of $98 billion over three years. The bill reduced the 1981 tax cut by about a quarter, with most of the restored revenue coming from corporate taxes. In his January 1981 State of the Union address, Reagan loudly condemned the view that budgets could be brought into balance by increasing taxes. Knowing that Reagan would not accept a tax increase, key aides sold the new legislation to the president by stressing its tax-reform nature, not its tax-raising elements.

A second deficit-reduction package containing tax increases was passed in 1984. It called for some $13 billion in spending cuts and another $50 billion in new taxes. The bill had no central goal other than to find politically feasible ways of reducing the deficit. Once again, Reagan quietly added his signature to a tax increase.

Two years later, after much debate, the Tax Reform Act of 1986 emerged from Congress.[27] This bill was based on a simple principle: achieve lower tax rates across the board by eliminating many loopholes. The measure was intended to be "revenue neutral" rather than a tax increase or decrease. The Reagan administration and members of Congress contributed extensively to the emergence of this legislation. Reagan liked the emphasis on simplicity, but his proposal did not garner strong support when it was made public in the fall of 1984. Reagan then contributed to his own problems when he stated (incorrectly) that no individual or corporation would suffer a tax increase. The Treasury Department, now led by James Baker, was asked to develop a new proposal. Reagan unveiled his new tax reform

82 *The High-Opportunity Presidents*

proposal in May 1985 amid considerable fanfare. He began with a presidential address and then went on the road, emphasizing the bill's populist themes and touting the tax cut it would provide for average Americans. Congress modified the bill and several loopholes crept back into the final measure before Reagan eventually signed it.

Social Security and Medicare

Social Security and Medicare changed considerably during Reagan's years in office. Reagan's first foray into this issue area was a poorly designed proposal for reducing benefits for retirees between the ages of 62 and 65. The response to the idea on Capitol Hill was dismay. In less than a week, the Senate passed a unanimous resolution calling for the president to abandon his proposal. Deciding not to fight Congress, Reagan signified his "surrender" with a note saying he was not wedded to any one approach to Social Security reform. Nevertheless, the administration later tried to achieve budgetary savings by reducing the minimum Social Security benefit, but opposition formed quickly, and the proposal was defeated. Congress also learned from the incident, abandoning the idea of gradually increasing the age of eligibility for Social Security from 65 to 68 and reducing cost of living adjustments (COLAs).

Reagan's strategy for handling Social Security shifted to top-level negotiation.[28] As the impacts of inflation (forcing higher cost-of-living increases) and a weak economy (reducing Social Security tax collections) intensified, the pressure for action intensified as well. In response, the president formed a bipartisan commission to review Social Security reform and release its recommendations after the 1982 midterm elections.

The result was a stalemate. In late November, observers feared that the Social Security Administration would have to halt some of its monthly benefit payments as of July 1983 unless an agreement could be reached. David Stockman briefed the president on the stalemate in the commission and then asked two specific questions: First, would he accept the basic outlines of a compromise that had produced partial commission agreement, and second, would he agree to have the White House initiate secret negotiations with the commission? Reagan, the pragmatist, decided that this was the best he could get and answered yes to both questions.

The resulting "gang of nine" commissioners operated in secret. After initial difficulties and periodic checking with Reagan and House Speaker Tip O'Neill, the gang of nine was able to reach a compromise agreement. The process was delicate: Both Reagan and O'Neill had to sign off as supporting the proposal before it could go back to the full commission and become public. Neither Reagan nor O'Neill was pleased with aspects of the agreement, but under the pressure of time they acquiesced.

Despite efforts by party leaders to sell the compromise as "shared pain," final congressional passage was not easy. The committee chairs were generally cooperative, but last-minute lobbying and different preferences in the House and Senate complicated reaching a final compromise. The final bill increased taxes, delayed COLA adjustments, and gradually raised the eligibility age.

Social Security issues cropped up again in 1985 amid Republican efforts in the Senate to develop a significant deficit-reduction package.[29] The Senate narrowly voted to eliminate that year's COLA, but Republicans in the House were less enthusiastic, with 67 writing their Senate colleagues suggesting that they change their position. Reagan then made a deal with O'Neill to delay COLA elimination in exchange for O'Neill's support of a slight increase in defense spending.

Regulatory Policy Changes

Despite his rhetoric, Reagan pursued a limited deregulation agenda, and changes in regulatory policy reflected his policy interests. Among other things, he pursued modification of regulations regarding savings and loan associations, cable television, and agriculture. Notably, changes shifting natural resources from preservation to aggressive development occurred through administrative policies of Interior Secretary James Watt.[30] Reagan did not contribute extensively to the public debate on these issues, and they were not high priorities. Nevertheless, the administration did speak publicly as certain proposals made their way through the legislative process.

The 1982 Garn-St. Germain legislation modifying regulations for savings and loan institutions represented a major step beyond the regulations issued in 1980. The problem was that in a period of high inflation, the institutions could not pay sufficient interest to attract savers and thereby generate the capital needed for home mortgage loans. In response to this situation, Congress relaxed the rules governing the kinds of loans that could be made and the level of interest rates that could be paid. The Reagan administration was supportive of the measure and it had strong backers in Congress. Unfortunately, the new bill would worsen an already difficult situation.

Civil Rights

Reagan had a long history of opposing affirmative action, civil rights legislation, and efforts to use the federal government to promote equality in the workplace. His views were based in part on his conservative philosophy, which called for a reduced role for the federal government in dealing with domestic issues, but they also stemmed from his inability to recognize racial and sexual discrimination as serious problems. When the

84 *The High-Opportunity Presidents*

Voting Rights Act came up for renewal in 1981, the White House firmly opposed the provision stipulating that one could use statistical results rather than prove intent in obtaining judgments that voting rights had been infringed.

In the debate over making Martin Luther King Jr.'s birthday a national holiday, opponents of the measure pointed to the costs incurred in losing a federal workday. The Reagan administration appeared to be supportive of that view. Ultimately, President Reagan decided against a veto of this legislation, stating somewhat grudgingly that he would go along with the measure due to its "symbolic importance."

Federalism Initiatives

One of Reagan's goals was to transfer power from the federal government to state governments, and he had modest success with his efforts. His most concerted attempt occurred in 1982 when he proposed that Washington and the states swap functions—for example, the states would accept total responsibility for Aid to Families with Dependent Children (AFDC), and the federal government would take over Medicaid. Reagan tried to sell the program to the public and even visited several state legislatures. Governors welcomed the greater discretion in some programs, but they were concerned about the possible long-term loss of funds. The legislation died in 1982.

In 1981, the administration tried, with partial success, to cut several programs, including AFDC and Medicaid. On Medicaid in particular, Reagan ran into strong and effective legislative resistance. Overall, Reagan succeeded in slowing the rate of growth in federal spending for federal-state programs. Whether intended or not, one important consequence was that the states began to raise taxes. As a result, the portion of state and local budgets coming from federal grants-in-aid declined from 25.8 percent in 1980 to 18.2 percent in 1987.[31]

Reagan and Congress

Reagan demonstrated a range of skills in promoting passage of his economic program in 1981. He focused his agenda, displayed unusual skill in his public appeals, worked hard to gain the votes of individual members of Congress, and showed a willingness to stand firm when others might have decided to compromise. Without such an effort, there would have been a tax cut in 1981, but not one nearly as large. Congress also played an important role, including making key changes in the original proposal that Reagan had been reluctant to request. Moreover, legislative leaders offered considerable help in the bargaining process.

A more distant view of Reagan's performance over his eight-year tenure reveals that it was not particularly strong. While the ingredients for increased legislative success may have been on hand, his success in 1981 was more the result of short-term calculations rather than a significant lasting realignment of views.[32] After 1981, Reagan pursued a limited legislative agenda and deferred to the policy initiatives emerging from Congress during his second term. A key example was Reagan's efforts on immigration, where he initially formed a task force for recommendations but ended up deferring to legislation provided by Congress in the form of the Immigration Reform and Control Act of 1986, which opened him up to criticism of taking an "amnesty" approach to immigration.[33]

An Assessment

Many have hailed the "Reagan Revolution" as a standard by which to judge the administration. But a better perspective is to consider the scope of Reagan's legacy in shaping government programs and economic performance in light of his goals, along with his impact on the presidency itself.[34]

During his years in the White House, Reagan clearly limited the potential expansion of the federal government's domestic activities. His rhetorical appeals contributed to this containment, but after 1981 the mounting federal deficit and the nation's trade deficit also became increasing constraints. The Reagan administration sharply curtailed the pace of new regulations and reduced some regulations already in place in specific areas. Similarly, the rates of increase in federal grants-in-aid slowed, and the states began to show somewhat greater independence.

Yet expansion did take place. The number of federal employees increased by more than 8 percent between 1980 and 1988. While taxes were cut in 1981, the government later sought additional revenue through both the tax code and the Social Security system. As a result, the portion of the nation's gross domestic product (GDP) being absorbed by the federal government declined only marginally—from 19 percent in 1980 to 18.4 percent in 1988.

A more significant legacy is found in the mix of spending for government programs. Spending on defense rose from $133 billion in 1980 to $290 billion in 1988, or from 4.9 percent to 5.9 percent of GDP. Within domestic categories, the expenditures held down were largely in the area of discretionary spending. Spending on entitlement programs such as Social Security and Medicare grew considerably, in part as a result of the legislation enacted in 1983.

Scholars and others continue to debate the strength of Reagan's economic performance. One clear area of improvement was the sharp decrease in the inflation rate—from 13 percent at the beginning of the Reagan administration to 4 percent in 1983. It remained low as well in the

86   The High-Opportunity Presidents

years that followed. Reagan was aided by a sharp drop in energy costs and a change in the inflation index itself that removed the cost of homes from annual inflation calculations.

Job creation efforts and growth appear to have been fairly good for the best years of 1983–1988, but more lackluster if the steep recession of 1982 is included. Growth averaged 2.4 percent in Reagan's first term and 3.3 percent in his second. By contrast, Carter's average was 3.1 percent, and the results under Reagan were well below growth levels achieved in the 1960s and 1990s. While some new jobs were created, the problem of stagnant hourly wages continued. Unemployment levels remained stubbornly high—an average of 7.5 percent over Reagan's eight years in office. More positively, the recession-free period following the early recession was unusually long.[35]

The sources of economic growth in the 1980s are often attributed to the ultimate impact of Reagan's policies, not his original plan. While Reagan had hoped to achieve additional savings and investment through tax policies, the result was actually a worse performance than in the 1970s. Deficits, while not planned, were nevertheless seen widely as providing exactly the kind of stimulus to the economy advocated by supporters of Keynesian views. Reagan's failure to match tax cuts with spending cuts led to a ballooning deficit. Reagan left office as a big spender who saddled his successor with a massive debt that increased threefold—from $700 billion in 1980 to over $2 trillion as Reagan left office. During his presidency, the United States went from being the world's largest creditor nation to the world's largest debtor nation.

Defenders of Reagan's economic performance have pointed out that because of the economic growth during the Reagan years, the deficit was less troublesome as a percentage of the GDP than might otherwise have been the case.[36] Detractors have viewed the accumulated debt as a more pressing problem. In particular, the large interest costs incurred, sometimes exceeding 15 percent, complicated later efforts to balance the budget.

Reagan, then, clearly did not lead a revolution, but he did leave his imprint on domestic policy. By using his various roles more forcefully throughout his presidency, he might have achieved greater policy change and done more to promote specific new policy techniques. Yet he faced a basic constraint—the public simply did not share his desire for a more dramatic change in the scope of domestic programs. Public sentiment constraining the president's actions was also evident in the intense opposition to Reagan's nomination of Robert Bork to the Supreme Court, due to Bork's extreme right-wing ideology.[37] Conservatives would later point to opposition to Bork based on ideology rather than legal qualifications as a defining event leading to the hyper-partisanship that would plague US politics decades later.

Finally, Reagan left a legacy in presidential leadership. His ability to reassure the public was important during the difficult period in which inflation was weakening the economy, and he showed that the bully pulpit could be used effectively. Perhaps most ironically, he showed unusual skill in publicly displaying himself as an ideologue who was not enthusiastic about the role of government while quietly compromising on a variety of issues.

But did Reagan's achievements meet the high opportunity level he encountered on entering office? Apart from his first-year successes, he did not achieve what might have been expected of a high-opportunity president. In this sense, he proved to be the least effective of the four high-opportunity chief executives.

Notes

1 Garry Wills, *Reagan's America: Innocents at Home* (Garden City, NY: Doubleday, 1985); and Lou Cannon, *President Reagan: The Role of a Lifetime* (New York: Simon and Schuster, 1991).
2 Gary G. Hamilton and Nicole W. Biggart, *Governor Reagan, Governor Brown: A Sociology of Executive Power* (New York: Columbia University Press, 1984).
3 Peggy Noonan, *What I Saw at the Revolution: A Political Life of Ronald Reagan* (New York: Random House, 2003), 154.
4 Helen Thomas, *Front Row at the White House: My Life and Times* (New York: Scribner, 2000), 335.
5 Noonan, *What I Saw at the Revolution*.
6 Cannon, *President Reagan*, 217.
7 Fred I. Greenstein, "Ronald Reagan—Another Hidden-Hand Ike," *P.S.: Political Science and Politics* 23 (March 1990): 7.
8 Ronald Reagan, *An American Life: The Autobiography* (New York: Simon and Schuster, 1990); and Martin Anderson, *Revolution: The Reagan Legacy* (Palo Alto, CA: Hoover Institute Press, 1990).
9 Joseph White and Aaron Wildavsky, *The Deficit and the Public Interest: The Search for Responsible Budgeting in the 1980s* (Berkeley: University of California Press, 1989), 67.
10 Stephen Hess and James Pfiffner, *Organizing the Presidency*, 4th ed. (Washington, DC: Brookings Institution, 2020).
11 Shirley Anne Warshaw, *Powersharing: White House-Cabinet Relations in the Modern Presidency* (Albany: State University of New York Press, 1996), 155–156.
12 Jane Mayer and Doyle McManus, *Landslide: The Unmaking of a President, 1984–1988* (Boston: Houghton Mifflin, 1988), 361–364.
13 Colin Campbell, *Managing the Presidency: Carter, Reagan, and the Search for Executive Harmony* (Pittsburgh, PA: University of Pittsburgh Press, 1986), 99.
14 Mark A. Peterson, *Legislating Together: The White House and Capitol Hill from Eisenhower to Reagan* (Cambridge, MA: Harvard University Press, 1990), 260.
15 Kenneth O'Reilly, *Nixon's Piano: Presidents and Racial Politics from Washington to Clinton* (New York: Free Press, 1995), ch. 9.

88 The High-Opportunity Presidents

16 William K. Muir Jr., *The Bully Pulpit: The Presidential Leadership of Ronald Reagan* (San Francisco: ICS Press, 1992).

17 Peter J. Boettke, "The Reagan Regulatory Regime: Reality vs. Rhetoric," in *The Economic Legacy of the Reagan Years: Euphoria or Chaos?* ed. Anandi P. Sahu and Ronald L. Tracy (Westport, CT: Greenwood Publishing, 1991), ch. 7.

18 Mary E. Stuckey, *The President as Interpreter-in-Chief* (Chatham, NJ: Chatham House, 1991), 115.

19 Mark Hertsgaard, *On Bended Knee: The Press and the Reagan Presidency* (New York: Farrar, Straus, Giroux, 1988).

20 Ibid., 2.

21 Barbara Hinckley, *The Symbolic Presidency: How Presidents Portray Themselves* (New York: Routledge, 1990), 75.

22 Muir, *Bully Pulpit*, 189.

23 Stephen J. Wayne, "Congressional Liaison in the Reagan White House: A Preliminary Assessment of the First Year," in *President and Congress: Assessing Reagan's First Year*, ed. Norman J. Ornstein (Washington, DC: American Enterprise Institute, 1982), 44–66.

24 See especially Anderson, *Revolution*; Samuel Kernell, *Going Public: New Strategies of Presidential Leadership*, 4th ed. (Washington, DC: CQ Press, 2006); Stockman, *Triumph of Politics*; Darrell M. West, *Congress and Economic Policymaking* (Pittsburgh, PA: University of Pittsburgh Press, 1987); and White and Wildavsky, *Deficit and the Public Interest*. At the Ronald Reagan Presidential Library, the personal files of David Gergen, O. M. Oglesby, and Murray Weidenbaum were examined, as well as an exit interview by Kenneth Duberstein.

25 Kernell, *Going Public*, 150.

26 William Greider, "The Education of David Stockman," *Atlantic Monthly*, December 1981.

27 Timothy J. Conlan, Margaret T. Wrightson, and David R. Beam, *Taxing Choices: The Politics of Tax Reform* (Washington, DC: CQ Press, 1990); and Jeffrey H. Birnbaum and Alan S. Murray, *Showdown at Gucci Gulch* (New York: Random House, 1987).

28 Paul C. Light, *Artful Work: The Politics of Social Security Reform* (New York: Random House, 1985); and White and Wildavsky, *Deficit and the Public Interest*, ch. 14.

29 George Hager and Eric Pianin, *Mirage: Why Neither Democrats nor Republicans Can Balance the Budget, End the Deficit, and Satisfy the Public* (New York: Random House, 1997), 140–143.

30 David M. Shafie, *The Administrative Presidency and the Environment* (New York: Routledge, 2020), 54.

31 David Mervin, *The Presidency and Ronald Reagan* (New York: Longman, 1990), 110.

32 West, *Congress and Economic Policymaking*, 80.

33 Craig A. Kaplowitz, "The Great Repudiator and Immigration Reform: Ronald Reagan and the Immigration Reform and Control Act of 1986," *Journal of Policy History* 30, no. 4 (2018): 635–656.

34 John L. Palmer and Isabel V. Sawhill, eds., *The Reagan Experiment: An Examination of Economic and Social Policies under the Reagan Administration* (Washington, DC: Urban Institute Press, 1982); Larry Berman, ed., *Looking Back on the Reagan Presidency* (Baltimore: Johns Hopkins University Press, 1990); Joseph Hogan, ed., *The Reagan Years: The Record in Presidential*

Leadership (New York: St. Martin's Press, 1990); and B. B. Kymlicka and Jean V. Matthews, *The Reagan Revolution?* (Chicago: Dorsey Press, 1988).

35 *Budget of the United States Government, FY 1998, Historical Tables* (Washington, DC: Government Printing Office, 1997).

36 Michael J. Boskin, *Reagan and the Economy: The Successes, Failures and Unfinished Agenda* (San Francisco: ICS Press, 1987), ch. 9.

37 Richard L. Vining, Jr. and Rachel Bitecofer, "Change and Continuity in Citizens' Evaluations of Supreme Court Nominees," *American Politics Research* (2022), https://doi.org/10.1177/1532673X221119402.

5 George W. Bush

A Resolute Decider with a Co-President

A president may enter office with one level of political opportunity, but events may disrupt the old order and create new opportunities, or erect roadblocks. Such was the case with George W. Bush (served 2001–2009).

During the 2000 presidential campaign, candidate Bush focused his attention on domestic affairs. A two-term governor from Texas, Bush was more comfortable discussing matters at home than abroad. In fact, when pressed by a campaign reporter, Bush could not identify the leaders of several strategically important nations. George W. Bush had a clear domestic agenda that he communicated often throughout his campaign: tax cuts, education reform, Social Security reform, energy reform, immigration reform, and aid to faith-based groups providing social services.

President Bush entered office under favorable conditions (peace and prosperity—including a budget surplus), yet his legitimacy was questioned. The 2000 election was disputed, with the vote in Florida determining the outcome. A 30-day postelection legal battle ensued between Bush's camp and Democratic nominee Al Gore's camp, only to be settled at the 11th hour when the Republican-controlled US Supreme Court awarded Florida's 25 electoral votes, and thereby the White House, to Bush. Moreover, Bush could not claim an electoral mandate, as he garnered less of the popular vote than Gore. Bush's inauguration was marred by public protests, with chants of "Hail to the Thief!" These were not ideal circumstances under which to enter office.

Thus, Bush came to office as a low-opportunity president. To the surprise of many, he was able to attain significant early legislative victories, specifically tax cuts and education reform. But then conditions changed—dramatically.

It is useful to see the presidency of George W. Bush in three very different stages: stage 1: inauguration to September 2001; stage 2: September 11, 2001, to the economic meltdown of 2008; and stage 3: the meltdown to the end of his presidency. These stages were emblematic of three very different presidencies and very different outcomes.

DOI: 10.4324/9781003426684-6

George W. Bush   91

During stage 1, Bush was an overachiever who, although facing a low level of opportunity, succeeded in getting two major pieces of legislation passed. With the 9/11 attacks in stage 2, Bush became a high-opportunity president, but his focus turned to foreign policy. It was during this period that he was, in the domain of domestic affairs, less successful. He created the new cabinet-level Department of Homeland Security and passed a major prescription drug law, but failed on his campaign promises of Social Security and immigration reform.[1] In stage 3, the economic crisis of 2008 gave the president unprecedented high opportunity, and a major bailout package was passed. Since we are focusing on the first terms of presidents, in this chapter we will analyze the first two stages of Bush's roller coaster of opportunity occurring during his first term.

Personal Characteristics

George W. Bush (1946–) was born in New Haven, Connecticut, the eldest of six children. At the time of his birth, his father—the future president—was attending Yale University. The family moved to Midland, Texas, after Bush Sr.'s graduation in 1948. Bush attended public school in Midland while his father set out to become an oilman. Bush Sr.'s success took the family to Houston, where George W. Bush attended prep school at Kinkaid Academy. He attended high school at the Phillips Academy boarding school in Andover, Maryland, where he played JV basketball and baseball and became the school's head cheerleader.

In the footsteps of his father and grandfather, Bush attended Yale University, and his activities there indicate that he followed their footsteps in form but not in substance. While there from 1964 to 1968, he, like his father, served as president of Delta Kappa Epsilon fraternity. Also like his father and grandfather, he was a cheerleader and was inducted into the Skull and Bones secret society. But unlike his father, Bush was not a very good student, earning only average marks. Also unlike his father, who played first base on Yale's baseball team that went to the College World Series, he was not a successful athlete.

Bush was able to avoid service in Vietnam by serving in the Texas Air National Guard. Although Bush made no personal appeals for help when applying for the Guard, he received a recommendation from Ben Barnes, a former Speaker of the Texas State House of Representatives and lieutenant governor. He was commissioned in 1968 and flew F-102 jet fighter aircraft first in Texas and then in Alabama.

Bush attended Harvard Business School from 1973 to 1975, becoming the first president to have earned an MBA. While on spring break in 1975, he visited Midland, Texas, and determined that the area afforded him the opportunity he needed to become a successful businessman. In the fall of 1975, he set up Bush Oil in a one-room office above a bank in Midland.[2]

92 *The High-Opportunity Presidents*

At a backyard cookout in 1977, he met Laura Welch, a school teacher and librarian. They were married three months later.

George W. Bush's presidency marked the second time in history that a father and his son had held the office, and his grandfather had been a US senator. But Bush's early years didn't mark him for greatness. By his own admission, prior to turning 40, he led a very undisciplined life, punctuated by alcoholism.[3] Bush never addressed allegations of illicit drug use, fearing he would set a bad example. But "W" (as he was often called) would overcome these personal problems to take a high-trajectory ride to the presidency.

Career Path

In his thirties and forties, Bush pursued the dual-occupational legacy of his family—business and politics. In his first attempt at public office, Bush secured the Republican nomination in 1978 to run for the US House of Representatives in Texas's 19th District. Although he expended a great deal of shoe leather to introduce himself to voters, he lost by 6 percent to Kent Hance, who portrayed Bush as an out-of-touch carpetbagger.

Following his defeat, Bush switched his focus back to becoming a successful oilman, forming a company called Arbusto (Spanish for "bush"). The company floundered for several years and then merged with Spectrum-7 in 1984, with Bush retained as chairman. Following the collapse in oil prices in the mid-1980s, Bush negotiated the sale of Spectrum-7 to Harken Oil. Bush was offered one share of Harken for every five of Spectrum-7. Allegations arose regarding Bush's involvement in insider trading, but an investigation by the Securities and Exchange Commission (SEC) concluded that Bush had insufficient information to engage in such trading.

In 1988, Bush switched his focus back to politics, moving to Washington, DC, to serve as senior adviser on his father's presidential campaign. Following the election, Bush moved to Dallas to put together a group of investors to purchase the Texas Rangers baseball team. In 1989, Bush was successful in helping his investment team purchase the Rangers and was named a managing general partner, earning a salary of $200,000 a year, even though his financial investment of $800,000 was comparatively small compared to the team's sale price of $89 million. Bush's job was to be the public face of the club, particularly in its lobbying efforts with the city of Arlington to secure a new stadium. When the Rangers were again sold in 1998, Bush received $14.9 million of the $250 million sale price.

In 1991, Bush again returned to politics, this time to work on his father's failed reelection campaign. In 1994, Bush tossed his hat into the ring for the Texas governorship as his brother, Jeb, concurrently ran for the Florida governorship. Bush easily won the Republican nomination and squared off against the popular incumbent, Ann Richards.

Bush's campaign team included Karl Rove and Karen Hughes, both of whom would eventually follow him to the White House. The campaign charted a course focused on the issues of education, welfare reform, tort reform, reforming the juvenile justice system, and permitting Texans to carry concealed handguns (Richards had vetoed a concealed-carry bill). Bush used these issues to position himself as a "compassionate conservative"—later a central presidential campaign theme.[4] Bush performed well in televised debates and upset Richards by almost eight points in the election.

Once in office, Bush made a strong push for tax cuts based on the state's budget surplus but ended up getting about a third of what he wanted from the state legislature. At the time, Texas had mandatory student testing in public schools, and scores improved on Bush's watch, as did teacher salaries. Bush ended the use of social promotion and put in place a program to promote reading by the third grade. During his tenure, he established himself as tough on law-and-order issues, executing 152 prisoners and proclaiming that "incarceration is rehabilitation."[5] Bush also extended state funding to faith-based organizations providing social services. Not only did his gubernatorial policies foreshadow his presidency, so did his management style—as he became known for his blunt speaking and punctuality.[6] In 1998, he won reelection in a landslide, capturing 69 percent of the vote.

With only five and a half years of experience in office under his belt, Bush announced his candidacy for the presidency in June 1999. Bush found himself surrounded by 11 other candidates in the primary field, but was able to out-fundraise all of them, causing many to drop out before the first contest. Bush selected Dick Cheney as his vice presidential running mate. This came as a surprise to many given Cheney's position as the head of the VP search committee, his age, his heart trouble, and the fact that he provided no strategic Electoral College benefit (Cheney was from the small, heavily Republican state of Wyoming). Bush campaigned as a "compassionate conservative," a "reformer with results," and a "uniter not a divider" who would be capable of working across party lines, as he had with the Democratically controlled Texas legislature. Bush campaigned on restoring honor and integrity to the White House, strengthening the military, and returning the budget surplus of the late 1990s to the taxpayers in the form of tax cuts. Ultimately, Bush prevailed by a razor-thin margin in the Electoral College with 271 votes. However, Bush couldn't claim a mandate as he had lost the popular vote to Gore by over half a million votes.

What Manner of Man?

Writings about George W. Bush's personal character invariably use the same adjective to describe him: resolute. But resoluteness may be positive in

94   *The High-Opportunity Presidents*

some situations, lending itself to heroic leadership in times of uncertainty, and negative in others, leading to stubbornness.[7] Bush's resoluteness meant an unwillingness to listen to alternatives when creating policy, and sticking with policies even though they appeared to be failing, apparently unable to admit error.[8] Bush valued loyalty above all else and would not stand for those who challenged his opinions.[9] His certitude in his actions has been traced to his inability to engage in introspection and to consider alternative viewpoints.[10] Other psychological profiles paint Bush as being superficial (not prone to complex thinking), outgoing, and impulsive.[11] Bush was largely a "faith-based" decision-maker who saw the world in very moral terms and preferred action to calculation.[12]

Bush's tendency to commit verbal gaffes—particularly his mispronunciation of the word "nuclear" and using jumbled words such as "misunderestimated" and "subliminable"—led to questions about his intelligence. While intelligence is not a correlate of successful presidential leadership, Bush's intelligence was a matter of much debate. Was he really worthy of degrees from two of the nation's leading universities, or did he skate by as an underachieving "legacy" student? Estimates of Bush's intelligence rate him with a robust IQ of about 120–125, which, although in the top 10 percent of the population, places him in the bottom quartile of all presidents.[13]

However, Bush excelled at interpersonal relationships. He was optimistic, warm, gregarious, and incredibly adept at remembering people's names, often giving them nicknames in order to facilitate recall. Many felt drawn to him, and he used these qualities to persuade others.

Policy Views

Although he didn't always articulate it well, Bush was better than his father at developing what they both called "the vision thing." He preferred big ideas to the minutiae of policy details. He had a clear idea of where he strategically wanted to move the country—a set of policies later dubbed the "ownership society." These policies stressed individual responsibility and free market principles to empower individuals to have ownership over their choices in life, which for him meant less government intrusion into those choices. Policies associated with this included his support for medical savings accounts, personal Social Security accounts, lowering taxes overall so that people had more economic freedom, and moving the responsibility for social services from government to faith-based organizations.[14] Tax cuts were central to his vision, and on the campaign trail he would frequently repeat that the budget surplus was "not the government's money, it's *your* money." Bush saw these ends as the logical outgrowth of the vision laid down by his hero, Ronald Reagan.

George W. Bush   95

Although receiving degrees from Harvard and Yale, Bush struck a populist chord with his Texas twang and anti-intellectualism. He did not seem curious about the world beyond our nation's borders. His only foreign travel prior to his presidency was to Mexico. However, he spoke Spanish and was familiar with issues facing migrant workers.

Challenges and Opportunities

The foremost challenge facing Bush as he entered office was his perceived illegitimacy, having lost the popular vote and having been awarded Florida's Electoral College votes by the Supreme Court, which split 5-4 on the case. Republicans lost seats in both chambers of Congress, so Bush could not claim any presidential coattails to overcome his lack of a popular mandate. He was met with an evenly divided Senate (50-50) and a very slim Republican majority in the House (221-212). This arrangement was unified government in name only, and many presumed that Bush would have to govern from the center in order to broker bipartisan compromise.[15]

There was little public mood for new governmental action. Polls found that Americans preferred that the budget surplus be used to shore up Medicare and Social Security, rather than used to promote new programs or to be returned as tax cuts. Just as many Americans preferred that the surplus be used to pay down the national debt as preferred the surplus be returned to them as tax cuts.[16] But the public mood shifted dramatically with the 9/11 terrorist attacks. Trust in government, which had been declining for decades, rose dramatically, as did support for government action and the desire of citizens to engage in self-sacrifice.[17] As a foreign policy influence, the 9/11 attacks and subsequent wars in Afghanistan and Iraq gave the president a tremendous amount of opportunity in his first term, less so as the wars dragged on in his second term.

Although the federal government was still running a budget surplus, the economy was sliding into a recession. The nation was ready for a new energy policy as gas prices ballooned just ahead of the 2000 elections. This was an area in which Bush and his advisers had a great deal of practical experience.

Bush saw the Department of Education as a tool for imposing accountability on a K-12 system that many found to be underperforming. The education system was widely perceived as bloated, inefficient, and sorely lacking in positive results. This issue also presented a great deal of opportunity for the administration, and Bush intended to implement his Texas reforms nationally.

Leadership Style

The paradox of Bush's presidency is that he was most skillful at a time when his opportunity was lowest. Bush's team was bent on getting a fast start.[18]

96   *The High-Opportunity Presidents*

Prior to 9/11, he had low opportunity and some good degree of policy success, compromising when necessary and going public in an attempt to overcome congressional opposition. With 9/11, the opportunity structure changed to meet his style. His "full speed ahead" manner of management would be thought to portend major achievements given the opportunities presented. But this was not the case. Post-9/11, Bush achieved little in the area of domestic policy. This largely hinged on his predominant focus on foreign policy, but other factors contributed to his lack of policy success. Particularly, the attacks caused Bush to see the world in black-and-white terms in both foreign and domestic policy, hindering his ability to compromise on the remainder of his domestic agenda.

The Advisory Process and Approach to Decision-Making

From the beginning of his administration, Bush had planned to augment the powers of his vice president. Bush was particularly influenced by how demeaned and useless his father had felt in the Reagan administration and wanted to make sure that Cheney had a more meaningful role.[19] Over time Bush became known for his heavy reliance on Cheney as his closest adviser. Many have questioned the degree to which he influenced Bush. Shirley Anne Warshaw's analysis suggests that Cheney did not usurp presidential power from Bush, as many critics assert. Rather, Bush delegated authority to him in many policy areas, such as the economy, energy, the environment, and national security, thus effectively creating a "co-presidency."[20] Cheney's authority in these areas consisted of staffing the agencies as well as decision-making.[21]

Cheney kept himself informed of all aspects of policy by integrating his staff with the president's and implementing "full transparency" of information between the two offices.[22] This meant that virtually every policy meeting and subsequent decision had input from both the president's and the vice president's staff members.[23] Moreover, Cheney worked tirelessly to expand the power of the presidency under the "unitary executive" theory. This led to his advocacy for Bush's many signing statements that he felt would help correct congressional interference in the actions of the administration.

Cheney was particularly influential when it came to decisions that straddled the policy domains of energy and the environment. Specifically, he was responsible for policies related to increased industrial emissions and the use of federal lands for purposes such as oil and gas drilling, as well as logging.[24] Cheney made sure that appointments to executive agencies were business-friendly and that enforcement budgets were slashed.[25]

Cheney used the transition process to control appointments, particularly within the areas of policy he cared about most.[26] Two cabinet members whom Cheney did not recommend were Secretary of State Colin Powell and Attorney General John Ashcroft, who famously and frequently feuded with the vice president and his staff during the president's first term.[27]

Bush surrounded himself with three close advisers, hoping to avoid his father's problems created by his chief of staff, John Sununu, who tried to dominate decision-making.[28] Two important advisers were holdovers from the campaign—Karl Rove and Karen Hughes. Karl Rove became senior adviser to the president. Karen Hughes, the campaign's press secretary, became counselor to the president and oversaw operation of White House communications. Bush family loyalist Andrew Card became White House chief of staff. But Attorney General Alberto Gonzales, National Security Advisor Condoleezza Rice, and, of course, Vice President Cheney all had direct access to the president.[29]

Bush was loathe to changes in his administration and rarely dismissed advisers, hoping they would provide steady and continued support. Bush liked to remain optimistic and certain, and he didn't like it when people brought him information that ran counter to his positions, particularly when it was bad news.[30] Subsequently, Bush's administration bore many of the hallmarks of groupthink. In Bush's White House, devil's advocates were not welcome as close advisers.[31] Eventually, three factions emerged in the administration: the "Christian conservatives," the "White House moderates," and the "pro-business appointees" led by Cheney.[32] By the second year, the conservative faction became dominant in the administration, and its sway became even greater when Karen Hughes departed, leaving Karl Rove as the president's most trusted adviser. Bush was surrounded mainly by conservative ideologues, making compromise difficult. Moreover, the reliance on Rove and the ideologues meant that policy details would receive less attention than political calculations. Indeed, very few white papers were prepared on policy pros and cons, and very few deliberations were held other than discussions of the politics of selling the agreed-upon alternative.[33]

Bush trusted the competence of his cabinet members, and he tended to delegate a great deal of authority to them. However, this came with a price—he expected loyalty, at least in the form of message discipline. Treasury Secretary Paul O'Neill, who enjoyed arguing ideas, was fired for his criticism of Bush's economic policy.[34]

Though Bush benefited from having a former president for a father, he rarely sought his counsel. Although he might talk to his father about his experiences with certain potential appointees, he did not seek his policy advice.[35]

Administrative Strategies

Bush felt unfettered in his use of administrative strategies and acted in concert with the unitary executive theory—that the president controls *all*

98 *The High-Opportunity Presidents*

of the executive branch and has the authority to make *all* decisions he deems necessary to run it. In a sense, Bush didn't see a great need to go to Congress for authority on issues, because he felt most actions were already his prerogative. This alienated him from Congress and affected his relationship with congressional leaders.

While the use of signing statements was nothing new, Bush used them in unprecedented numbers. It was clear by the use of these statements that the president asserted discretion in terms of which provisions of the law to enforce.[36] In this sense, Bush had a "presidentialist" philosophy, which might be called "ultra-separationist."[37]

Bush undertook some notable executive actions and rulemaking that would have lasting effects. On August 9, 2001, he ordered that federal funds could be used in stem cell research only from existing embryonic stem cell lines. Both the Office of Faith-Based Initiatives and the Office of Homeland Security were created by executive order. The administration was notorious for denying congressional requests for information, placing a high premium on secrecy.[38] In late 2001, Bush issued an executive order making it more difficult to obtain presidential records. Shortly after coming into office, Bush reversed Clinton's 11th-hour rule limiting arsenic in drinking water, but reversed course again when public opinion went against him.

Public Leadership

In the history of measured presidential job approval, George W. Bush is the recipient of the most dramatic spike and enjoyed the highest peak, jumping 40 points, from 51 percent to 91 percent.[39] The 9/11 rally in public opinion created tremendous opportunity for the president. However, over the course of 2002, his approval ratings slipped down to the mid-50s but spiked back up to the mid-70s with the Iraq invasion in March 2003. But just before he left office, his approval rating plummeted to 25 percent. Bush is frequently criticized for not having taken advantage of the spirit of patriotism following 9/11. Bush could have used the opportunity to engage more Americans in civic life and volunteerism, instead of telling them to "go shopping."

Though he was widely ridiculed for his less-than-stellar public speaking, his direct, simple, and to-the-point style was effective with audiences, especially in smaller forums. Other than his speech on 9/11, none of Bush's major addresses can be tied to any shift in public opinion.[40] By the time of his reelection, the country was deeply divided. He remained wildly popular with Republicans but was reviled by Democrats (90 percent of Republicans approved of his job performance, whereas only 15 percent of Democrats did).[41]

Congressional Leadership

In terms of dealing with Congress, Bush preferred to leave the heavy lifting to his party's leadership and his liaison staff, taking a one-on-one approach with individual legislators only when absolutely necessary at the last minute. He would meet with his party's leadership and key committee members in the Oval Office but left it up to them to secure passage of his agenda. He developed a strategy of working first with the House to get a bill to his liking, and then he negotiated from a far-right position with the more moderate Senate, often yielding a center-right compromise.[42] Also, it was easier to secure first passage of bills in the House because his party controlled the rules for debate and amendment, unlike in the Senate.

When Bush came to office, Republicans had a slim majority in the House and the Senate was evenly divided. But soon Republicans lost control of the Senate when Senator Jim Jeffords (VT) became an independent, faulting Bush for having campaigned as a moderate but governing from a hard-right position. In a reversal of the usual midterm election trends, Bush's party picked up seats in 2002 in the House and regained control of the Senate.

In his two terms, Bush issued 161 signing statements, affecting over 1,100 provisions of federal law. He issued most of them (111) during his first term. What is most important is that Bush's signing statements were far more likely than those of his predecessors to be about constitutional objections. Bush had little tolerance for congressional interference in how he saw fit to discharge his duties.

Legislative Enactments

Bush's "ownership society" agenda, combined with his emphasis on "compassionate conservatism," meant a number of new legislative proposals. At the forefront were tax cuts, education reform, and faith-based social services initiatives. Bush had success with all of these in Texas and was confident of their success at the national level.[43] Ultimately, he achieved four pieces of landmark legislation on domestic policy: tax reform, education reform, Medicare reform, and homeland security. The last could be thought of as a logical outgrowth of the war on terror, having significant linkage to foreign policy. Bush's faith-based initiative legislation stalled in the Senate, yet he established the office via executive order. Other legislation failed due in part to the struggling economy, but mostly due to the president's emphasis on foreign policy after the 9/11 attacks.

Tax Cuts (Economic Growth and Tax Relief Reconciliation Act, 2001)

Tax cuts were Bush's most high-profile campaign promise and became his most important domestic policy achievement. With the Senate split 50-50

100 *The High-Opportunity Presidents*

and Vice President Cheney casting the tiebreaking vote, Bush had to forge a coalition to avoid a Democratic filibuster. But congressional Democrats gave momentum to the president by proposing their own plan of between $800 million and $900 million in cuts.[44] Congressional Republicans greased the rails by separating the tax cuts from the regular budget process. The Senate Budget Committee was deadlocked, so Majority Leader Trent Lott (R-MS) bypassed the committee and moved the bill directly to the floor for a vote. The bill passed the Senate with a number of sweeteners for members. When the bill went to conference, Democrats were excluded from the committee.

Evidence that the economy was in recession did not materialize until sometime after Bush took office. This meant that the government's revenue estimates in early 2001 were overly optimistic. Initially, Bush was given to believe that, even after the cuts, there would be a significant surplus left over for new domestic programs and debt reduction. Once the declining revenue projections came in, Bush started to sell the tax cuts as a way to stimulate the economy.

Concerns about the affordability of the tax cuts given the economic uncertainty did not deter the president. Neither did the lack of public support and concern that the bulk of the cuts went to the highest income earners. Fed Chairman Alan Greenspan initially backed the cuts, giving the president political cover. Later though, he and Treasury Secretary Paul O'Neill advocated that the tax cuts be conditional upon the health of the budget.[45] Bush forged ahead, mindful of the political consequences suffered by his father when he broke his "read my lips, no new taxes" pledge.

Bush originally wanted $1.6 trillion in cuts to a number of taxes, including the income tax, and wanted to increase child tax credits and eliminate the estate tax (which he referred to as the "death tax") as well as the "marriage penalty." Congress gave him $1.35 trillion in cuts over ten years and more in subsequent years. Bush's big push for the tax cuts included "going public" in the states he won in 2000 that had incumbent Democratic senators. However, his coordinated public offensive seemed not to move the needle in the aggregate and didn't attract any new votes in the Senate.[46] Bush got help from right-leaning interest groups to publicize his cause, and the Club for Growth ran advertisements targeting Senators Voinovich (R-OH) and Snowe (R-ME), who were unwilling to support the president's proposal. Eventually, Voinovich voted for the bill but was motivated more by enticements than Bush's public pressure.[47] But this achievement came at a price. On May 24, Senator Jim Jeffords, a moderate Republican, left the party to become an Independent, giving control of the Senate to the Democrats. Jeffords told Bush prior to the vote on tax cuts that he planned to leave the party, but Bush convinced him to do so after the vote on the cuts. Essentially, Bush paid for the cuts with his party's control of the Senate.

On May 23, 2001, the tax cuts passed by 240-154 in the House, carrying all Republicans, 28 Democrats, and 1 independent. In the Senate, the tax cuts passed 58-33, with 12 Democratic votes. In May 2003, Bush signed another tax cut—the Jobs and Growth Tax Relief Reconciliation Act, which raised the alternative minimum tax exemption and reduced the capital gains tax. The 2003 bill was much more controversial as the country waged two wars with declining revenues. The House voted nearly on party lines, with the bill prevailing 231-200, and the Senate deadlocked 50-50 with Vice President Cheney casting the tiebreaking vote. Together, these were known as the "Bush tax cuts" and were set to sunset in 2010. They had the most profound impact on domestic policy of any of Bush's initiatives, ballooning the deficit by decreasing revenues as wartime spending increased.

No Child Left Behind (2002)

Bush was determined to have bipartisan support for his signature education policy, and he secured the "liberal lion" of the Senate, Ted Kennedy, as one of the bill's sponsors. The policy reflected Bush's conception of an "ownership society"—that all individuals, regardless of ethnicity, should be given the same opportunities in life by having quality K-12 education. This policy called for a tremendous overhaul of a system that had many entrenched interests, including school administrators and teachers. Bush's tendency for pushing hard without regard to alternative considerations actually helped his efforts in this case. Had he been too cautious, he might have suffered a stinging defeat, as Bill Clinton did during his first-term health care loss. In the interest of bipartisanship and speeding the process along, Bush made one major concession—to remove a provision for private school vouchers. The bill mandated standardized testing and a number of punitive steps if schools missed their yearly progress testing goals. This conformed with Bush's penchant for measures and accountability.

The bill sailed through Congress with little resistance and was signed into law in January 2002. The act was a major accomplishment in terms of bipartisan cooperation, and it was an issue in which Bush himself became deeply involved. Over time, the policy received low marks from the public and was unpopular with Republicans and Democrats alike. Democrats wanted more funding for schools; Republicans wanted vouchers. Teachers felt forced to "teach to the tests." Ten years later, an even less sanguine legacy was apparent, as most felt that the law had made no difference or had worsened the quality of education.[48]

102 *The High-Opportunity Presidents*

Department of Homeland Security (Homeland Security Act, 2002)

A commission chaired by former senators Gary Hart and Warren Rudman investigated US preparedness for a terrorist attack prior to 9/11, but its reports, released in 1999, 2000, and January 2001, were ignored by the Bush administration. The final report made sweeping recommendations. Key to the recommendations was consolidating a number of government agencies, including the Federal Emergency Management Agency (FEMA), the Customs Service, the Coast Guard, and the Border Patrol, under one roof. Soon after the terrorist attacks of September 11, 2001, Bush appointed former Pennsylvania governor Tom Ridge the head of the Office of Homeland Security, and he began serving in October 2001. Bush and Congress then moved quickly to establish the Transportation Security Administration (TSA) as part of the Aviation and Transportation Security Act, signed on November 19, 2001. But more was needed, as Ridge had no authority over the myriad of government agencies tasked with preventing terrorism.

Bush used his 2002 State of the Union address to call for more funding for homeland security but resisted changes to its administrative structure. As reports continued to trickle out regarding the lack of coordination of agencies prior to 9/11 and their mishandling of intelligence, Congress ramped up its push for a new Department of Homeland Security (DHS). As Congress began to move on the bill, Bush reversed course and called for a sweeping DHS overseeing 22 agencies. Bush was determined to get out ahead of public opinion and to have a voice in the matter if Congress was prepared to move legislation without his input.[49]

House Speaker Dennis Hastert paved the way by helping to avoid standing committees' parochial concerns and objections by referring them to an ad hoc committee. The Senate bill was drafted by Joe Lieberman (D-CT), generally a supporter of the president's security policies. But the president ran into difficulties with Lieberman, who felt that the Bush proposal did little to provide protection from another attack.[50]

A controversial policy concern was whether TSA employees would be federal employees and be allowed civil service protections from termination and to unionize. Congress adjourned before the 2002 midterm elections without having finished work on the bills. During the elections, national security and homeland protection became wedge issues, and Republicans portrayed Democrats as siding with special interests at the expense of the security of the nation and charged them with a lack of patriotism. Republicans took control of the Senate in the elections, and Democrats were forced into negotiating from a position of weakness, giving Bush most of what he asked for during the lame-duck session. The legislation was enacted in November 2002 without the union-friendly measures and without including the FBI and CIA under the DHS umbrella.

On this issue, Bush was being led more than he was leading. When Congress looked to act, he tried to jump out ahead with a hastily put-together plan. Again, Bush worked with friendly members of the House to get a right-leaning bill before sending it to the more moderate Senate. The election benefited him tremendously, and the Democrats came to him with concessions in the end. Fortune more than skill favored Bush on this issue as the administration concentrated on ongoing war and preparations for another.

Prescription Drugs (Medicare Modernization Act, Medicare Part D, 2003)

Bush saw adding a prescription benefit to Medicare as a gift to Democrats that would instead benefit him at the polls come reelection. It would be the equivalent of what welfare reform did for Bill Clinton—inoculate him against the criticism of being too ideologically extreme.[51] But in reality, Democrats didn't like the provisions of the bill, and many Republicans felt it was fiscally irresponsible. The process became highly partisan, with committees voting entirely on party lines. President Bush and Republican Party leaders had met with small groups of legislators to apply pressure to get the initial bill passed. The bill passed the House by one vote, and a much more moderate bill, drafted by Ted Kennedy, passed overwhelmingly in the Senate. The House version contained a provision that forced Medicare to compete with private health plans. This provision was favored by Bush but was a deal breaker for Senate Democrats. The compromise bill made the competition provision merely experimental.

In the House, voting was held open late, and at 3:00 a.m. on November 22, it appeared to be failing. Hastert held the voting open while leaders could pressure dissenting Republicans to switch their votes, promising campaign assistance. At 5:00 a.m., Bush was awakened so that he could call Republicans and urge them to vote yes.[52] The final vote was 220-215 in the House, with 16 Democrats voting for it and 25 Republicans voting against it. The bill passed the Senate 55-44.

The bill was originally estimated by the Congressional Budget Office (CBO) to cost $395 million over ten years. The Bush administration knew the CBO estimate was low but did not disclose that Medicare's chief actuary estimated the program to cost $534 billion.[53] Bush signed the bill on December 8, 2003. He used up a great deal of political capital to secure the legislation, and it would prove to be the last landmark policy he could negotiate with Congress.

George W. Bush and Congress

A major loss for Bush was his faith-based initiative, which was the essence of the "compassionate conservatism" that he invoked during the 2000

104 *The High-Opportunity Presidents*

election campaign. This policy united those who wanted to shrink government with the Christian conservatives. However, it legitimized the welfare state, which was anathema to many conservative Republicans. The idea was that faith-based organizations are better at doing the work of social services—they would be more efficient and have more compassion than government bureaucrats. Bush had a special place in his heart for these ministries, as he credits his faith for helping him overcome his alcohol problem. Questions surrounding the presumption of the effectiveness of faith-based organizations as well as the separation of church and state stalled congressional action. Ultimately, with congressional interest waning and the 9/11 attacks taking his focus, Bush gave up on the legislative path.

Items not on the Bush agenda came as efforts of Congress to respond to public pressure. The first dealt with the accounting and management scandals at firms such as Enron, WorldCom, and others that first came to light in late 2001. Bush was not inclined to push for a strong bill and recommended increasing prison sentences for those convicted. Congress pushed forward on a strong bipartisan effort, known as Sarbanes-Oxley, that would strengthen oversight of financial auditors by creating the Public Company Accounting Oversight Board, reduce any conflicts of interest, enhance financial disclosure rules, and augment SEC resources and responsibilities, among other measures. Bush felt that the law was too rigid, yet given the overwhelming vote in Congress (423-3 in the House, 99-0 in the Senate), and as more accounting fraud at large companies was exposed, his hand was forced (although he used a signing statement to water down its effectiveness).[54] Bush also felt compelled to sign the Bipartisan Campaign Reform Act due to similar public support for the measure.

After 9/11, the Bush administration tried to push domestic issues as "national security," including drilling in the Alaskan National Wildlife Refuge (ANWR) and fast-tracking trade authority. Bush believed he could overwhelm Congress by sheer force of his popularity and could focus his energy on foreign policy. Energy legislation was stuck in conference as the House and Senate bills appeared irreconcilable—the Senate bill promoted conservation and did not allow drilling in the ANWR.[55] Senate Democrats tired of Republicans' tactic of railroading legislation by excluding Democrats from conference committees, and successfully filibustered the bill.

As with his Medicare reform, Bush thought that his Clear Skies initiative of emissions trading would establish his bona fides with the political center on the issue of the environment.[56] The Clear Skies initiative had both regulatory and legislative elements. The administration's efforts at regulatory reform were implemented prior to the legislative push but were eventually struck down by the courts. Christine Todd Whitman, administrator of the

Environmental Protection Agency, became engaged in a drawn-out fight with Cheney's National Energy Policy Development group over rulemaking. Republicans on the Hill were intransigent as they felt that they could not defend Bush's proposal without technical details, which he refused to release.[57] The proposal failed in 2003. Beyond energy policy, Bush suffered other major legislative failures during his first term: medical malpractice reform, welfare reform with enhanced work requirements, and conservative modifications to Head Start.

The main principles of Bush's congressional strategy were to push a limited agenda and not to compromise until it was absolutely necessary. Bush was famous for underscoring his principled stances by telling his legislative liaisons, "I will not negotiate with myself."[58] His use of the House as the first option on legislation was effective due to the House's stricter rules on floor debate.[59] Hastert had a close relationship with Bush, making sure the president would not be embarrassed by having to veto any bill he sent him.[60] The MBA president delegated this job to the Republican House leadership, with only moderate success.

An Assessment: The Rise of the Administrative Presidency

The biggest challenge Bush faced was accomplishing anything at all at the start of an illegitimate presidency. The fact that Bush achieved major accomplishments before 9/11 is impressive. But less impressive is how he squandered his post-9/11 political capital. He had tremendous opportunity as well as resources, but he didn't accomplish as much as he could have. Bush failed to anticipate opposition to his policies, particularly on the faith-based initiatives and on homeland security. Bush's failure to examine policies in detail and to invite devil's advocates is similar to his rigid (and erroneous) belief that Iraq possessed weapons of mass destruction. Bush's failure to anticipate opposition is similar to his sentiment that the United States would be greeted as liberators by the Iraqis.

Bush was most powerful during his honeymoon and right after 9/11. He was less effective at other times. Bush squandered his post-9/11 political power the same way he squandered his second-term electoral mandate (in failing on Social Security and Immigration reform). Presidents generally enjoy a great deal of success with Congress during wartime, moving in the president's direction on domestic policy.[61] Crises provide focus for the public and for policy makers, facilitating new ideas and change.[62] In this sense, Bush woefully underperformed after 9/11.

As this book amply demonstrates, even under the best of circumstances, presidents have a hard time leading Congress. If the president's party has control of both houses, the way might be a bit smoother. Yet even then, a variety of political and institutional roadblocks litter the president's path. Some presidents try to overcome this by "going public," believing that if

106 *The High-Opportunity Presidents*

they can sway public opinion, they can also sway Congress. Others put time and capital into "going Washington" and playing the insider game of bargaining with, persuading, and pressuring key members of Congress. Still others, frustrated with congressional gridlock, are tempted to go beyond the law, as Reagan did in the Iran–Contra scandal.

Another strategy, as old as the presidency itself, yet given new life in the modern era, is to rely on the administrative capacity of the office. In this way, presidents circumvent Congress and unilaterally make policy. This includes the use of signing statements. Article II, Section 1 says that "all executive power shall be vested in a President of the United States of America." While the "all" at the beginning of the sentence seems to suggest a presidential exclusivity in the executive function, elsewhere in the Constitution (e.g., Article I, Sections 8 and 9) certain managerial or executive functions are given to Congress. From this, one might conclude that while the president is the chief executive officer, he must share certain executive powers with Congress.

Recent presidents have begun to interpret the "vesting clause" expansively, using administrative methods to set policy. Using this old power in a new way, Richard Nixon, facing a Congress controlled by Democrats yet determined to leave his mark, decided that an expansive view of his managerial power gave him significant opportunities to get around Congress and set policy in several legislative areas.[63] Bush used administrative authority to engage in a high degree of rulemaking, and his rate of rules proposed to those that became binding law was higher than the rates of his three predecessors.[64] His successors would find this course of action appealing as well.

Notes

1 John Robert Greene, *The Presidency of George W. Bush* (Lawrence, KS: University of Kansas Press, 2022), 260.

2 Stanley A. Renshon, *In His Father's Shadow: The Transformations of George W. Bush* (New York: Palgrave Macmillan, 2004).

3 Robert Draper, *Dead Certain: The Presidency of George W. Bush* (New York: Free Press, 2007); Bill Minutaglio, *First Son: George W. Bush and the Bush Family Dynasty* (New York: Times Books, 1999); and George W. Bush, *Decision Points* (New York: Broadway, 2010).

4 William G. Mayer, *The Uses and Misuses of Politics: Karl Rove and the Bush Presidency* (Lawrence, KS: University of Kansas Press, 2021), ch. 10.

5 Alan Dershowitz, "Bush's Ill-Advised Silence," *New York Times*, August 21, 1999.

6 Renshon, *In His Father's Shadow*, 97.

7 For an interesting discussion on the merits and drawbacks of Bush's resoluteness, see Robert Maranto, Tom Lansford, and Jeremy Johnson, eds., *Judging Bush* (Stanford, CA: Stanford University Press, 2009).

8 Robert Maranto and Richard E. Redding, "Bush's Brain (No, Not Karl Rove): How Bush's Psyche Shaped His Decision Making," in *Judging Bush*, ed.

Robert Maranto, Tom Lansford, and Jeremy Johnson (Stanford, CA: Stanford University Press, 2009), 21–40.

9 Paul O'Neill, *The Price of Loyalty* (New York: Simon and Schuster, 2004).

10 Steven J. Rubenzer and Thomas R. Faschingbauer, *Personality, Character, and Leadership in the White House: Psychologists Assess the Presidents* (Washington, DC: Potomac Books, 2004).

11 See Justin Frank, *Bush on the Couch: Inside the Mind of the President* (New York: HarperCollins, 2004); and Aubrey Immelman, "The Political Personality of U.S. President George W. Bush," in *Political Leadership for a New Century: Personality and Behavior among American Leaders*, ed. Linda O. Valenty and Ofer Feldman (Westport, CT: Praeger, 2002), 81–103.

12 James P. Pfiffner, "George W. Bush: Policy, Politics and Personality," in *New Challenges for the American Presidency*, ed. George C. Edwards III and Phillip John Davies (New York: Longman, 2004), 161–181.

13 Maranto and Redding, "Bush's Brain."

14 Steven E. Schier, *Panorama of a Presidency: How George W. Bush Acquired and Spent His Political Capital* (Armonk, NY: M.E. Sharpe, 2009), ch. 4.

15 Gary C. Jacobson, *A Divider, Not a Uniter* (New York: Pearson Longman, 2006), 69.

16 Pew Research Center for the People & the Press, "Bush Lost Battle over the Surplus, but Won Tax Cut War," May 11, 2001, www.people-press.org/2011/05/11/bush-lost-battle-over-the-surplus-but-won-tax-cut-war/.

17 See Virginia A. Chanley, "Trust in Government in the Aftermath of 9/11: Determinants and Consequences," *Political Psychology* 23, no. 3 (2002): 469–483.

18 Donald F. Kettl, *Team Bush: Leadership Lessons from the Bush White House* (New York: McGraw-Hill, 2003).

19 Shirley Anne Warshaw, *The Co-Presidency of Bush and Cheney* (Stanford, CA: Stanford University Press, 2009).

20 Ibid.

21 Shirley Anne Warshaw, "The Cheneyization of the Bush Administration," in *Judging Bush*, ed. Robert Maranto, Tom Lansford, and Jeremy Johnson (Stanford, CA: Stanford University Press, 2009), 41–57.

22 Warshaw, "The Cheneyization of the Bush Administration."

23 Karen Hughes, *Ten Minutes from Normal* (New York: Penguin, 2004).

24 Barton Gellman, *Angler: The Cheney Vice Presidency* (New York: Penguin, 2008).

25 Warshaw, "The Cheneyization of the Bush Administration."

26 See Martha Joynt Kumar, "The Presidential Transition of 2001: Scholars Offer Expertise and Analysis," *PS: Political Science and Politics* 35, no. 1 (2002): 9–12.

27 Warshaw, "The Cheneyization of the Bush Administration."

28 Andrew Rudalevige, "'The Decider': Issue Management and the Bush White House," in *The George W. Bush Legacy*, ed. Colin Campbell, Bert A. Rockman, and Andrew Rudalevige (Washington, DC: CQ Press, 2008), 144.

29 Schier, *Panorama of a Presidency*, 67.

30 Draper, *Dead Certain*.

31 Ron Suskind, *The Price of Loyalty: George W. Bush, the White House, and the Education of Paul O'Neill* (New York: Simon and Schuster, 2004).

32 Warshaw, "The Cheneyization of the Bush Administration."

33 Gary Mucciaroni and Paul J. Quirk, "Deliberations of a 'Compassionate Conservative': George W. Bush's Domestic Presidency," in *The George W. Bush*

108 *The High-Opportunity Presidents*

Presidency: Appraisals and Prospects, ed. Colin Campbell and Bert A. Rockman (Washington, DC: CQ Press, 2004), 162–163.

34 Suskind, *The Price of Loyalty*.

35 Draper, *Dead Certain*.

36 James P. Pfiffner, "President Bush as Chief Executive," in *Judging Bush*, ed. Robert Maranto, Tom Lansford, and Jeremy Johnson (Stanford, CA: Stanford University Press, 2009), 71.

37 Charles O. Jones, "The US Congress and Chief Executive George W. Bush," in *The Polarized Presidency of George W. Bush*, ed. George C. Edwards III and Desmond S. King (New York: Oxford University Press, 2007), 401.

38 John E. Owens, "Bush's Congressional Legacy and Congress's Bush Legacy," in *Assessing George W. Bush's Legacy: The Right Man?* ed. Iwan Morgan and Phillip John Davies (New York: Palgrave Macmillan, 2010), 66.

39 George C. Edwards III, *Governing by Campaigning: The Politics of the Bush Presidency* (New York: Pearson Longman, 2008), 147.

40 George C. Edwards III, *On Deaf Ears: The Limits of the Bully Pulpit* (New Haven, CT: Yale University Press, 2006), 32.

41 Ronald Brownstein, *The Second Civil War: How Extreme Partisanship Has Paralyzed Washington and Polarized America* (New York: Penguin, 2007).

42 Barbara Sinclair, "Living (and Dying?) by the Sword: George W. Bush as Legislative Leader," in *The George W. Bush Legacy*, ed. Colin Campbell, Bert A. Rockman, and Andrew Rudalevige (Washington, DC: CQ Press, 2008), 168.

43 Mucciaroni and Quirk, "Deliberations of a 'Compassionate Conservative,'" 163.

44 Ibid., 166.

45 Suskind, *The Price of Loyalty*.

46 Edwards, *Governing by Campaigning*, 95–96.

47 Ibid., 97–98.

48 Lydia Saad, "No Child Left Behind Rated More Negatively Than Positively," *Gallup Politics*, August 20, 2012, www.gallup.com/poll/156800/no-child-left-behind-rated-negatively-positively.aspx.

49 Brandice Canes-Wrone, *Who Leads Whom? Presidents, Policy, and the Public* (Chicago: University of Chicago Press, 2005).

50 Mucciaroni and Quirk, "Deliberations of a 'Compassionate Conservative,'" 180.

51 Jonathan Oberlander, "The Bush Administration and the Politics of Medicare Reform," in *Building Coalitions, Making Policy: The Politics of the Clinton, Bush & Obama Presidencies*, ed. Martin A. Levin, Daniel DiSalvo, and Martin M. Shapiro (Baltimore: Johns Hopkins University Press, 2012), 154.

52 Sinclair, "Living (and Dying?) by the Sword," 179.

53 Bruce Bartlett, "Republican Deficit Hypocrisy: Remember the Medicare Drug Benefit?" *Forbes*, November 20, 2009.

54 Ashley Moraguez, "Does Bipartisanship Pay? Executive Manipulation of Legislative Coalitions During the George W. Bush Presidency," *Congress & the Presidency* 49, no. 1 (2020): 62–91.

55 Sinclair, "Living (and Dying?) by the Sword," 176.

56 David Emer, "Bush's Clear Skies Initiative and the Politics of Policymaking," in *Building Coalitions, Making Policy: The Politics of the Clinton, Bush & Obama Presidencies*, ed. Martin A. Levin, Daniel DiSalvo, and Martin M. Shapiro (Baltimore: Johns Hopkins University Press, 2012), 245.

57 Ibid., 253.

58 John D. Graham, *Bush on the Home Front* (Bloomington: Indiana University Press, 2010), 6.
59 Ibid.
60 Sinclair, "Living (and Dying?) by the Sword," 180.
61 William G. Howell, Saul P. Jackman, and Jon C. Rogowski, "The *Wartime President:* Insights, Lessons, and Opportunities for Continued Investigation," *Presidential Studies Quarterly* 42, no. 4 (2012): 802.
62 See John W. Kingdon, *Agendas, Alternatives, and Public Policies* (New York: Longman, 2002); and David Mayhew, "Wars and American Politics," *Perspectives on American Politics* 3, no. 3 (2005): 473–493.
63 See Richard P. Nathan, *The Administrative Presidency* (New York: Wiley, 1983).
64 Jason Webb Yackee and Susan Webb Yackee, "Is the Bush Bureaucracy Any Different? A Macro-Empirical Examination of Notice and Comment Rulemaking under '43,'" in *President George W. Bush's Influence over Bureaucracy and Policy*, ed. Colin Provost and Paul Teske (New York: Palgrave Macmillan, 2009), 45.

Part II

The Moderate-Opportunity Presidents

6 Harry S. Truman
A Broker with Beliefs

On April 12, 1945, Vice President Harry Truman walked to the special Capitol Hill basement office used by House Speaker Sam Rayburn (D-TX) for an after-hours conversation and a glass of bourbon with some of his friends in Congress. On arrival, he was told that Stephen Early, President Franklin Roosevelt's press secretary, wanted him to call the White House. Early's strained voice and instructions for coming to the White House warned the vice president that all was not well. In fact, ashen-faced, Truman proclaimed, "Jesus Christ and General Jackson" as he put down the phone. Not many minutes later he entered the White House, where First Lady Eleanor Roosevelt awaited him. As she put her arm on his shoulder, she told him the bad news: "Harry, the President is dead." For a moment the vice president was unable to speak. Then he said, "Is there anything I can do for you?" Eleanor replied, "Is there anything we can do for you, for you are the one in trouble now."[1]

In the midst of a world war, an uncertain nation wondered what kind of leadership would be provided by a president who had been regarded by many only a decade earlier as a senator of little stature and the product of a political machine. Yet, despite some low points in public support, Harry Truman (served 1945–1953) generally managed to land on his feet and govern quite effectively.

Personal Characteristics

Harry S. Truman (1884–1972) was born in Lamar, Missouri, the oldest of the three children of Martha and John Truman, a mule trader. Harry's parents wanted to give him a middle name in honor of one of his grandfathers, but, unable to decide which one, they settled on simply a middle initial—"S"—which stands for nothing.

DOI: 10.4324/9781003426684-8

114 *The Moderate-Opportunity Presidents*

After graduating from high school in Independence, Missouri, Harry, unable to afford college, took a series of jobs in nearby Kansas City that included railroad timekeeper and bank clerk. At age 22o he took over management of his grandmother's 600-acre farm and became a self-described "dirt farmer." After returning in 1919 from distinguished military service in France during World War I, Harry opened a haberdashery store in Kansas City with a war buddy. The shop failed in the wake of a recession that decimated sales for select menswear.

Career Path

Truman's political career in Missouri began with his election as a county judge in 1922, aided by Kansas City political boss Tom Pendergast. Such judgeships were administrative—not judicial—so Truman controlled hundreds of patronage jobs and many public works projects. Truman acquired valuable political experience that he later put to good use. He served as judge for 10 of the next 12 years before gaining election to the US Senate in 1934. In 1940, he retained his seat against a strong challenger despite the pall cast by sponsor Tom Pendergast's conviction for tax evasion. During his second term, Truman gained considerable public exposure as he headed the Senate Committee to Investigate the National Defense Program, which audited wartime contracts.

In 1944, his selection as the Democratic vice presidential candidate came amid intense political maneuvering. Roosevelt felt that Henry Wallace, his current vice president, was too liberal to warrant renomination. Truman, however, seemed to be a plausible candidate—he apparently appealed to different segments of the party, and he had gained considerable visibility from his Senate committee investigations. After a long delay, Truman was offered the second spot on the ticket by FDR at the Democratic convention in Chicago.

Truman's career path left little room to accumulate experience in foreign policy, and FDR contributed to his vice president's foreign policy gap by unwisely excluding Truman from strategic wartime deliberations. He came into office with other valuable experience, however. According to Harold Gosnell, Truman profited from skills he had developed earlier in his career while acting as a broker among different groups. In Kansas City, as a county administrator allied with the Pendergast machine, he balanced the claims made by various ethnic groups, including a large African American population. His brokering skills were especially evident later, in 1940, when he needed to build an electoral coalition of diverse urban ethnic groups, small-town residents, and farmers.[2] Truman also entered the White House with extensive knowledge of the country from his wide travels with his Senate committee and of American history from his voracious appetite for books.

What Manner of Man?

Truman possessed several traits that would later serve him well as a president cast into difficult circumstances. One was his diligence and capacity for hard work. As a youngster he had read a set of encyclopedias from A to Z. In the Senate, he studied night after night, going over railroad financial reports as part of his committee responsibilities. As president he often was seen lugging six- to eight-inch stacks of folders into the family quarters of the White House for his evening reading. His habit of rising early originated in his younger days on the farm, and he stuck to that schedule throughout his years in politics.

Truman was one of the more knowledgeable presidents on the subject of American political history. Although he was largely self-taught and tended toward some uncritically accepted popular views, his studies had included an analysis of the leadership approaches and performances of each of his predecessors in the White House. When Truman set out to learn something, he tended to dig into the specifics of issues but to the exclusion of an examination of broader theoretical considerations. For example, he knew a great deal about the federal budget but made no pretext of having studied economics.

As for other qualities, historian Donald R. McCoy found Truman to be "an honest man who abhorred having anyone kicked around."[3] Former House Speaker John Garner (D-TX), who knew Truman from his days in Congress, remarked as Truman assumed the presidency that he was "honest and patriotic and has a head full of horse sense. Besides, he has guts."[4] Indeed, when his business venture failed, he resisted the bankruptcy route taken by his partner and struggled for more than a decade to fully repay his debts. And, despite being the product of a political machine and facing financial pressures from past debts, Truman did little to seek personal profit.

Years ago Americans were fond of pointing out that Roosevelt proved that a rich man could be president, Truman proved that anybody could be president, and Eisenhower proved that they did not need a president. Putting the other two aside for now, it is clear that Truman was in some ways simply an average American in the White House. He enjoyed a glass of bourbon with friends who shared his background, energetically pursued his poker games, and sometimes spoke in a gruff and profane manner. More importantly, however, he also possessed considerable political skill within a personality more complex than some of the assessments of him have suggested.

Policy Views

Truman's policy views were liberal—but with some moderate tendencies. During his Senate years he supported Roosevelt during the "Second

116   *The Moderate-Opportunity Presidents*

New Deal" in 1935 and stood firmly shoulder to shoulder with organized labor. In his second term in the White House, he opposed moves by many Republicans and conservative Democrats to terminate FDR's National Youth Administration, National Resources Planning Board, Farm Security Administration, and aspects of the Tennessee Valley Authority.[5]

An important strain running through Truman's policy orientation was his dislike of the large eastern corporate interests. This dislike stemmed not only from his Missouri roots but also from his resentment over his own unsuccessful business venture. In some respects, Truman's views reflected an earlier America of farms, small towns, and main streets rather than large bureaucracies, corporate structures, and large metropolitan areas. In accordance, Truman would label his domestic program the "Fair Deal."

Truman's policy views on civil rights changed considerably from his judgeship days in Missouri to his presidential days in the White House.[6] Early in his political life he displayed little sensitivity to racial issues, and he repeated racial stereotypes and epithets. In the Senate, he supported antilynching laws but did not speak out, probably because of political expediency. In fact, he reportedly told a friend who opposed the antilynching measure that his sympathies were with him but that the black vote was too important in Kansas City and St. Louis.[7] Those views changed when he reached the White House.

Challenges and Opportunities

Truman was thrust into the presidency in a situation presenting significant constraints and few advantages. As an "understudy" president following a popular predecessor, he often was compared unfavorably with FDR, especially in his public speaking. Additionally, he did not have the legitimation gained from having been elected president in his own right. Weak public support also proved to be a problem. Truman enjoyed a surge of popularity in the first months in office but saw a dramatic slide in 1946 from which he only partially recovered.

The public also had no enthusiasm for new government programs. A Gallup poll conducted in 1945 revealed very limited interest in any major new initiatives beyond aid to veterans. Indeed, only 16 percent of the electorate wanted Truman to move to the left, 18 percent preferred a move to the right, and 55 percent preferred the middle of the road.[8]

The Democratic Party coalition also presented difficulties. The presidential ticket had won in 1944 by Roosevelt's lowest margin—only 53 percent. In Congress, Democrats had slim majorities in the House and Senate. Furthermore, on many votes Truman could anticipate the formation of the same conservative Democratic and Republican voting bloc that had derailed so many of Roosevelt's domestic initiatives. The strength of that bloc was enhanced by the greater dominance of southern Democrats on key committees following a major reorganization in 1946. To make matters worse, in the 1946 midterm elections the Republicans added 55 seats in the House and 12 in the Senate as they regained control of both houses of Congress. Truman also faced an anticommunist witch hunt led by Republican senator Joseph McCarthy of Wisconsin, who accused Truman and members of his administration of being soft on, and even harboring, communists.

The surge of Republican strength in 1946 placed Truman in a weak position, closely resembling that of Bill Clinton and Barack Obama after their significant midterm losses in their second year. Truman's popularity was low, and the Republicans had found voter responsiveness to their line "To err is Truman." Democratic Party leaders made no secret of their interest in having a different candidate in 1948, but they were unable to settle on an alternative. Truman entertained thoughts of stepping down with the prospect of General Dwight Eisenhower running as the Democratic Party nominee. Later, though, he resolved to run in 1948 and scornfully dismissed the suggestion of Senator William Fulbright (D-AK) that he step down, labeling Fulbright "Sen. Halfbright."[9]

Truman was in a difficult position regarding promising issues. Roosevelt had preferred experimentation and administrative adaptation in major programs and had left little in the way of a "blueprint" to be followed. Few had anticipated that the war would end abruptly in mid-1945.[10] The shift from a wartime economy to a peacetime footing presented an enormous challenge and few guidelines. The combination of wage and price controls and massive deficits had produced a tremendous surge of economic growth. The questions now were: How should controls be eliminated? To what extent can a peacetime economy provide the necessary consumer goods once pent-up demand is unleashed?

Economic and budgetary conditions presented some potential opportunities. With the end of the war, federal spending plummeted from $98 billion in 1945 to $33 billion in 1946. This drop raised opportunities to reduce taxes, lower the deficit, and create new programs—but only if majorities in Congress could be achieved. The economy was much larger than in the 1930s; the gross national product (GNP) had surged from $101 billion to $215 billion during five years of wartime production. After initial postwar sluggishness, the economy grew by 4.1 percent in 1948. The larger economy offered an opportunity for new programs, but paradoxically it also served to undercut public support for the view that a larger government role was needed to ensure adequate growth.

Along with his domestic challenges, Truman faced an enormous number of foreign policy issues. His first decision was to order the use of atomic bombs against two Japanese cities—a move that ended the war in the Pacific. As postwar relations with the Soviets deteriorated, he successfully put in place the Truman Doctrine (1947), declaring that the United

118   *The Moderate-Opportunity Presidents*

States would aid governments threatened by communist subversion. He also implemented the Marshall Plan (1949), providing economic assistance for Western Europe, and the North Atlantic Treaty Organization (1949), providing for the collective defense of eleven North American and European countries. Key events in 1948 included recognition of the new state of Israel and Truman's decision to provide airlift assistance to West Berlin as the Soviets sought to isolate and control the city.

Foreign policy challenges rather than domestic opportunities defined Truman's tenure in the presidency. He had campaigned on some domestic issues, but primarily in the spirit of preserving the New Deal rather than engaging in broad new initiatives. Foreign policy issues then quickly took over as issues such as agriculture and Social Security reform were quickly "overshadowed by ominous events occurring around the world."[11] The 1949 defeat of Nationalist forces in China precipitated an intense debate over "Who lost China?" and charges that the Truman administration had been soft on communism. The war in Korea meant that he had to contend with an increasingly unpopular war during his last 30 months in office.

Leadership Style

Acting on his extensive study of earlier presidents, Truman strongly emphasized the importance of the presidency as an institution. He also firmly believed in the importance of speaking out for all of the people. His tendency to present Congress with lengthy lists of program objectives stemmed in part from his sense that a president should promote broad, inclusive goals.

The Advisory Process and Approach to Decision-Making

"Accidental" presidents face unique problems in staffing their presidencies. Truman made the appropriate gesture of asking FDR's people to stay. However, some did not want to work for another president, some preferred to leave low-paying government jobs, and others he could not trust, so the cabinet and staff changed quite quickly.[12]

Truman proceeded along traditional lines with his staff organization and recruitment. His key aides for daily operations included Matthew Connelly, appointments secretary; Donald Dawson, coordinator of patronage; George Elsey, speech writer and legislative analyst; and Press Secretary Charles Ross. Charles Murphy drafted bills and prepared Truman's September 1945 long message to Congress, and David Niles was responsible for minority groups. He never appointed a chief of staff, but his special counsel to the president, Clark Clifford, acted as such in addition to various other roles. John Steelman, in some respects, filled a role that resembled that of chief of staff later in Truman's presidency.[13]

Truman's advisory processes often produced lively debates over policy options. The leading proponent of the more liberal positions was Clark Clifford. A lawyer and native of St. Louis, Clifford had left his legal practice to take a series of Washington positions, and Truman found him to be a lucky inheritance. Described by journalist Patrick Anderson as both "smooth as silk and tough as nails," Clifford occupied the large office next to Truman's and got along very well with the president.[14]

Administrative Strategies

Truman used administrative decisions extensively in order to craft policy. He was especially interested in "good government" issues in the wake of the rapid expansion of agencies begun with the New Deal and the war effort. Republicans in Congress had a similar interest. Thus, in 1947 the Republican-controlled Congress established the Commission on the Organization of the Executive Branch of the Government to help a new president cope with the problems of executive branch organization. Truman, pledging his full cooperation, appointed former president Herbert Hoover to head the new commission. To the Republicans' dismay, however, Truman was the president to benefit from the commission's findings after he surprisingly defeated Dewey in the election of 1948. Truman was pleased with the 19 extensive reports produced by 1949 because he believed the commission had acted in a nonpartisan manner. In part because of Truman's strong public endorsement, all of the Hoover Commission's recommendations were later signed into law.[15]

Early in his tenure, Truman was confronted with labor disputes. The nation's labor unions had grown considerably—to the point that they had 14.8 million members, or a third of the labor force. Once the unions were freed from the wartime agreement not to strike, a wave of labor disputes spread throughout major sectors of the economy. In his overall responses to labor strikes, Truman showed a willingness to use administrative actions to defend what he saw as the larger public interest, particularly with regard to railroads and coal mining. In one of the more significant setbacks of his presidency, however, Truman's 1952 seizure of the nation's steel mills during the Korean War in response to an industry-wide labor strike was overturned by the Supreme Court.[16]

Ultimately, the most important area in which Truman applied his administrative strategies was civil rights, where the same forces that had prevented Senate passage of measures like the antilynching bill in the 1930s persisted. Truman's early prejudices about race had given way to a more enlightened view. He became, in some ways, a champion of civil rights at a time when it was potentially dangerous to do so. Before taking administrative action in this area, Truman sought other lines of influence such as advocating civil rights measures in major addresses. In a January 3, 1946, radio speech, he went public and criticized the "small handful of Congressmen" in the House Rules Committee who had prevented a vote on a permanent Federal Employment Practices Commission (FEPC), which would have continued the operation established by FDR in 1941.[17] In the face of the expected Senate filibuster, Truman briefly reiterated his support, but he could not change the outcome. Despite organized protests led by the National Association for the Advancement of Colored People (NAACP), the fate of the FEPC had been decisively determined. Truman continued some limited protections against employment discrimination, but his fact-finding authority did not include an enforcement function.

Truman finally turned to administrative action on civil rights issues with the creation in December 1946 of the Presidential Commission on Civil Rights (PCCR). His action was prompted by his disgust with several gruesome incidents in the South. The distinguished members of the PCCR were given the substantial time and broad mandate they would need to prepare a report that, Truman hoped, would provide additional momentum on civil rights issues.[18] A year later the PCCR issued its lengthy and sweeping report, *To Secure These Rights*. Although the commission's findings dealt with problems confronting many different minority groups, African Americans were the main focus of the report's 34 major recommendations on voting rights, personal security, the need for a Fair Employment Practices Committee, laws prohibiting housing discrimination, school desegregation in Washington, DC, and other issues. The report received widespread public attention. The Truman White House mailed out 25,000 copies, publisher Simon and Schuster sold some 36,000 copies for a dollar apiece, and the report was summarized by many newspapers, religious organizations, and interest groups. William White, the executive secretary of the NAACP, praised the report for having "stirred America's conscience."[19]

Truman then used the PCCR report to prompt additional action. In February 1948, he sent a message to Congress calling for a broad range of civil rights protections. Major recommendations included the establishment of a permanent FEPC as well as the passage of measures designed to eliminate southern practices preventing African Americans from registering and voting and to end discrimination in interstate rail, bus, and airplane travel. But for legislative leaders and Truman himself, the result was predetermined: While some legislation might pass the House, a Senate filibuster could not be defeated, and the civil rights bills would not pass.

Determined to make progress on this front anyway, Truman turned once again to administrative action. By executive order, he established a Fair Employment Board within the Civil Service Commission to address job discrimination. A more dramatic step, however, was his July 26 executive order requiring the nation's military leaders to undertake steps to desegregate the armed forces.

Political calculations clearly influenced Truman's actions. He had not included the PCCR recommendation for desegregation of the armed services in his February 1948 message to Congress, and he was still uncertain of what he would do as late as May 11.[20] He was concerned in part about a significant drop in his public approval but also saw an opportunity to burnish his credentials with African American voters.[21] The announcement of his executive order on July 26 came at a time when he supported a softer civil rights plank than Hubert Humphrey, then the young mayor of Minneapolis, was advocating for the Democratic Party platform.[22] Truman was obviously hoping to keep the South from bolting the Democratic Party. Yet, while acting as a broker among competing interests, he also was manifesting aspects of personal beliefs in his administrative strategies.

Public Leadership

In his public role, Truman was handicapped by his staunchly partisan, sometimes overly blunt persona. Once at a press conference he responded to an inquiry about why he had granted an exclusive interview to *New York Times* journalist Arthur Krock by saying, "I'll give interviews to anyone I damn please." Clark Clifford recognized Truman's image problems and in his reelection memo recommended (to no avail) that Truman be seen more often with famous people such as scientists.[23] Unsurprisingly, one study found Truman to be the least successful president in maintaining his popularity.[24]

Truman's approach to press conferences differed markedly. At times, Truman's forthright replies drew favorable responses because of their candor. But at other times he stumbled because of his bluntness and, in general, did not offer specific policy objectives.

Truman's rhetorical skills were invariably compared with those of FDR, placing him at a disadvantage. Clark Clifford assessed Truman's speaking style: "He generally reads poorly from written texts, his head down, words coming forth in what the press liked to call a drone."[25] He tended to emphasize a careful collection of facts in his speeches but had little interest in developing a more effective rhetorical style. In his early days in the White House, Truman was reluctant to make public addresses, and he had his lengthy September 1945 State of the Union-type address read by the clerks in Congress. Later, he shed that reluctance and even exceeded the average number of major presidential addresses. Moreover, Truman was the first president to deliver an entire address solely on the subject of civil rights. In a speech made before a Washington audience of 10,000 members and supporters of the NAACP, he harshly criticized racial discrimination as he proclaimed, "One immediate task is to remove the last remnants of the barriers

122 *The Moderate-Opportunity Presidents*

which stand between millions of our citizens and their birthright.... We cannot wait another decade or another generation to remedy these evils."[26]

Congressional Leadership

Most of the president's senior professional staff dealt with Congress to some degree, typically hashing out policy and serving as a representative of the president. For example, Clark Clifford worked on a variety of policy issues, while John Steelman handled individual cases pertaining to public works and federal grants to particular districts.[27] Truman held meetings with Democratic legislative leaders on a regular basis, and he established "back door" access for not only Speaker Sam Rayburn but also many members of Congress through the use of short morning appointments.

As noted, Truman favored placing a large number of issues on the congressional agenda through messages and speeches. Whether the issues were acted on or not, Truman felt presidents were obligated to present a broad agenda. This view was especially evident in his September 1945 message to Congress. In 1948, he similarly outlined a broad agenda in his State of the Union address and in a message to Congress on civil rights issues as he sought in part to highlight differences between his positions and those of the Republican congressional majorities.

Truman pursued strategies beyond efforts at agenda setting. He engaged in some bargaining, but sometimes with a reluctance that could be traced to his belief in the importance of congressional independence. That belief, however, did not prevent him from becoming involved on occasion in the organization of Congress. For example, he encouraged Sam Rayburn to seek the minority party leadership position in the House after he lost the speakership after Democratic losses in the 1946 midterm elections. On several occasions, Truman sought to mobilize public support for specific legislation. On other occasions, he tried to prompt action on measures that had become stalled in committee.

Truman also employed a strong veto strategy as he vetoed several labor and tax bills, as well as a price decontrol measure. Some of his vetoes were overridden—a reflection of both Republican strength in Congress after the 1946 elections and his willingness to stand firm in the face of likely defeat. During 1947–1948, posturing for the 1948 presidential campaign became his primary objective, and the veto strategy was effective at signaling to the electorate his differences with the Republican Congress.

Legislative Enactments

Congress faced enormously important and complicated issues during Truman's years in office. At first, the agenda was largely set by the need to end the war and convert to a peacetime economy. Economic planning, elimination of wage and price controls, labor-management relations, and tax policy changes were paramount. Yet Truman also sought to shape the congressional agenda and to promote aspects of his Fair Deal, especially as a source of national strength in the fight against communism.[28] One indication of the scope of his agenda was found in his September 1945 message to Congress that broadly called for measures such as increased unemployment compensation, tax reform, crop insurance for farmers, national health insurance, construction of the St. Lawrence Seaway, federal aid for housing, and an increase in the minimum wage.[29] Republicans acted with surprise and anger at the scope of the program being pushed by an unelected chief executive, using phrases such as "more bureaus and more billions." Although Truman often was unable to mobilize support, his leadership efforts helped to shape various domestic policy responses.

Economic Planning and Price Controls

Truman entered office in the midst of an ongoing struggle over economic policy that eventually would produce the landmark Employment Act of 1946. A conflict about power, the struggle pitted liberal supporters of strong government roles in the economy against Republican and business interests who longed for a return to their position of power and prestige in postwar America. Elaborate arguments about Keynesian economics and the use of tax policies and deficit spending to achieve economic goals often bypassed key aspects of the underlying conflict.

Although Truman contributed to passage of the Employment Act, it largely owed its life to interest group politics in Congress. The initial legislation was developed through extensive committee deliberations begun in 1944. The interest group response was intense, with labor unions energetically supporting the legislation and prominent business groups such as the US Chamber of Commerce, the National Association of Manufacturers, and the American Farm Bureau expressing their equally vocal opposition. Truman contributed to passage of the act by instructing his legislative lieutenants to ensure that it received priority and exerting pressure at a key point to get the legislation out of committee. He offered a modest amount of ongoing public commentary and made a radio address in November 1945 that sought, with apparently little impact, to rally public support when the legislation appeared to be stalled in committee.

The question of how to end wartime-induced price controls presented Truman with enormous difficulties because ending such controls was far more difficult than establishing them.[30] Americans had gone along with controls during World War II, and the country had achieved an admirable record of controlling inflation as prices had increased only 30 percent over the duration of the war. By contrast, during World War I, when no

124 *The Moderate-Opportunity Presidents*

controls had been imposed, prices had rapidly doubled. Once World War II ended, however, public enthusiasm for controls fell off sharply, and rationing was quickly eliminated.[31]

Congress was of little help to Truman in his dilemma—Republicans perceived an excellent election issue. When Republican Senate leader Robert Taft of Ohio was asked what might be done, he responded rather cryptically that people should "eat less."[32] Truman's efforts to control prices and reduce inflation were repeatedly rebuffed by the Republican-controlled Congress. The failure of Congress to respond to Truman's overtures led the president to denounce the "do-nothing" Congress, and the episode became a major campaign issue in Truman's surprising 1948 election victory.

Taft-Hartley Act

Although President Truman and Congress disagreed on labor union organizing rights, they agreed in 1945 on legislation tackling the problem of racketeering in unions.[33] This came as Truman successfully vetoed an initiative sponsored by Senator Robert Taft (D-OH) that would have restricted unions' rights. Regulatory policies for unions became a hot issue in the wake of the 1946 campaign. Unions were roundly condemned as corrupt and charged frequently with being under communist control and at the root of the surge of inflation and the extensive work stoppages. In this context, Truman introduced his own legislative proposals, and no fewer than 17 bills were sent to the Speaker of the House.[34]

Senator Taft became the predominant player in Congress with the 1947 emergence of the Taft-Hartley Act, a management-supported bill seeking to reverse gains won by unions. The bill made certain union practices such as a closed shop (only union members) illegal and authorized the president to obtain a court order blocking (for up to eight days) any strike that imperiled the "national health or safety." The act also increased the size of the National Labor Relations Board (NLRB) from three to five and established the Office of the General Counsel to determine whether to act on a complaint. Despite labor's opposition to many of his views, Taft was a firm believer in the right of labor to strike and to bargain collectively with management. As a result, some of his fights were with legislators who wanted a more restrictive bill than he preferred. But Taft and his colleagues prevailed in the end, thanks in part to a clever political ploy in which few efforts were made to soften a House bill extremely harsh on unions. This allowed Taft and some of his supporters to argue that he was promoting a more moderate version in the Senate, which labor strongly opposed but business interests strongly supported.

Once the bill was delivered to him on June 7, Truman had to decide whether to sign it. Views were mixed. The White House received over half a million messages from the American public—most of which urged a veto.

Overall, however, public opinion was more divided, with 46 percent preferring presidential acquiescence and 38 percent supporting a veto.[35] Union officials and many members vociferously denounced the Taft-Hartley Act. A survey of Democratic Party workers revealed that even in the pro-business, conservative South, the vast majority recommended a veto.

The president's cabinet strongly supported a presidential bill-signing ceremony. Proponents of a signature argued that a veto would in any event be overridden. Additionally, the legislation spoke to Truman's concern about the arrogant use of power by some union leaders. The most influential advocate of a veto was Clark Clifford, who argued that the legislation was inconsistent with what the president had proposed in January. He further argued that a veto would put Truman on the side of most working Americans.

Taking his own counsel, the president submitted a lengthy, harshly written veto message to Congress. He argued that the Taft-Hartley Act would produce more government intervention, encourage distrust in labor-management relations, and prove to be unworkable for the NLRB. He followed his veto message with a national radio address in which he reiterated the goals of his January proposals and argued that the bill was bad for labor, bad for management, and bad for the country. Later that evening, Senator Taft also made a radio address in which he charged that Truman had grossly misrepresented the bill. After the shouting was over, Congress, as expected, voted by large margins to override Truman's veto.

Tax Policies

The stakes in new tax policy during the Truman years were high. In the face of the rapid decline in tax revenues after World War II, Republicans believed a significant reduction in taxes was necessary. Truman also supported a tax cut but more modest in size. In this instance, Congress was more willing to go along with Truman's proposals, as the enacted reduction was close to his original proposal. However, both the White House and Congress realized that broader changes would be considered later. As soon as the 1946 midterm election results became known, Harold Knutson (R-MN) presented a tax-reduction bill designed to cut off much of the government's income and compel it to retrench. The Republicans also wanted a large tax cut to ward off any efforts by Truman to promote new government programs. Rep. Albert Gore (D-TN) led his party's fight in the House as he claimed that this proposal was "right out of the Andrew Mellon primer on special privilege."[36] The bill was changed in an effort to reduce the portions of the tax cut being directed toward those with high incomes, but Truman vetoed the measure in 1947, calling it "the wrong tax at the wrong time."

126 *The Moderate-Opportunity Presidents*

Housing Policy

Although Truman set his sights on housing policy almost immediately upon entering the White House, his first proposals in 1945 drew only a limited response as Congress was more interested in addressing the pressing issue of housing assistance for veterans. Indeed, the lack of an adequate supply of housing was forcing some veterans to go from door to door in search of a room to rent. Congress responded with the Veterans' Emergency Housing Act of 1946. It provided for price ceilings on new homes for veterans and assistance to producers of building materials for veterans' housing.

Landmark housing legislation emerged in Truman's second term in 1949 as he successfully pushed forward a measure providing for both public housing and urban renewal projects for older urban areas. The president had promoted the issue during the 1948 campaign and then submitted a proposal to Congress in early 1949. He also promoted this policy in his public addresses. Despite strong resistance from the real estate lobby, the initiative remained largely intact as it made its way through Congress.

Health Policy and Social Security

Truman's efforts to handle the New Deal agenda in the areas of health and Social Security produced mixed results. In 1946, Congress quickly rejected his call for national health insurance. Instead, it took more limited action, passing the Hill-Burton Act, which launched a program for much-needed hospital construction. Unlike other aspects of Truman's health proposals, the final version of this measure was supported by the American Medical Association (AMA). But to satisfy the AMA, the bill's drafters had to maximize state and local control while giving the federal government little opportunity for modifying decisions made at that level.[37]

Truman made his most aggressive effort to establish national health insurance in the wake of his 1948 campaign when he promoted the issue with gusto. Although initial public opinion polls showed majorities in support, he quickly ran into difficulty. His majorities in Congress were modest, and he faced the continued resistance of southern Democrats. In the battle for public opinion, the AMA viewed his proposal as a life-or-death struggle and spent the unprecedented sum of $1.5 million in a public relations blizzard that claimed Truman's plan would impose the judgments of politicians over those of doctors. Then, in a turn of events not unlike that faced by President Bill Clinton a generation later, a sharp drop in public support eroded his chances for a broad new program.

Changes in Social Security proved far easier to achieve. Truman turned to Social Security reform in his second term as pressures began mounting for expanding a system that had remained unchanged for over a decade.

The Social Security Administration and recipients of its benefits led the campaign more forcefully than the Truman administration, but the president was a strong supporter. These efforts were aided by the public's fondness for Social Security, the most popular of the New Deal programs. By the time Congress finished enacting Social Security reforms in 1950, benefits had been expanded by some 77 percent, and many more Americans found themselves eligible for Social Security.

Truman and Congress

On the grand scale of things, Harry Truman did not have much success with Congress on domestic issues. Although he was not overly eager to engage in bargaining tactics, his lack of success stemmed largely from the strength of the same conservative coalition of Republicans and southern Democrats who had curtailed Roosevelt's reform efforts in 1937. But Truman was able to pursue a few strategies with some success, especially vetoes and veto threats. Agenda setting may not have motivated Congress to act, but it did help to perpetuate stalled New Deal issues. Truman also correctly sensed that he could promote his agenda while portraying Republicans as extremists after they seized control of Congress in the 1946 elections. In short, Truman was more effective in keeping Democratic issues alive and blunting Republican initiatives through the use of defensive strategies than in leading the charge toward new initiatives.

An Assessment

Perhaps the most dramatic assessment of Truman's skills—and the underlying strength of the Roosevelt coalition—was given by the voters in the 1948 presidential election. Defying all odds, as well as the early polling results and the unanimous thumbs-down prediction by the top 50 political pundits, Truman managed a narrow victory.[38] He had succeeded in following through with his strategy of maintaining the Roosevelt coalition. That strategy consisted of skillfully contrasting Republican positions with his own through veto strategies with Congress and strong public statements. When crowds cried, "Give 'em hell, Harry," there was no doubt who "'em" was. Truman campaigned with fervor as he wound his way through the pivotal midwestern states on a whistle-stop tour with a campaign message of protecting New Deal programs from assault by his opponent in 1948, Republican Thomas Dewey. Truman was no mere interloper in these states, as he had visited many of them for non-electoral policy speeches during his administration, making him look less of an opportunist.[39] In retrospect, Truman was aided by having a majority coalition of party identifiers, even though his party was divided between northern

128 *The Moderate-Opportunity Presidents*

liberals and southern conservatives on many issues ranging from civil rights to national health insurance. An improving economy also helped his cause.

Progress on civil rights was Truman's most important domestic legacy—notably his 1948 actions to desegregate the nation's armed services. The process took several years to implement but went surprisingly well, providing important new opportunities for African Americans. A half century later, the military was regarded as the nation's most successfully integrated institution. Supreme Court Justice Thurgood Marshall, who once represented the NAACP, observed that Truman, in promoting civil rights, "took over and told the southern bloc where to go."[40] Whatever the case, Truman clearly acted as a broker in making some of his civil rights decisions as he sought to minimize the loss of southern support. He changed his personal views on the issue. Longtime aide George Elsey strongly rejected the view that Truman acted out of political expediency: "I don't think there was anything phony at all. It wasn't a sham, it wasn't a pretense, it wasn't a lot of hot air just for political purposes." Ronald Sylvia concluded similarly based on his comparative study of presidents: "Truman reacted to events based on his personal belief in fairness and equity."[41]

Although Truman was less directly responsible for them, two important economic policy legacies also emerged. The landmark Taft-Hartley Act was a central legacy of Truman's first term. This legislation was strongly opposed by some union leaders, and those on the political left within the labor movement also regretted that this law reduced the potential for a broad, class-based labor movement. Nevertheless, unions did well in their organizational efforts during the 1950s. Passage of the Employment Act in 1946, with its creation of the CEA, was not used as a basis for bold fiscal policy steps by either Truman or Eisenhower. By the 1960s, however, the council and its underlying rationale for assertive federal action was serving Presidents Kennedy and Johnson quite effectively in their economic policy proposals.[42]

As a moderate-opportunity president, Truman occupied the presidency during a very difficult time and often shaped policy by successfully opposing aspects of legislation being promoted by the conservative coalition. His distinctive leadership style aided his efforts. Although all presidents seek to balance good policy and good politics in various ways, Truman's performance, more than those of his predecessors, included a stronger emphasis on the effort to do the right thing.

Notes

1 David McCullough, *Truman* (New York: Simon and Schuster, 1992), 341–342. For other sources on Truman's background, see especially Robert H. Ferrell, *Harry S. Truman: A Life* (Columbia: University of Missouri Press, 1994); and Alonzo L. Hamby, "The Mind and Character of Harry S. Truman," in *The*

Truman Presidency, ed. Michael Lacey (New York: Cambridge University Press, 1989), ch. 1.

2 Harold F. Gosnell, *Truman's Crises: A Political Biography of Harry S. Truman* (Westport, CT: Greenwood Press, 1980), 259.

3 Donald R. McCoy, *The Presidency of Harry S. Truman* (Lawrence: University Press of Kansas, 1984), 16.

4 Robert J. Donovan, *Conflict and Crisis: The Presidency of Harry S. Truman, 1945–1948* (New York: Norton, 1977), 7.

5 Gosnell, *Truman's Crises*, 175.

6 Ferrell, *Harry S. Truman*. For representative discussions of this issue, see also Gosnell, *Truman's Crises*, 275–276; McCullough, *Truman*, 588–592; William C. Berman, *The Politics of Civil Rights in the Truman Administration* (Columbus: Ohio State University Press, 1970), ch. 1; and Kenneth O'Reilly, *Nixon's Piano: Presidents and Racial Politics from Washington to Clinton* (New York: Free Press, 1995), 145–164.

7 Ferrell, *Harry S. Truman*, 193.

8 George Gallup, *The Gallup Poll, 1935–1971*, Vol. 1 (New York: Random House, 1972), 523.

9 Susan M. Hartmann, *Truman and the 80th Congress* (Columbia: University of Missouri Press, 1971), 3.

10 It is now uncertain just how long top foreign policy experts felt the war would continue without the use of the atomic bomb. The possibility that the war would end quickly was nevertheless not a part of domestic planning activities at the time of Roosevelt's death. For a recent review of this issue, see Robert Jay Litton and Greg Mitchell, *Hiroshima in America: Fifty Years of Denial* (New York: Putnam's Sons, 1995).

11 Robert J. Donovan, *Tumultuous Years: The Presidency of Harry S. Truman, 1949–1953* (New York: Norton, 1982), 127.

12 Gosnell, *Truman's Crises*, 234.

13 Charles E. Walcott and Karen M. Hult, *Governing the White House: From Hoover through LBJ* (Lawrence: University Press of Kansas, 1995), 149.

14 Patrick Anderson, *The Presidents' Men: White House Assistants of Franklin D. Roosevelt, Harry S. Truman, Dwight D. Eisenhower, John F. Kennedy, and Lyndon B. Johnson* (Garden City, NY: Doubleday, 1968), 113. Also see Clark M. Clifford, *Counsel to the President: A Memoir* (New York: Random House, 1991); and Douglas Frantz and David McKean, *Friends in High Places: The Rise and Fall of Clark Clifford* (Boston: Little, Brown, 1995).

15 According to Peri E. Arnold, the Hoover Commission was a uniquely broad and successful effort. Peri E. Arnold, *Making the Managerial Presidency: Comprehensive Reorganization Planning, 1905–1980* (Princeton, NJ: Princeton University Press, 1986), 154.

16 *Youngstown Sheet and Tube Co. v. Sawyer*, 343 U.S. 579 (1952).

17 Phillips, *Truman Presidency*, 31.

18 Barton J. Bernstein, "The Ambiguous Legacy: The Truman Administration and Civil Rights," in *Politics and Policies of the Truman Administration*, ed. Barton J. Bernstein (Chicago: Quadrangle Books, 1970), 281.

19 Donald R. McCoy and Richard T. Ruetten, *Quest and Response: Minority Rights and the Truman Administration* (Lawrence: University Press of Kansas, 1973), 100.

20 Ruth P. Morgan, *The President and Civil Rights: Policy-Making by Executive Order* (New York: St. Martin's Press, 1970), 18.

130 *The Moderate-Opportunity Presidents*

21 Myunghoon Khan, "Presidential Unilateral Action as a Tool of Voter Mobilization," *Presidential Studies Quarterly* 50, no. 1 (2020): 107–128.
22 Samuel G. Freedman, *Into the Bright Sunshine: Young Hubert Humphrey and the Fight for Civil Rights* (New York: Oxford University Press, 2023).
23 McCullough, *Truman*, 556.
24 Paul Brace and Barbara Hinckley, *Follow the Leader: Opinion Polls and the Modern Presidents* (New York: Basic Books, 1992), 32–35.
25 Halford R. Ryan, *Harry S. Truman: Presidential Rhetoric* (Westport, CT: Greenwood Press, 1993), 8.
26 Berman, *Politics of Civil Rights in the Truman Administration*, 62.
27 Walcott and Hult, *Governing the White House*, 35.
28 Jeremy L. Strickler, "The Historical Presidency: A Strategy of Strength: The Truman Presidency and the Rhetorical Linkage of Warfare and Welfare," *Presidential Studies Quarterly* 50, no. 3 (2019): 650–665.
29 McCullough, *Truman*, 468.
30 Problems with postwar economies are effectively reviewed in Hugh Rockoff, *Drastic Measures: A History of Wage and Price Controls in the United States* (New York: Cambridge University Press, 1984).
31 Robert H. Ferrell, *Harry S. Truman and the Modern Presidency* (Boston: Little, Brown, 1983), 87–88.
32 McCullough, *Truman*, 520.
33 James T. Patterson, *Mr. Republican: A Biography of Robert A. Taft* (Boston: Houghton Mifflin, 1972), 305–306.
34 The legislative history of the Taft-Hartley Act is extensively reviewed in R. Alton Lee, *Truman and Taft-Hartley: A Question of Mandate* (Lexington: University of Kentucky Press, 1966).
35 See Laurie L. Rice and Samuel Kernell, "Presidents' Vetoes and Audience Costs," *Presidential Studies Quarterly* 49, no. 1 (2018): 130–152.
36 John F. Witte, *The Politics and Development of the Income Tax* (Madison: University of Wisconsin Press, 1985), 132.
37 Paul Starr, *The Social Transformation of American Medicine* (New York: Basic Books, 1982), 350.
38 McCullough, *Truman*, 710.
39 Shannon Bow O'Brien, *Why Presidential Speech Locations Matter: Analyzing Speechmaking from Truman to Obama* (Cham: Palgrave MacMillan, 2018), 107.
40 Carl T. Rowan, *Dream Makers, Dream Breakers: The World of Justice Thurgood Marshall* (Boston: Little, Brown, 1993), 415.
41 Ronald D. Sylvia, "Presidential Decision Making and Leadership in the Civil Rights Era," *Presidential Studies Quarterly* 25 (1995): 398.
42 John P. Frendreis and Raymond Tatalovich, *The Modern Presidency and Economic Policy* (Itasca, IL: F. E. Peacock, 1994), ch. 10.

7 Dwight D. Eisenhower
A Skilled Centrist

In 1952, a nation frustrated with a stalemated war in Korea turned to a highly esteemed former military leader. Dwight Eisenhower (served 1953–1961), affectionately called "Ike," proved to be a popular president who easily won reelection in 1956. His critics, however, often painted him as lazy and ineffective. After he recovered from his September 1955 heart attack, some even enjoyed suggesting a broader role for his chief of staff as they asked, "Now what do we do if Sherman Adams gets sick and Eisenhower has to be president?" In 1960, presidential scholar Richard Neustadt expressed his own doubts about Eisenhower's leadership skills in his classic study *Presidential Power*, thereby echoing the already widespread skepticism.[1] When staffers such as speechwriter Arthur Larson depicted a president who was politically astute and deeply involved in the direction of his administration, they were expressing a minority view.

More recent analyses have been far more complimentary. In 1967, liberal journalist Murray Kempton concluded, "He was the great tortoise upon whose back the world sat for eight years. We laughed at him; we talked wistfully about moving; and all the while we never knew the cunning beneath the shell."[2] Fred Greenstein's 1982 portrayal of a president who defended the dignity of the office while working actively behind the scenes as a "hidden hand" president was followed by other, more favorable works.[3] In view of these wide-ranging assessments, perhaps yet another look at Eisenhower's leadership style will reveal whether his achievements matched his moderate opportunities.

Personal Characteristics

Dwight David Eisenhower (1890–1969), like nineteenth-century presidents Zachary Taylor and Ulysses S. Grant, became president by virtue of his status as a war hero. But he was the only president with a lengthy military career to serve in the twentieth century. Although his election in 1952 led many pundits to wonder publicly whether he had sufficient experience for

DOI: 10.4324/9781003426684-9

132 *The Moderate-Opportunity Presidents*

the job, his career path included a surprisingly diverse set of relationships. Historian Stephen Ambrose challenged the conventional wisdom when he concluded that "Eisenhower knew Washington and its modus operandi at least as well as any of his predecessors, and far better than most."[4]

Ike grew up in Abilene, Kansas, the third of seven sons. His father worked as a mechanic for a creamery operated by the River Brethren, a branch of the American Mennonite sect to which the Eisenhowers belonged. After graduating from high school and putting a brother through college for one year, Ike sought an appointment to West Point. At West Point, Ike displayed considerable athletic talent until a knee injury ended his football career. In 1915, he graduated in the top half of a class that produced, remarkably, 59 generals.[5]

After graduation Ike was sent by the army to San Antonio, Texas, where he met Marie "Mamie" Doud, the daughter of a wealthy Denver meat packer. They married in 1916 and had two sons, one of whom died of scarlet fever. Ike's other son, John Sheldon Eisenhower, was the father of David Eisenhower, who married the daughter of Ike's vice president, Richard Nixon.

Career Path

Eisenhower's military career was tremendously diversified in his responsibilities. During World War I he commanded a tank training center, earning along the way the Distinguished Service Medal and a promotion to captain. Ike showed a keen interest in staff relationships from the outset and in 1926 graduated first in his class at the army's elite command and general staff school. While stationed in Washington in the early 1930s and serving as aide to the army chief of staff, General Douglas MacArthur, Eisenhower testified before congressional committees on the army's budget, among his many other duties. His Washington years also gave him an opportunity to closely observe the Roosevelt presidency. While there, his brother Milton was a high-ranking official in the Department of Agriculture. From Washington, Eisenhower accompanied MacArthur to the Philippines, where his activities included speechwriting and observing MacArthur's zealous self-promotion.

With the advent of World War II, Eisenhower's career skyrocketed and he eventually became a national hero—a phenomenon that stemmed not only from his military achievements but also from his public relations skills. His public acclaim grew as he ultimately became commander of the Supreme Headquarters, Allied Expeditionary Force, with the responsibility for planning and coordinating the 1944 Normandy invasion. In that role he often was praised for his ability to coordinate and manage other military leaders with diverse personalities into an effective organization.

After the war Eisenhower served for three years as the army chief of staff, two years as president of Columbia University, and then as commander of the North Atlantic Treaty Organization (NATO). In the spring of 1952 he resigned the NATO post to pursue the Republican Party's presidential nomination.

Despite Eisenhower's widespread popularity, the contest for the Republican nomination was very close. Ohio senator Robert Taft had the support of many party loyalists and isolationists. Eisenhower also was handicapped by his late entry into the race.

In the fall campaign, Eisenhower was aided by his likable personality and his foreign policy themes.[6] Voters were frustrated over the endless war in Korea and hoped that Eisenhower, who had promised to go to Korea if elected, would be able to end the conflict. Republican stalwarts, and even a large number of Democratic Party identifiers, proudly wore his campaign button proclaiming "I like Ike."[7]

Domestic issues took a back seat in Eisenhower's campaign. He was far more familiar with and interested in foreign policy, and he recognized that he was the candidate of a party with sharp divisions between those wanting to largely maintain existing programs and arch-conservatives who sought to roll back New Deal programs. Subsequently, Eisenhower could claim no mandate to pursue any specific domestic policy.

What Manner of Man?

Although at first Eisenhower was not really sure he wanted to be president, he was quite confident that he would succeed in the office once he made the commitment. In his eyes, he was simply the best man to make important decisions, and he thought himself a better judge of people than many politicians. Of course, he did not consider himself to be a politician.

Eisenhower was known for his idealism and optimism, but his aides sometimes wished for a bit more cynicism. Chief of Staff Sherman Adams remarked: "In a determination to reach a difficult but desired objective, the idealistic and optimistic Eisenhower would reveal a faith in the higher motives of mankind that astonished the more cynical members of his cabinet."[8] In his dealings with others, Eisenhower was surprisingly mild for a military leader. As president, Eisenhower worked assiduously to establish cordial, productive relationships, even with his former opponent Robert Taft. Overall, he viewed his relationships with others as educational and seemed to make surprisingly few enemies.

As for Eisenhower's intellectual capabilities, some observers guessed him to be intelligent but untutored. National Security Council official Robert Bowie found that the president had considerable talent for pulling together people with diverse views and cutting through to get at the heart of an issue. Others recognized his effective cognitive style (explicit reasoning

134 *The Moderate-Opportunity Presidents*

about means and ends), which allowed him to consider both the long-term and short-term consequences of an action and perceive more comprehensive patterns.[9] Yet Eisenhower was not very assertive in his search for new, substantive domestic policies. He seldom read serious books. He generally preferred the company of successful businessmen and almost never associated with academicians even though he had served briefly as president of Columbia University.

Policy Views

Although Eisenhower was quite conservative in his policy views, he felt the Republican Party had to move to the "middle of the road" to compete effectively with Democrats. He had been raised as a Republican and remained one throughout his military career. As of 1952, he regarded any expansion of Democratic domestic policy as harmful to the nation. The view that he was a moderate was fostered in part by Democratic Party efforts to recruit him as its nominee in 1948.

Of the few policy goals stated in the 1952 campaign, a central one was to reduce spending and achieve a balanced budget. He also vowed not to cut popular programs, especially Social Security.[10] As for agricultural policies, he promised to continue price support programs at least through 1954. Other campaign positions included amending the Taft-Hartley Act, providing supplementary aid to health care and education, and promoting a tax cut.

Although he rarely demonstrated a clear ideological bent in public, the private Eisenhower was fairly conservative politically.[11] Among other things, he argued that the Tennessee Valley Authority was an example of "creeping socialism" and a flawed policy because it asked taxpayers in other regions to help finance public power that would be used to attract industry away from their own states. But on some issues, such as housing assistance and Social Security, Eisenhower saw an appropriate role for the government.

On civil rights and race, Eisenhower's stance was said to be a combination of "sympathy, understanding, and empathy with paternalism and some racist notions."[12] Several years after the 1954 Supreme Court decision overturning the concept of "separate but equal" for the nation's schools,[13] Eisenhower confided to aide Arthur Larson, "I personally think the decision was wrong."[14] For Eisenhower, the route toward desegregation would be best achieved not by decisions and laws but by changes in attitudes.

Once in office, Eisenhower proceeded with a fairly definite set of policy goals. One analysis of his legislative programs for 1953 and 1954 concluded that he set out to balance the budget, lower taxes, encourage private enterprise, and reduce the scope of federal activity.[15] He was strongly committed to fighting inflation but expressed less concern about unemployment. According to journalist Robert Donovan, Eisenhower's primary goals were to modify and modernize New Deal programs that had demonstrated their worth by their successful longevity.[16]

Challenges and Opportunities

During his eight years in office, Eisenhower had many opportunities to act on his preference for dealing with foreign rather than domestic issues. He began by putting the stalled Korean peace talks back on track, and an armistice ending the Korean War was signed in July 1953. In the spring of 1954, he finessed US action in North Vietnam in the face of the looming defeat of the French by Vietnamese nationalists.

On the home front, Eisenhower faced a related foreign policy challenge in the form of Senator Joseph McCarthy's intensifying charges that communist infiltration of the federal government had contributed to the 1949 communist victory in China and a weakening of the overall US position. Eisenhower was reluctant to take on McCarthy directly but made some mild, behind-the-scenes efforts to strengthen opposition to the senator's actions. He was afraid a public battle with McCarthy might divide the Republican Party and focus too much attention on an issue the president wanted to ignore. "I will not," Eisenhower said to his brother Milton, "get into a pissing contest with that skunk."[17]

After delaying action on school desegregation in 1953, a unanimous Supreme Court ruled on May 17, 1954, that "in the field of public education, the doctrine of 'separate but equal' has no place."[18] The Court instructed the attorneys in the case to return to the Court in a year to argue the issue of remedies to segregation. Based on those arguments, the Court ruled in 1955 that desegregation plans must proceed with "all deliberate speed."[19] The struggle between segregationists and civil rights activists would last for years, with Eisenhower drawn into the fray as a result of the decision.[20]

When Eisenhower entered office in 1953, several factors seemed to be operating in his favor. His victory margin of almost 11 percent over his opponent, Illinois governor Adlai Stevenson, was the third largest since 1932. His first-year popularity average of 68 percent also ranked third, and his four-year average of 69 percent was surpassed only by President John Kennedy during his three years in office.

Nevertheless, Eisenhower faced several constraints. The campaign had produced few new issues, and short of a major dismantling of New Deal programs, there did not seem to be many promising new ideas. Eisenhower also faced budget difficulties and an awkward situation in Congress. The 1952 election had produced a moderate Republican gain in House seats (22), giving Eisenhower an eight-vote margin. He had only a two-vote

136 *The Moderate-Opportunity Presidents*

margin in the Senate. Yet the Republicans were divided on key issues between the "old guard," often from the Midwest and the West, and those desiring accommodation with New Deal programs.[21] In the midterm elections of 1954, Republicans lost control of the House.

Eisenhower's reelection to office in 1956 was more a reaffirmation of his strong emphasis on foreign policy and his personal popularity than evidence of support for new initiatives. The successful launch in 1957 of a Soviet space vehicle called *Sputnik* produced outcries for new educational and research efforts, but congressional support for such initiatives was less clear. Eisenhower's determination to balance the budget each year (indeed, he produced surpluses for three of his eight years in office) served to further limit his options.

Leadership Style

Eisenhower came to the presidency with specific ideas about how a president should lead. Despite his personal popularity, he firmly resisted the "cult of personality" style that his old boss General Douglas MacArthur had displayed in 1951 upon his return to the United States after being abruptly dismissed from his post by President Harry Truman. "Our public life can have no solid base in wishful reliance on a hero, or savior," asserted Ike.[22] Instead, he saw leadership as a process and often commented that it was surprising how much a person could accomplish if not concerned with gaining credit for his or her actions.

Eisenhower told aide Arthur Larson that he did not believe presidents crusade for good causes that were not assigned to them by the Constitution—that is, presidents enjoyed all the powers formally bestowed by the Constitution and did not need any more.[23] As for a president's relationship with Congress, Eisenhower preferred a partnership between the two branches. He was quick to criticize FDR's assertive efforts to provide congressional leadership and was unusually reluctant to assume a strong role. Eisenhower's definition of leadership was often stated as "deciding what needs to be done and then getting others to do it."[24] Despite Richard Neustadt's negative portrayal of Eisenhower in *Presidential Power*, Ike's view of leadership was completely in keeping with Neustadt's: Effective presidential influence requires skillful persuasive abilities.

The Advisory Process and Approach to Decision-Making

General Lucius Clay, chairman of the board of Continental Can Company, and Herbert Brownell, a New York attorney who had played a key role in drafting Eisenhower for the Republican nomination and in the 1952 campaign, helped the president select his cabinet. Of those chosen, no one was an old friend, many were strangers. Only Brownell, who became attorney general, and Postmaster General Arthur Summerfield had been active in his election campaign.

Eisenhower's cabinet operations were in some ways unique.[25] A formal agenda for each meeting was prepared by Chief of Staff Sherman Adams, and cabinet members were given background papers to be read before each meeting. The meetings themselves, generally held on Friday morning, typically lasted for three hours. In an effort to achieve some kind of follow-up and follow-through, Eisenhower hired a cabinet secretary. He was the first president to do so.

A few cabinet members figured prominently in domestic policy matters both in cabinet meetings and in their individual advisory roles. George Humphrey, an Ohio businessman and secretary of the Treasury, spoke extensively on issues such as the need to balance the budget. Agriculture Secretary Ezra Taft Benson from Utah was a strong advocate of steps that would reduce the government's role in the nation's farm economy. Oveta Culp Hobby, a Texan who had switched to the Republican Party in 1952, became the first secretary of the new Department of Health, Education, and Welfare and contributed a conservative view on most issues. More liberal views were expressed by Attorney General Brownell. Vice President Richard Nixon advised the president on how Congress might react to particular policies and the electoral response they might evoke.[26]

When asked whether a president should have a chief of staff, Eisenhower drew on his military experience, responding: "Why should I be my own Sergeant Major?"[27] He selected Sherman Adams to fill the role of chief of staff. Adams, a former member of Congress who had worked on Eisenhower's campaign while serving as governor of New Hampshire, monitored activities both in the domestic departments and agencies and in Congress. Two other staff members with important domestic policy roles were Bryce Harlow, an Oklahoman with considerable experience on Capitol Hill, and General Wilton Persons, whose experience included lobbying Congress for Pentagon programs. Persons headed the Office of Legislative Liaison for a time and made periodic contributions to domestic policy decisions.[28]

Eisenhower tended to focus his personal involvement in domestic affairs on economic policy and budgetary issues. On economic matters, he was briefed weekly by Council of Economic Advisers head Arthur Burns and his assistant for economic policy, Gabriel Hague. According to cabinet records and the memoirs of cabinet members, the president reviewed economic policy options extensively, particularly during the recession of 1954.[29] On budgetary matters, Eisenhower consulted with Bureau of the Budget director Joseph Dodge to review his options, particularly in the fall of 1953 when he was trying to cut the budgets of many programs. One of the top officials in the Bureau of the Budget found Eisenhower "more budget minded" than any executive he had ever known.[30]

138 *The Moderate-Opportunity Presidents*

In weighing some policy decisions, Eisenhower sought the "middle of the road" and "progressive, forward looking policies"—both keys to the success of the Republican Party.[31] He often spoke of the need to create "Modern Republicanism" and asserted that "the Republican party must be known as a progressive organization or it will sink." His underlying concern was that permanent dominance by the Democrats was not healthy for American politics and would likely produce too many "wild-eyed, pinkish, programs."[32]

In his decision-making role, Eisenhower looked at himself as something of a national steward. For example, he pointed out the national security implications of the proposed St. Lawrence Seaway and the federal interstate highway program—two projects he supported. He also looked for ways in which private economic activity, such as private development of atomic energy as a source of electric power, could strengthen expanded government programs. Yet his fiscal conservatism, coupled with his desire to pursue a variety of policies, often produced very modest initiatives.

Administrative Strategies

Eisenhower took a distinctly positive approach to the "good government" aspects of administrative reform. To Herbert Hoover's regret, however, this did not include creating another Hoover Commission. In fact, Hoover found Ike's approach a sign of weakness, but political scientist Peri Arnold found it an indication of Eisenhower's confidence in his ability to use his political skills in other ways.[33]

In his administrative responses to desegregation issues, Eisenhower acted decisively where the federal law was clear. In 1954, he took steps to end segregation of the public school system in the nation's capital when the Supreme Court established the legal basis for doing so.[34] He also took the final steps toward complete desegregation of the nation's military forces. In 1957, in the face of open resistance to desegregation of Central High School in Little Rock, Arkansas, Eisenhower committed federal troops to keeping order and ensuring that the enrollment of African American students would proceed in an orderly fashion.

The president was more cautious about administrative roles involving new federal commitments. While he did not recommend legislation providing for a Federal Employment Practices Commission, he forced government contractors to comply with nondiscrimination policies. Attorney General Herbert Brownell had hoped to follow the precedent of Truman's Justice Department in taking a clear position in support of desegregation, but when he sought Eisenhower's support, the president remained cautious. If the Court asked him a direct question, Eisenhower instructed, Brownell should state that he personally believed that segregation was unconstitutional.[35]

Dwight D. Eisenhower 139

Eisenhower's administrative actions in the area of race relations were based on some political considerations, as he hoped to increase Republican support in the South and had good working relationships with many southern Democrats in Congress. His own skepticism about the effectiveness of government action on race relations was evident as well. Yet in his search for the middle ground on race relations, he made more civil rights-friendly appointments to the judiciary in the South than several of his successors.[36]

Public Leadership

Eisenhower's lengthy experience with public relations and his view of the president's proper role were in evidence in his approaches to public leadership. For example, he sought to defend the dignity of the presidency by avoiding any personal conflict with Senator Joseph McCarthy. He also sought to present the persona of a president who was not simply "another politician."

Eisenhower's personal popularity was impressive, and he is tied with Kennedy (behind Reagan's leading performance) in sustaining popularity. This translated into favorable press coverage—at least at the outset of his administration. In October 1953, ten months into his administration, one reporter commented that his readers were not yet ready for critical interpretations of the president.[37]

Several strategies contributed to Eisenhower's success. He chose veteran reporter James Hagerty as his press secretary and drew upon his considerable skills. Hagerty adroitly handled the news media, including in the aftermath of Eisenhower's heart attack in September 1955. Hagerty also sat in periodically on policy discussions, a further indication of the importance of his role in the Eisenhower White House.

Eisenhower's interest in public relations prompted him to agree to televised press conferences in 1955. However, these were delayed telecasts (Kennedy began live press conferences in 1961). Eisenhower carefully prepared for the conferences with the help of Hagerty, and he was the first president to allow reporters to use direct quotes from the event. Eisenhower and Hagerty could generally anticipate about 90 percent of the questions, and the president also employed a strategy of occasionally either "playing dumb" or giving rambling answers to avoid a specific answer that might have unwanted consequences. In fact, he would often respond to Hagerty's suggestion that he not answer a question by saying, "Oh, leave it to me, Jim, I'll confuse them."[38]

The president was fond of the "lightning rod" strategy—that is, he would try to avoid taking the political heat for an unpopular policy or blunder by distancing himself from the problem and swinging criticism toward an aide or cabinet member. Agriculture Secretary Ezra Taft Benson, who frequently took hotly disputed policy positions, proved useful in

140 *The Moderate-Opportunity Presidents*

deflecting criticism from the president. Blunt statements by Vice President Richard Nixon cast him in the role of Eisenhower's "hatchet man." Chief of Staff Sherman Adams became the man the conservative old guard in Congress could easily hate, as was Herbert Brownell, Eisenhower's attorney general.[39]

On some issues, Eisenhower was reluctant to speak out at all. Most notably, he made virtually no use of the bully pulpit to encourage efforts toward desegregation. At his first press conference after the Supreme Court's 1954 school desegregation decision, he was asked the question he doubtlessly anticipated: Do you have any advice to give to the South on how to react? "Not in the slightest," Eisenhower replied. "The Supreme Court has spoken and I am sworn to uphold the constitutional process in the country; and I will obey."[40]

In choosing a less public, or hidden hand, brand of leadership, Eisenhower limited his use of the bully pulpit aspects of the presidency. Eisenhower did not have General MacArthur's flair for drama or Adlai Stevenson's gift of lyrical prose, but he was a shrewd rhetorical strategist and tactician. Moreover, he profited from his ability to focus on middle-of-the-road policies yet generally stay above the fray of partisan battles. Eisenhower also had a unique ability to capitalize on his reputation, obvious sincerity, and winning smile, while not appearing superficial.[41]

Congressional Leadership

Eisenhower was known for his modest domestic policy initiatives. In fact, he introduced no major legislation his first year in office. However, he is credited with creating the first office of legislative liaison in the White House, tasked with promoting presidential policies on Capitol Hill. He also held weekly meetings with legislative leaders and members of the cabinet who would explain major legislative proposals. At these meetings, participants would review the timing of various legislative activities for the next week. In some instances, Eisenhower modified his positions on the basis of those discussions.

In dealing with legislative leaders, Eisenhower found that he worked surprisingly well with Robert Taft, the Republican majority leader in the Senate. Taft died, however, in July 1953. The leadership efforts of his successor, William Knowland (R-CA), first as majority leader and then as minority leader, did not please Eisenhower. On the House side, he was generally happy with the performance of the Republican majority leader, Charles Halleck of Indiana (served 1953–1954), and included him in the leadership breakfasts even when Joseph Martin (R-MA) took over the top Republican position after the Republicans lost control of the House in 1954.[42] There were obvious partisan differences when Democrats and fellow Texans Sam Rayburn in the House and Lyndon Johnson in the

Senate assumed the top leadership positions in 1955. Eisenhower sought to achieve good working relations by periodically inviting Rayburn and Johnson to drop by the family quarters of the White House for a cocktail and some casual conversation.

Particularly in his first year in office, Eisenhower was reluctant to push legislators very hard, and he was willing to listen to legislators' concerns at considerable length. In 1953, he invited every member of Congress to group dinners or luncheons at the White House simply for the purpose of listening. In other settings, he relied on gentle persuasion. Also in the first year, he was in contact with his party's legislative leaders on a daily basis. Senator Taft was welcome to visit any time, and the president instructed Sherman Adams that any member of Congress who wanted to see him should be granted that access. In meetings with legislators, Eisenhower sometimes went beyond his "patient education" approach to legislative relations. Although he personally disliked patronage, both he and Sherman Adams used it on some occasions. In 1953, for example, in the major fight over postponement of a tax cut, Eisenhower made it clear that patronage decisions would be influenced by the degree of support given to his positions.

Legislative Enactments

The Eisenhower years saw the passage of only a moderate amount of new legislation. The first year was especially slow, in part because of what the press saw as a very limited presidential agenda—statehood for Hawai'i, restoration of the oil-rich tideland regions to the states, and modification of the Taft-Hartley Act. Perhaps the most noteworthy occurrence during the first few months was Eisenhower's reluctance to promote his own agenda even on an issue like tidelands oil. Eisenhower had his greatest legislative impact in 1954, and his second term produced a landmark civil rights enactment but often stalemates on newer issues.

Taxation and the Budget

Taxation and budgetary issues were high on the list of Eisenhower's legislative concerns. During his 1953 State of the Union address, Ike was greeted with noisy Republican opposition when he made balancing the budget his top priority and relegated a tax cut to a lowly fifth-place mention. "Reductions in taxes will be justified only as we show we can succeed in bringing the budget under control," Eisenhower told his clearly underwhelmed audience.[43]

In taking his position against a tax cut, the president was staring at a projected deficit for fiscal 1954 of approximately $9.4 billion, which was

142 *The Moderate-Opportunity Presidents*

well over 10 percent of total projected spending. Furthermore, Eisenhower felt that some of Truman's defense spending commitments had been grossly underfunded. His budget difficulties were significantly improved, however, by the end of the Korean War.

The president was able to make substantial headway in reducing the deficit by making cuts of approximately $4 billion. One of his main contributions was to hold down defense spending in the midst of cold war hysteria—an accomplishment perhaps only someone with Ike's military record could have done. When he told legislative leaders that there could be no tax decrease in 1953, Taft loudly protested that the Republicans were committed to a tax cut. Eisenhower, however, would not be deterred, and he proceeded in 1953 to steer legislators and others away from a tax reduction until budget cuts could be achieved. Taxes were reduced slightly, but Eisenhower used a successful television appeal to help retain an excise tax scheduled to expire on January 1, 1954. Although the fight left some congressional Republicans wounded, Eisenhower's diplomacy prevented any bitterness, and his key opponent complimented him on "a good fight" in a cordial letter.

With his budget cuts in place, Eisenhower was able to set his sights on a longer-term tax cut in 1954, enacted in the Omnibus Tax Act. The proposed tax legislation reduced taxes for both individuals and corporations. Individual changes included more medical deductions, changes in the calculation of dependency for children who worked, and a child care tax deduction for working women. Corporations were aided by a liberalization of depreciation allowances, but the general corporate rate remained the same.

The Eisenhower administration played a prominent role in passage of the Omnibus Tax Act. A *New York Times* reporter characterized the White House staff operations as "the smoothest working machine Capitol Hill has seen in years."[44] When the Democrats proposed a larger dependency deduction than he had requested, Eisenhower went on television opposing the change and the $2.5 billion in lost revenue it represented. As part of the sales effort, Secretary of the Treasury Humphrey invited all but three senators to lunch in order to explain the details of the program. In the end, Eisenhower was able to maintain strong Republican support, and the bill he called the cornerstone of his administration emerged from conference committee closely resembling his initial recommendations. This situation again represented shared policymaking, but with a strong presidential role.

Atomic Energy Act

The Atomic Energy Act in 1954 called for the development of nuclear energy for civilian purposes. Its passage reflected both Eisenhower's commitment to the private sector and his style of legislative leadership. Efforts to develop new atomic energy legislation had received considerable attention in the Atomic Energy Commission (AEC) under President Truman, and the Eisenhower administration was moving rather slowly toward promoting additional action. After repeated urging by the Joint Congressional Committee on Atomic Energy (JCCAE), the AEC prepared a preliminary draft of the legislation that the JCCAE used in 1953, but a bill cleared by the White House was not available until 1954.

In early 1954, Eisenhower proposed another bill that included both international and domestic components. The international component, with its provisions for greater international cooperation, was the less controversial of the two. The importance of that aspect of the proposed new legislation was dramatized by an important presidential address, entitled "Atoms for Peace," delivered in December 1953 at the United Nations. President Eisenhower, spurred by the Soviet Union's detonation of its first nuclear device, starkly depicted the horror of modern warfare but also pointed out how such a destructive power could be harnessed for productive civilian purposes. On the domestic side, proponents of public and private nuclear power development created substantial conflict. Senate deliberations on the bill were slowed in part by a filibuster by legislators wanting a greater commitment to public power, but in both the House and the Senate, Eisenhower was able to muster substantial Republican support. The Atomic Energy Act was signed by Eisenhower on August 30, 1954, allowing private companies access to restricted information and permitting foreign nations seeking peaceful nuclear power greater exchange of information.

Interstate Highway System

Establishment of the interstate highway system was the most important domestic policy action of the Eisenhower administration. Like many members of the American military, Ike was impressed by Germany's autobahn system. Highway construction was viewed as a priority because both the White House and Congress recognized that the tremendous increase in automobile use in the years after World War II required a large-scale federal effort to provide the needed roads.

Eisenhower provided important support for the new system but ultimately found he had to compromise with Congress on the funding mechanism. He began promoting the idea by forming an advisory committee on a national highway program and then having Vice President Nixon gain some favorable publicity by presenting the plan at the July 1954 meeting of the Governors' Conference in New York. On February 22, 1955, Eisenhower sent Congress a message calling for a $101 billion, ten-year program that would include $31 billion in federal assistance to the states. Legislators agreed that a major program was needed but disagreed on the financing mechanism. Democratic leaders preferred greater use of gasoline taxes and some other direct taxes

144   *The Moderate-Opportunity Presidents*

over Eisenhower's financing mechanism, which called for the sale of $20 billion in bonds. At the beginning of the 1956 session of Congress, the president renewed his support of the legislation and indicated he would not resist the taxing mechanisms preferred by many Democrats. The result was strong bipartisan support for the bill, which Eisenhower signed in June.[45]

Social Security

Even though he was uncertain about the Social Security program, Eisenhower followed up on action taken in 1950 to expand its coverage and benefits. The US Chamber of Commerce and conservatives such as Senator Carl Curtis (R-NE) proposed redesigning the system so that all senior citizens would be immediately eligible, thereby reducing reliance on the "contributory principle" that had been at the heart of Franklin Roosevelt's original proposal. The immediate inclusion of all elderly as recipients would, conservatives believed, reveal the program's total cost and thus would provide a basis for generating political support for reductions in benefits. Faced with this controversy, the Eisenhower administration, possessing limited expertise on Social Security, was uncertain about the best course of action. After reviewing the options, the Eisenhower administration chose to avoid a major political battle and recommended "more of the same" to Congress.

In 1954, Congress extended eligibility for Social Security to some 10.5 million persons, increased monthly benefits, and enacted several significant reforms. Given the popularity of Social Security among both the general public and many members of Congress, the primary role of the Eisenhower administration took on was one of providing greater legitimacy for the original design of the Social Security system, rather than trying to influence the outcome of the final vote.

In 1956 Congress passed a second major change in the Social Security system—some coverage of the disabled—despite some opposition from the Eisenhower administration. The Social Security Administration, Democratic leaders in Congress, and organized labor supported the change. Senate Majority Leader Lyndon Johnson was responsible for lining up a winning coalition. Because several key votes were close, Johnson, to achieve passage of the bill, had to enlist Republican support even in the face of opposition from the Eisenhower administration. House passage came more easily.[46]

Civil Rights

In 1956, believing the Supreme Court had addressed school desegregation issues, Eisenhower encouraged Attorney General Brownell to prepare legislation dealing with voting rights. Brownell, who persistently advocated a larger federal role in civil rights, eagerly developed a legislative proposal calling for federal district courts to ensure citizens' access to the polls and for a bipartisan commission to look into instances of discrimination against African Americans. While these recommendations were far short of the measures hoped for by the growing civil rights movement, they alarmed defenders of the status quo in the South. Meanwhile, on another front, 103 members of Congress from the southern states (excluding Lyndon Johnson and a few others) were supporting legislative action seeking to overturn the 1954 *Brown v. Board of Education* decision.

In these turbulent times, then, the voting rights legislation was defeated. Some in the Eisenhower administration blamed the Democrats, including Majority Leader Lyndon Johnson, for not taking a more supportive role. Others argued that the administration's actions suggested an ambivalence toward the proposal since the president had not played a public role in gathering support for the bill. The conclusion reached by Elmo Richardson seemed to fairly assess this situation: "In retrospect, neither party seemed overly anxious to take up the controversial issue in an election year."[47]

The 1957 legislative session produced a very different result. Eisenhower resubmitted his 1956 legislation, with provisions to ensure voting rights as the main component. Passage occurred fairly easily in the House, but the Senate once again posed a formidable obstacle. Lyndon Johnson reasoned that the best way to get the measure through was to accede to southerners' demands for a jury trial in cases involving voting rights violations. Eisenhower was reluctant to agree to the demand, but he did not have the votes. Some civil rights groups were opposed to the jury trial provision but ultimately urged Eisenhower to sign the final bill. The Civil Rights Act of 1957 was the first since the end of Reconstruction. It established a framework for a judicial approach to voting rights violations and established a fact-finding commission.

The Civil Rights Act of 1960 stemmed from the realization that earlier legislation was not working effectively and concerns with racial violence that included bombings of African American schools and churches. The key component of the Eisenhower proposal that became law called for the appointment of federal court referees to investigate situations in which discrimination was preventing African Americans from registering to vote. Although Eisenhower claimed a major victory, later events did not support that optimism.

Eisenhower and Congress

Eisenhower's legislative performance was quite successful, even though he had a limited agenda. According to Mark Peterson, who compared presidents' relationships with Congress between 1953 and 1990, Eisenhower ranked next to the lowest (ahead of only Gerald Ford) in the number of tough proposals submitted each year. Yet he was remarkably successful in

146 *The Moderate-Opportunity Presidents*

enacting those tough proposals. Eisenhower, Peterson concludes, "achieved much by limiting the targets of his interest and efforts."[48] To a striking degree, his successes came in his second year, in which, by his own calculations, 13 of his 19 major proposals were enacted, together with 150 of 232 other proposals he had submitted.[49]

Eisenhower's success stemmed from multiple strategies. He sometimes was able to "go public" effectively with focused appeals such as those for changes in agricultural price supports and tax changes in 1954. And he employed a veto strategy to a moderate degree; his average of 2.21 vetoes per month was the third highest among modern presidents.[50] Eisenhower also played a conciliatory role in his dealings with Congress, especially after 1954 with Democratic Party leaders. Overall, however, he was a contributor but not a central player as major new policies (and, often, larger commitments than he preferred) emerged from Congress.

An Assessment

Eisenhower displayed considerable talent as president. Among other things, he recruited highly competent staffers, and he dealt with the public shrewdly to sustain his popularity. Yet he also engaged in several focused efforts to sell specific legislative measures. In his relationship with Congress, his pursuit of a limited agenda and use of a conciliatory approach were relatively successful. Some of his aides thought he resembled a decathlon athlete—not necessarily the best performer on any given dimension but without significant weaknesses.

Greater debate surrounds the extent to which Eisenhower used his opportunities. The interstate highway system is arguably his most lasting domestic policy legacy, and he will be known for his balanced budgets. Eisenhower achieved either two or three balanced budgets, depending on how they are calculated, during his eight years in office. In 1960, critics such as John Kennedy argued that the emphasis on balanced budgets contributed to insufficient economic growth. Eisenhower's defenders countered that he had contained inflation. He also worked to keep the deficit down. Not only was he able to reduce the projected 1953–1954 deficit from approximately $9 billion to $3.1 billion, but he kept the deficit under $4 billion over the next two years.

Few major new initiatives or actions to curtail existing programs were evident during the Eisenhower years. His limitations as an initiator became even more evident in his second term as the public pressed for actions on federal aid to education and health insurance for the elderly. He perhaps worked hardest to curtail agricultural price supports. While he achieved some legislative success, he was forced to recognize that the sheer productive capacity of American farmers was largely overwhelming his efforts. Fundamental change in agricultural programs would not occur until the

1990s. The Tennessee Valley Authority (TVA) was another favorite target. There he sought to prevent expansion rather than to achieve a retrenchment. "No one has worked harder than I have to stop the expansion of TVA," Eisenhower boasted.[51]

Along the way, he managed to legitimize policies he inherited from the New Deal presidents. Economist John Witte found that Eisenhower's actions in 1954 validated the programs he had inherited. This, coupled with his decision not to pursue additional tax reform while in the White House, further legitimized the tax system that had been broadened during World War II to finance the nation's military efforts.[52] Similarly, Eisenhower's decision to support expansion of Social Security in 1954 helped ensure the longevity of one of the New Deal's most popular programs.

The absence of a broader civil rights legacy continues to generate debate. Attorney General Brownell believed Eisenhower was trying to prevent national polarization over the issue by seeking a middle way.[53] On this issue, the critics have been quite harsh. Historian Stephen Ambrose has argued that Ike passed up a major leadership opportunity by not speaking out and offering no encouragement to those seeking steps toward peaceful desegregation. At the same time, he allowed opponents of desegregation to assert that the president was on their side. It is clear that the president who touted the importance of attitudes and the "feelings in one's heart" as the key to modifying race relations chose not to participate in efforts to change those attitudes.

Viewed on his own terms, Eisenhower could claim considerable success. His middle-of-the-road policies did not turn the Republicans into a majority party, but they did often corral what he saw as excesses in more liberal proposals. He was able to leave office untainted by a far-reaching scandal. Finally, although the critics were increasingly characterizing the government as stalemated by the end of his second term, he headed toward retirement feeling vindicated that his rather traditional view of the president's role had produced sustained public support.

Notes

1 Richard E. Neustadt, *Presidential Power* (New York: Wiley, 1960).
2 Arthur Larson, *Eisenhower: The President Nobody Knew* (New York: Scribner, 1968), 200.
3 Fred I. Greenstein, *The Hidden Hand Presidency: Eisenhower as Leader* (New York: Basic Books, 1982).
4 Stephen E. Ambrose, *Eisenhower: The President* (New York: Simon and Schuster, 1985), 18.
5 Robert F. Burk, *Dwight D. Eisenhower: Hero and Politician* (Boston: Twayne, 1986), 21; Greenstein, *Hidden Hand Presidency*; Elmo Richardson, *The Presidency of Dwight D. Eisenhower* (Lawrence: Regents Press of Kansas, 1979).

148   *The Moderate-Opportunity Presidents*

6 On the importance of foreign policy issues and Eisenhower's popularity, see Angus Campbell et al., *The American Voter* (New York: Wiley, 1960).

7 See John Robert Greene, *I Like Ike: The Presidential Election of 1952* (Lawrence, KS: University Press of Kansas, 2017).

8 Sherman Adams, *Firsthand Report: The Story of the Eisenhower Administration* (Westport, CT: Greenwood Press, 1961), 7.

9 See John Burke and Fred I. Greenstein (with Larry Berman and Richard Innerman), *How Presidents Test Reality: Decisions on Vietnam, 1954 and 1965* (New York: Russell Sage Foundation, 1989), 66.

10 Michael G. Krukones, *Promises and Performances: Presidential Campaigns as Policy Predictors* (New York: University Press of America, 1984), 76; Barton J. Bernstein, "The Election of 1952," in *History of American Presidential Elections, 1789–1968*, ed. Arthur M. Schlesinger Jr. (New York: McGraw-Hill, 1971), 3215–3266.

11 In fact, Eisenhower was described by a former speechwriter as being "closer to Hoover than the New Dealers." William Bragg Ewald Jr., *Eisenhower the President: Crucial Days, 1951–1960* (Englewood Cliffs, NJ: Prentice-Hall, 1981), 42.

12 Michael S. Mayer, "Eisenhower and Race," in *Dwight D. Eisenhower: Soldier, President, Statesman*, ed. Joan P. Krieg (Westport, CT: Greenwood Press, 1987), 39.

13 *Brown v. Board of Education of Topeka*, 347 U.S. 483 (1954).

14 Larson, *Eisenhower*, 124.

15 Gary W. Reichard, *The Reaffirmation of Republicanism: Eisenhower and the Eighty-Third Congress* (Knoxville: University of Tennessee Press, 1975), 230.

16 Robert J. Donovan, *Eisenhower: The Inside Story* (New York: Harper, 1956), 229.

17 Quoted in Stephen E. Ambrose, "The Eisenhower Revival," in *Rethinking the Presidency*, ed. Thomas E. Cronin (Boston: Little, Brown, 1982), 107.

18 *Brown v. Board of Education of Topeka*, 347 U.S. 483 (1954). Also see Carl T. Rowan, *Dream Makers, Dream Breakers: The World of Thurgood Marshall* (Boston: Little, Brown, 1993), 217.

19 *Brown v. Board of Education of Topeka*, 349 U.S. 294 (1955).

20 Robert C. Smith, "Presidential Responsiveness to Black Interests From Grant to Biden: The Power of the Vote, the Power of Protest," *Presidential Studies Quarterly* 52, no. 3 (2022): 648–670.

21 Reichard, *Reaffirmation of Republicanism*, chs. 1 and 2.

22 Marcus Childs, *Eisenhower: Captive Hero* (New York: Harcourt Brace, 1958), 12. MacArthur was dismissed for defying Truman's wish to avoid expanding the Korean conflict.

23 Larson, *Eisenhower*, 54.

24 Ibid., 15.

25 On Eisenhower's use of his cabinet, see in particular James P. Pfiffner, *The Strategic Presidency: Hitting the Ground Running*, 2nd ed. (Lawrence: University Press of Kansas, 1996); and Stephen Hess, *Organizing the Presidency*, rev. ed. (Washington, DC: Brookings Institution, 1988).

26 Ewald, *Eisenhower the President*, 177.

27 Ambrose, *Eisenhower*, 52.

28 Charles E. Walcott and Karen M. Hult, *Governing the White House: From Hoover through LBJ* (Lawrence: University Press of Kansas, 1995), 38–43.

29 Donovan, *Eisenhower*, 209–229.

30 Ewald, *Eisenhower the President*, 64.

Dwight D. Eisenhower   149

31 Donovan, *Eisenhower*, 151.
32 Robert H. Ferrell, ed., *The Eisenhower Diaries* (New York: Norton, 1981), 288.
33 Peri E. Arnold, *Making the Managerial Presidency: Comprehensive Reorganization Planning, 1905–1980* (Princeton, NJ: Princeton University Press, 1986), 202.
34 *Bolling v. Sharpe*, 347 U.S. 483 (1954).
35 Herbert Brownell, *Advising Ike: The Memoirs of Attorney General Herbert Brownell* (Lawrence: University Press of Kansas, 1993), 193.
36 Michael Mayer, "Eisenhower and the Southern Federal Judiciary: The Sobeloff Nomination," in *Reexamining the Eisenhower Presidency*, ed. Shirley Anne Warshaw (Westport, CT: Greenwood Press, 1993), 57–75.
37 Peter Lyon, *Eisenhower: Portrait of a Hero* (Boston: Little, Brown, 1974), 483.
38 Milton S. Eisenhower, "Portrait of a Brother," in *The Eisenhower Presidency: Eleven Intimate Perspectives of Dwight D. Eisenhower*, ed. Kenneth W. Thompson (New York: University Press of America, 1984), 9.
39 Richard J. Ellis, *Presidential Lightning Rods: The Politics of Blame Avoidance* (Lawrence: University Press of Kansas, 1994).
40 Ambrose, *Eisenhower*, 190.
41 See Bernard K. Duffy, foreword to *Dwight D. Eisenhower: Strategic Communicator*, by Martin J. Medhurst (Westport, CT: Greenwood Press, 1993), xi; and David Haven Blake, *Liking Ike: Eisenhower, Advertising, and the Rise of Celebrity Politics* (Oxford: Oxford University Press, 2016).
42 Henry Z. Scheele, "President Dwight D. Eisenhower and the U.S. House Leader Charles A. Halleck: An Examination of an Executive-Legislative Relationship," *Presidential Studies Quarterly* 23 (Spring 1993): 289.
43 Reichard, *Reaffirmation of Republicanism*, 98.
44 Ibid., 112.
45 Robert L. Branyan and Lawrence H. Larsen, *The Eisenhower Administration: 1953–1961* (New York: Random House, 1971), 537–562.
46 Martha Derthick, *Policymaking for Social Security* (Washington, DC: Brookings Institution, 1979), 304.
47 Richardson, *Presidency of Dwight D. Eisenhower*, 112.
48 Mark A. Peterson, *Legislating Together: The White House and Capitol Hill from Eisenhower to Reagan* (Cambridge, MA: Harvard University Press, 1990), 235.
49 Dwight D. Eisenhower, *Mandate for Change* (Garden City, NY: Doubleday, 1963), 303.
50 Richard A. Watson, *Presidential Vetoes and Public Policy* (Lawrence: University Press of Kansas, 1993). Also see Robert J. Spitzer, *The Presidential Veto: Touchstone of the American Presidency* (Albany: State University of New York Press, 1988).
51 Richardson, *Presidency of Dwight D. Eisenhower*, 50.
52 John F. Witte, *The Politics and Development of the Federal Income Tax* (Madison: University of Wisconsin Press, 1985), 144.
53 On the question of political motivations and the 1956 election, coverage of his speeches showed a measure of change. See Earl Black and Merle Black, *The Vital South: How Presidents Are Elected* (Cambridge, MA: Harvard University Press, 1992), 180.

8 John F. Kennedy
A Quest for Heroic Leadership

John Kennedy (served 1961–1963) very narrowly won election in 1960 with a campaign proclaiming the need to "get the country moving again." In foreign affairs, he asserted the importance of increased defense spending and a staunch anticommunist posture. Domestically, he stressed economic growth and endorsed a lengthy list of initiatives. To achieve those goals, he promised "decisive and vigorous" presidential leadership. His promise, however, was short-lived. In November 1963, his term was cut short by an assassin's bullet. How well did he perform in his short time in office?

Public evaluations of the Kennedy presidency have been strikingly high. For example, one major study in 1983 placed Kennedy at the top of the former presidents the public would like to see in office again. Kennedy was chosen by 30 percent of the respondents, outdistancing Franklin Roosevelt by 10 percent.[1] In 2021, a poll found that Kennedy ranked only behind Lincoln (and ahead of Washington) in public favorability.[2] Kennedy's high evaluations stem in part from factors unrelated to the merits of his performance. Some respondents seem nostalgic for a period in which it seemed that pressing social and economic problems could be successfully addressed. Additionally, the Kennedys as a family hold a special and glamorous place in the American imagination. Kennedy's adroit handling of the media, which helped to generate high levels of personal popularity, also contributed to a widespread sense of martyrdom after his assassination.

Members of the Kennedy administration and some presidential scholars have praised Kennedy's leadership as well. Kennedy's outstanding rhetorical skills and a unique ability to digest information quickly from staff aides and documents are a common theme, as is his growth in office. Many see Kennedy as a young president who matured in the presidency to become an increasingly effective promoter of civil rights legislation and a major tax cut.[3] Kennedy's handling of the 1962 Cuban missile crisis also received high praise, especially considering the lessons he learned from the Bay of Pigs fiasco.

DOI: 10.4324/9781003426684-10

Other evaluations of the Kennedy presidency have been sharply critical. Some critics contend that Kennedy cultivated popularity by keeping the spotlight on his young, attractive "First Family" while displaying reluctance to work on his domestic agenda.[4] In his dealings with Congress, other critics say, Kennedy was overly deferential. His efforts to build close ties with business interests and his early reluctance to address civil rights issues have drawn criticism as well. In fact, some critics have likened Kennedy's leadership to a rocking chair: it moved a lot but never seemed to get anywhere.

Personal Characteristics

John Fitzgerald Kennedy (1917–1963) inherited his political aspirations from his intensely ambitious father, Joseph Kennedy. Joseph made a fortune in various business enterprises, including the purchase of undervalued businesses and a scotch distributorship, and invested in the movie industry. He also found time for government service. In the Roosevelt administration he served as head of the new Securities and Exchange Commission and as US ambassador to England. By 1960, his estate was worth an estimated $250 million, and he was priming one of his nine children, John, for a run for the presidency.

After graduating from a Connecticut preparatory school and spending some time at the London School of Economics and Princeton University (he was forced to withdraw because of illness), John entered Harvard University in 1936 and studied economics and political science. He graduated with honors in 1940. His senior thesis, "Why England Slept," examined British appeasement of fascism before World War II.

Kennedy served in the navy during the war. On August 2, 1943, his patrol torpedo boat was rammed and sunk by a Japanese destroyer. He led the 11 survivors on a four-hour swim to a nearby island, towing an injured crew member by a life preserver strap. After the ordeal, Kennedy returned to the States and was hospitalized for malaria. In 1944, he underwent back surgery and was honorably discharged from the navy the next year.

In 1951, JFK, then an eligible bachelor and US senator, met Jacqueline Lee Bouvier at a Washington dinner party. They were married two years later. The young first lady (only 31 when John became president) made the White House a center for culture and the arts and became a fashion trendsetter in her own right.

Career Path

John Kennedy's political career began with election to the House of Representatives from a lower-income Boston district in 1946. Six years later, Kennedy successfully challenged Massachusetts Republican Henry

152 *The Moderate-Opportunity Presidents*

Cabot Lodge for his Senate seat and won despite Dwight Eisenhower's strength at the top of the ticket. In 1956, Kennedy sought second place on a Democratic presidential ticket headed by former Illinois governor Adlai Stevenson but lost to Senator Estes Kefauver of Tennessee. His defeat ultimately worked to his advantage, however, in that he gained greater national attention and avoided the stigma of defeat in the 1956 campaign.[5]

His plans for a presidential bid in 1960 were several years in the making but were not actually announced until January 2, 1960. He decided to showcase his electability through primary victories, and he won several important states, including West Virginia, which proved to be pivotal.[6] Lyndon Johnson, who had belatedly entered the race, was selected as his vice presidential nominee to help carry the South.

Kennedy's narrow general election victory over Richard Nixon (by only 114,000 votes) can be attributed to many factors. Kennedy benefited from winning the first presidential debate. And when civil rights leader Martin Luther King Jr. was jailed in Georgia on a driver's license infraction, he called King's wife to offer his sympathy and support. That expression, which Nixon had considered and rejected, helped with African American voters. He also was aided by a higher-than-usual degree of Catholic support in the North for the Democratic ticket. Conversely, Nixon succeeded in attracting Democratic white Protestant voters who were reluctant to have a Catholic in the White House—a factor that helped explain JFK's very narrow margin of victory.

What Manner of Man?

According to historian James Giglio, "No president in the twentieth century combined [Kennedy's] rhetoric, wit, charm, youth, and Hollywood appearance."[7] His disarming use of self-deprecating sense of humor was often on display as well. In early 1960, JFK's opening statement at the Gridiron Club gathering of Washington's leading journalists revealed his skill at diffusing potential criticism with humor. At a time when the scope of his father's financial and personal assistance was drawing skeptical questioning from some quarters, Kennedy began his speech by stating that he had just received a telegram from his father saying: "DON'T BUY A SINGLE VOTE MORE THAN NECESSARY. I'LL BE DAMNED IF I'M GOING TO PAY FOR A LANDSLIDE."[8]

More broadly, Kennedy was extremely effective in handling public relations. In fact, he once commented that he thought he might be best suited for a career in real estate sales after his presidency.[9] Running through all his public relations endeavors was his father's influence—and some of these endeavors were stained with charges of deception.[10] The most disputed aspect of JFK's early efforts came with publication of his book *Profiles in Courage*, for which much of the research and writing was done by others.[11]

In his dealings with other people, Kennedy was said to be efficient at extracting information and getting to the core of problems. He was skilled at drawing out differing ideas from aides. When conflicts among them erupted, he resorted to his own personal charm to resolve them. More broadly, he was able to cajole, persuade, soothe, and inspire others.[12]

Other frequently noted traits were his high degree of competitiveness and his willingness to take some calculated risks. Some observers described him as being "half Harvard and half Irish"—with at least the Irish side willing to contest elections very tenaciously. His willingness to take risks did not cover all endeavors, however. In 1961, for example, he proceeded cautiously with Congress. He tended to take more risks when his reputation was on the line in a policy struggle. Although Kennedy displayed little vindictiveness, he was willing to engage forcefully with others, as he did with his angry, heavy-handed response in 1962 when the steel companies sought price increases at a time when the president was trying to keep inflation in check.

Since a young age, Kennedy had suffered from several serious medical ailments—even more than were recognized before his death.[13] He was afflicted with Addison's disease (caused by a hormonal deficiency) and suffered from chronic back problems that frequently required the use of crutches. In fact, some of his medical problems were so severe that he received the last rites on no fewer than four occasions, including twice during delicate back surgery in 1955. Given his multiple health problems, his brother Robert may not have exaggerated when he asserted that JFK lived half of his days on earth in intense pain.[14]

Policy Views

In his approach to domestic policy, Kennedy firmly believed that problems could be solved—but with pragmatism rather than conventional ideologies. During his days in the House and Senate, he supported a wide variety of liberal measures such as increases in Social Security and low-income housing assistance, but in part because of their popularity with his constituents. According to journalist Richard Reeves, "He was not a liberal moralist—he did not call himself any kind of liberal—but rather a managerial politician."[15] In a similar vein, political scientist Lewis Paper concluded, "No one would ever mistake John Kennedy for a radical who would always stand on principle."[16] In addition to his preference for pragmatic solutions over liberal orthodoxy, Kennedy desired good government-business relations as an avenue toward improved economic growth. On civil rights, he generally preferred caution.

154   *The Moderate-Opportunity Presidents*

Although Kennedy advocated no overall economic policy during his presidential campaign, he repeatedly asserted the need to improve the nation's rate of economic growth—primarily because to keep up with the Soviet Union. More broadly, in his domestic agenda, which he called the "New Frontier," he endorsed many traditionally Democratic measures. These included medical care for the elderly, increases in Social Security, additional commitments to housing programs, aid to depressed areas, assistance for the poor, aid to education, and reform of agriculture policies.

Because of Kennedy's sheltered family life, he had had virtually no meaningful contact with African Americans or other groups suffering during the Depression. Similarly, his years in Washington produced little direct involvement with the problems facing African Americans. In his eyes, at least at first, desegregation was rational but not necessarily a moral issue, and civil rights protests were simply domestic problems that had to be managed.[17]

Challenges and Opportunities

President Kennedy's foreign policy challenges consumed much of his time in 1961 and, indeed, throughout his presidency. During his first year in office, he confronted a difficult relationship with Soviet leader Nikita Khrushchev, tension over Berlin, and problems in both Vietnam and Laos. Having made the prior administration's apparent failings in dealing with Cuba a campaign issue, Kennedy sought to get rid of Cuban leader Fidel Castro, an endeavor that ate up a good deal of his time. Kennedy's spectacular Bay of Pigs failure was later followed by his adroit handling of the Cuban Missile Crisis. Before his death, Kennedy successfully promoted an atomic weapons test ban treaty but was facing renewed problems in Vietnam in the wake of the assassination of South Vietnamese leader Ngo Dinh Diem.

Kennedy's opportunities were not very promising for a president seeking to "get the country moving again" and reenergize a sluggish economy. A few factors, however, were operating in his favor. Although his popularity declined in 1963, he had enjoyed high popularity throughout his first two years. However, since his popularity was not clearly tied to his domestic agenda, it was a somewhat ambiguous resource.

Another advantage welcomed by the young president was the large number of proposals developed in Congress during Eisenhower's second term. These proposals had not gained the support needed for passage or, in some cases, the support needed to override an Eisenhower veto. The list included Medicare for the elderly, which JFK had promoted during his last two years in the Senate; federal aid to education; aid to depressed areas; and several environmental measures.[18]

Although many of these proposals were favored by a majority of citizens, Kennedy confronted several obstacles in the legislative arena that limited his opportunities. Kennedy could not deal with Congress by claiming a mandate from having stressed a few strong themes in his campaign or from having achieved a decisive victory. Moreover, the Democrats lost 21 seats in the House—the worst outcome produced by any incoming president—leaving Kennedy with no sense of momentum.

At the outset, Kennedy endured bumpy relations with some congressional leaders. In the Senate, Mike Mansfield (D-MT), Vice President Lyndon Johnson's successor as majority leader, proved to be well liked on both sides of the aisle, but he lacked Johnson's assertiveness. In the House, Speaker Sam Rayburn's declining health and death in the fall of 1961 elevated John McCormack (D-MA) into that key position. McCormack, however, possessed only modest skills and a personal dislike of John Kennedy, stemming from earlier political conflicts. The important committee, mostly elderly and often conservative, remembered JFK only as a young and not very influential senator.

Economic conditions further complicated Kennedy's opportunities. The economy slumped in early 1961 as unemployment rose to 7.7 percent. This made congress more receptive to measures such as aid to depressed areas than might otherwise have been the case. By 1963, with the inflation level lowered, the president was indicating his willingness to experiment with deficit spending, but the improvement in the economy also made government borrowing more difficult to promote in Congress.

The president found the public's high level of trust in government to be a positive resource, but he was less certain about whether the public really wanted to participate in a period of renewed government activism. Kennedy was familiar with the theory of cycles espoused by aide Arthur Schlesinger Jr., and he hoped that his presidency would coincide with a new cycle of activism. But, despite his inaugural pleas for action, many believed the election produced little indication that the public supported assertive action.

Leadership Style

Kennedy entered the presidency with a heroic view of presidential leadership.[19] His study of political leadership led him to identify with the role played by Prime Minister Winston Churchill, who dramatically rallied British public opinion during World War II. Through family discussions led by his father, he also was thoroughly grounded in key dimensions of Franklin Roosevelt's leadership style.[20] Kennedy may have disagreed with some aspects of FDR's foreign policies, "but he admired Roosevelt's ability to articulate the latent idealism of America, and he greatly envied Roosevelt's capacity to dominate a sprawling government."[21]

156 *The Moderate-Opportunity Presidents*

The Advisory Process and Approach to Decision-Making

Kennedy sought White House staff and cabinet members with different backgrounds. For example, from his Senate staff and election campaigns he selected people whose political judgment he trusted—among them, Theodore Sorensen and Richard Goodwin from his Senate staff and former campaign aides Lawrence O'Brien and Kenneth O'Donnell. Perhaps reflecting his interest in a problem-solving approach to public policy, Kennedy recruited from academia prominent Boston scholar Arthur Schlesinger Jr. as a general aide and Harvard dean McGeorge Bundy as national security advisor. By selecting some more conservative advisers—such as Bundy, as well as investment banker Douglas Dillon as Treasury secretary and former Ford Motor Company president Robert McNamara as defense secretary—Kennedy hoped to broaden his political base in the wake of his narrow election victory.

Sorensen, whose role at points resembled that of chief of staff, and legislative assistant Mike Feldman helped shape Kennedy's domestic policy initiatives with the assistance of an extensive network of presidential task forces established during Kennedy's first year in office. Other architects of the president's domestic policy were Walter Heller, an economist from the University of Minnesota who was appointed chairman of the Council of Economic Advisers, and Bureau of the Budget director David Bell, a former Truman staffer who taught economics at Harvard. As part of a group known as the "Quadriad," they often worked closely with Treasury Secretary Dillon and William McChesney Martin, chairman of the Federal Reserve Board.

The assessments of Kennedy's band of recruits were mixed. Long before some fell under intense criticism for their roles in the deepening war in Vietnam in the mid-1960s, they often were called the "best and brightest." JFK's effort to gather various policy ideas from the nation's universities was particularly welcomed by segments of the nation's academic community but criticized by others. Washington insider Clark Clifford, however, viewed the Kennedy recruits as "the cockiest crowd I'd ever seen at the White House."[22]

Administrative Strategies

Kennedy's administrative strategies included modest efforts at "good government" reform and one dramatic use of administrative action for policy purposes. His disinterest in the federal bureaucracy stemmed primarily from his belief that it acted too slowly and had too few new policy ideas. His frustration with the bureaucracy, however, did not motivate him to press for structural reforms.[23]

Kennedy's first executive order was to direct Agriculture Secretary Orville Freeman to make more food available to the needy in some states, such as West Virginia. In 1962 Kennedy responded decisively to an announced price increase by US Steel. The whole episode, which some likened in importance to the 1962 Cuban missile crisis,[24] began when the Kennedy administration pursued a policy called "jawboning"—that is, encouraging businesses to adopt only modest price increases while encouraging labor to limit its demands for wage increases. Following that policy, Secretary of Labor Arthur Goldberg had pressured his former employer, the United Steelworkers of America, to accept a wage increase of 2.5 percent, which was well within the Kennedy administration's guidelines. But on April 10, 1962, US Steel president Roger Blough met Kennedy at the White House and presented him with a memorandum calling for a price which exceeded the administration's guidelines. Blough and Kennedy argued briefly about whether US Steel had specifically agreed to the earlier guidelines, and Blough departed. That same day, seven other steel companies announced similar price increases.

Kennedy, sensing a threat to his administration, acted forcefully and resolutely. Arthur Goldberg responded immediately to his call and, on hearing of US Steel's actions, offered to resign. Kennedy rejected his offer and proceeded to draft a statement to the press citing how other Americans had heeded his call for sacrifice—including those who had gone to Vietnam—and making it clear that he wanted the price increases rescinded. At his press conference Kennedy described the steel companies' actions as "a wholly unjustifiable and irresponsible defiance of the public interest." He then added, "Some time ago I asked each American to consider what he would do for his country and I asked the steel companies. In the last twenty-four hours we had their answer."[25]

Determined that nothing would hamper his ability to continue with his anti-inflation strategy, Kennedy proceeded to throw the full power of the federal government into his effort to obtain a reversal by the steel companies. Steel executives were subpoenaed to appear at a grand jury investigation, and the Federal Trade Commission and congressional committees were encouraged to investigate. The administration also applied economic leverage by promising to steer new contracts to any firm that did not go along with the general steel price increase.

Then, just 72 hours after it began, the conflict ended. A small steel company decided to rescind the price increase and all the other companies quickly followed suit. Kennedy was able to attribute his success to his public efforts as well as his administrative powers. Although he tried to quiet the furor it produced, his widely reported remark, "My father always told me that all businessmen were sons-of-bitches, but I never believed it till now" generated resentment. In the following months, however, the president made a more concerted effort to court business support through various tax packages.

158 *The Moderate-Opportunity Presidents*

Until 1963, administrative action also constituted Kennedy's primary approach to civil rights issues. In 1961, he concentrated on appointing African Americans to top government posts, but his choice of nominees drew mixed reviews. Civil rights leaders found fault with his continuing tendency to show deference to southern leaders in Congress by appointing federal judges to the Fifth Circuit Court of Appeals (which covered the southern states) whom southerners would not find threatening.

Housing desegregation policies were another area in which reliance on administrative strategies proved difficult. Fearing conflict with southerners in Congress and resistance to actual implementation, Kennedy avoided issuing the executive order on housing he had promised to sign "with the stroke of a pen" during the 1960 campaign.[26] In their frustration over his delay, civil rights supporters mailed him pens at the White House. As the midterm elections approached, the president decided to delay his order once more until voters had cast their ballots. When it was finally signed on Thanksgiving Eve 1962, the executive order dealing with housing segregation disappointed civil rights leaders. The order's provisions were not retroactive and applied only to a limited number of federal housing loans.

Public Leadership

In his public role, President Kennedy was known for his idealistic, motivating rhetoric. In his widely acclaimed inaugural address he proclaimed:

> Let the word go forth ... to friend and foe alike, that the torch has been passed to a new generation, born in this century, tempered by war, disciplined by a hard and bitter peace, proud of our ancient heritage.... [We] shall pay any price, bear any burden, meet any hardship ... to assure the survival and the success of liberty.

The president also was known for circumventing his own press secretary in his courting of the press. But his courtship had its limits. Reporters who wrote less-than-flattering accounts of the president found themselves distanced from personal contact with him. The result was generally quite favorable press coverage.

Press conferences were a key component of Kennedy's public relations and support-building strategies. Unlike Eisenhower, who used a taped delay for his press conferences, Kennedy appeared live—the first president to do so. The large audiences his press conferences attracted were taken with his witty responses and his willingness to respond at length on policy issues—much more so than either Truman or Eisenhower. In fact, press conferences were JFK's principal forum for reaching the public. Convinced that citizens tire of formal speechmaking, Kennedy went before the cameras only nine times during his presidency to deliver a formal address.

Thus, like Roosevelt, Kennedy tended to limit his major addresses and save them for the most urgent problems.[27] Until his third year in office, most of these speeches addressed foreign policy issues.

To implement his style of heroic leadership, Kennedy aggressively used the bully pulpit, espousing causes such as fighting inflation, building backyard bomb shelters, and participating in physical fitness programs. In fact, some criticized him for using the bully pulpit too much.[28] Kennedy also promoted the importance of government service through agencies such as the Peace Corps. According to Mary Stuckey,

> Kennedy made the country feel as if government service, national service, was a high, even a noble calling. He never denigrated politics while acting politically. Instead, he was much more likely to exalt politics, perhaps creating inflated expectations, but assuring that people would have respect for and faith in their national government.[29]

Congressional Leadership

Despite adviser Richard Neustadt's suggestion that he abolish the White House Office of Legislative Relations (OLR) Eisenhower had created, Kennedy chose to expand it. OLR director Lawrence O'Brien included 40 legislative liaison people from various departments in well-orchestrated and highly energetic efforts.[30] To his credit, O'Brien continued as OLR director during much of Johnson's presidency.

Kennedy made several important strategic choices in his dealings with Congress. At the outset, he chose to help Speaker Sam Rayburn expand the size of the House Rules Committee, improving his chances of breaking up the southern Democrat/Republican roadblocks. In 1961, he used a partial fast-start strategy as he pushed successfully on measures such as aid to depressed areas and a job training program. However, he proceeded cautiously on the potential landmark issues of Medicare and federal aid to education, despite their position at the top of his agenda, and he submitted no civil rights legislation.[31] In 1963, the president undertook a major third-year shift as he moved aggressively on civil rights and a sweeping tax-cut proposal.

Kennedy found flattery to be quite effective in working with individual members of Congress such as Senate Minority Leader Everett Dirksen (R-IL) and Senate Finance Committee Chairman Harry Byrd Jr. (D-VA), whose birthday party JFK attended by helicopter. On some occasions, he lobbied quite heavily for specific votes. Frequently, however, he was faced with resistance from southern committee chairmen and was reluctant to aggressively seek a change in their positions. Finally, he preferred to persuade through policy arguments rather than "arm twisting" and bargaining. According to Senator Claiborne Pell (D-RI), Kennedy often assumed

160   *The Moderate-Opportunity Presidents*

that a rejection of his reasoned arguments indicated that the time was not ripe for action.

Legislative Enactments

During Kennedy's years in the White House, Congress enacted a moderate amount of major legislation but reached a stalemate on some key issues, such as federal aid to education, Medicare, and civil rights. During his third year in office, he became more assertive in the areas of fiscal policy and civil rights and established some momentum, only to fall prey to an assassin's bullet.

Federal Aid to Education

Kennedy faced a long-standing controversy as he sought action on federal aid to education in 1961. Legislators and the public had debated the issue at length in the late 1950s as the surge of baby boomers in the nation's school systems created intense financial pressures. Further complicating the matter were the related issues of race and religion. The racial question concerned whether aid would go to segregated school districts, and the religious controversy surrounded whether the program would include aid to parochial schools.

As the nation's first Catholic president, Kennedy found the aid to education question difficult to address.[32] Moreover, he faced a set of antagonistic interest groups that had fought the issue to a standstill. Kennedy's response was to continue to oppose aid for parochial schools—a stand he had taken during the campaign. His legislative proposal closely paralleled a bill the Senate passed in 1960 providing aid for school construction and teachers' salaries. Although he gave no major address on the topic, he advocated his position in several televised news conferences. The White House made no specific reference to leveraging this aid to force additional desegregation, and on Capitol Hill a conflict was temporarily avoided when Adam Clayton Powell (D-NY), a prominent African American in the House, agreed to refrain from raising the issue until there was a more favorable climate for civil rights.

Employment-Related Policies and the Environment

Kennedy was able to use a fast-start strategy to address the problems of unemployment and stagnant wages in 1961. Enactment of the Area Redevelopment Act in June 1961 marked the conclusion of a struggle that had begun in the late 1950s as Congress sought to address the economic problems of depressed areas, including coal mining communities. The legislation provided for funding of commercial and industrial development, technical assistance in community planning, and the retraining of unemployed workers.

Changes in minimum wage provisions proved to be more controversial. The Democratic Party platform had included an increase to $1.25 an hour, and Kennedy also promoted the measure in his February 13, 1961, message to Congress. Legislators wrangled over the extent of coverage as well as the size of the increase from the existing $1.00 an hour. Senator Paul Douglas (D-IL), a prominent economist who had written on this subject, promoted expansion, while business groups such as the Chamber of Commerce argued against a major expansion. The president's original bill called for extending the minimum wage to 4.3 million workers, but Congress exempted more than 700,000 employees—mainly those working for laundries and small interstate businesses.

Environmental concerns emerged in Congress in the late 1950s, but legislators made few tangible commitments. By 1963, public support had expanded enough to allow passage of the Clean Air Act, which focused largely on automobile emissions. Kennedy threw his weight behind the measure as it made its way through Congress. He also advocated conservation measures and the importance of a clean environment and committed some federal funding to these efforts.

Social Security, Welfare, and Health

Although it faced a deadlock over Medicare, the Kennedy administration pursued changes in Social Security and welfare policy. Kennedy, specialists in Congress, and advocates within the Social Security Administration promoted a proposal that would give men the same rights to partial benefits at age 62 that women had received in 1956. Kennedy included these reforms in his February 13 message to Congress outlining his program for economic growth and recovery. The proposal was further aided by Social Security Administration analyses indicating that the expansion could be absorbed without additional Social Security taxes. Congress passed the reforms easily by the end of June 1961. Congress further expanded Social Security benefits in 1962.

In 1961, Congress followed the president's lead by providing assistance to the children of unemployed parents. Legislators' favorable response to welfare reform proposals stemmed in part from a study conducted by an ad hoc committee headed by Abraham Ribicoff, secretary of Health, Education, and Welfare (HEW), and a nationally publicized crackdown on welfare fraud. Kennedy's initial proposal to Congress focused on the rehabilitation of welfare recipients through community work programs. In presenting his proposal to Congress, he stressed that public welfare must be "more than a salvage operation" and asked legislators to raise federal funding of state programs from 50 percent to 75 percent.

162   *The Moderate-Opportunity Presidents*

The new program attracted the support of the National Social Welfare Assembly and many Democratic members of Congress. Republicans argued that federal involvement should not be expanded. HEW Assistant Secretary Wilbur Cohen, who had worked hard on this issue, noted that one of the surprising dynamics surrounding passage of the legislation was the relative lack of conflict.[33]

Tax Policies

Kennedy's efforts to pass tax legislation began in 1961 under the leadership of Douglas Dillon, secretary of the Treasury, and Harvard law professor Stanley Surrey, who was serving as assistant secretary and had chaired Kennedy's task force on tax reform. As the recession worsened in Kennedy's first weeks in office, the planning effort turned from a single comprehensive reform bill to a two-stage strategy in which a quick stimulus bill would be passed in 1961 followed by a major reform measure in 1962 or 1963. The president's initial proposal in April 1961 focused primarily on the use of tax incentives to businesses to expand and modernize production facilities and equipment.[34]

Despite the attractiveness of several provisions granting tax reductions in exchange for investment, some businesses remained skeptical of Kennedy. Conflicts emerged among business sectors over the distribution provisions. Kennedy spoke privately of his disappointment with the reactions of business leaders but was restrained in his public responses. Although early opposition prevented quick action on the tax incentive package, it was finally enacted in 1962. During an often highly partisan process, numerous changes were made in the legislation at the committee stage in each house.

Kennedy urged public support for the tax reform legislation. He promoted the measure in press conferences and used a scheduled June 11, 1962, commencement appearance at Yale University to deliver a major address that stressed the importance of fiscal policies in achieving more rapid economic growth. Reaction to the speech was mixed, and some concluded that it was difficult to analyze economic issues in a commencement speech. Nevertheless, many supporters of Keynesian views on tax policy inside the president's administration were delighted with his strong stand. The level of resistance declined for the 1962 reforms, and Kennedy signed them into law in October.

In January 1963, Kennedy submitted a tax-cut package to Congress. Under the tutelage of Walter Heller, Kennedy had become increasingly confident in his own analysis and saw tax cuts as a broader vehicle toward growth than redevelopment programs. The administration consulted many business and some labor groups to gain an understanding of provisions likely to draw the greatest support.[35] The final result was a tax proposal that represented two important "firsts." Kennedy was the first president to promote a tax cut when the government was operating with a deficit and the first to promote a tax cut when the economy was performing well.

The program Kennedy submitted to Congress in January 1963 called for tax reductions in all brackets, a reduction in the corporate tax rate from 52 percent to 47 percent, and special tax breaks for small businesses. The total package called for reducing taxes by $13.6 billion with $11 billion going to individuals and $2.6 billion to corporations. Because it was anticipated that the 1962 reforms would add $3.4 billion in revenue, this package represented a reduction of $10.2 billion in revenue. In designing his proposed reductions, Kennedy paid careful attention to measures that would cut the capital gains tax, expand policies related to child care, change deductions for charitable giving, and alter the taxes of the elderly. In order to maximize congressional support, the president was careful to project revenue decreases below Eisenhower's largest recession-driven deficit of $12.4 billion.[36]

Despite the administration's efforts to design a politically attractive measure, the House Ways and Means Committee introduced extensive changes. Virtually unanimous Republican opposition in the House was offset by strong support from southern Democrats. Kennedy undertook both radio and television appeals that touted the benefits of the tax cut to individual families and how the bill would lead to long-term economic growth and prevent a recession.

The Senate Finance Committee held extensive hearings over a three-month period. Floor opposition was led by liberals who unsuccessfully attacked the bill on equity grounds. The final bill passed easily with bipartisan support and moved to the conference committee. In accepting changes as his bill moved through Congress, Kennedy was quite willing to compromise and see reforms eliminated as a necessary price for gaining passage of the tax cuts he felt would stimulate the economy. When it finally passed in January 1964, the bill became the first landmark enactment under the Johnson administration.[37]

Housing Policy

Kennedy did not succeed in his effort to make the Federal Housing Administration (FHA) into a cabinet-level Department of Urban Affairs. His major housing proposal was successful because, unlike the proposed Department of Urban Affairs, it enjoyed southern and bipartisan support. It also had the support of a variety of interest groups since it promised to distribute a wide variety of benefits.[38] In further expanding on the measure's wide appeal, the Kennedy administration added sweeteners as the bill was being debated in committee to help generate support from southern Democrats and members from rural areas. The final bill broadened and extended programs such as urban renewal, public housing, and housing

164 *The Moderate-Opportunity Presidents*

for the elderly and college students, as well as offered a new middle-income housing program and funding for mass transportation facilities and open spaces in the cities.

Civil Rights

In 1963 Kennedy abandoned his mild administrative strategies for dealing with civil rights issues and changed direction.[39] Events were transforming the civil rights movement and white attitudes outside the South. In trying to desegregate public facilities in Birmingham, Alabama, movement leader Martin Luther King Jr. was pursuing a conscious strategy of taking on the toughest case in the hope of forcing decisive action. The protest campaign included sit-ins at department stores, street marches, and pray-ins. When King was jailed for a brief time, he wrote his famous "Letter from the Birmingham Jail," which made an eloquent defense of civil disobedience and nonviolent protest.

In dealing with the demonstrators, Birmingham Police Chief Eugene "Bull" Connor provided the nation with gripping, repugnant television footage. Cameras showed lunging police dogs and police using high-pressure fire hoses on small children. As a result, the national sentiment swung further toward an end to segregation. Community leaders of all stripes called on the Kennedy administration to find ways to achieve desegregation while also eliminating violent confrontations.

In the face of this crisis, Kennedy was jolted into reassessing his cautious approach and pursuing a more resolute course on civil rights. He proposed additional civil rights legislation, and, in an address to the nation on June 11, 1963, he became the first president to specifically condemn segregation on moral grounds. In that address, he stated:

> We are confronted primarily with a moral issue. It is as old as the scriptures and is as clear as the American Constitution.... We face therefore, a moral crisis as a country and as a people. It cannot be met by repressive police action. It cannot be left to increased demonstrations in the streets. It cannot be quieted by token moves or talk. It is a time to act in Congress, in your State and local legislative body and, above all in our daily lives.[40]

After his address, the administration took action. At the White House, Kennedy himself met with a wide array of opinion leaders. His brother, Attorney General Robert Kennedy, maintained close contact with leading civil rights leaders. Both brothers were initially apprehensive about King's plans for a march on Washington, but they decided that the best strategy was to ensure that it would be peaceful. That strategy proved to be successful, when on August 28, 1963, some 300,000 men and women, black

John F. Kennedy 165

and white, participated in a peaceful and dignified gathering at the base of the Lincoln Memorial.

As for civil rights legislation, the administration promoted its bill widely and consulted extensively with Congress, both before and after the bill was submitted. According to Burke Marshall, Kennedy was even willing to defer his tax-cut proposal if that was required to gain passage of the civil rights bill.[41] By the time of Kennedy's death, this legislation had made substantial headway on Capitol Hill.

Kennedy and Congress

Overall, Kennedy succeeded only to a moderate degree with Congress. He was able to promote some new legislation, but he did not see passage of his landmark bills. His inability to achieve landmark legislation was not especially surprising, however, since presidents without high-opportunity levels have had very little success. On some measures of moderate importance before Congress, a stronger bargaining role might have produced different results. On the minimum wage, for example, Lewis Paper concluded that Kennedy may have conceded coverage for laundry workers too soon.[42]

An Assessment

Because John Kennedy died in office, his performance as president is not easy to evaluate. Enough is known, however, to address several of the issues raised at the beginning of this chapter.[43]

Policy Legacy

Kennedy's civil rights record is destined to remain the central component of his domestic policy legacy. Although he was highly cautious during his first two years in office, there was little opportunity for passing a new civil rights bill in 1961. Civil rights aide Harris Wofford had hoped for a stronger administrative role, but he did not fault the absence of a legislative initiative.[44] Beginning in the spring of 1963, however, Kennedy submitted a landmark proposal and pursued a broad range of legislative strategies. He also employed forceful rhetoric and held numerous meetings with various opinion leaders and civil rights advocates.

Kennedy also had a role in advancing interest in the use of fiscal policy to stimulate the economy. He helped to achieve some major domestic enactments and pushed legislation that would gain passage after his death. His successors continued to promote fiscal policy well into the 1970s when challenges to this approach arose. Kennedy's major domestic policy enactments included welfare and Social Security reform, several changes

166 *The Moderate-Opportunity Presidents*

in regulatory policy, and the Area Redevelopment Act. Although JFK did not succeed on many major initiatives, he was able to make progress that provided momentum for the Johnson administration.

Performance

Kennedy's efforts to provide heroic leadership allowed him to blend that aspect of his persona into a highly effective public relations effort. In his call for new action, he successfully motivated large numbers of college-age students to pursue careers in the public sector.[45] Despite his initial desire to avoid civil rights issues, his lofty rhetoric may have had an impact on the civil rights movement. In fact, Robert Moses, who served as director of the Mississippi Council of Federated Organizations, believed that a new generation of African Americans seemed to respond to the question of what they could do for their country in ways that Kennedy had not specifically intended.[46] Although he had not tried to educate the public on civil rights issues, his public address on June 11, 1963, did forcefully frame this domestic issue in moral terms.

As for his use of his presidency as a bully pulpit, critics abound. And his rate of major voluntary domestic policy addresses is lower than that of any other president. Moreover, some critics find that his emphasis on dramatic rhetoric risked overreaction, such as his statements during the steel price increase controversy.

Was Kennedy an underachiever? Some harder bargaining might have helped, yet it seems doubtful that he could have accomplished much more in his situation with a different leadership style. Michael Harrington concluded that Kennedy did relatively well given his circumstances and his political values.[47] Taking into account his successes with smaller programs as landmark efforts failed, Mark Peterson found that "there was more to Kennedy's legislative performance than symbols."[48] Some Kennedy administration insiders held that the president could have achieved greatness if his life had not been cut short. Other observers were not so optimistic. The situation in Vietnam and the possibility of public scandals arising from his personal behavior may have waylaid a promising future. Nevertheless, Kennedy's record reveals that overinflated initial adulation followed by highly critical revisionism has made it too easy to obscure his respectable, but by no means outstanding, performance.

Notes

1 Larry Berman, *The New American Presidency* (Boston: Little, Brown, 1987), 236.
2 Matthew Smith, "The Most and Least Popular US Presidents, According to Americans," YouGovAmerica, last modified July 27, 2021, https://today.you-

gov.com/topics/politics/articles-reports/2021/07/27/most-and-least-popular-us-presidents-according-ame.

3 The highly favorable interpretations of the Kennedy presidency include James David Barber, *The Presidential Character: Predicting Performance in the White House*, 4th ed. (Englewood Cliffs, NJ: Prentice Hall, 1992); and Theodore Sorensen, *Kennedy* (New York: Harper and Row, 1965).

4 See in particular Garry Wills, *The Kennedy Imprisonment: A Meditation on Power* (Boston: Little, Brown, 1982); and Bruce Miroff, *Pragmatic Illusions: The Presidential Politics of John F. Kennedy* (New York: David McKay, 1976).

5 See Fredrik Logevall, *JFK: Coming of Age in the American Century, 1917–1956* (New York: Random House, 2020).

6 Robert Rupp, *The Primary That Made a President: John F. Kennedy and West Virginia* (Knoxville, TN: University of Tennessee Press, 2020).

7 James N. Giglio, *The Presidency of John F. Kennedy* (Lawrence: University Press of Kansas, 1991), 1.

8 James Reston, *Deadline: A Memoir* (New York: Random House, 1991), 288.

9 Ralph G. Martin, *A Hero for Our Time: An Intimate Story of the Kennedy Years* (New York: Macmillan, 1993), 564.

10 See Wills, *Kennedy Imprisonment*; and John Blair and Clay Blair, *The Search for JFK* (New York: Berkeley Publishing, 1975).

11 Historian Herbert Parmer, after reviewing materials at the John F. Kennedy Library, concluded that while Kennedy had sponsored and shaped the work, the research and drafts had been done by several people, particularly Professor Jules Davids of Georgetown University and Senate staffer Theodore Sorensen. Giglio, *Presidency of John F. Kennedy*, 11.

12 Patricia Dennis Witherspoon, *Within These Walls: A Study of Communication between Presidents and Their Senior Staffs* (New York: Praeger, 1991), 42.

13 This discussion is drawn from John R. Bumgarner, *The Health of the Presidents: The 41 United States Presidents through 1993 from a Physician's Point of View* (Jefferson, NC: McFarland & Co., 1994), 234–249.

14 Martin, *Hero for Our Time*, 97. The discussion of Kennedy's background also draws from Wills, *Kennedy Imprisonment*.

15 Ibid., 480.

16 Lewis J. Paper, *John F. Kennedy: The Promise and the Performance* (New York: Crown, 1975), 46.

17 Harris Wofford, *Of Kennedy and Kings: Making Sense of the Sixties* (New York: Farrar, Straus, Giroux, 1980), 128.

18 James L. Sundquist, *Politics and Policy: The Eisenhower, Kennedy, and Johnson Years* (Washington, DC: Brookings Institution, 1968).

19 This concept and interpretation draws from Bruce Miroff, *Icons of Democracy: American Leaders as Heroes, Aristocrats, Dissenters, and Democrats* (New York: Basic Books, 1993), ch. 8.

20 At the outset of his administration, JFK showed a knowledge of Neustadt's recommended techniques as he asked Neustadt and Clark Clifford to prepare recommendations for the organization of his presidency and key strategies. He did not want them to work together, however, so he would gain the value of two different reports. Neustadt subsequently served as ambassador to Great Britain and periodically suggested overall strategies to Kennedy.

21 Arthur M. Schlesinger Jr., *A Thousand Days: John F. Kennedy in the White House* (Boston: Houghton Mifflin, 1965), 120.

22 Martin, *Hero for Our Time*, 300.

168 The Moderate-Opportunity Presidents

23 Charles E. Walcott and Karen M. Hult, *Governing the White House: From Hoover through LBJ* (Lawrence: University Press of Kansas, 1995), 111.
24 This discussion draws from Giglio, *Presidency of John F. Kennedy*, 129–133; and James F. Heath, *John F. Kennedy and the Business Community* (Chicago: University of Chicago Press, 1969), 68–73.
25 Quoted in Schlesinger, *A Thousand Days*, 636.
26 Charles M. Lamb, Joshua Boston, and Jacob R. Neiheisel, "Power Plus Persuasion: The Anatomy of Kennedy's Housing Order," *Congress & the Presidency* 40, no. 1 (2019): 109–134.
27 Sorensen, *Kennedy*, 329.
28 As one indication of at least a measure of interest in actual impact, Kennedy asked Sorensen at the end of 1961 to provide a list of what he had asked the citizens themselves to do. The list produced some 15 items.
29 Mary E. Stuckey, *The President as Interpreter-in-Chief* (Chatham, NJ: Chatham House, 1991), 63.
30 Ibid., 223.
31 Paul C. Light, *The President's Agenda: Domestic Policy Choice from Kennedy to Carter* (Baltimore: Johns Hopkins University Press, 1981), 70. Somewhat less emphasis on Medicare as a goal is suggested in Alan Shank, *Presidential Policy Leadership: Kennedy and Social Welfare* (Lanham, MD: University Press of America, 1980), 93.
32 On this issue, see Barbara Kellerman, *The Political Presidency: The Practice of Leadership from Kennedy through Reagan* (New York: Oxford University Press, 1986), ch. 4; and Hugh D. Graham, *The Uncertain Trumpet: Federal Education Policy in the Kennedy and Johnson Years* (Chapel Hill: University of North Carolina Press, 1984).
33 Edward D. Berkowitz, *Mr. Social Security: The Life of Wilbur J. Cohen* (Lawrence: University Press of Kansas, 1995), 150–151.
34 John F. Witte, *The Politics and Development of the Federal Income Tax* (Madison: University of Wisconsin Press, 1985), 155.
35 Records kept by Theodore Sorensen indicate consultation with all of the peak business groups and more than 20 more specific groups. Despite JFK's rancorous dealings with Roger Blough in April, he was surveyed, along with more than a dozen prominent business figures. Many individuals had specific suggestions but generally showed considerable support. George Meany, speaking for the AFL-CIO, stressed tax cuts for lower-income brackets. Memo, "Private Groups and Individuals in Favor of a Tax Cut," Sorensen Papers, Box 59, Legislative Affairs, 1961–1964, John F. Kennedy Library, Boston.
36 Witte, *Politics and Development of the Federal Income Tax*, 158.
37 Support for the view that this legislation was destined to pass can be found in Giglio, *Presidency of John F. Kennedy*, 139.
38 Shank, *Presidential Policy Leadership*, 66.
39 The lengthy literature on Kennedy's civil rights actions now includes an increasing number of sources that have used not only interviews but also extensive archival research. Carl M. Bauer strongly emphasizes Kennedy's commitments and influence in his book *John F. Kennedy and the Second Reconstruction* (New York: Columbia University Press, 1977). Two important recent interpretations are contained in Hugh Davis Graham, *Civil Rights and the Presidency: Race and Gender in American Politics, 1960–1972* (New York: Oxford University Press, 1992); and Mark Sloan, *Calculating Visions* (New Brunswick, NJ: Rutgers University Press, 1992). Helpful recent interpretations also can be found in Irving Bernstein, *Promises Kept: John F. Kennedy's New Frontier*

(New York: Oxford University Press, 1991); and Giglio, *Presidency of John F. Kennedy*.

40 *Public Papers of the Presidents of the United States: John F. Kennedy, 1963* (Washington, DC: Government Printing Office), 468, 469.

41 Burke Marshall, "Congress, Communication, and Civil Rights," in *The Kennedy Presidency: Seventeen Intimate Perspectives of John F. Kennedy*, ed. Kenneth W. Thompson (New York: University Press of America, 1985), 71.

42 Paper, *John F. Kennedy*, 275.

43 For a review of several issues raised in this discussion, see Thomas Brown, *JFK: History of an Image* (Bloomington: Indiana University Press, 1988), ch. 5.

44 Wofford, *Of Kennedys and Kings*.

45 David S. Broder, *Changing of the Guard: Power and Leadership in America* (New York: Simon and Schuster, 1980).

46 Gerald Strober and Deborah Strober, *"Let Us Begin Anew": An Oral History of the Kennedy Presidency* (New York: HarperCollins, 1993), 272–273.

47 Michael Harrington, *The Other America: Poverty in the United States* (New York: Collier Books, 1997).

48 Mark A. Peterson, *Legislating Together: The White House and Capitol Hill from Eisenhower to Reagan* (Cambridge, MA: Harvard University Press, 1990), 241.

9 Barack Obama

A Negotiator without a Partner

In 2008, the conditions were ripe for a "throw the bums out" election. President George W. Bush's approval ratings were in the 20 percent range, the Republican brand was badly damaged, the United States was bogged down in two unpopular wars, and the economy had tanked due to a combined housing and financial crisis. On the Democratic side, Barack Obama emerged as a highly charismatic candidate, promising "hope" and "change." Republicans were outspent roughly four to one, and their standard-bearer, John McCain, ran a poor presidential campaign. These conditions should have brought about one of the biggest Democratic landslides in history. The Electoral College results exaggerated Obama's victory over McCain, 365-173, but the popular vote showed a much closer election: 53 percent to 46 percent, a comfortable victory but no blowout.

Barack Obama (served 2009–2017) thus entered office with some political capital but with many conditions—especially the economy—dragging down his opportunities for success. As promised in the election, he immediately focused on the economy and on health care reform. After a painstakingly long process, he was able to pass a good portion of what he had promised. But throughout his first term, his efforts were hampered by the Great Recession—with unemployment hovering around 9 percent and stagnant economic growth. After only one year in office, a backlash against his presidency emerged in the form of the TEA Party movement, which became the face of opposition within the Republican party. By the 2010 midterm elections, Democrats had lost their majority hold on the House of Representatives and had their hold on the Senate shaved by four seats, down to a slim majority of 53-47. Obama called the results a "shellacking" and watched his approval rating drop to around 40 percent.

Obama was able to get a stimulus bill and financial reform passed, and he succeeded in maneuvering his health care bill through Congress during the 2010 lame-duck session. However, he failed on other significant pieces of legislation, such as his jobs bill, and failed to even get his immigration reform bill introduced. The last two years of Obama's first term were

DOI: 10.4324/9781003426684-11

marked with few successes as he faced an empowered and intransigent opposition party in Congress.

Personal Characteristics

Barack Hussein Obama (1961–) was born in Honolulu, Hawai'i, to Ann Dunham (originally from Wichita, Kansas) and Barack Obama Sr. (from Kenya). His parents met while studying at the University of Hawai'i at Mānoa, where Obama Sr. was an exchange student. They were married seven months before his birth and separated a few weeks after he was born. His parents officially divorced in 1964, and Dunham remarried Lolo Sotero, an Indonesian citizen. Dunham and Barack moved to Indonesia with Sotero in 1967, where the family spent four years. During this time, Obama attended Indonesian-language grammar schools and his mother conducted homeschooling in English. Obama returned to Hawai'i with his maternal grandparents in 1971 and attended the private Punahou School. While there, Obama wrote for the school's literary journal and played on the school's state-champion varsity basketball team. Obama's father came to visit his son only once when Obama was eleven years old. In 1974, Obama's mother returned to Hawai'i for graduate studies. Between 1976 and 1977 she returned to Indonesia for fieldwork, but Obama did not join her, continuing to live with his grandparents in Honolulu. In 1979, Obama graduated from Punahou and moved to Los Angeles to attend Occidental College.[1] Obama's teenage years might have resulted in more personal upheaval and identity crises than they did if he had not spent them in Honolulu—the most culturally diverse metropolitan area in the United States. In Honolulu, mixed-race parents were the norm, and there was no dominant ethnic group.[2] Still, his identity crisis caused a bit of psychological stress, and Obama admits to having dabbled in marijuana and cocaine in his teenage years as a result.[3]

A childhood in a nontraditional family is not a sentence to low achievement. Instead, it may lead to increased personal introspection and a more crystallized sense of identity, stimulating ambition and achievement.[4] Upon moving to Los Angeles, Obama focused on his studies and was able to transfer to Columbia University in his third year. In 1983, Obama graduated from Columbia with a BA in political science and soon thereafter took a job with the New York Public Interest Research Group. In 1985, Obama moved to Chicago and spent three years as a community organizer, and this experience would later shape his views and hone his political skills. In 1988 he began his studies at Harvard Law School, where he was elected editor of the *Harvard Law Review* in 1990. He graduated *magna cum laude* the following year and returned to Chicago, where he worked for a law firm while lecturing at Chicago Law School. During this time, he

172 *The Moderate-Opportunity Presidents*

became involved in voter registration drives and by the mid-1990s turned his attention toward elective office.[5]

Career Path

Obama's first political race was in 1996 for the Illinois State Senate seat from the Third District, which comprised areas of Chicago's South Side. The seat had been held by Alice Palmer, who endorsed Obama to fill her open seat as she pursued a seat in the US Congress. Palmer failed to secure the seat in a special election and decided to challenge Obama to retain her state senate seat. But she and two other would-be challengers fell short of the signature requirement when their petitions were challenged by Obama's campaign. Obama won the Democratic primary unopposed and cruised to a landslide (82 percent) victory in the general election in the strongly Democratic district.

Obama won a two-year term in the Illinois State Senate in 1996 and needed to defend his seat in 1998. He faced no opposition in the Democratic primary and cruised to an easy general election victory, amassing 89 percent of the vote. In 2000, Obama faced his first significant electoral test as he set his eyes on Illinois' First Congressional District seat. The seat was held by Bobby Rush, who had badly lost his mayoral campaign against Richard M. Daley the year before. Rush portrayed Obama as a carpet-bagger who was out of touch with the needs of the long-term residents of Chicago. Although Obama matched Rush in fundraising, he lost by a 2-1 margin.

Obama's loss in his first contested election taught him the importance of solidifying his stance with the city's entrenched power base of African American politicians and clergy. He spent his next two years in the state senate building these political bridges as well as enhancing state funding to his district. He secured the passage of legislation that included mandatory videotaping of confessions in potential death penalty cases and an anti-profiling bill.

Obama geared up for his 2004 US Senate run early, beginning polling, fund-raising, and recruiting staff in late 2002. Although the Democratic field vying for the open seat was crowded, Obama won the March primary handily, carrying 53 percent of the vote. Obama's Republican general election opponent, Jack Ryan, was forced to withdraw due to the release of sordid details in his divorce case. Obama did not use the information against Ryan and cautioned his supporters not to do so, but the press gave the scandal a great deal of coverage. Obama's star brightened, and he was chosen to give the keynote address at the 2004 Democratic Convention—a speech that turned him into a national figure. Obama easily beat Ryan's replacement, Alan Keyes.

Obama's political rise was meteoric. He had served eight years as a state senator and two years as a US senator, and had lost only one political campaign before announcing his candidacy for president in early 2007. His primary campaign throughout 2007–2008 pitted him against a number of Democratic foes, but by the end of January 2008 the field quickly winnowed down to a race between Obama and former first lady Hillary Clinton, who was serving as US Senator from New York. Clinton proved to be a formidable opponent, and Obama only received enough delegates to secure the nomination by winning the war for Democratic "superdelegates." Obama's campaign themes of "hope" and "change," combined with his soaring rhetorical skills, were on clear display as he gave his acceptance speech in Denver at the Democratic National Convention.

In the general election, Obama faced off against longtime US Senator John McCain of Arizona. The contrast between Obama's youth and vigor and McCain's age and detachment was evident. Obama chose Delaware Senator Joe Biden as his running mate, who balanced the ticket with age and foreign policy experience. McCain chose Sarah Palin, the recently elected governor of Alaska. The McCain campaign hoped Palin would appeal to the Christian conservative wing of the party as well as to women voters. Palin was ridiculed in the press for her lack of basic policy information and her poor performances in TV interviews. But Palin wasn't the only factor working against McCain—the economy was slowing into recession, the banking industry was in crisis, housing foreclosures were increasing, and two drawn-out and expensive wars in Afghanistan and Iraq had diminished public favor with the Republican Party. Obama won the electoral vote easily, even taking the traditionally Republican electoral strongholds of Indiana, North Carolina, and Virginia.

What Manner of Man?

Barack Obama has often been characterized as cool, detached, and aloof, but at the same time charismatic, earning the nickname "No Drama Obama."[6] He is highly intelligent and often comes off as professorial. However, in private, he has been known at times to lose his temper.[7] Obama is much more interested in crafting and explaining good policy than in playing the political game of securing legislative victories. He is willing to compromise, and his tendency to indicate his openness to do so frequently angered his base of supporters who feared he gave away too much too soon.

Obama's demeanor has caused observers to label him the "Rorschach President,"[8] in that Americans projected their hopes and fears onto him. Obama himself noticed this tendency among his supporters.[9] For liberals, he was the wellspring of hope and change. For conservatives, he was a Muslim socialist from Kenya steeped in dirty Chicago-style politics, intent

174   *The Moderate-Opportunity Presidents*

on confiscating guns and trampling the Constitution.[10] In fact, a poll taken in the summer of 2012 found that a third of conservative Republicans thought Obama was a Muslim.[11] And polls show Obama to have been a deeply divisive president.

Despite rumors at the time, Obama identifies as a Christian, though he grew up in a nonreligious household. Obama's Christianity became a campaign issue in 2008 as details emerged of radical statements having been made by his pastor, Jeremiah Wright of Trinity United Church of Christ. When these statements came to light, Obama left Trinity Church and distanced himself from Wright's words.

Obama takes pride in being a "family man," trying to provide the positive father figure for his two daughters that he lacked growing up. Obama has been criticized for being too much of a family man, preferring to eat dinner with his children as opposed to dining with congressional leaders. Unlike his predecessor, Obama enjoys an occasional beer and became the first president to brew his own beer in the White House. In fact, Obama's penchant for inviting political opponents to have a beer with him at the White House was dubbed "Beer Diplomacy," reminiscent of Reagan inviting Tip O'Neill to the White House for drinks.

Policy Views

The overarching theme of Barack Obama's policy views is "fairness."[12] Obama insisted in his policy statements that all people—from suspected terrorist detainees in Guantanamo Bay to elite Wall Street bankers—play by the same set of rules. Specific policies that flowed from this belief include repealing the Bush-era tax cuts for the wealthy, upholding equal pay for equal work, providing medical coverage for all Americans, and passing rules to ensure fair play in the financial and housing markets.

Obama's stance on gay marriage was initially in opposition, but by 2012 his position had "evolved" to where he became a supporter of marriage equality. Obama's shift on the issue created the paradox of his administration simultaneously enforcing the Defense of Marriage Act while arguing against it in the courts.[13] Obama was careful to discuss issues of social justice in racially blind terms in order to not alienate white voters. His tendency to do so made some civil rights leaders question Obama's commitment to the African American community.[14]

Because Obama came to office in the middle of the greatest economic downturn since the Great Depression, many thought he would adopt New Deal-style policies. However, Obama's preferences were less grandiose. Rather than a focus on creating make-work jobs to combat unemployment, Obama saw the recession as an opportunity to retool the economy for the new century by providing assistance to businesses investing in high-technology and green energy innovations.

Challenges and Opportunities

The major challenge—and opportunity—facing Obama's presidency was the Great Recession. Normally, an economic crisis gives the president a governing opportunity, as the public demands action and other political actors look for leadership. Or as summed up by Rahm Emmanuel (Obama's first chief of staff) in his famous quote: "You never want a serious crisis to go to waste ... it's an opportunity to do things that you think you could not do before."[15] Combined with Obama's charisma, his electoral victory, and his campaign themes of hope and change, this might have been the case. However, this opportunity was limited by a huge budget deficit and a desire of many in Congress not to deepen it. George W. Bush's tax cuts and two wars had ballooned the deficit by the time Obama took office, sapping support for large spending initiatives.

With a mid-60 percent job approval rating, Obama enjoyed relatively high public support at the beginning of his term.[16] His poll numbers began to decline in the summer of 2009, and an organized opposition was born in the form of the TEA Party movement. Obama's approval rating hovered in the 40s for most of the remainder of his first term, gradually building back to just over 50 percent as his reelection drew nearer. Obama's polling numbers were not terrible, but they masked the intensity of the opposition. Stoked by the TEA Party, congressional Republicans were emboldened to resist his legislative efforts and unrelentingly attack the president.

Obama had significant opportunity in terms of the legislative setting—in the elections of 2008, he boosted the Democratic advantage in each chamber, bringing with him 21 new House members and eight new senators. The Democrats' margin in the Senate briefly reached a filibuster-proof 60-seat majority when Arlen Specter (PA) switched parties to become a Democrat. However, Democrats were never able to use their antifilibuster majority effectively as Senator Ted Kennedy was largely absent due to health issues before his death in August 2009. Obama had difficulty holding a governing coalition together, losing a few conservative Democrats on important policy matters. Worse, Republicans stood steadfastly united against him. In fact, in October 2010, Senate Minority Leader Mitch McConnell proclaimed that his number-one priority was to make Obama a one-term president. While there was some opportunity for Obama on paper, the reality was different. In the midterm election that year, Democrats lost control of the House while retaining the Senate with a narrow margin, further limiting Obama's opportunity.

A promising issue that was ripe for action when Obama took office was the Lilly Ledbetter Fair Pay Act. The legislation failed to pass in the 110th Congress but was reintroduced in January 2009, clearing both chambers a week after Obama's inauguration. The bill allowed Obama to claim an early legislative victory.

176 *The Moderate-Opportunity Presidents*

Handling two wars was a challenge for Obama. While he worked to develop an exit strategy from Iraq, he simultaneously oversaw a "surge" of troops into the war in Afghanistan. Moreover, the president failed to close the Guantanamo detention facility as he had promised, and he became deeply involved in the targeted assassination drone program. These foreign policy pressures diverted Obama's attention from his domestic policy agenda.

Leadership Style

Obama's plan to enact sweeping changes to deal with the economic crisis he inherited was often hampered by how he attempted to achieve them. Instead of building big-ticket reform packages that would instantaneously attract public and congressional attention and push them through, Obama preferred to negotiate down to basic frameworks for policies that then might be improved or altered along the way. Obama truly believed that change was incremental and that he needed to negotiate "little steps" in order to build consensus.[17] While this approach may have been the most pragmatic and realistic, it did not provide the type of transformative leadership many of the public wanted, or thought it was getting, based on Obama's lofty campaign rhetoric.

Obama's pursuit of compromise was based on both pragmatism and his campaign promise to change the tone in Washington. From a pragmatic standpoint, Obama believed that compromise produced a partnership of actors invested in a policy's success. From the campaign promise standpoint, he could not tell Americans that he planned to change the culture of Washington by ignoring the minority party and railroading legislation through unified control of Congress—something for which he criticized his predecessor.

Obama's leadership style was known to be cool, cerebral, detached, and nonconfrontational. Obama and his staff believed that they could think their way through legislative. Moreover, Obama believed that he had the ability to broker peace between the entrenched parties in Washington.[18] But Obama was not terribly active in congressional policy negotiations by most presidential standards. Except for financial reform and some last-minute bargaining on health care, Obama generally left the details of negotiating votes to congressional leadership. This reflected his reverence for Madisonian separation of powers as much as his preference to stay above the fray of the partisan fighting. The end result was compromised policy that often veered away from his initial pledges,[19] resulting in his difficulty in explaining the policies to the American people. This, in turn, allowed for misinterpretation, demonization, and the backlash brought on by the TEA Party.

Late in his first term, Obama tried to go public to put pressure on obstructionist lawmakers. But many members of Congress were more fearful of primary challenges from TEA Party-supported candidates if they were seen as too cozy with the president. Obama's last-ditch effort was to attempt to charm Republican congressional leaders. But despite his attempts at beer diplomacy, golf diplomacy, and even dinner diplomacy, Obama wasn't very effective at waging "charm offensives" with an opposition uninterested in being charmed.

The Advisory Process and Approach to Decision-Making

Prior to assuming the presidency, Obama, like some of his predecessors, had no executive experience. This caused many to question his preparation and the extent to which he would lean on campaign operatives when governing.[20] To help solve the economic crisis and to provide confidence to financial markets, Obama brought in a number of Wall Street insiders, whom many felt were to blame for the crisis. Conflicts on economic policy were a persistent characteristic of the administration.[21]

In his deliberations with advisers, Obama used multiple advocacy, but decision-making was centralized in the White House. He did not employ an "honest broker" to cull out and relay additional alternative perspectives.[22] This is not to say that deliberations were not open; in fact, they were managed by the president himself, who was careful to solicit multiple perspectives, often demanding dissent in policy discussions.[23]

Vice President Joe Biden did not wish to retain the unusual amount of power wielded by his predecessor, Dick Cheney. But neither did he want the office to return to insignificance. Biden's penchant for outspokenness and his constant questioning of policy arguments provided a devil's advocate role to assist Obama in policy making.[24] His relationship with members of the Senate proved invaluable, especially when he was able to negotiate a postponement of the debt ceiling vote and get Senate Minority Leader Mitch McConnell (R-KY) to agree to restore taxes on wealthy Americans to pre-Bush-tax-cut levels. For his efforts, Biden was known as the "McConnell Whisperer."

Early in Obama's administration, a controversy arose surrounding Obama's expanded use of "policy czars." These czars are appointed by the president and given authority over certain aspects of policy but do not have the legal authority to implement policy themselves.[25] Though the administration did not use the term "czar," the number of these advisers expanded and their existence was controversial due to the lack of Senate confirmation. The use of czars reflected Obama's concern with being at the center of policymaking and making sure he had as much high-quality policy information as possible at his disposal.

178 *The Moderate-Opportunity Presidents*

Administrative Strategies

In keeping with his campaign theme of changing the tone in Washington, Obama wanted to work with Republicans instead of moving unilaterally toward his policy goals.[26] But he was met with fierce Republican resistance and eventually felt compelled to turn to administrative strategies to achieve policy change. While Obama's use of executive orders and proclamations was on par with his predecessors in terms of numbers, they were qualitatively more sweeping.[27] Many included reversals of Bush-era executive orders, including the issues of family planning, stem cells, and organized labor.[28] Later in his presidency, Obama used an executive order to reshape immigration in line with the DREAM Act, which was languishing in Congress. In the wake of the Sandy Hook massacre, he issued 23 presidential directives to reduce gun violence.

With the slow progress of the economic recovery and the "shellacking" of the 2010 midterm elections, Obama decided a shakeup of his economic team was in order. He appointed a team that was more pragmatic and politically oriented, including Clinton administration figures that strengthened Obama's bona fides with the business community.[29]

Public Leadership

Considering Obama's formidable rhetorical powers displayed during his campaign, it seemed he would be a natural at using the bully pulpit. But his successes going public were marginal. Obama came to be known for his overreliance on his teleprompter and was much less polished without it. His first press conference fell flat, with observers describing him as overly long-winded and professorial in his answers. Obama's tendency to be overly cautious extended to his public leadership, and he often seemed led by public opinion rather than engaging in an effort to shape it, as evidenced by his "evolved" position on gay marriage.

Analysis of Obama's weekly radio address demonstrated that, compared with other recent presidents, Obama's speeches had high levels of integrative complexity—the interrelationships in the description of public policy.[30] This didn't translate well into explaining in simple terms how his policies would help average Americans. While Obama maintained the traditional rate of press conferences set by his predecessors, he provided far more one-on-one interviews than they had.[31]

Shortly after Obama took office in 2009, resistance in the form of the TEA Party began. Egged on by right-wing talk radio show hosts and FOX News, and funded by right-wing donors, these groups staged numerous protests in 2009 and 2010. "TEA" stood for "taxed enough already," but the party's agenda also included opposition to health care reform. Some noted that these issues may have been a mask for racial antipathy toward the nation's first African American president, as many members held racially antagonistic views.[32] The TEA Party was effective in holding Republican members of Congress accountable to their agenda, limiting Obama's ability to find a willing negotiating partner. In 2010, many upstart candidates donned the TEA Party's mantle and achieved primary election upsets of long-serving congressional Republicans. On the left, Obama was outflanked by the Occupy Movement protesting economic inequality and the disproportionate political power of the wealthy.

Much of the resistance to Obama's efforts at public leadership can be attributed to the nature of the times. Access to new internet media had given voice to conspiracy theorists and fringe opposition groups, including the "birther" movement that challenged Obama's citizenship. Public discourse had coarsened, and during a speech to a joint session of Congress in September 2009, Representative Joe Wilson (R-SC) angrily interrupted by yelling "You lie!" at the president when Obama insisted that illegal immigrants would not be covered under his health care proposal. Obama was not immune to this trend—when he attempted to prove that he was not detached from the Gulf of Mexico oil spill cleanup, he declared that he needed more facts to know "whose ass to kick."

The Obama team was eager to take lessons from its electoral victory, particularly the use of new media, into governance.[33] In an effort to let people's voices be heard, Obama established the Office of Public Engagement. But the office turned out to be less effective than planned, and some observers decried it as merely a front, while interest groups worked the usual backroom deals behind the facade.[34]

Congressional Leadership

Obama's "fast-start" plans for his first hundred days focused on stimulating the economy, particularly with the passage of the American Recovery and Reinvestment Act (ARRA). His strategies for dealing with policy details and negotiations varied by issue—being moderately involved with the ARRA, hands-off with health care reform until the last minute, and more deeply involved in financial reform. In each case, he tried to stay above the fray when it was dangerous and was more deeply involved when his hand was strongest.

The 2010 midterm elections caused Obama's first term to be a tale of two Congresses—some significant success with the 111th but virtually none with the 112th. Obama's way of dealing with congressional intransigence was to identify legislators facing a "permission structure" that would make them amenable to compromise—that they would face no ill effects, especially in coming elections, for compromising. Obama's approach was informed by behavioral social science literature on patterns of cooperation, and he was the first to use it. But the method could not overcome

180 *The Moderate-Opportunity Presidents*

the hyper-partisanship of the TEA Partiers in Congress, to whom John Boehner owed his speakership. Boehner simply could not broker a moderate compromise with the president in the 112th Congress.

Legislative Enactments

During Obama's first week in office, the House and Senate passed the Lilly Ledbetter Fair Pay Act, and he signed it on January 29, 2009. While the legislation did not require much effort on Obama's part, it gave him momentum going into his negotiations on his first major challenge: the stimulus bill. Despite the array of interests that quickly lined up against him, Obama achieved three major legislative victories in his first term: the economic stimulus package, health care reform, and financial reform. And though he was successful in getting these policies passed, public approval did not redound to him for his efforts as his job approval dropped during his second year in office.[35]

American Recovery and Reinvestment Act (ARRA, 2009)

The economic troubles facing Obama upon inauguration were worse than those facing any of his predecessors since FDR. Real gross domestic product (GDP) for 2008 had declined by 6.8 percent, and the unemployment rate stood at 7.7 percent when he took office.[36] Home sales had dropped precipitously, and the foreclosure crisis had begun. Obama knew that quick action was required not just to turn around the recession but to restore business and consumer confidence.

Prior to his inauguration, Obama met with congressional leaders of both parties. All agreed on the importance of stimulating the economy, with Democrats preferring a large spending bill and Republicans preferring a smaller bill based on permanent tax cuts. Although Obama's bill passed easily through the House with the Democratic majority, negotiations with Republicans in the Senate were necessary as Democrats were one vote shy of a filibuster-proof majority.

Complicating matters, Senator-elect Al Franken of Minnesota had yet to be seated due to a contested election, and Ted Kennedy was absent due to illness. This forced the administration to pick a handful of senators to sway. First, it was necessary to appease conservative Democrat Ben Nelson of Nebraska to keep him in the fold. Next, the administration sought out moderate Republican allies—Susan Collins and Olympia Snowe from Maine, and Arlen Specter of Pennsylvania. Most of the convincing was done with earmarked projects, but Specter's main concern was the size of the bill, so Obama negotiated a smaller package to his liking.[37] The bill that passed the Senate was substantially different from the House bill.

Obama dispatched Rahm Emmanuel as well as Peter Orzag, chief of the Office of Management and Budget, to negotiate with congressional leadership. The final bill was pared back to an estimated $787 billion (two-thirds spending, one-third tax cuts) before it passed on February 13, 2009. Only three Senate Republicans voted for it, and no House Republicans. Final estimates a few years later put the total cost at $862 billion over eleven years, with the heaviest expenditures in the first year.[38] Less than one month into his presidency, Obama had his first major legislative victory.

To help sell the ARRA to the public, the http://Recovery.gov website was designed to provide transparency in the awarding of contracts, as well as build support for the policy by allowing individuals to see how the money was being spent in their area. But ultimately, the stimulus became the first in a line of policies that Obama failed to adequately explain to the public. Even though one-third of the bill was tax cuts that reduced taxes on 95 percent of Americans, many mistakenly thought the bill raised their taxes.[39] At first, some Republican-leaning states blustered that they would refuse the ARRA "government handout." But the resources proved too tempting, given many states' budget problems due to declines in their tax revenue. Particularly tempting was $87 billion to help states with Medicaid, as more out-of-work people qualified. The full impact of the stimulus was muted by state reductions in spending. The end result was a policy that could have done more to hasten recovery but did ameliorate some of the worst effects of the economic downturn. In addition to strengthening the social safety net, the act also provided initiatives in science, health, infrastructure, and green energy. In order to create immediate stimulus in the economy, ARRA construction funds were designated only for "shovel ready" projects. A few of the investments in green energy companies, particularly Solyndra, failed, fueling Republican criticism.

Patient Protection and Affordable Care Act (PPACA, 2010)

Prior to Obama taking office, 15 percent of Americans lacked health insurance, and many more were dissatisfied with their coverage, with 90 percent of Americans believing the system required fundamental change.[40] A whopping 62 percent of all personal bankruptcies were attributed to medical costs.[41] The United States had the most expensive system in the world, with one in six dollars spent on health care, but health outcomes lagged behind other nations. Despite the failure of previous presidents to secure a national program, the direness of the situation presented an opportunity for Obama.

From the beginning, and to the consternation of the liberal wing of his party, Obama assured Americans that he would not support the "single payer" system (often called "socialized medicine") that exists in most other industrialized democracies. Instead, Obama left it to Congress to

182   *The Moderate-Opportunity Presidents*

work out the major details of policy. The most controversial plan was the "public option," which would allow a public insurance entity to compete against private companies, with the goal of lowering costs through competition. Obama championed this idea in speeches, but there proved to be inadequate support.

Just as with Clinton's health care reform proposal, entrenched interests quickly lined up in opposition. As legislators returned to their districts in the summer of 2009, they were met with angry outbursts at town hall meetings. Many constituents opposed to the legislation worried about nonexistent care-rationing "death panels" (a term popularized by Sarah Palin).

In Congress, Democratic leadership found it difficult to keep their own party onboard with their proposal, especially Senators Ben Nelson (D-NE) and Joe Lieberman (D-CT). In the Senate, negotiations eventually produced 60 votes to invoke cloture, and it was passed on Christmas Eve 2009. But the House and Senate bills were different enough that any compromises in conference could peel away votes, dooming the legislation.[42] Worse for Obama, Republican Scott Brown won the late Ted Kennedy's Massachusetts Senate seat in January 2010, denying the Democrats the ability to invoke cloture on a compromise bill.

A series of tricky parliamentary maneuvers were necessary to bring about the bill's passage. First, the House had to pass the Senate's version of the bill. Second, the House would pass a bill "correcting" the Senate bill to satisfy the concerns of House members. And finally, both would be bundled into a filibuster-proof budget reconciliation bill that would be passed by the Senate. The process worked by the slimmest of margins, with Obama involved in last-minute arm-twisting, including traveling with Rep. Dennis Kucinich (D-OH) onboard Air Force One to make a speech in Kucinich's district providing political cover.

The bill was signed into law on March 23, 2010, with Biden candidly remarking to Obama (over what he did not know was a live microphone) that the occasion was "a big fucking deal." Despite the fact that the final bill reflected an approach championed by the conservative Heritage Foundation, the policy was incredibly unpopular among Republicans, who repeatedly tried to repeal it. The policy headed to the Supreme Court for review, particularly the aspect of the individual insurance mandate. On June 28, 2012, the Court upheld the individual mandate but struck down mandates on states for Medicaid. Obama had won, but the policy would not be fully implemented until after his reelection, too late for him to achieve any political benefit.

Wall Street Reform and Consumer Protection Act (Dodd-Frank, 2010)

The rollback of banking regulations in the mid-1990s allowed predatory lending and a number of questionable and complex financial transactions to go unnoticed by federal regulators. The resulting subprime mortgage crisis in 2007 presaged deep recession. To fix the problem, legislation known as "Dodd-Frank" was designed to prevent future bailouts of banks that had become "too big to fail" by enhancing federal oversight of financial trading markets and protecting consumers.

By the time Obama turned his attention to financial reform, the sector had partially recovered thanks to the Troubled Asset Relief Program (TARP) bailout, making reform seem less imperative. Moreover, the industry was well situated to mount a coordinated opposition to his proposals.[43] Obama intended for his administration to be deeply involved in the details of policymaking from the beginning, and the bill was drafted by the Treasury Department.[44]

A controversial aspect to the legislation was the "Volcker Rule," advocated by former Fed chief Paul Volcker. The rule would reinstate the Glass-Steagall (1933) provision that prohibited commercial banking from dealing in securities. The measure met with resistance from the industry and its lobbyists and was even opposed by Treasury Secretary Timothy Geithner. Eventually, the Volcker Rule was included after Obama came out in support of it, but it was watered down to allow banks a percentage of dealings in securities. The bill became law on July 21, 2010.

Obama and Congress

In addition to the three major policy successes, Obama had a number of more modest ones. These included child health care, hate crimes, public lands management, smoking prevention, extension of unemployment benefits, 9/11 first responders' health care, and the repeal of the military's "Don't Ask Don't Tell" policy. Obama achieved little significance during the second half of his first term.

Obama's dealings with Congress ranged from hands-off in some instances to being more deeply involved in others. His deference to congressional leadership led to the passage of financial reform but the death of immigration and energy reform.[45] Aside from financial reform, Obama preferred to stay above the partisan fray of Congress, out of concern for either his reputation or his Madisonian respect for separation of powers.

The Bush tax cuts were set to expire on December 31, 2010, meaning taxes would be raised on all Americans. Both sides wanted to continue the tax cuts for low- and moderate-income earners, but Obama wanted to raise the rate on those with incomes over $250,000 back to the Clinton-era rates. Republicans, emboldened by their 2010 election victory, would not budge during the lame-duck session. The tax rates were extended for all until 2012, with an extension in unemployment benefits and a payroll tax cut.

184   *The Moderate-Opportunity Presidents*

In late July 2011, Obama and congressional leaders engaged in what became known as the "debt ceiling showdown." Republicans in the House of Representatives were emboldened by the TEA Party caucus to force a bargain on taxing and spending by using the debt ceiling extension as a bargaining chip. They demanded that for the debt limit to be extended, an equal amount of spending must be cut from the federal budget. Moreover, Republicans were not willing to accept revenue increases (i.e., tax increases) to fill the gap. Obama was hamstrung by the left wing of his party, while House Speaker Boehner was hostage to TEA Partiers.[46] Obama and Boehner attempted to broker a "grand bargain" that would extend the debt ceiling while bringing the federal budget into balance over the long term, but this failed. Instead, the sides negotiated $1 trillion in cuts over the next ten years, but that was only half of what was needed. Harry Reid proposed that a "supercommittee" be formed to find the rest of the spending cuts. The deal extended the debt ceiling but created mandatory sequestration as the supercommittee failed to find the needed cuts.

The failed grand bargain of early August 2011 created mandatory sequestration as of January 1, 2013. At that time, the Bush tax cuts were already set to expire for all individuals, and the sequestration would cause federal spending to be slashed by 2–3 percent across the board. This deadline was set so that both parties would take the issue seriously after the election. Republicans wanted to protect defense spending and Democrats wanted to protect social programs. Obama, with Biden's help, then negotiated a tax increase for those making over $400,000 as part of a deal to extend the debt ceiling. The sequester was kicked down the road until March 1, 2013, when it went into effect.

Obama confronted an immigration system widely seen as "broken." Republicans had failed to achieve immigration reform in the George W. Bush years and had begun using illegal immigration as an issue on which to attack Obama. In 2013, a group of senators known as the "Gang of Eight" proposed a comprehensive immigration reform bill. While passing the senate with a strong majority vote of 68-32, House Speaker John Boehner refused to act on the bill. After failing to make headway with Congress, Obama devised an administrative strategy. Obama announced a "deferred action" plan that would allow approximately half of illegal immigrants to remain in the United States (a previous strategy employed by George H. W. Bush). The DACA (Deferred Action for Childhood Arrivals) plan affected approximately 1.5 million people. Obama argued that by "acting where Congress has failed… [he hoped] to work with both parties to pass a more permanent legislative solution. And the day I sign that bill into law, the actions I take will no longer be necessary."[47] That day never came for Obama.

Occasionally, Congress gave the president the opportunity to succeed and to take credit for policy. One case was the Lilly Ledbetter Act, another was the repeal of the "Don't Ask Don't Tell" rule on gay service in the military. In the latter case, Congress gave Obama political cover by requiring a Pentagon study into the effects on military preparedness. Once the study was in hand, Obama was able to take credit.

But more often than not, Obama failed to sell his policies to the public. For example, the more people knew about the provisions of the Affordable Care Act, such as the provision to allow adults under 26 years of age to remain on their parents' policies and the prohibition against discrimination based on preexisting conditions, the more they liked it. But Obama wasn't able to make his case. Obama bears part of this responsibility, but much of it lies with the advent of partisan niche media, which fueled the TEA Party resistance and the resulting conflation of presidential job approval with partisanship.[48]

An Assessment

The Great Recession, as it came to be known, was the worst economic downturn in US history since the Great Depression. The stimulus stopped the recession from becoming worse, but that sentiment was cold comfort to out-of-work Americans. The economic problems facing the nation were severe and should have given the president more opportunity if he hadn't been faced with a Congress cautious about borrowing and reluctant to bargain with a Democrat in the White House. Obama's economic policies had a positive impact on the economy, but they did not have a similar effect on his job approval.[49]

Efforts to stimulate the economy in addition to the ARRA included the Home Affordable Modification Program to limit foreclosures (but did not include a moratorium). The Cash for Clunkers program was also supposed to stimulate the economy through new auto sales. But these cautious efforts were not bold enough to deal with the magnitude of the economic crisis, and recovery was glacial.

While some consider the number of pieces of landmark legislation passed in Obama's first two years to be remarkable, the three major policies were not as bold as the president wanted. They were compromised pieces of legislation that ended up being quite moderate and inadequate to deal with the economic downturn and the health care crisis. Additionally, Obama failed to turn his policy successes into political capital. In fact, there was a backlash among states in terms of their resistance to ARRA and health care, with some states' attorneys general hinting at nullification. Obama was not directly responsible for TARP, although he did vote for it as senator, but he was associated with it as it was implemented primarily on his watch. A majority of Americans felt that the loans to large financial institutions had hurt the economy more than they had helped. Americans were evenly divided on the ARRA and felt that the auto bailouts and bank

186 *The Moderate-Opportunity Presidents*

regulations were helpful.[50] Ultimately, Obama's good deeds did not go unpunished.

With intransigence in Congress, Obama looked to administrative tools to achieve a greater measure of policy success.[51] In a move that many viewed as unpopular, the Obama administration subsidized loans to the struggling US auto industry to the tune of $62 billion—on top of the $13.4 billion authorized by the Bush administration. The loans helped the auto industry rebound, and many of them were paid back early and in full. Using $4.35 billion from the stimulus, Obama funded "Race to the Top" grants to encourage K-12 education reform, providing incentives to the underfunded No Child Left Behind policy of the Bush administration.

Obama's economic concerns in his first term led him to de-prioritize environmental issues, even though climate change was a deep personal concern of his.[52] Obama's administrative efforts, along with the signing of the Paris Climate Agreement in his second term, would be quickly undone by Donald Trump. In Obama's last two years, Senate Majority Leader Mitch McConnell would stall Obama's judicial nominations, including a critical swing seat on the Supreme Court. This allowed for the filling of the judiciary with Trump appointees, who would work to undo Obama's administrative legacy.

Obama was best, though, when helping the nation through crisis. Even though the Gulf oil spill lasted a prolonged time, and Republicans tried to label it "Obama's Katrina," the president was seen as successful in managing the catastrophe. And with his response to the devastation caused by Hurricane Sandy, Obama won the praise of staunch Republican governor Chris Christie. At certain times in his presidency, when times were the worst, Obama's public leadership helped an anxious nation.

"No Drama Obama" seemed at times to lack the fire in his belly, and many working-class Americans felt left out of a recovery that seemed to prioritize Wall Street, big banks, and the auto companies. President Obama did not speak to those who felt left out and left behind, opening the door for Donald Trump to emerge—speaking directly to this audience and drawing working-class voters away from the Democrats.

Notes

1 See Stanley A. Renshon, *Barack Obama and the Politics of Redemption* (New York: Routledge, 2012), 285–286.

2 See Michael Haas, ed., *Barack Obama, the Aloha Zen President: How a Son of the 50th State May Revitalize America Based on 12 Multicultural Principles* (Westport, CT: Praeger, 2011).

3 Barack Obama, *Dreams from My Father: A Story of Race and Inheritance* (New York: Times Books, 1995), 93; and Katharine Q. Seelye, "Barack Obama, Asked about Drug History, Admits He Inhaled," *New York Times*, October 24, 2006.

4 See Renshon, ch. 7.
5 Ibid., 287–288.
6 Ibid., 3.
7 Ibid.
8 These include Stanley Renshon, Charles Kolb, Gary Younge, and Deepak Chopra, among others.
9 Barack Obama, *The Audacity of Hope* (New York: Three Rivers Press, 2006), 11.
10 See Martin A. Parlett, *Demonizing a President: The "Foreignization" of Barack Obama* (Santa Barbara, CA: Praeger, 2014).
11 The Pew Forum on Religion and Public Life, "Little Voter Discomfort with Romney's Mormon Religion, Only about Half Identify Obama as Christian," July 26, 2012, www.pewforum.org/2012/07/26/2012-romney-mormonism-obamas-religion/.
12 See chapter 5 of Renshon for a discussion of how Obama's morality of "fairness" ties to his political ambition.
13 Peter Baker, "For Obama, Tricky Balancing Act in Enforcing Defense of Marriage Act," *New York Times*, March 28, 2013.
14 See Ama Mazama and Molefi Kete Asante, eds., *Obama: Political Frontiers and Racial Agency* (Washington, DC: CQ Press, 2009); and Matt Bai, "Is Obama the End of Black Politics?" *New York Times*, August 6, 2008.
15 Originally quoted in an interview with the *Wall Street Journal*, November 19, 2008.
16 "Presidential Job Approval Center," *Gallup*, www.gallup.com/poll/124922/Presidential-Approval-Center.aspx.
17 Justin S. Vaughn, "No Place for a Community Organizer: Barack Obama's Leadership of Congress," in *The Obama Presidency: Change and Continuity*, ed. Andrew J. Dowdle, Dirk C. Van Raemdonck, and Robert Maranto (New York: Routledge, 2011), 112.
18 Sasha Abramsky, *Inside Obama's Brain* (New York: Portfolio, 2009).
19 See Vaughn, "No Place for a Community Organizer," 113–114; Lawrence R. Jacobs and Theda Skocpol, *Health Care Reform and American Politics: What Everyone Needs to Know* (New York: Oxford University Press, 2010).
20 See Edward Klein, *The Amateur: Barack Obama in the White House* (Washington, DC: Regnery, 2012).
21 See Ron Suskind, *Confidence Men: Wall Street, Washington, and the Education of a President* (New York: HarperCollins, 2011); and Robert Kuttner, *A Presidency in Peril: The Inside Story of Obama's Promise, Wall Street's Power, and the Struggle to Control Our Economic Future* (White River Junction, CT: Chelsea Green, 2010).
22 James P. Pfiffner, "Decision Making in the Obama White House," *Presidential Studies Quarterly* 41 (June 2011): 244–262.
23 Ibid., 260.
24 Richard M. Yon, "Vice President Joe Biden: Perpetuating Influence or Restoring Historical Insignificance?" in *The Obama Presidency: A Preliminary Assessment*, ed. Robert P. Watson, Jack Covarrubias, Tom Lansford, and Douglas M. Brattebo (Albany: State University of New York Press, 2012), 377.
25 Justin S. Vaughn and José D. Villalobos, "The Policy Czar Debate," in *The Obama Presidency: A Preliminary Assessment*, ed. Robert P. Watson, Jack Covarrubias, Tom Lansford, and Douglas M. Brattebo (Albany: State University of New York Press, 2012), 317–318.

188 *The Moderate-Opportunity Presidents*

26 Graham G. Dodds, "Unilateral Directives," in *The Obama Presidency: A Preliminary Assessment*, ed. Robert P. Watson, Jack Covarrubias, Tom Lansford, and Douglas M. Brattebo (Albany: State University of New York Press, 2012), ch. 21.

27 Ibid., 345.

28 Ibid., 346–347.

29 M. Stephen Weatherford, "Economic Crisis and Political Change: A New New Deal?" in *The Obama Presidency: Appraisals and Prospects*, ed. Bert A. Rockman, Andrew Rudalevige, and Colin Campbell (Washington, DC: CQ Press, 2012), 317.

30 Peter Suedfeld, Ryan W. Cross, and Jelena Brcic, "Two Years of Ups and Downs: Barack Obama's Patterns of Integrative Complexity, Motive Imagery, and Values," *Political Psychology* 32 (November 2011): 1007–1033.

31 Martha Joynt Kumar, "Continuity and Change in White House Communications: President Obama Meets the Press," in *The Obama Presidency: Change and Continuity*, ed. Andrew J. Dowdle, Dirk C. Van Raemdonck, and Robert Maranto (New York: Routledge, 2011), 91–106.

32 For a discussion, see Theda Skocpol and Vanessa Williamson, *The TEA Party and the Remaking of Republican Conservatism* (New York: Oxford University Press, 2012), 69.

33 Diane J. Heith, "Obama and the Public Presidency: What You Got Here Won't Get You There," in *The Obama Presidency: Appraisals and Prospects*, ed. Bert A. Rock-man, Andrew Rudalevige, and Colin Campbell (Washington, DC: CQ Press, 2012), 123–148.

34 Lawrence R. Jacobs, "The Privileges of Access: Interest Groups and the White House," in *The Obama Presidency: Appraisals and Prospects*, ed. Bert A. Rockman, Andrew Rudalevige, and Colin Campbell (Washington, DC: CQ Press, 2012), 149–170.

35 Gary C. Jacobson, "Legislative Success and Political Failure: The Public's Reaction to Barack Obama's Early Presidency," *Presidential Studies Quarterly* 41 (June 2011): 100.

36 Ted Gayer, "Economic Policymaking during the Great Recession," in *The Obama Presidency: Change and Continuity*, ed. Andrew J. Dowdle, Dirk C. Van Raem-donck, and Robert Maranto (New York: Routledge, 2011), 137.

37 Weatherford, "Economic Crisis and Political Change," 309.

38 Gayer, "Economic Policymaking during the Great Recession," 146.

39 Sean J. Savage, "The First Hundred Days: FDR and Obama," in *The Obama Presidency: A Preliminary Assessment*, ed. Robert P. Watson, Jack Covarrubias, Tom Lansford, and Douglas M. Brattebo (Albany: State University of New York Press, 2012), 317–318.

40 Joel Roberts, "Poll: The Politics of Health Care," *CBS News*, June 14, 2010, www.cbsnews.com/2100-500160_162-2528357.html.

41 David U. Himmelstein, Deborah Thorne, Elizabeth Warren, and Steffie Woolhandler, "Medical Bankruptcy in the United States, 2007: Results of a National Study," *American Journal of Medicine* 122 (August 2009): 699–788.

42 See Mark Carl Rom, "President Obama's Health Care Reform: The Inevitable Impossible," in *The Obama Presidency: Change and Continuity*, ed. Andrew J. Dowdle, Dirk C. Van Raemdonck, and Robert Maranto (New York: Routledge, 2011), 159.

43 Weatherford, "Economic Crisis and Political Change," 311.

44 Ibid., 312.

45 Vaughn, "No Place for a Community Organizer," 114.

46 See Bob Woodward, *The Price of Politics* (New York: Simon and Schuster, 2012); and David Corn, *Showdown: The Inside Story of How Obama Fought Back against Boehner, Cantor, and the Tea Party* (New York: HarperCollins, 2012).

47 Quoted in Joaquin Jay Gonzalez, *Immigration and America's Cities* (Jefferson, NC: McFarland, 2016), 277.

48 See Kathleen Hall Jamieson and Joseph N. Cappella, *Echo Chamber: Rush Limbaugh and the Conservative Media Establishment* (New York: Oxford University Press, 2010); Natalie Jomini Stroud, *Niche News: The Politics of News Choice* (New York: Oxford University Press, 2011); and Raphael Small and Robert M. Eisinger, "Whither Presidential Approval," *Presidential Studies Quarterly* 50, no. 4 (December 2020): 845–863.

49 M. Stephen Weatherford, "The Wages of Competence: Obama, the Economy, and the 2010 Midterm Elections," *Presidential Studies Quarterly* 42, no. 1 (March 2012): 8–39.

50 Pew Research Center for the People & the Press, "Auto Bailout Now Backed, Stimulus Divisive," February 23, 2012, www.people-press.org/2012/02/23/autobailout-now-backed-stimulus-divisive/; see Jacobson, "Legislative Success and Political Failure," 226.

51 Andrew Rudalevige, "The Contemporary Presidency: The Obama Administrative Presidency: Some Late-Term Patterns," *Presidential Studies Quarterly* 46, no. 4 (December 2016): 868–890.

52 David M. Shafie, *The Administrative Presidency and the Environment: Policy Leadership and Retrenchment from Clinton to Trump* (New York: Routledge, 2020), 18.

10 Donald Trump
Outsider, Disruptor, Norm-Buster, Dissembler

The goal of this book is to evaluate and ultimately rank how successful different presidents were in achieving their domestic policy goals. Each president has brought different strengths, weaknesses, baggage, agendas, operating styles, and hopes to the White House. Donald Trump presents something of a conundrum for scholars. His background, goals, rhetoric, and style of leadership were far different than any other president. When comparing Trump with other presidents, it often feels like comparing apples to oranges.

Donald Trump won the 2016 election in one of the most stunning upsets in presidential history. Virtually no one, including those in Trump's own campaign, thought he would win. And while he lost the popular vote to rival Hillary Clinton by roughly 2.9 million votes, he won the key swing states of Pennsylvania, Michigan, and Wisconsin by a combined 77,774 votes, delivering an electoral college victory. How would this president, the first with no governmental experience, execute an agenda in this situation to fulfill his promise to "Make America Great Again"?

Personal Characteristics

Donald John Trump (1946–) was born in Queens, New York. He attended Fordham University in New York, transferred to the University of Pennsylvania, and graduated with a bachelor's degree. Shortly thereafter, he became president of his father's real estate company, and renamed it The Trump Organization. He has written 19 books, mostly how-to books on wealth creation. Throughout his career in business, he would repeatedly comment on political issues, often on the Howard Stern radio program. Always a showman and a salesman, Trump realized early on that hyperbole and exaggeration were effective tools for garnering attention, and Trump developed a public persona that was flamboyant and often overblown.

Trump's oversized personality and razor-sharp tongue led some to believe that in due time, Trump would have to become less belligerent

DOI: 10.4324/9781003426684-12

Donald Trump 191

and more presidential—that Washington would tame Donald Trump. But Trump refused to be tamed or silenced; in fact, he tamed nearly the entire Republican party.

Career Path

Donald Trump took a very unusual career path to the presidency. He neither served in the military nor had he ever held an elected or governmental office. Trump had spent his entire adult life running the family real estate business that his father started. In that capacity, Trump had a bumpy financial ride. His real estate and casino business declared bankruptcy six times. Trump fared better when he licensed his name to others to run businesses featuring the Trump "brand." Over the years, Trump was best at building the Trump brand, self-promoting, and selling his name as a lifestyle to be purchased.

As the head of a family business, Trump prided himself as being the "decider." He did not have to deal with or answer to a board of directors or stockholders, only family members who primarily were his children. He did have to negotiate "deals" and he claimed to be a master dealmaker. One of his more lucrative ventures was to have ghost writers produce books under his authorship, mostly dealing with self-promotion, or providing self-help books on how to win, how to make a deal, and how to make money. He often seemed more media gadfly than businessman. One of his most significant ventures was to be the face and voice of the television show, *The Apprentice*, where he developed his famous tag line: "YOU'RE FIRED!" The television program brought Trump into the living rooms of millions of Americans each week, making him a media star.

Donald Trump was also a casino owner, owned the New Jersey Generals football team of the defunct United States Football League, owned the Miss Universe, Miss USA, and Miss Teen USA pageants. He also started Trump University, which sold real estate training courses priced from $1,500 to $35,000.[1] In 2013, the state of New York filed a $40 million civil suit against Trump University, claiming the company made false statements and defrauded consumers. In 2017, Trump agreed to payments to settle the case. He also started his own private charity, The Donald J. Trump Foundation. In 2018, the attorney general of New York filed suit against the Foundation and against President Trump and his adult children. In November of 2019, a New York judge ordered Trump to pay $2 million to several charities for misusing Foundation funds (some Foundation money went to financing Trump's presidential campaign).[2]

Over the years, Trump had toyed publicly with the idea of running for president, promoting a bogus "birther" campaign, accusing Barack

192   *The Moderate-Opportunity Presidents*

Obama of having been born outside the United States. He made his official announcement on June 16, 2015, which included a tirade against immigrants and Mexico. Many surmised Trump's motivation was to get even after Barack Obama had mocked him at the 2011 White House Correspondent's dinner (Trump denies this).[3] Nonetheless, it was curious how determined Trump was to undo all of Obama's accomplishments once he achieved office.

What Manner of Man?

Donald Trump is a self-promoter who has exhibited narcissistic qualities and is a serial liar.[4] He acts in aggressive and bullying ways, often calling his rivals vile names and repeatedly insulting women by demeaning their appearance. He was married three times, and during the 2016 presidential campaign, paid several women *not* to tell their stories of marital infidelity with him. During the campaign, a tape was released from the television program *Access Hollywood*, wherein Trump was caught on tape advocating and excusing sexual assault.

One can also see in Donald Trump's rhetoric a tendency to over-personalize issues and attack anyone who questions or challenges him. During the Republican primaries, he engaged in repeated personal attacks against his rivals, calling them names (e.g., Little Marco, or Lyin' Ted). This overly hot rhetoric followed Trump into the White House where he continued to verbally belittle opponents and rivals (e.g., Little Rocket Man, for North Korea's dictator, Kim Jong Un). Trump's attack style may have served him well in business but was of limited utility in politics. His adversarial style made bargaining and compromising—the deal-making which Trump claimed to be the master of—difficult to impossible.

Numerous amateur and professional psychologists have tried to come to grips with the personality and alleged personality disorders Trump exhibits. And while it is improper to do diagnosis at a distance (known as the "Goldwater Rule" in psychology, dating back to psychologists who attempted to analyze the 1964 Republican candidate),[5] numerous critics (including his niece) have asserted that Trump exhibits narcissistic personality disorder.[6] It is not possible to confirm these suspicions, and Trump the salesman may have demonstrated a style of governing that is built on the belief that by being demanding and self-centered, he actually helps himself stake out a strong position and gain the political upper-hand.[7]

Policy Views

As a newcomer to the national policy scene, Donald Trump did not so much have policy goals and views, as feelings, instincts, and attitudes. He was a grievance collector and many of what emerged as his policy views stemmed from these grievances. Trump was a populist and a nationalist and viewed the U.S. government as a business that had made many bad deals. What specific views he had were often expressions of what he thought his 2016 electoral coalition wanted to hear. To that end, he reversed the pro-choice abortion position he had taken earlier in his life.[8]

The 2016 election was the first post-Obama election, and after eight years in office, some voters were desperate for a change. Candidate Trump reached out to these disgruntled voters and promised to become their champion. He particularly spoke to the resentment of voters who felt economic and status anxiety as they watched women and people of color rising in American society.[9] He signaled his views on race by running an aggressive campaign against immigrants, promised to "build a wall" to keep Mexican "rapists and criminals" out of the United States, and insisted that he would make Mexico pay for the wall. He also promised to re-create industrial jobs the United States had lost to China over the prior decades. Trump became a grievance candidate, speaking to the resentments and fears of white voters in a way that prior national figures had only insinuated in the past.[10] Where President Barack Obama worked to create a post-racial America, Donald Trump worked to gin up racial resentments. Combined with activating nationalism, sexism, and appealing to religious identities, this approach proved to be an effective approach to running for president.[11]

Donald Trump played to the anger and resentment of voters during his campaign mega-rallies. His mean-spirited, authoritarian message was punctuated by his promise to pay for the legal fees of anyone who physically attacked protestors at his rallies (he later reneged on the promise).[12] He even childishly mocked a reporter with a disability at one rally.[13]

Donald Trump's voter coalition represented a mix of old Republican faithful (though many traditional Republican leaders identified as "Never Trumpers"), angry white voters, newly enfranchised white supremacists, and traditionally Democratic white working-class voters. This coalition became known as "the base," and it would be deeply loyal to Trump throughout his term and thereafter. Trump recognized this loyalty early on, saying during the 2016 campaign "I could stand in the middle of 5th Avenue and shoot somebody and I wouldn't lose voters."[14]

Challenges and Opportunities

Although Donald Trump came to office having lost the popular vote, he rode a tide of public dissatisfaction with government and traditional politicians. In fact, one can say that, combined with Democratic-Socialist Bernie Sanders's near-upset victory over Hillary Clinton in the Democratic primary, 2016 was a "smash the system" type of election. In fact, 12 percent

194 *The Moderate-Opportunity Presidents*

of Sanders' primary supporters voted for Trump in the general election.[15] The public mood was decidedly anti-establishment.

To compound problems, the new president's inaugural address was dark, confrontational, macabre, and a direct warning (or threat) to the old elite—many of whom were seated right behind the new president. With his new constituency, Trump was determined to crush the old order and establish a new "America First" approach to governing. Critics often referred to the speech as the "American Carnage" speech.[16] The speech was so unusual for an inaugural address that it caused former President George W. Bush to remark that it was "some strange shit."[17]

The legislative setting was advantageous to Trump, with Republicans continuing to enjoy majorities in both the House and the Senate. However, the two-vote margin in the Senate promised to make legislating difficult. Worse yet for Trump, Republicans lost six House seats and two Senate seats in the 2016 election, earning him no presidential coattails. Republicans in Congress had done little to tee up any promising issues for the new president, other than a promise to "repeal and replace" Obamacare. Republicans had no plan on the "replace" aspect of the promise, and Trump only ambiguously promised "something terrific" during his campaign.[18]

Donald Trump inherited a strong and growing economy. While the nation was still running a deficit, the size of deficits had decreased markedly over Obama's term in office.[19] Trump made China's rise, and consequent loss of U.S. jobs, a key issue in his campaign, forcing it onto his foreign policy agenda. Terrorism by the Islamic State remained a threat, and Trump promised "a total and complete shutdown of Muslims entering the United States until our country's representatives can figure out what is going on."[20] Beyond these foreign policy issues forced onto the agenda by Trump, the war in Afghanistan continued to be a lingering problem, as did North Korea's pursuit of nuclear weapons and ballistic missile technology.

Leadership Style

Donald Trump's leadership can best be described as "a bull in a China shop." He was a norm-busting disrupter who was uninterested in the niceties of civil interaction or working within the established order.[21] He slept very little, yet he spent hours on end watching television, tweeting, and phoning friends, instead of engaging in presidential duties (time blocked off as "Executive Time" in his official calendar).[22] Trump demanded loyalty from his advisors and appointees,[23] and was notoriously thin-skinned when criticized, to the extent of attempting to use the power of his office to silence critics.[24]

Advisory Structure and Decision-Making

As Trump prepared to take power, critics worried that his hotel business empire could create conflicts of interest in his decision-making. Trump did little to assuage these concerns. Unlike prior presidents who had put their assets into blind trusts, Trump asserted that he would have no interest in his businesses as he would turn them over to his sons to manage and that his sons would not discuss business or national policy matters with him.[25] Trump's further assertions that he would not benefit from foreign nationals staying at his hotels and resorts in order to curry favor rang hollow with critics, and resulted in two lawsuits asserting violations of the emoluments clause of the constitution (the cases were dismissed by the Supreme Court).[26] Questions surrounding nepotism in elevating his daughter Ivanka and his son-in-law Jared Kushner into high positions in the administration (and their coincidental economic windfalls in their own business dealings) cast a pall on the administration's ethics and independence.[27]

Team Trump mangled the process of the presidential transition. Chris Christie had been managing the transition but was fired and replaced with Trump's son-in-law Jared Kushner after the election. When Christie was ousted, Trump confidants Michael Flynn and Steve Bannon gleefully tossed his binders of information on potential administration picks into the dumpster.[28] Kushner had to start from scratch to make good on Trump's promises to "drain the swamp" and hire "the best people." By inauguration day, there were large numbers of important staff and agency positions unfilled, and the policy agenda seemed confused and in limbo.[29]

As president, Donald Trump believed he did not need much help from a staff to advise him on issues. He has called himself a "stable genius" and he rarely relied on written reports and evidence when making up his mind. In fact, advisors were forced to alter the format of presidential briefings so he would read them—making them shorter, using visual aids, and featuring his name repeatedly in the memos in order to keep him interested.[30]

Upon leaving the administration, Trump aides painted unflattering images of the workings of the Trump White House and of the president himself. Advisors fretted over Trump's lack of knowledge of what constituted inappropriate or even illegal actions. Staff Secretary Rob Porter said that "A third of my job was trying to react to some of the really dangerous ideas that [Trump] had and try to give him reasons to believe that maybe they weren't such good ideas."[31]

Tell-all books from former Trump staff members became a cottage industry, with each revealing more and more chaos and dysfunction in the White House.[32] It is no wonder that his White House had the highest staff turnover rate of any modern president.[33]

196 *The Moderate-Opportunity Presidents*

Administrative Strategies

Donald Trump often resorted to executive authority to expand his power and achieve his policy goals. It did not always go well, but it was a strategy that was compatible with Trump's style, and one that recognized his weaknesses as a legislative president and consensus-builder.[34]

President Trump had an expansive view of his executive authority. Article II, he often said, gave him the authority to do whatever he wished.[35] He saw himself as head of a "unitary executive" that gave him total control of the executive branch, unencumbered by Congress, the courts, or shared government authority. This conception of power was certain to conflict with the interests, powers, and needs of the other branches. Consequently, Trump faced considerable pushback from Congress, the courts, and various states' attorneys general (especially California, which filed over 100 lawsuits against the Trump administration).

Trump recognized he would have difficulty getting his agenda through Congress, especially after the midterm elections when the Republicans lost control of the House. Trump therefore relied heavily on an administrative route to making policy. However, the setbacks with the presidential transition severely limited Trump's effectiveness in his first year.[36] On his own authority, he pulled out of international agreements (e.g., Paris Climate Accords, Iran nuclear agreement), issued executive orders (on travel bans, and immigration issues), and relied on executive authority to "go it alone" where possible, with a particular focus on undoing Obama's accomplishments.[37] Due to Republican enablers in Congress, Trump managed to get away with numerous power grabs.

The "go it alone" strategy was not the invention of President Trump, but he used it aggressively and with purpose. Conservative writer Rich Lowry noted at the time that "The Trump administration has been exhaustingly eventful, but almost none of the events have involved Congress," adding that "Until further notice, this is the American model—government by and of the president. We live in an age of unilateral rule."[38]

At times, Trump's inexperience and inattention to administrative leadership worked against him. . He hired and fired frequently, demanded total loyalty, refused to be guided by data or science, alienated experienced officials, publicly demeaned others (as he did to his first Attorney General Jeff Sessions), all of which created a "hollow executive branch."

Trump overtly politicized an already political administrative team. Constitutionally, executive branch employees are to serve the President, but also be bound by their constitutional oaths. But Donald Trump only wanted loyalty. He even said that those working for him would be pardoned if they broke the law in serving the will of the President.[39] No president politicized the Department of Justice more than did President Trump, with the willing support of Attorney General William Barr. Barr had been a cheerleader for an extreme version of the unitary executive, and openly used the levers of justice to help the President and hurt critics of the administration, (as was the case when Barr previewed the release of the Mueller Report by sanitizing the findings and declaring Trump innocent).[40] When federal employees objected, as did many Inspectors General, Trump fired them and found a willing replacement who would do the President's bidding. Trump kept many high-level positions vacant or filled by temporary, "acting," heads in order to ensure loyalty and flexibility.[41]

Public Leadership

Donald Trump loved an audience and fed on their adoring and rapt attention. He came to life when addressing a rally or large group. To see him at rallies with his loyal base was to see him in his element. They adored him and he performed for them. While Donald Trump wasn't the first candidate to use Twitter in his campaigns, he was undoubtedly the most effective. Trump knew that the more outrageous his claims, the more media attention he would create. He enjoyed watching the likes and re-tweets going up "like a rocket" when he "put out a beauty" of a post.[42] It has been estimated that Trump was able to generate $5 billion in free media attention during the 2016 campaign, much of it due to his Twitter posts.[43] But Twitter wasn't just a way for Trump to generate broadcast media coverage; he used it frequently as a way to reach out directly to his constituency without the filtering effect of the mainstream media—which he often characterized as peddling "fake news."

After the election and before his inauguration, Trump held eight "victory rallies," in key swing states that helped deliver the presidency to him.[44] He continued this attack-style politics as president. Unlike virtually all other presidents, Trump based his public rhetoric on ginning up conflict and criticism. Both during his campaign and as president, Trump often made incendiary comments, used foul language, and almost always demeaned opponents and rivals. Such conflictual language divided the nation but unified his base.

Trump continued to use his Twitter account as his presidential "bully pulpit."[45] He defended its use by tweeting: "My use of social media is not Presidential—it's MODERN DAY PRESIDENTIAL."[46] He also used Twitter as a means to govern, using it to make several "official" governmental proclamations.[47] His frequent deletions of tweets caused great concern among those worried about erasure of the public record.[48] On January 6, following his supporters' attack on the US Capitol, Twitter suspended Trump's account, citing a risk of further incitement to violence.[49] Trump claimed censorship and unsuccessfully sued to be reinstated, with his case being thrown out by the Supreme Court.[50]

198　*The Moderate-Opportunity Presidents*

During his presidency, Donald Trump never rose above 50 percent in popularity. Every other president since these polls were taken reached over 50 percent often, but Trump seemed to always fluctuate between 41 and 45 percent. Unlike other presidents, his popularity seemed somewhat immune to good or bad news. In terms of his job approval, Trump's highest ratings were the lowest in history, but his numbers never fell very low. His low ceiling but high floor reflected the divisiveness of his presidency as well as the blind loyalty of his base.

While Trump took aim at the mainstream media, he maintained a critical ally in FOX News. Trump would often call in to FOX news shows live during his "executive time" to explain his positions as well as to air his grievances. At the end of his term, when Trump downplayed the COVID pandemic, FOX News was complicit in denigrating public health measures that might have otherwise saved lives.[51]

Congressional Leadership

Donald Trump touted his skills at deal-making, and even wrote (with the help of a ghostwriter)[52] a best-selling book titled *Trump: The Art of the Deal*.[53] Many thought these deal-making abilities would translate into success in bargaining with members of Congress. However, Trump did not have a robust legislative agenda beyond tax cuts, repealing Obamacare, and funding his wall on the border with Mexico. He did not like negotiating with Congressional leaders, and often left the heavy lifting to Republican members in Congress. In contrast to Eisenhower, who exhibited a hidden-handed brand of leadership, Trump exhibited an absentee brand of leadership regarding Congress.

Republican lawmakers in Congress were eager to act on improving U.S. infrastructure, passing comprehensive immigration reform, and repealing and replacing Obamacare. Members received virtually no help or guidance from the administration on any of these issues. It seemed that the White House was promising every week that it was "Infrastructure week," although there was no action to go along with the proclamation. Trump's plan of "something terrific" to replace Obamacare never materialized, and efforts to repeal it fell short when Senator John McCain gave the effort a dramatic thumbs-down deciding vote.

Trump had a basic misunderstanding of the powers that members of Congress wield. Furthermore, he failed to recognize their distaste for his Twitter call-outs and the strong-armed tactics used by those in his administration.[54] While many members may have had misgivings about him personally, Trump's legislative victories can be attributed more to Republican leaders in Congress working on his agenda items and less to the efforts of Trump and his administration.[55] Trump's control over the most vocal and active wing of the Republican electorate kept members on his side,[56] especially through two impeachment votes and after the January 6th insurrection.

Legislative Enactments

Donald Trump's legislative legacy is sparse. Tax cuts and pandemic relief were his most significant legislative achievements. Trump achieved a couple of minor legislative successes on criminal sentencing reform and opioid addiction but failed on his major goals of funding his wall on the border with Mexico, replacing Obamacare, and passing an infrastructure bill. Much of Trump's failure with Congress can be attributed to his personal approach to deal-making, his aversion to detailed preparation of proposals, his failure to do the hard work of negotiating with Congress, and his preference for quick, personal action.

Tax Cuts and Jobs Act of 2017

Trump's lone piece of landmark legislation was the Tax Cuts and Jobs Act (TCJA) of 2017. The TCJA constituted the biggest restructuring of corporate and personal taxes since 1986.[57] Under the TCJA, the corporate tax rate was lowered to a flat 21 percent from a progressive rate of 15 to 39 percent. Other notable features of the act included a limit on deductions of state and local taxes and setting the penalty for the Obamacare individual insurance mandate at zero. The act simplified taxes in some ways but complicated them in others, mostly in ways that were a boon to large corporations and the wealthy.

While the bill received vocal support from several administration figures, it was primarily hammered out between Republican leaders in the House and Senate. Fortunately for Trump, this was an issue on which Republicans were united and eager to act, unlike with some of Trump's positions that did not align with Republican orthodoxy. The president and administration officials played the role of cheerleaders for the bill, both in terms of pushing leaders to advance the bill quickly and building public support.[58] Treasury Secretary Mnuchin claimed the tax cut would pay for itself[59] and Trump's chief economic advisor Gary Cohn said that the wealthy would not be getting a tax cut.[60] Trump himself asserted that, as a wealthy individual, the tax plan was "not good for me."[61]

Outgoing Senator Rob Corker (R-TN) became a holdout on the bill on the principle of fiscal responsibility. Trump and Corker engaged in a public feud, trading insults.[62] Republicans in the Senate handled the issue themselves, with Senator Pat Toomey (R-PA) negotiating with Senator Corker. The final negotiated size of the expected deficit was 1.5 trillion over ten years, and Corker thought this was the best he could get without

200   *The Moderate-Opportunity Presidents*

his committee (Banking, Housing, and Urban Affairs) being bypassed by a different bill with a higher deficit figure.[63]

The budget reconciliation process was used to get the bill to pass the Senate with 51 votes. Republicans then voted on a continuing budget resolution that contained a waiver to the 2010 PAYGO rule that would have mandated spending cuts to offset the expected deficits.[64] President Trump signed both bills on December 22, 2017. Three months later, the Treasury Department revised the expected deficit impact of the tax cuts from $1.5 to $2.3 trillion.[65]

Pandemic Response and Relief

The Coronavirus pandemic of 2020 threatened to cost the lives of millions of U.S. citizens and to grind the economy to a halt. The crisis necessitated several responses from the administration and Congress. In each case, the administration made small requests for funding, but Democrats, who controlled Congress, led the way in drafting the legislation and up-sizing the dollar figures. Democratic leaders negotiated with Treasury Secretary Steve Mnuchin and White House Chief of Staff Mark Meadows, with Trump updated but not involved in any negotiations.[66] Republicans were deeply divided in the Senate and were unable to come up with an alternative set of bills that could secure passage. Trump was ultimately left with no option other than to sign bills he was presented in order to appear responsive to the crisis.

Ultimately, Congress passed three key bills in March of 2020. The Coronavirus Preparedness and Response Supplemental Appropriations Act provided $8.3 billion for research and development of vaccines, health care preparedness, and medical supplies. The Families First Coronavirus Response Act provided $3.5 billion for paid leave for workers, free Coronavirus testing, expanded unemployment benefits, and an increase in funding for food stamps. Finally, the Coronavirus Aid, Relief, and Economic Security Act (CARES), at a price tag of $2.2 trillion, became the largest single economic stimulus in U.S. history. It included $300 billion in direct cash payments to individuals in the form of cash cards. In an effort at credit-claiming, letters were sent to taxpayers bearing the president's signature announcing the payment. The measure increased unemployment benefits and established the Paycheck Protection Program, which provided forgivable loans to businesses.

Other Enactments

Three other less significant pieces of legislation passed during Trump's term, both with limited presidential involvement (although the president was happy to claim credit for them). The first was the First Step Act, which dealt primarily with reforming federal prisons and criminal sentencing laws. Trump was not initially inclined to support the bill, but his son-in-law and political adviser, Jared Kushner, used a number of tactics (including meetings with celebrities and advocacy from Vice President Pence) to get the president on board with the bill.[67] With strong bipartisan support, the issue with passage had more to do with the president's buy-in and willingness to sign the bill than with negotiations between the parties on Capitol Hill.

Another bill with strong bipartisan (in fact, nearly unanimous) support dealt with attempts to remedy the opioid crisis.[68] Titled the SUPPORT for Patients and Communities Act, the measure reflected a politically ripe issue whose time had come for action. Once again, the president offered nothing in the way of securing passage other than a meeting at the White House and signaling his support.

Donald Trump had railed against the North American Free Trade Agreement (NAFTA) and the Trans-Pacific Partnership (TPP) during his presidential campaign as part of his economic nationalism agenda.[69] These trade deals were a key point of Trump's domestic policy agenda and deserve mention. During his first debate with Hillary Clinton, Trump labeled NAFTA as "the single worst trade deal ever"[70] and promised to renegotiate it.[71] Trump played no direct role in renegotiating the deal, yielding responsibilities to U.S. Trade Representative Robert Lighthizer, Senior Political Advisor Jared Kushner, and U.S. Ambassador to Canada Kelly Craft. The USMCA, as it came to be called, was signed by the three countries in 2018. Trump was desperate to get the pact approved by Congress, and in negotiations Lighthizer yielded concessions to Democrats on nearly everything they demanded.[72] House Speaker Nancy Pelosi gleefully summarized the negotiations: "We ate their lunch."[73] The final agreement included items that could hardly be considered Republican free-trade orthodoxy, including a boost for U.S. auto manufacturing, the strengthening of labor laws, and environmental protection.[74] Trump's handling of the TPP and his economic negotiations with China are discussed below in the Administrative Governance section.

Notable Failures

Donald Trump failed to achieve meaningful progress on a number of issues that propelled him to office. First and foremost was the issue of immigration, including his signature promise to build a wall on the southern border, and to force Mexico to pay for it. Trump was unable to achieve any of his desired changes in immigration law and failed to secure $19.1 billion requested for funding his border wall. Trump's fight with Congress over wall funding resulted in a shutdown of the federal government that lasted over a month (December 2018 to January 2019),

202 *The Moderate-Opportunity Presidents*

with the president finally capitulating to a bi-partisan agreement with no funding for his wall.[75] Two weeks later, Trump declared a national emergency and redirected $8 billion, mostly from the Department of Defense, to build the wall.[76] Ultimately, only 453 miles of the 1,951-mile border wall were built, with 373 miles composed of retrofitting existing barriers and only 80 miles of new construction.[77] Other notable legislative failures include Trump's promise to repeal and replace Obamacare and to pass an infrastructure bill. It became a running joke that at the beginning of each week, the administration would declare that it was turning its attention to the subject and the coming week would be "Infrastructure Week."[78]

Trump and Congress

Trump's divisive campaign style did not translate into success with Congress.[79] Members of Congress who could be considered the "insider Washington establishment" that Trump targeted were wary of working with him. In fact, House Speaker Paul Ryan condemned Trump's attack on a Hispanic judge (sitting on a case involving Trump University) as "the textbook definition of a racist comment."[80] Whether they liked Trump or not, or the direction he was leading their party, Republican leaders reluctantly supported some of the president's initiatives while allowing Trump to take a back seat in the legislative process. Aside from the few legislative enactments mentioned above, Trump had a good deal of success in refashioning the federal courts. Doing so had been a pet project of Senate Majority Leader Mitch McConnell, who shepherded through a new cadre of young, conservative judges, including three new Supreme Court Justices (one appointment of which McConnell denied to Obama). To date, the reshaping of the Supreme Court has been the most lasting and impactful legacy of Trump's presidency.

Impeachments

President Trump handed the Democrats an impeachable case when he pressured the President of Ukraine to help him dig up dirt on Trump's likely 2020 election rival Joe Biden. The House tried to get information and testimony from the White House, but the President stonewalled. On December 18, 2019, the Democratically controlled House voted to impeach the president in a largely partisan vote. When the case went to the Senate for trial, the Republican Senators refused to call witnesses, all but ending any chance for the House Democrats to make its case. In January 2020, the Senate voted to acquit the president on the two charges against him: 52-48 on the charge of abuse of power (with Mitt Romney joining Democrats), and 53-47 on the charge of obstruction of Congress (on straight party lines).

Trump was again impeached just prior to leaving office for his encouragement of the January 6, 2021, insurrection that disrupted the counting of the 2020 electoral votes. The president had encouraged his followers to march to the Capitol and to "fight like hell." Insurrectionists scaled the walls of the Capitol, broke windows and doors, and forcefully occupied the Senate chamber, causing congress members and Vice President Pence to hide. Seven people died during and after the melee. The House voted to impeach Trump shortly before he left office, and delivered the charges to the Senate just after Trump left office. Senate Republicans who had spoken out against the President's support and encouragement for the attack on January 6 quickly changed their tune and rallied to his side. Ultimately, only seven Republicans in the Senate voted to convict Trump. The Trump takeover of the Republican party remained nearly complete even after he left the presidency, as Republican lawmakers continued to see their personal electoral fate tied to the former president.

Administrative Governance

While contemporary presidents have responded to difficulties with Congress by resorting to administrative tools, for Trump, it was a matter of preference. In his acceptance speech at the 2016 Republican convention, Trump repeatedly declared about America's ills: "I alone can fix it."[81] Trump did not have the patience or the inclination to work with Congress; he preferred swift, decisive action that made him look as though he was unilaterally in control of government.[82]

A few days into his term, Trump signed an executive order removing the United States from the Trans-Pacific Partnership (TPP), keeping a campaign. The TPP had been part of the Obama Administration's "Pivot to Asia," and officials had argued that the agreement was necessary to counter the economic threat of a rising China. Trump asserted that he would negotiate directly with China in order to "cut a better deal."[83] In 2018, Trump placed a number of tariffs on Chinese-manufactured goods, claiming (erroneously) that China would pay the tariffs and the U.S. treasury would make money (in actuality, U.S. consumers bore the brunt of the tariffs).[84] Trump's promise of a new deal never materialized, as the two nations reached agreement on only the first phase of a negotiation process with multiple phases.

On immigration, Trump took numerous administrative steps. He banned nationals of eight majority-Muslim countries from entering the United States (the "Travel Ban" was forced to be re-written after being struck down in the courts). He reduced refugee admissions to the lowest level since 1980. He canceled the Deferred Action for Childhood Arrivals

(DACA) program and ended the Temporary Protective Status of immigrants from several nations. He initiated Title 42 during COVID, which gave immigration officials the ability to expel migrants (including asylum seekers) to their home country or the country they were last in on their way tot he United States. Trump's "zero-tolerance" immigration policy resulted in prolonged separation of children from adult family members who were jailed.

Shortly after his election, then-President-elect Trump promised to remove two federal regulations for every new one enacted.[85] This effort was a continuance of Trump's motivation to undo whatever Obama had done. Trump's success was marginal in this regard, due mostly to self-inflicted errors in process that resulted in a substantial number of legal challenges.[86] The greatest area of success for the administration was in rolling back environmental regulations.[87]

Trump's biggest challenge as president was his response to the COVID-19 pandemic. In December of 2019, an outbreak of the virus was detected in Wuhan, China. Within weeks, the virus had spread across the globe. The first confirmed case of COVID-19 in the United States was on January 20, 2020. The spread of the virus was quick and deadly. Initially, President Trump downplayed the threat of the virus, assuring the public that it would soon "just disappear."[88] Then, at a time when the United States should have been gearing up to fight the virus, the Trump administration underplayed its hand. The virus struck New York City especially hard. The President, instead of springing into action, tried blaming governors for a weak response to the threat. He kept asking governors to praise him, suggesting that aid might be linked to public praise for the president.[89] The virus continued to spread and the president did little. Trump seemed more worried about the stock market falling and, with it, his electoral prospects, than he did about public health. Trump mocked people who wore masks and refused to wear one himself in most cases. He held rallies and large public gatherings in the middle of the pandemic. Few wore masks, there was virtually no social distancing, and the presence of large crowds made for super-spreader events.[90] And then, the president himself contracted COVID-19. He spent several days in the hospital and then quickly resumed his reelection campaign, again irresponsibly holding large rallies with few mask-wearers and no social distancing.

If Trump frequently exercised administrative overreach, there were also times when he chose to exercise executive underreach. This can be seen in his underwhelming response to the COVID-19 pandemic of 2020. He even went so far as to publicly ask his crisis response team to look into whether injecting disinfectants (such as bleach) into patients could help wipe out the virus.[91] Though most of Trump's administrative response to the virus was insufficient to the task, the "Operation Warp Speed" initiative helped to speed up the production of vaccines.

Donald Trump's flamboyant personality and inner drive for power shaped his administrative approach. His ceaseless tweeting about issues undermined his administration's rationales regarding administrative decisions and invited lawsuits.[92] Overall, his approach caused needless problems and embarrassments, and he might have achieved more with a nuanced, more politically sensitive and cooperative approach. But that was not Trump. His wins, as well as his losses, were a function of his political personality, not a thoughtful management design.

An Assessment

President Trump's personalistic and unilateral view of executive power had its benefits, but also its drawbacks. It increased Trump's power but led to a series of problems. In asserting power, the president was aided by willing enablers in his party in Congress, but he also faced stiff opposition, and the courts sometimes provided pushback. In direct opposition to the Eisenhower hidden-handed approach to managing the executive branch, Trump exercised a high-energy, high-profile, power-grabbing style.[93] This approach, while lacking subtlety, served as a hammer to continually force his preferred issues onto the public agenda, winning some while losing others. This unhidden-handed form of leadership reflected Trump's limited experience, as well as his domineering personality. It is not a model that could easily be exported to other administrations.

Donald Trump is difficult to compare with other presidents because he was so very different. He did not measure himself as past presidents did. Most presidents hope to leave a legacy of bold legislative achievements. Donald Trump, either because he was not especially gifted at the give-and-take of Washington, DC politics, or because he did not know how to accomplish his goals through the legislative process, or because he found a way to make changes that was better suited to his style, defies simple or traditional analysis.

By most conventional measures, Trump's was a failed presidency. A thin legislative achievement record, low popularity ratings, reflections of chaos in the White House in book after book from administration insiders, leaving behind a COVID crisis as well as an economic crisis, having been impeached twice, and dividing the nation while undermining America's position as global leader, and then losing in his bid for reelection, all would place Trump near the bottom of the list of presidential greatness.

Trump was elected by many voters who wanted an outsider who could shake up the system.[94] Trump governed in a way that flouted traditional norms, preferring a politics of transgression.[95] The approach got him impeached twice—once for engaging in illegal campaign activity and another for his attempt to retain his position by force. Trump didn't begin the politics of hyper-partisanship, but he threw gas on the flames. Efforts

206 *The Moderate-Opportunity Presidents*

to hold him accountable for his actions resulted in Republicans (in government and the media) protecting him in order not to offend his supporters. Any evaluation of the Trump presidency must conclude with the condemnation of the damage his presidency inflicted on the intuitions that support and protect what Lincoln called "our great experiment" in democratic self-rule.

Notes

1 Michael Barbaro, "New York Attorney General Is Investigating Trump's For-Profit School," *The New York Times*, May 19, 2011, https://www.nytimes.com/2011/05/20/nyregion/trumps-for-profit-school-said-to-be-under-investigation.html.
2 Luis Ferré-Sadurní, "Trump Pays $2 Million to 8 Charities for Misuse of Foundation," *The New York Times*, December 10, 2019, https://www.nytimes.com/2019/12/10/nyregion/trump-foundation-lawsuit-attorney-general.html.
3 Amy Wang, "Did the 2011 White House Correspondents' Dinner Spur Trump to Run for President?" *Chicago Tribune*, February 26, 2017, https://www.chicagotribune.com/nation-world/ct-white-house-correspondents-dinner-trump-20170226-story.html.
4 For a tally of Trump's lies in office, see Glenn Kessler, Salvador Rizzo, and Meg Kelly, "Trump's False or Misleading Claims Total 30,573 Over 4 Years," *Washington Post*, January 24, 2021, https://www.washingtonpost.com/politics/2021/01/24/trumps-false-or-misleading-claims-total-30573-over-four-years/.
5 For a discussion, see Alan Stone, "The Psychiatrist's Goldwater Rule in the Trump Era," *Lawfare*, April 19, 2018, https://www.lawfareblog.com/psychiatrists-goldwater-rule-trump-era.
6 For example, see Mary L. Trump, *Too Much and Never Enough: How My Family Created the World's Most Dangerous Man* (New York: Simon & Schuster, 2020); and Den P. McAdams, *The Strange Case of Donald Trump: A Psychological Reckoning* (New York: Oxford University Press, 2020).
7 For two very different views on the Trump psychology, see: Bandy X. Lee et al., ed., *The Dangerous Case of Donald Trump: 37 Psychiatrists and Mental Health Experts Assess a President, Updated and Expanded Edition* (New York: Thomas Dunne Books, 2019); and Stanley Renshon, *The Real Psychology of The Trump Presidency* (New York: Palgrave Macmillan, 2020).
8 Philip Bump, "Donald Trump Took 5 Different Positions on Abortion in 3 Days," *The Washington Post*, April 3, 2016, https://www.washingtonpost.com/news/the-fix/wp/2016/04/03/donald-trumps-ever-shifting-positions-on-abortion/.
9 See Alan Abramowitz and Jennifer McCoy, "United States: Racial Resentment, Negative Partisanship, and Polarization in Trump's America," *The Annals of the American Academy of Political and Social Science* 68, no. 1 (2019): 137–156; Marc Hooghe and Ruth Dassonneville, "Explaining the Trump Vote: The Effect of Racist Resentment and Anti-Immigrant Sentiments," *PS: Political Science and Politics* 51, no. 3 (2018): 528–534; Matthew D. Luttig, Christopher F. Federico, and Howard Levine, "Supporters and Opponents of Donald Trump Respond Differently to Racial Cues: An Experimental Analysis," *Research & Politics* 4, no. 4 (2017), https://doi.org/10.1177/2053168017737411; Brenda Major, Alison Blodorn, and Gregory Major Blascovich, "The Threat

of Increasing Diversity: Why Many White Americans Support Trump in the 2016 Presidential Election," *Group Processes & Intergroup Relations* 21, no. 6 (2018): 931–940; Tyler T. Reny, Loren Collingwood, and Ali A. Valenzuela, "Vote Switching in the 2016 Election: How Racial and Immigration Attitudes, Not Economics, Explain Shifts in White Voting," *Public Opinion Quarterly* 83, no. 1 (2019): 91–113; and Emmitt Riley and Clarissa Peterson, "Economic Anxiety or Racial Predispositions? Explaining White Support for Donald Trump in the 2016 Presidential Election," *Journal of Race and Policy* 14, no. 1 (2019): 5–24.

10 For a discussion of the nationalist roots of Trump's appeal, see Matthew Dallek, *Birchers: How the John Birch Society Radicalized the American Right* (New York: Basic Books, 2022), especially ch. 12. For more on Trump's appeals and their historical roots, see Jelani Cobb, "Donald Trump, a Frightening Window Into the American Present," *The New Yorker*, March 15, 2016.

11 John Sides, Michael Tesler, and Lynn Vavreck, *Identity Crisis: The 2016 Campaign and the Battle for the Meaning of America* (Princeton, NJ: Princeton University Press, 2018).

12 Philip Bump, "Donald Trump Reverses Course on Paying Legal Fees for Man Who Attacked Protester. But Could He Do It?" *The Washington Post*, March 15, 2016, https://www.washingtonpost.com/news/the-fix/wp/2016/03/10/trump-once-said-he-would-pay-legal-fees-for-people-who-beat-up-protesters-now-that-its-happened-can-he/.

13 Jose A. DelReal, "Trump Draws Scornful Rebuke for Mocking Reporter with Disability," *Washington Post*, November 26, 2015, https://www.washington-post.com/news/post-politics/wp/2015/11/25/trump-blasted-by-new-york-times-after-mocking-reporter-with-disability/.

14 Colin Dwyer, "Donald Trump: 'I Could ... Shoot Somebody, And I Wouldn't Lose Any Voters,'" *NPR: The Two-Way*, January 23, 2016, https://www.npr.org/sections/thetwo-way/2016/01/23/464129029/donald-trump-i-could-shoot-somebody-and-i-wouldnt-lose-any-voters.

15 Sides, Tesler, and Vavreck, *Identity Crisis*, 160.

16 Cornelius Hirsch and Giovanna Coi, "Biden and Trump's Inauguration Speeches Compared," *Politico*, January 20, 2021, https://www.politico.eu/article/joe-biden-donald-trump-presidential-inauguration-speeches-compared/.

17 Yashar Ali, "What George W. Bush Really Thought of Donald Trump's Inauguration," *New York Magazine*, March 29, 2017, https://nymag.com/intelligencer/2017/03/what-george-w-bush-really-thought-of-trumps-inauguration.html.

18 Sarah Ferris, "Trump: I'll Replace ObamaCare with 'Something Terrific,'" *The Hill*, July 29, 2015, https://thehill.com/policy/healthcare/249697-trump-replace-obamacare-with-something-terrific/.

19 See https://fred.stlouisfed.org/series/FYFSD.

20 Jessica Taylor, "Trump Calls for 'Total and Complete Shutdown of Muslims Entering' U.S.," *NPR*, December 7, 2015, https://www.npr.org/2015/12/07/458836388/trump-calls-for-total-and-complete-shutdown-of-muslims-entering-u-s.

21 Kenneth R. Mayer, "Is President Trump Conventionally Disruptive, or Unconventionally Destructive?" in *The 2016 Presidential Election: The Causes and Consequences of a Political Earthquake*, ed. Amnon Cavari, Richard J. Powell, and Kenneth R. Mayer (New York: Lexington Books, 2017), 189; and Michael Pocalyko, "The Businessman President," *Survival: Global Politics and Strategy* 59, no. 1 (2017): 51–57.

208   *The Moderate-Opportunity Presidents*

22 Alexi McCammond and Jonathan Swan, "Scoop: Insider Leaks 'Trump's 'Executive Time'-filled Private Schedules," *Axios*, February 3, 2019, https://www.axios.com/2019/02/03/donald-trump-private-schedules-leak-executive-time. Eliana Johnson and Daniel Lippman, "9 Hours of 'Executive Time': Trump's Unstructured Days Define His Presidency," *Politico*, October 29, 2018, https://www.politico.com/story/2018/10/29/trump-daily-schedule-executive-time-944996.

23 See Zack Budryk, "Trump Offered Kelly FBI Director's Job, Demanded Loyalty: Report," *The Hill*, August 30, 2020, https://thehill.com/homenews/administration/514369-trump-offered-kelly-fbi-directors-job-demanded-loyalty-report/; Michael Kruse, "'I Need Loyalty'," *Politico*, March/April, 2018, https://www.politico.com/magazine/story/2018/03/06/donald-trump-loyalty-staff-217227/; and Michael S. Schmidt, "In a Private Dinner, Trump Demanded Loyalty. Comey Demurred," *The New York Times*, May 11, 2017, https://www.nytimes.com/2017/05/11/us/politics/trump-comey-firing.html.

24 See Asawin Suebsaeng and Adam Rawnsley, "Trump White House Pressured Disney to Censor … Jimmy Kimmel," *Rolling Stone*, February 26, 2023, https://www.rollingstone.com/politics/politics-news/trump-white-house-pressure-disney-censor-jimmy-kimmel-1234686853/.

25 Isaac Arnsdorf, "Trump Asks Public for Blind Trust," *Politico*, January 12, 2017, https://www.politico.com/story/2017/01/donald-trump-business-conflicts-interest-233520.

26 See Adam Liptak, "Supreme Court Ends Emoluments Suits Against Trump," *The New York Times*, February 21, 2021, https://www.nytimes.com/2021/01/25/us/emoluments-trump-supreme-court.html; and Karen Yourish and Larry Buchanan, "Trump Still Makes Money from His Properties. Is This Constitutional?" *The New York Times*, July 10, 2019, https://www.nytimes.com/interactive/2018/12/17/us/politics/trump-emoluments-money.html.

27 See Jay Willis, "How Don Jr., Ivanka, and Eric Trump Have Profited Off Their Dad's Presidency," *GQ*, October 14, 2019, https://www.gq.com/story/trump-kids-profit-presidency; and Sui-Lee Wee, "Ivanka Trump Wins China Trademarks, Then Her Father Vows to Save ZTE," *The New York Times*, May 28, 2018, https://www.nytimes.com/2018/05/28/business/ivanka-trump-china-trademarks.html.

28 John P. Burke, "'It Went Off the Rails': Trump's Presidential Transition and the National Security System," *Presidential Studies Quarterly* 48, no. 4 (2018): 838.

29 Michael A. Genovese, *The Trumping of American Politics: The Strange Case of the 2016 Presidential* (Amherst, NY: Cambria Press, 2017); and Michael A. Genovese, *How Trump Governs: An Assessment and a Prognosis* (Amherst, NY: Cambria Press, 2017), chs. 2, 3, and 4.

30 Rebecca Savransky, "NSC Officials Include Trump's Name as Often as Possible So He Reads Memos: Report," *The Hill*, May 17, 2017, https://thehill.com/homenews/administration/333788-nsc-official-include-trumps-name-as-often-as-possible-so-he-reads/.

31 Bob Woodward, *Fear* (New York: Simon & Schuster, 2018), xix.

32 See Aaron Blake, "What Trump Aides Who Wrote Tell-all Books Said, Before and After," *The Washington Post*, May 13, 2022, https://www.washingtonpost.com/politics/2022/05/13/what-trump-aides-who-wrote-tell-all-books-said-before-after/; and Thom Poole, "I Read All those Trump Tell-alls. Here's What I Learned," *BBC News*, September 12, 2020, https://www.bbc.com/news/world-us-canada-53970246.

33 Martha Joynt Kumar, "Energy or Chaos? Turnover at the Top of President Trump's White House," *Presidential Studies Quarterly* 49, no. 1 (2019): 219–236.

34 For a spirited defense of President Trump's use of executive authority, see John Yoo, *Defender in Chief: Donald Trump's Fight for Presidential Power* (New York: All Points Books, 2020).

35 Michael Bryce-Saddler, "While Bemoaning Mueller Probe, Trump Falsely Says the Constitution Gives Him 'The Right to Do Whatever I Want,'" *The Washington Post*, July 23, 2019, https://www.washingtonpost.com/politics/2019/07/23/trump-falsely-tells-auditorium-full-teens-constitution-gives-him-right-do-whatever-i-want/.

36 David E. Lewis, Patrick Bernhard, and Emily You, "President Trump as Manager: Reflections on the First Year," *Presidential Studies Quarterly* 48, no. 3 (2018): 480–501.

37 Clodagh Harrington and Alex Waddan, *Obama v. Trump: The Politics of Rollback* (Edinburgh: Edinburgh University Press, 2022).

38 Rich Lowry, "The Age of Unilateral Rule," *Politico*, June 1, 2017, https://www.politico.com/magazine/story/2017/06/01/rich-lowry-donald-trump-unilateral-rule-215214/.

39 Paul Rosenzweig, "'Take the Land': Trump Promises Pardons for Law-Breaking," *Lawfare*, September 3, 2019, https://www.lawfareblog.com/take-land-trump-promises-pardons-law-breaking.

40 See Nicholas Fandos, Katie Benner, and Charlie Savage, "Justice Dept. Officials Outline Claims of Politicization Under Barr," *The New York Times*, July 10, 2020, https://www.nytimes.com/2020/06/24/us/politics/justice-department-politicization.html; and Matt Zapotosky and Karoun Demirjian, "Analysts Say Barr Is Eroding Justice Department Independence — Without Facing Any Real Personal Consequence," *The Washington Post*, June 24, 2020, https://www.washingtonpost.com/national-security/analysts-say-barr-is-eroding-justice-department-independence--without-facing-any-real-personal-consequence/2020/06/24/459778ca-b647-11ea-a8da-693df3d7674a_story.html.

41 Philip Bump, "Trump Relies on Acting Cabinet Officials More than Most Presidents. It's Not an Accident," *The Washington Post*, April 8, 2019, https://www.washingtonpost.com/politics/2019/04/08/trump-relies-acting-cabinet-officials-more-than-most-presidents-its-not-an-accident/.

42 Katie Rogers, "White House Hosts Conservative Internet Activists at a 'Social Media Summit'," *The New York Times*, July 11, 2019, https://www.nytimes.com/2019/07/11/us/politics/white-house-social-media-summit.html.

43 Peter L. Francia, "Free Media and Twitter in the 2016 Presidential Election: The Unconventional Campaign of Donald Trump," *Social Science Computer Review* 36, no. 4 (2017): 440–455.

44 Stephen Hess and James Pfiffner, *Organizing the Presidency*, 4th ed. (Washington, DC: Brookings, 2021), 191.

45 Derek Robertson, "How @realDonaldTrump Changed Politics — and America," *Politico*, January 9, 2021, https://www.politico.com/news/magazine/2021/01/09/trump-twitter-ban-suspended-analysis-456817.

46 Quoted in Rebecca Morin, "Trump: My Social Media Use Is 'Modern Day Presidential,'" *Politico*, July 1, 2017, https://www.politico.com/story/2017/07/01/trump-tweets-modern-day-presidential-240170.

47 Masha Gessen, "How Trump Governs by Tweet: Start with Outrage, then Escalate," *The New Yorker*, October 11, 2017, https://www.newyorker.com/news/news-desk/how-trump-governs-by-tweet-start-with-outrage-then-escalate.

48 Rachel Treisman, "As President Trump Tweets and Deletes, the Historical Record Takes Shape," *NPR*, October 25, 2019, https://www.npr.org/2019/10/25/772325133/as-president-trump-tweets-and-deletes-the-historical-record-takes-shape.

49 Bobby Allyn and Tamara Keith, "Twitter Permanently Suspends Trump, Citing 'Risk of Further Incitement of Violence'," *NPR*, January 8, 2021, https://www.npr.org/2021/01/08/954760928/twitter-bans-president-trump-citing-risk-of-further-incitement-of-violence.

50 Mark Sherman, "Supreme Court Dismisses Case over Trump and Twitter Critics," *AP* News, April 5, 2021, https://apnews.com/article/supreme-court-dimisses-case-trump-twitter-critics-bcdfcc37052e9c737ac5a1318b02a71c.

51 Marion R. Just and Ann N. Crigler, "Learning from the News in a Time of Highly Polarized Media," in *U.S. Election Analysis 2020: Media, Voters and the Campaign*, ed. Daniel Jackson, Danielle Sarver Coombs, Filippo Trevisan, Darren Lilleker, and Einar Thorsen, https://www.electionanalysis.ws/us/2020/.

52 Jane Mayer, "Donald Trump's Ghost Writer Tells All," *The New Yorker*, July 18, 2018, https://www.newyorker.com/magazine/2016/07/25/donald-trumps-ghostwriter-tells-all.

53 Donald J. Trump with Tony Schwartz, *Trump: The Art of the Deal* (New York: Random House, 2015).

54 Jon R. Bond, "Which Presidents Are Uncommonly Successful in Congress? A Trump Update," *Presidential Studies Quarterly* 49, no. 4 (2019): 905.

55 Ibid., 906.

56 Gary C. Jacobson and Huchen Lieu, "Dealing with Disruption: Congressional Republicans' Responses to Donald Trump's Behavior and Agenda," *Presidential Studies Quarterly* 50, no. 1 (2020): 4–29.

57 William G. Gale, Hilary Gelfond, Aaron Krupkin, Mark J. Mazur, and Eric J. Toder, "Effects of the Tax Cuts and Jobs Act: A Preliminary Analysis," *National Tax Journal* 71, no. 4 (2019): 589–612.

58 Jim Tankersley and Alan Rappeport, "How Republicans Rallied Together to Deliver a Tax Plan," *The New York Times*, December 19, 2017, https://www.nytimes.com/2017/12/19/us/politics/republican-tax-bill.html.

59 Damian Paletta and Max Ehrenfreund, "Trump's Treasury Secretary: The Tax Cut 'Will Pay for Itself,'" *Washington Post*, April 20, 2017, https://www.washingtonpost.com/news/wonk/wp/2017/04/20/trumps-treasury-secretary-the-tax-cut-will-pay-for-itself/.

60 Louis Nelson, "Cohn: 'The Wealthy Are Not Getting a Tax Cut,'" *Politico*, September 28, 2017, https://www.politico.com/story/2017/09/28/trump-tax-reform-tax-cuts-243246.

61 Annie Lowery, "Trump Says His Tax Plan Won't Benefit the Rich—He's Exactly Wrong," *The Atlantic*, September 29, 2017, https://www.theatlantic.com/business/archive/2017/09/trump-tax-plan-benefit-rich/541584/.

62 Jacob Pramuk, "Republican Sen. Bob Corker Unloads on Trump, Says He 'Debases the Country,'" *CNBC.com*, October 24, 2017, https://www.cnbc.com/2017/10/24/trump-blames-sen-bob-corker-for-fighting-tax-cuts.html.

63 There was some speculation as to what was called a "Corker Kickback" that might personally benefit Senator Corker (called the "pass-through" business deduction), but Corker insists he did not know the details of the compromise that included this item. See Seung Min Kim, "Why Corker Flipped on the Tax Bill," *Politico*, December 18, 2017, https://www.politico.com/story/2017/12/18/bob-corker-tax-bill-kickback-republicans-respond-302482.

64 Christina Wilkie, "Trump Signs GOP Tax Plan and Short-term Government Funding Bill on His Way Out of Town," *CNBC.com*, December 22, 2017, https://www.cnbc.com/2017/12/22/trump-signs-gop-tax-plan-short-term-government-funding-bill.html.

65 David Rogers, "POLITICO Analysis: At \$2.3 Trillion Cost, Trump Tax Cuts Leave Big Gap," *Politico*, February 28, 2018, https://www.politico.com/story/2018/02/28/tax-cuts-trump-gop-analysis-430781.

66 George C. Edwards III, "Was Donald Trump an Effective Leader of Congress?" *Presidential Studies Quarterly* 51, no. 1 (2021): 4–34.

67 See Brian Bennett, "How Unlikely Allies Got Prison Reform Done—With an Assist from Kim Kardashian West," *Time*, December 21, 2018, https://time.com/5486560/prison-reform-jared-kushner-kim-kardashian-west/; and Annie Karni, "The Senate Passed the Criminal Justice Bill. For Jared Kushner, It's a Personal Issue and a Rare Victory," *The New York Times*, December 14, 2018, https://www.nytimes.com/2018/12/14/us/politics/jared-kushner-criminal-justice-bill.html.

68 Marianna Sotomayor, "Trump Signs Sweeping Opioid Bill with Vow to End 'Scourge' of Drug Addiction," *NBCNews.com*, October 14, 2018, https://www.nbcnews.com/politics/congress/trump-signs-sweeping-opioid-bill-vow-end-scourge-drug-addiction-n923976.

69 See Matthew J. Baltz, "'Americanism Not Globalism Will Be Our Credo!': An Analysis of the Economic Nationalism(s) of Trump's Administration and an Agenda for Further Research," *Nations and Nationalism* 27, no. 3 (2021): 797–815; and Jasmin Habib and Michael Howard, "The Political Economy of Donald J. Trump," in *Reading Donald Trump: A Parallax View of the Campaign and Early Presidency* (New York: Palgrave Macmillan, 2019).

70 Maggie Severns, "Trump Pins NAFTA, 'Worst Trade Deal Ever,' on Clinton," *CNN.com*, September 26, 2016, https://www.politico.com/story/2016/09/trump-clinton-come-out-swinging-over-nafta-228712.

71 Jen Kirby, "USMCA, Trump's New NAFTA Deal, Explained in 600 Words," *Vox.com*, July 1, 2020, https://www.vox.com/2018/10/3/17930092/usmca-mexico-nafta-trump-trade-deal-explained.

72 Edwards, 15.

73 Emily Cochrane, Ana Swanson, and Jim Tankersley, "How a Trump Trade Pact Won Over Democrats," *New York Times*, December 19, 2019, https://www.nytimes.com/2019/12/19/us/politics/trump-trade-deal.html.

74 Katie Lobosco, "NAFTA Is Officially Gone. Here's What Has and Hasn't Changed," *CNN.com*, July 1, 2020, https://www.cnn.com/2020/07/01/politics/usmca-nafta-replacement-trump/index.html.

75 Andrew Restuccia, Burgess Everett, and Heather Caygle, "Longest Shutdown in History Ends after Trump Relents on Wall," *Politico*, January 25, 2019, https://www.politico.com/story/2019/01/25/trump-shutdown-announcement-1125529.

76 Rebecca Shabad, Alex Moe, Frank Thorp V., and Kristen Welker, "Trump to Declare National Emergency, Announce \$8 billion for Border Wall," *NBCNews.com*, February 14, 2019, https://www.nbcnews.com/politics/congress/government-shutdown-vote-border-bill-trump-n971576.

77 Melissa Correa, "VERIFY: How Much of President Trump's 450-Mile Border Wall Is Actually a New Barrier?" *KHOU.com*, January 13, 2021, https://www.khou.com/article/news/verify/verify-how-much-of-president-trumps-450-mile-border-wall-is-actually-a-new-barrier/285-ce164c2a-c8d7-4ded-b82b-6141b980d61b.

212 *The Moderate-Opportunity Presidents*

78 Jason Scott Smith, "Infrastructure during the Trump Presidency," in *The Presidency of Donald Trump: A First Historical Assessment*, ed. Julian E. Zelizer (Princeton, NJ: Princeton University Press, 2022), 169.

79 Jon Herbert, Trevor McCrisken, and Andrew Wroe, *The Ordinary Presidency of Donald J. Trump* (New York: Palgrave MacMillan, 2019), 157.

80 Jennifer Steinhauer, Jonathan Martin, and David M. Herszenhorn, "Paul Ryan Calls Donald Trump's Attack on Judge 'Racist,' but Still Backs Him," *The New York Times*, June 7, 2016, https://www.nytimes.com/2016/06/08/us/politics/paul-ryan-donald-trump-gonzalo-curiel.html.

81 Yoni Appelbaum, "'I Alone Can Fix It," *The Atlantic*, July 21, 2016, https://www.theatlantic.com/politics/archive/2016/07/trump-rnc-speech-alone-fix-it/492557/.

82 Sidney M. Milikis and Nicholas Jacobs, "'I Alone Can Fix It' Donald Trump, the Administrative Presidency, and Hazards of Executive-Centered Partisanship," *The Forum* 15, no. 3 (2017): 583–613.

83 Ryan Hass and Abraham Denmark, "More Pain than Gain: How the US-China Trade War Hurt America," *Brookings.com*, August 7, 2020, https://www.brookings.edu/blog/order-from-chaos/2020/08/07/more-pain-than-gain-how-the-us-china-trade-war-hurt-america/.

84 Geoffrey Gertz, "Did Trump's Tariffs Benefit American Workers and National Security?" *Brookings.com*, September 10, 2020, https://www.brookings.edu/policy2020/votervital/did-trumps-tariffs-benefit-american-workers-and-national-security/.

85 Clyde Wayne Crews Jr., "Donald Trump Promises to Eliminate Two Regulations for Every One Enacted," *Forbes*, November 22, 2016, https://www.forbes.com/sites/waynecrews/2016/11/22/donald-trump-promises-to-eliminate-two-regula-tions-for-every-one-enacted/?sh=500ecd3e4586.

86 Philip A. Wallach and Kelly Kennedy, "Examining Some of Trump's Deregulation Efforts: Lessons from the Brookings Regulatory Tracker," *Brookings*, March 8, 2022, https://www.brookings.edu/research/examining-some-of-trumps-deregulation-efforts-lessons-from-the-brookings-regulatory-tracker/.

87 See David M. Shafie, *The Administrative Presidency and the Environment: Policy Leadership and Retrenchment from Clinton to Trump* (New York: Routledge, 2020); and Nadja Popovich, Livia Albeck-Ripka, and Kendra Pierre-Louis, "The Trump Administration Rolled Back More Than 100 Environmental Rules. Here's the Full List," *The New York Times*, January 20, 2021, https://www.nytimes.com/interactive/2020/climate/trump-environment-rollbacks-list.html.

88 Dan Goldberg, "'It's Going to Disappear': Trump's Changing Tone on Coronavirus," *Politico*, March 17, 2020, https://www.politico.com/news/2020/03/17/how-trump-shifted-his-tone-on-coronavirus-134246.

89 Kathleen Ronayne and Jonathan Lemire, "Flatter or Fight? Governors Seeking Help Must Navigate Trump," *Associated Press*, March 26, 2020, https://apnews.com/article/donald-trump-ap-top-news-virus-outbreak-mi-state-wire-public-health-f9fb8c41b7f8acc215e3ec78ca32210a.

90 Susan B. Glasser, "Donald Trump's 2020 Superspreader Campaign: A Diary," *The Atlantic*, November 2, 2020, https://www.newyorker.com/news/letter-from-trumps-washington/donald-trumps-2020-superspreader-campaign-a-diary.

91 Katie Rogers, Christine Hauser, Alan Yuhas, and Maggie Haberman, "Trump's Suggestion That Disinfectants Could Be Used to Treat Coronavirus Prompts

Aggressive Pushback," April 24, 2020, https://www.nytimes.com/2020/04/24/us/politics/trump-inject-disinfectant-bleach-coronavirus.html.

92 See Todd L. Belt, "The Unforced Errors of Norm and Rule Violations: The Trump Administration's Domestic Policy," *Palgrave: Politics in Practice*, June 20, 2020, https://www.palgrave.com/gp/blogs/perspectives-in-politics-international-studies/todd-belt-blog.

93 See Mark Shanahan, "Outsider Presidents: Comparing Trump and Eisenhower," in *The Trump Presidency: From Campaign Trail to World Stage*, ed. Mara Oliva and Mark Shanahan (New York: Palgrave MacMillan, 2019).

94 For further discussion on Trump's impact in this regard, see Michael Haas, *Shaking Things Up: How Donald Trump Changed the Government in Washington* (New York: Peter Lang, 2023).

95 Julia Azari, "The Trump Presidency Thrives on Norms," *The Mischiefs of Faction*, May 8, 2020, https://www.mischiefsoffaction.com/post/the-trump-presidency-thrives-on-norms.

Part III

The Low-Opportunity Presidents

11 Richard Nixon

An Activist with an Enemies List

The administration of President Richard Nixon (served 1969–1974) imploded in 1974 when the president's role in the imbroglio known as the Watergate scandal became known. Nixon resigned in disgrace on August 9, 1974. Since that time, new perspectives have emerged on Nixon's domestic policy leadership. In her reassessment, historian Joan Hoff Wilson wrote that Nixon accomplished far more than many people thought: "During his first term in office, Nixon acted as an agent of change in five areas of domestic reform: welfare, civil rights, economic policy, environmental policy, and reorganization of the federal bureaucracy."[1] Has Nixon, the first of the low-opportunity presidents, been overlooked and underrated as a domestic policy president?

Personal Characteristics

The early years were not easy for Richard Milhous Nixon (1913–1994). His mother, a Quaker who grew up in Whittier, California, married Frank Nixon, who possessed only a sixth-grade education. Frank was known to be "volatile, unpredictable, and explosive" and a "tyrant who intimidated his children."[2] The deaths of two of Richard's brothers added to the emotional stress. As the family struggled, Richard was pressed into working at his father's grocery store at an early age.

The family's limited finances prevented Richard from attending the eastern schools that had accepted his applications. Consequently, Richard attended nearby Whittier College in California, but was later able to attend Duke University Law School in North Carolina. He was a good student and did well in debate tournaments. At Duke, he lived very frugally, residing for a time in an abandoned shack. He was a determined student and graduated third in his class, humorously crediting his "iron butt" (studying without moving for hours on end).

When his dream of a job with a prominent eastern law firm did not materialize, Richard returned to Whittier to practice law. His involvement in a local drama group led to a romance and later marriage to Thelma

DOI: 10.4324/9781003426684-14

218   *The Low-Opportunity Presidents*

Catherine "Pat" Ryan, a high school typing teacher. During World War II, Nixon worked briefly for a price control agency in Washington and then served as an officer in the navy. While stationed in the Pacific, he was known among his peers as an excellent poker player. After the war, he joined many other veterans in the pursuit of political office.

Career Path

In his first foray into politics, Nixon successfully challenged five-term U.S. House incumbent Jeremiah "Jerry" Voorhis of California and joined the surge of Republican victors in 1946. In Washington, Nixon burst into the national spotlight when he supported the claims of journalist Whittaker Chambers that Alger Hiss, a former State Department official and prominent member of the eastern establishment, had associated with communists during the 1930s. The evidence Chambers uncovered and Nixon highlighted led to Hiss's conviction on perjury, but his guilt has long been debated. In a 1950 Senate bid, Nixon successfully challenged Helen Gahagan Douglas, a movie actress turned politician. He successfully tarred her as the "Pink Lady"—her "crime," according to Nixon, was the number of times she had voted with a known communist in the House.

Nixon was chosen by Republican Dwight Eisenhower as his vice presidential nominee in 1952 to add youth to the ticket, provide regional balance, and please the conservative wing of the party. But after it was revealed that Nixon had received personal financial support from a group of wealthy California businessmen, Eisenhower debated removing him. In a melodramatic televised address on September 23 that was viewed by 60 million people, Nixon denied any wrongdoing and claimed that he and his family lived simple lives. He admitted receiving only a dog as a gift, which his children had named Checkers, and insisted he would not give it back. The Checkers speech drew a strong public response, and the flood of telegrams to Eisenhower's campaign saved Nixon's position on the ticket.

As vice president, Richard Nixon stood by during Eisenhower's illnesses and had few responsibilities. He enjoyed traveling and in 1959 captured the spotlight when he engaged in a spontaneous "kitchen debate" with Soviet leader Nikita Khrushchev in Moscow over the merits of capitalism and communism. Eisenhower was uneasy about retaining Nixon in 1956, but because he had few alternatives, he decided to leave him on the ticket.

In 1960, Nixon narrowly lost the presidency to John Kennedy. Then, in 1962, he challenged the incumbent governor of California, Edmund "Pat" Brown, and lost. Afterward, he announced his retirement from politics with the now-famous line "You won't have Nixon to kick around anymore." In the wake of Republican Barry Goldwater's crushing defeat in 1964, Nixon quietly cultivated party support for his comeback. His chance finally came in 1968. With his more restrained demeanor, some suggested he was reinvented as a "New Nixon."[3] In the general election campaign, he promised to enforce law and order and to carry out a plan to end the war in Vietnam, but he did not have a lengthy domestic agenda.

What Manner of Man?

Elliot Richardson, the attorney general in the Nixon administration who resigned rather than fire the Watergate special prosecutor, once commented on his former boss's strategic intelligence:

> He is a realist whose realism … is infused with cynicism. This tough-minded outlook is a contributor to the range of his perspective on unfolding events, and it is permanently associated with his thinking. He takes the long view, and that capacity helps to explain the fact that he is perhaps the leading strategist we have had in the White House since World War II. He constantly thought about how to adapt the policies of the United States so as to accommodate our more long-term national interests.[4]

Nixon also was an introvert who suffered from low self-esteem. He even described himself as "an introvert in an extrovert's profession."[5] The magnitude of Nixon's loner tendencies was evident in his Oval Office relationships; he sometimes spent more time with Chief of Staff H. R. "Bob" Haldeman than Haldeman would have preferred and spent considerable time alone. Haldeman at one point recruited a staff member to be the president's "designated friend."

On an even more negative note, Nixon often expressed intense hostility and hatred toward individuals and institutions. On occasion he revealed a generous side, yet more generally he appeared cynical, suspicious, and mean-spirited. Targets of his hostility included liberals, the eastern establishment, the Kennedys, academics, and the press. His final words to staff members as he resigned showed that he recognized the problems his attitudes could create: "Always remember, others may hate you—but those who hate you don't win unless you hate them, and then you destroy yourself."[6]

Despite his frequent hostilities toward others, Nixon also displayed a desire to avoid personal conflict. In fact, he preferred to hand over difficult tasks such as firing people to Bob Haldeman. Nixon aide John Ehrlichman expressed a similar view when he stated, "We've got the reputation of … building a wall around the President. The fact is that he was down under the desk saying, 'I don't want to see those fellows' and we were trying to pull him out."[7]

Nixon was known as well for his propensity to stretch the truth and for the cavalier manner in which he stated complete falsehoods. Some of his

220 *The Low-Opportunity Presidents*

truth-stretching was of limited significance, such as his incorrect claim that his wife, Pat, was born on St. Patrick's Day (which she was not) and that (in addressing a French audience) he had majored in French in college. Once he was in the White House, Nixon's most fateful use of falsehoods was his insistence that he knew nothing about a White House cover-up of the administration's involvement in the break-in at the Democratic National Headquarters in the Watergate hotel/office complex in Washington. In fact, the president had been involved in the cover-up efforts since at least June 23, 1972—over two years before his tapes would tell the true story to the public. According to presidential biographer Fawn Brodie, Nixon enjoyed lying and considered it an important ability. She says he told a friend long before Watergate: "You don't know how to lie. If you can't lie, you'll never get anywhere."[8]

Policy Views

Nixon presented himself within the Republican Party as a moderate, and that in some respects is where he stood. Bryce Harlow, who served as a senior aide to both Eisenhower and Nixon, found Eisenhower more conservative than Nixon.[9] In his views of the use of government, Nixon certainly was no Lyndon Johnson, but he had a greater interest in putting government to work for the people than any of the other Republican presidents serving since 1933.

During the 1968 campaign, Nixon departed from his record of general support for civil rights measures earlier in his career. He denounced "forced busing" as a tool for school desegregation and endorsed the "freedom of choice" plans strongly preferred by white southerners. A hard line on "law and order" also emerged as a major theme, but with few specific proposals.[10] Yet on questions such as welfare reform, Nixon said little while actually denouncing the type of reform he would propose in 1969. The strongest themes of Nixon's 1968 campaign were ending the war in Vietnam and representing the interests of the middle class against what he believed were the failed social policies of liberals and Washington elites.

Challenges and Opportunities

Nixon entered the presidency facing significant challenges. Elected with only 43 percent of the vote, he was the first new president in 120 years to face a Congress in which the opposing party controlled both chambers. Republicans clearly were the minority party in the electorate as well. Nixon's popularity levels were a modest 59 percent on average the first year. Although he inherited a one-year budget surplus (in the wake of the 1968 tax increase) from his predecessor, Lyndon Johnson, he faced strong inflationary pressures and intense budget difficulties stemming from

Richard Nixon   221

a combination of continued spending on the Vietnam War and calls for additional domestic outlays.

Nixon assumed office with the nation bitterly divided. Urban unrest contributed to the tension, as did uncertainty about the Vietnam War. A majority of the public viewed the war as a mistake,[11] but no consensus existed on how the nation should end it. Growing war protests and the June 1971 publication of the top-secret, war-related document known as the *Pentagon Papers* in the *New York Times* and *Washington Post* produced intense resentment in the White House. These events led to administrative efforts to carry out campaign intelligence activities that became part of the Watergate scandal.

Other foreign initiatives competed consumed the president's attention. By means of highly secret negotiations, Nixon was able to open US relationships with China and made a state visit in 1972. In American relationships with the Soviet Union, Nixon promoted a policy known as "detente"— the use of agreements and treaties to reduce weapons and lessen tensions between nations. Indeed, detente seemed to be the right road toward bringing down future military spending as the nation moved into what was called an "Age of Limits."[12]

On the domestic front, the most important policy advantage was an activist public and Congress. A good deal of policy proposals were "in the pipeline," and interest groups were pushing for enactment of environmental and consumer protection measures. Later, at the end of his first term, it seemed that Nixon had met some of his challenges and might well enjoy new opportunities. Then, in April 1973, his presidency began to look increasingly fragile as top aides were asked to resign, and the nation had become focused on a series of abuses labeled Watergate.[13]

Leadership Style

Richard Nixon admired the leadership shown by Presidents Theodore Roosevelt and Woodrow Wilson. While clearly more interested in fulfilling a statesman's role and dealing with foreign policy rather than domestic matters, he also believed that a stable domestic policy base was a requisite for an effective foreign policy. He stated in his *Memoirs* that he was determined to be an activist president in domestic affairs, and at his first cabinet meeting he spurred its members to action, stating that "we do not want the record written that we were too cautious."[14] Health, Education, and Welfare (HEW) secretary and longtime friend Robert Finch, recognizing Nixon's desire, told his deputy John Veneman,

> You watch that man. He's going to surprise people. He wants to be remembered in history, and, as a student of Theodore and Franklin

222   *The Low-Opportunity Presidents*

Roosevelt, he knows that only presidents who come up with progressive social programs are likely to make a name.[15]

In designing his sweeping 1969 welfare proposal, Nixon also liked to remind his staff that it was Benjamin Disraeli, the conservative nineteenth-century British prime minister, who carried out reforms often advocated by liberals.

The Advisory Process and Approach to Decision-Making

In forming his cabinet, Nixon recruited a group of white men who drew little praise for their leadership or managerial skills.[16] He tried to recruit Whitney Young, an African American head of the Urban League, as secretary of housing and urban development but was unsuccessful.[17] In the end, Nixon surrounded himself with several former Republican governors and came to regret several of his appointments. Nixon thought cabinet-level deliberations were largely a waste of time, forcing different department heads to listen to others' problems.[18]

Campaign aide and public relations specialist Bob Haldeman became Nixon's very powerful chief of staff. As Watergate unfolded, Haldeman was roundly criticized by the press for his authoritarian, heavy-handed approach. Nevertheless, Stephen Ambrose found that Haldeman had desirable qualities for a chief of staff: He was intelligent, hardworking, efficient, ruthless, loyal, and tough enough to stand the pressures of a difficult job.[19]

During his first year in office, Nixon's domestic advisory process evolved significantly. At the outset, he was influenced by Daniel Patrick Moynihan, a former official in the Johnson administration and an "anti-bureaucratic" liberal. Pitted against Moynihan was economist Arthur Burns. Leonard Garment, a former law partner of Nixon's in New York, worked on minority issues, while Harry Dent, a South Carolinian with strong ties to Republican senator Strom Thurmond, brought a Southern perspective to many policy issues.

The emergence of John Ehrlichman as chief domestic adviser came in the wake of an intense fight over welfare policy in the first half of 1969. Promoters of a major change called a Family Assistance Plan (FAP) included Moynihan, Shultz, and several figures from HEW. Arthur Burns was adamantly opposed to the idea. After that fight, Ehrlichman's role grew, Burns moved to the Federal Reserve Board, and Moynihan saw his influence decline, and he resigned in late 1970. Nixon then formally created a Domestic Council and placed a large staff under Ehrlichman's direction. Ehrlichman, who saw himself as a centrist, periodically came under fire from both conservatives and liberals.[20]

Nixon's preference for foreign policy over domestic issues permeated his presidency. Indeed, he once stated that a president is needed for foreign policy, but in domestic affairs, the cabinet can run the country.[21] Given Nixon's propensity to delegate much of the domestic decision-making, it was fortunate that the Domestic Council performed well. It prepared well-documented analyses for the president's contemplation and generally was aware of and responsive to policy concerns in the country.[22] As for Nixon's staff overall, John Greene concluded that "this was a remarkable group of advisers, quite simply the most powerful and efficient presidential staff of the postwar era."[23]

Administrative Strategies

In its first term, the Nixon administration altered governmental structures, pursued civil rights goals, and established economic controls in 1971. Indeed, administrative strategies were an unusually important part of Nixon's leadership approach, largely because of the difficulties he faced in dealing with Congress.[24] But in his endeavors, the president did not count the bureaucracy among his friends. As Nixon commented to Bob Haldeman in 1971, "96% of the bureaucracy are against us, they're bastards who are here to screw us."[25]

Nixon appointed a commission, headed by business executive Arthur L. Ash, to reorganize the Bureau of the Budget. In its reincarnation, it became the Office of Management and Budget (OMB). This was the most significant domestic reform of the Nixon administration—and one that was accomplished by means of a well-developed lobbying effort on Capitol Hill.[26] Had Watergate not intervened, Nixon also would have pursued a major reorganizational effort aimed at collapsing the existing cabinet structure into fewer "super-cabinet" structures headed by lieutenants highly loyal to him.[27]

Nixon also attempted to transform the Office of Economic Opportunity (OEO), created in 1964 to coordinate the War on Poverty, but he was less successful. Nixon persuaded Donald Rumsfeld, a Republican member of Congress from Illinois, to head OEO and moved to extend OEO for two years. Rumsfeld carried out a number of reforms, but Nixon persisted in his opposition by vetoing two bills that would have extended OEO's mandate beyond the two years. Ultimately, Nixon was prevented from substantially dismantling OEO by a court order.[28]

Nixon tackled social policy issues, including crime and civil rights, not only through administrative actions but also through the judiciary appointment process. Nixon made changing the Warren court part of his 1968 campaign.[29] In 1969 Nixon got his opportunity, and nominated Warren Burger as the new chief justice. Burger nicely fit Nixon's criteria for justices who would be "tough on crime."[30] Nixon's efforts to appoint a southerner

224 *The Low-Opportunity Presidents*

to the Court failed twice. Clement Haynesworth, nominated in May 1969, was a competent judge but concerns about his financials and other improprieties led to his rejection by the Senate. Nixon's second nominee, G. Harrold Carswell, was quickly perceived by all but the most loyal Nixon defenders as a mistake. Carswell had a record of supporting racial segregation, and had one of the highest decision reversal rates of any sitting judge. His nomination was also defeated. Nixon turned away from his southern strategy with his other appointments.

Nixon's appointees to the high court surprised him. In particular, Harry Blackmun would write the famous *Roe v. Wade* abortion rights decision in 1973. Significantly, most of Nixon's nominees voted against President Nixon in the 1974 ruling that required him to release portions of his Watergate tapes.

Nixon also applied his administrative strategies to civil rights issues. Nixon proceeded with a series of steps seeking to reduce federal desegregation efforts. First, he and others leaned on administrators to move away from the Johnson administration's strategy of cutting off federal funds to segregated school districts. Second, Nixon and his aides made it very clear that anyone working in the Nixon administration should do nothing that was not absolutely required by law. Third, Nixon had federal lawyers push for Supreme Court agreement to a delay in HEW-approved school desegregation plans for 33 school districts in Mississippi.[31] The Supreme Court, headed by Nixon's newly appointed chief justice, Warren Burger, unanimously rejected the appeal.

In 1969, in an unexpected move, the Nixon administration introduced its "Philadelphia Plan" to push for affirmative action in the construction industry. Nixon believed that jobs were an important factor in improving race relations, but he also realized that, politically, it would pit organized labor against civil rights leaders. When the construction unions sought a congressional ban on the plan, the Nixon administration was able to sidetrack the effort. Ultimately, the Philadelphia Plan was adopted in 55 cities across the country.

In the summer of 1971, Nixon adopted a position that seemed to defy his long criticism of government bureaucracies. On August 15, he announced in a major national address that he was using his congressional authority to establish wage and price controls. As often happens, at the beginning of controls, the public response was quite positive. Scholars have quarreled as to whether this was merely a reelection ploy by the president.[32]

In response to public and congressional desires for action, Nixon created the Council on Environmental Quality by executive order in 1969. But when Congress responded to environmental initiatives with appropriations Nixon judged to be excessive, he took steps to slow action. In 1971, he impounded as much as 50 percent of the total spending appropriated by Congress for a water bill. In 1972, Nixon went along with Congress, though somewhat reluctantly, in establishing the Environmental Protection Agency.

Public Leadership

Nixon had an intense desire to draw public attention to favorable developments and seemed to believe that any policy problem could be solved by good public relations. Yet he also viewed the press as hostile and slanted against him and his programs. Despite his dislike of the press, Nixon actually had some success in shaping press coverage in his first term. Press conferences played only a very small role in Nixon's public leadership. The few he had were oriented toward foreign policy, and he made virtually no attempt to use them to help shape support for his domestic programs. As his first term progressed, press conferences were held less often—only about once every two months.[33]

Major national addresses and secondary speaking roles were a more important part of Nixon's strategies. Although he had difficulties with television because of his halting style of speaking, some of his addresses were effective. He achieved his greatest success in generating support for his welfare reform initiative, as 75 percent of the public thought his welfare plan was a good idea. In other speeches, Nixon talked extensively about crime, law enforcement, school desegregation, and, to a lesser degree, environmental issues.

Vice President Spiro Agnew also was a quite visible—and vocal—part of the administration's public face. Agnew's angry denunciations of liberals, the media, "unpatriotic war protesters who need to grow up," and "pointy-headed intellectuals" became a part of Nixon's "us vs. them" approach to politics. Agnew's efforts were at the forefront of the Nixon administration's attempt to benefit through cultural confrontation and divisiveness.

Congressional Leadership

Nixon recruited several Washington veterans for his legislative liaison efforts. His top aide was initially Bryce Harlow, a veteran of the Eisenhower administration who was instrumental in some of the Nixon administration's early coalition-building efforts. Harlow's relationship with Haldeman and Ehrlichman deteriorated, however, and he resigned.[34] He was followed by William Timmons, a former aide to Representative William Brock III (R-TN), and then Clark MacGregor, a former Republican member of Congress from Minnesota.

226 *The Low-Opportunity Presidents*

In allocating his time to congressional leadership, particularly during the first two years in office, Nixon made moderate efforts. Internal staff figures for the years 1969–1972 reveal the following yearly pattern: hours with GOP leadership meetings: 24, 16, 13, and 15; hours with senators: 125, 121, 94, and 23; hours with representatives: 87, 115, 69, and 30; and phone conversations with members: 204, 140, 180, and 61.[35] The falloff in time spent—quite common in a president's first term—reflected Nixon's frustration with Congress after his party fared poorly in the 1970 midterm elections.

Nixon displayed rather limited skill in dealing with members of Congress. Despite his earlier service there, Capitol Hill was still rather foreign to him, and he had difficulties in relating to the Senate in particular. Nixon was inept at small talk and often came off as awkward in his interactions with members of Congress.[36] Despite his often gruff, "in-your-face" demeanor, he found it hard to ask legislators for their votes. Recognizing that tendency, legislative liaison aide William Timmons at one point added a note at the bottom of Nixon's talking points for a meeting with a member of Congress, "ASK HIM FOR HIS VOTE."[37]

Nixon's chief strategy was to assume the role of centrist. To gain legislative victories, he started with the Republican core and then tried to coax into the fold Democrats from various factions depending on the nature of the issue. For example, House passage of the FAP in 1970 relied on a coalition of Republicans and liberal Democrats. And to slow school desegregation plans, he attempted to build a coalition of Republicans and conservative Democrats.[38] In fact, Nixon often found some of his best working relationships with southern Democrats.[39] After 1970, however, he adopted a strategy of increasingly going against Congress. As he told Bob Haldeman in a staff meeting at Key Biscayne on November 7, 1970, "Agreed, we don't work with Congress, we go against them."[40]

Vetoes were an important aspect of Nixon's legislative strategies, and he used the threat of a veto quite often as a bargaining tool. His threats were real—in the frequency with which he vetoed legislation, Nixon ranks near the middle among modern presidents.[41]

Legislative Enactments

During Nixon's first term in the White House, the number of major domestic enactments equaled 85 percent of those passed during Johnson's full term in office. The action was limited in 1969, reflecting in part Nixon's sparse first-year agenda and the bruising fights over Supreme Court nominees. The largest number of bills were enacted in 1970. Although Nixon exercised little presidential leadership during his abbreviated second term, some additional major legislation was enacted.

Tax Reform

In 1969, Congress enacted the most sweeping tax reform bill since 1913—a bill that had its origins in the Johnson administration, specifically Treasury Secretary Joseph Barr. Barr had warned of the prospects of a "taxpayers revolt," spurred on by increased public awareness of tax inequities, specifically the public's belief that millionaires were paying no personal income taxes.[42] The Nixon administration submitted proposals and got some of them approved, but the Democratic-controlled Congress drastically changed those proposals and added many of its own. Senate Minority Leader Hugh Scott (R-PA) was rather pointed in telling the White House staff that they should listen because specialists in Congress knew more about taxes than they did.[43] President Nixon was largely silent before the public on this issue, but he did use a veto threat, and he sought the aid of Republican legislators at a breakfast meeting at the White House. Ultimately, however, Nixon had to accept tax reforms he did not prefer. In assessing the overall effort, John Witte concluded that the tax reform measure was "basically a congressional tax bill."[44]

Crime Legislation

By making law and order a theme of his 1968 campaign, Nixon sparked the interest of both Congress and the public in law enforcement issues. By the time President Nixon and Congress proposed new crime legislation, they appeared to be responding to a major concern of average Americans. In the end, three major bills were enacted. The Organized Crime Control Act of 1970 was a comprehensive effort to address organized crime, including the creation of a witness protection program. The second measure, the Omnibus Crime Control Act of 1970, provided a wide variety of crime control provisions, including mandatory sentencing provisions. And the third, a narcotics control program, established several new drug control initiatives.

General Revenue Sharing

The general revenue sharing legislation enacted in 1972 was the Nixon administration's most significant domestic policy accomplishment. This strategy, which entailed having the federal government return tax dollars to state and local governments for use as they saw fit, appealed to Nixon for several reasons. In part, it would reduce the dependency on categorical grants, which had grown considerably in the Johnson presidency. It was also a means of providing additional aid to the suburbs and small towns, which fit nicely into Nixon's reelection concerns.

Nixon began his promotion of the idea in his January 1971 State of the Union address. He further pursued public support for it by unleashing a

228 *The Low-Opportunity Presidents*

mobilization effort, headed by Governor Nelson Rockefeller of New York, that surpassed the effort made for any other single piece of legislation. Indeed, according to one analyst, it was largely through Rockefeller's efforts that revenue sharing passed.[45] The administration also undertook an extensive legislative liaison effort to mobilize support in Congress and to decide on strategy as various alternative proposals emerged. In the end, then, Nixon largely prevailed; the program finally agreed on included about $5 billion in new revenues and a total of $16 billion over the 1973–1975 period.

Welfare, Social Security, and Health

Welfare, Social Security, and health care were highly salient legislative issues during Nixon's years in office. Interest in welfare reform heightened dramatically in August 1969 when Nixon unveiled a landmark proposal known as the Family Assistance Plan (FAP). FAP would have abolished Aid to Families with Dependent Children (AFDC) and Medicaid and replaced them with a guaranteed annual income of $1,600 for a family of four. In an attempt to provide work incentives, the plan also offered health benefits to families with incomes considerably above that level.

Nixon had several motivations in seeking broad welfare reform. Rapidly climbing welfare costs for AFDC were causing alarm in many quarters, and Nixon felt that, with his bold proposal, he might be able to gain credit for a historic change. Nixon's desire to aid the "deserving poor" had roots in his own childhood experiences. Other motivations were the president's desire to answer critics who had concluded by March 1969 that he had little in the way of a domestic program. It also reflected his desire to please those who opposed his civil rights policies. Finally, it reflected his desire to promote a plan that would lessen the role of federal officials and social workers.[46]

Democrats altered the bill so that Nixon would have to face the costs his plan would produce while he was in office. "The Democrats did this to trap us with an unworkable plan," he told Bob Haldeman. By the summer of 1970, Nixon had decided the plan should go nowhere. As Bob Haldeman put in his notes: "About Family Assistance Plan, wants to be sure it's killed by Democrats, and that we make a big play for it, but don't let it pass, can't afford it."[47]

Other welfare policy changes that took place during Nixon's first term were an expanded food stamp program and a major new federal commitment known as Supplementary Security Income (SSI). Nixon played a role in expanding the food stamp program when in May 1970 he requested a $1 billion-a-year increase. The Senate and House fought over the size of some of the provisions and finally passed a somewhat larger measure. The measure establishing the SSI program was passed in 1972, in a last-minute compromise. The program provided a floor income (initially $140 a month for individuals living alone and $190 a month for couples) for the aged, blind, and disabled.

Action on Social Security was even more extensive, with increases passed in 1969, 1971, and 1972. The generous increase in 1972, coupled with indexing, set the stage for funding problems as early as 1977. In each instance, Nixon's proposed figures were lower than the figures Congress adopted. As for indexing for annual cost of living adjustments (COLAs), Nixon had expressed an interest as early as 1969 as a way to eliminate a pattern of Democrats promoting increases in election years.[48] The actual decision-making process surrounding the 1972 legislation reflected electoral politics, with Nixon eager to cultivate the support of senior citizens.[49] Although he contributed little to the actual passage of the 1972 Social Security legislation, Nixon eagerly included references to the benefit increase he had signed in the mailings of the October benefits payments.

Nixon displayed considerable interest in health policy. In a February 1971 message to the American people, Nixon sought to respond to liberal calls for a system of national health insurance by promoting the concept of prepaid health plans. These plans, formerly opposed by conservatives, are now called health maintenance organizations (HMOs). His proposals included a call for private mandates—later to be echoed by Clinton's plan and included in "Obamacare." In the face of strong resistance by the American Medical Association, Nixon reduced his level of support for HMOs. Meanwhile, Democratic senator Edward Kennedy of Massachusetts was trying to broaden the scope of HMO development while Nixon was trying to reduce the funding levels being proposed in Congress. Thus, legislation was stalemated during Nixon's first term. Later, however, in 1973, a measure encompassing many of Kennedy's desires for a broad program but with funding levels closer to Nixon's preferences was passed.

On a second major health enactment, Nixon succeeded in helping to promote expansion of the federal government's cancer research effort. He proposed the legislation and promoted it publicly to a moderate degree. After elaborate compromises, the National Cancer Institute was created in 1971. But just as with welfare, final legislation was not as broad as the initial proposal.

Environmental and Consumer Protection Policies

A dramatic surge in environmental protection legislation, and to some extent consumer protection and health policies, occurred during Nixon's first term. Congress enacted the National Environmental Protection Act in 1969 and made sweeping changes in 1970 that included a major expansion of the effort to achieve clean air. The same year, Congress passed a clean water act and then a second water pollution control act in 1972. The year 1970 also saw the establishment of the Occupational Safety and Health

230　*The Low-Opportunity Presidents*

Administration within the Department of Labor. Other legislation passed in Nixon's first term tackled pesticide control, increased the funds spent on cancer research, and provided for an expanded organizational structure, banned cigarette advertising, and established the Consumer Product Safety Commission. President Nixon was not a significant voice in the sudden emergence of environmental issues in Washington.

The task facing the Nixon administration was one of acquiescing to this emerging interest while not accepting measures seen as extreme. Nixon also was determined that his potential rival in the 1972 election, Senator Edmund Muskie (D-ME), who had specialized in water pollution issues, not gain too much credit from passage of remedial legislation. After a very active year on environmental issues in 1970, Nixon lost interest. "The environment is not an issue that's worth a damn to us," he told aide Bob Haldeman.[50]

A close look at legislative action on major environmental policies during Nixon's first four years reveals several different patterns. In the area of pesticide controls, the Nixon administration's actions were pivotal to congressional adoption of new measures. According to Christopher Bosso, "Nixon's active intervention on the environment (based upon whatever motives) derailed the pesticides subgovernment and paved the way to substantial policy change."[51] In many other instances, the Nixon administration often sought to reduce the controls imposed on business by new legislation. On the Clean Air Act Amendments of 1970, for example, the administration supported some aspects of that sweeping legislation but unsuccessfully fought against amendments that would force the automobile industry to develop technologies that would reduce polluting auto emissions by 90 percent.

Civil Rights

During Nixon's first term, Congress extended the Voting Rights Act of 1965 and strengthened the enforcement provisions for the Equal Employment Opportunities Commission. On the extension of the Voting Rights Act, Nixon indicated his interest in softening some of its provisions, but the president did not speak out publicly in opposition. Congress ultimately prevailed, and the legislation was extended basically intact. The legislation expanding the enforcement powers of the Equal Employment Opportunity Commission was the culmination of a seven-year drive. The bill became the subject of a filibuster in the Senate, and two cloture votes failed. The legislation finally passed, however.

Nixon and Congress

According to a study by Mark Peterson, Nixon's relationship with Congress had many dimensions.[52] Despite his minority status, the president was more antagonistic than conciliatory toward legislators right from the outset and at times seemed unwilling to compromise. Yet he was willing to push hard for some of his bold programs, and in Peterson's study he did relatively well in gaining support for the large policy measures he submitted to Congress.

Congressional dominance was apparent in the shaping of domestic policy when the times were ripe for action and there were many policy ideas being promoted. At the same time, Nixon promoted some issues successfully, sought to define centrist positions in a number of areas, and displayed an interest in policy changes, which also contributed to an unusually extensive outpouring of legislation. Although he had to accept liberal reforms passed by Congress, Nixon consistently attempted to moderate or reduce congressional efforts while not openly operating against congressional or public opinion.

Watergate and the Ford Interregnum

The abuse of power in the Nixon administration will forever be somewhat mislabeled "Watergate."[53] That label was drawn from the burglary attempt at the headquarters of the Democratic National Committee on June 17, 1972. There is no hard evidence that Nixon knew in advance of the break-in, and there is considerable disagreement even today about the actual motivation for it.

But the abuse of power in the Nixon administration cannot be confined to events occurring at a hotel/office complex a few blocks from the White House, however fascinating.[54] The Nixon administration also engaged in illegal surveillance activities.[55] In the process, "as a wartime president, Nixon and his aides trampled again and again on the civil rights of antiwar protesters and other groups and individuals critical of the government."[56] One extreme case was the September 1971 break-in at a psychiatrist's office in Beverly Hills, California, so the intruders could examine the records of war protester Daniel Ellsberg. This break-in, like other activities, was carried out by a group known as the "Plumbers" because of their desire to plug leaks.

Another abuse of power was the administration's "enemies list"— prominent journalists, intellectuals, business and labor leaders, and others who might be targeted for harassment through tax audits, prosecution, and other government actions. The administration used the FBI and the Internal Revenue Service to harass political opponents.[57] At a May 1971 meeting attended by Nixon, plans were made to disrupt the campaigns of the strongest potential Democratic challengers. One of those disruptions was a fake letter written by Nixon campaign operatives attacking Edmund Muskie's wife. In an effort to defend his wife's honor, Muskie gave a very

232 The Low-Opportunity Presidents

emotional impromptu speech. Reactions to the episode led to Muskie's withdrawal from the race.

Nixon's final Watergate-related abuse—and the easiest for the public to understand—was his orchestration of a cover-up that included the payment of hush money to the Watergate burglars from funds kept in the White House. In October 1973, Nixon set the impeachment process in motion when he fired two attorneys general who would not dismiss the special prosecutor looking into the affair. He also resisted turning over his tapes of White House conversations to congressional committees and bungled the release of a sanitized version. The release of those tapes, which showed his involvement in the cover-up since June 23, 1972, led to bipartisan support for impeachment by the House of Representatives and his resignation as conviction in the Senate became increasingly certain.

Nixon's abuse of power was not confined to his domestic enemies. He also conducted a secret expansion into neutral Cambodia during the Vietnam War. On April 30, 1970, Nixon went on television to report that American troops had entered Cambodia. Significantly, the House drew up an article of impeachment based on the president's actions in Cambodia, but it was voted down in the House Judiciary Committee, which realized this could become a difficult issue within Congress.

With Nixon's resignation in 1974, Vice President Gerald Ford succeeded to the presidency. Ford faced enormous difficulties as president and compounded his problems by pardoning Nixon shortly after assuming office. His efforts to "put our national nightmare behind us" could be defended on some grounds, but the pardon fueled a drop in Ford's popularity from which he never recovered. The 1974 midterm election saw the Republicans lose 48 seats in the House and their ranks of party members shrink to only 144. The fairly promising pre-Watergate domestic agenda, which included health care reform, was dead. Efforts to end wage and price controls contributed to inflationary pressures, and the rising high unemployment figures jeopardized any fruitful policymaking. In foreign policy, the fall of Saigon to the North Vietnamese in April 1975 was a sad ending to virtually two decades of American involvement in Southeast Asia. It was not surprising, then, when Ford, in early 1976, was confronted with a tough nomination challenge from fellow Republican Ronald Reagan and was eventually defeated by Jimmy Carter.

An Assessment

As one would expect from a Republican president facing an activist Congress controlled by Democrats, Nixon seldom designed, promoted, and sold to Congress specific policy measures. His activism on some issues energized Congress. In his efforts to constrain what he saw as Democratic excesses, he also helped shape the domestic legacy that emerged. Environmental policy constitutes an important example of these forces. More programs of lasting duration were created by the Nixon administration than by any of those that followed.

Nixon's interest in the structure of the federal government also led to significant changes. The new OMB helped Nixon and future presidents better address management issues. Although his general revenue sharing scheme would not survive budget cuts by Reagan, that legislation provided for new flexibility in federal-state relations. Nixon also saw the establishment of Amtrak and the creation of the U.S. Postal Service as an independent agency.

The president had a moderate impact as well on the expansion of welfare and Social Security that occurred on his watch. Congress approved the indexing of Social Security for inflation. On welfare reform, it enacted only a small portion of what the president had proposed, but he initiated the idea of federal support of a minimum income—a notion that Congress had balked at and then enacted a much smaller program.

Nixon also contributed to changes in civil rights policies—some good, some bad, as civil rights leaders saw it. In dealing with the nation's schools, he reflected majority white opinion in opposing broad programs such as metropolitan-wide busing. He also expressed little support for some of the innovations that were beginning to emerge, such as magnet schools. He also established the first affirmative action program with his Philadelphia Plan.

A less positive Nixon legacy was the buildup of inflationary pressures that became increasingly troublesome throughout the 1970s. In fighting inflation, Nixon put into effect wage and price controls along with expansionary fiscal and monetary policies as part of his 1972 reelection bid. A change was warranted at that time, yet Nixon himself saw the problems down the road:

> The August 15, 1971, decision to impose [wage and price controls] was politically necessary and immensely popular in the short run. But in the long run I believe that it was wrong. The piper must always be paid, and there was an unquestionably high price for tampering with the orthodox economic mechanisms.[58]

Viewed in a broader perspective, Nixon's domestic performance suffers in one fundamental respect: he tended more to create divisions than to lessen them. Granted, presidents can do only so much to change the nation's climate of opinion, but underlying Nixon's rhetoric was a divisive "us versus them" tone. Since most of this rhetoric was directed toward protesters of the war in Vietnam, another cost of that war is apparent.[59]

234 *The Low-Opportunity Presidents*

This being said, Nixon was able to maintain in early 1973 that some of his goals had been met. He could rightly claim credit for some domestic policy changes, including a slowing of school desegregation efforts. Overseas, he had pursued innovative foreign policies with both China and the Soviet Union. The Paris peace accord, while less than he wanted, had provided an end to American involvement in Vietnam. In addition, the 1972 election had given him his coveted reelection—and by a margin that exceeded Eisenhower's. In overall terms, then, Nixon did reasonably well in achieving his domestic policy goals, especially for a low-opportunity president.

Yet Watergate cannot be ignored in any assessment of the Nixon presidency.[60] At a minimum, Watergate contributed to innumerable changes—almost all of them negative—in the presidency and American politics. Among other things, the public grew more cynical and less trusting of government, the level of political discourse has become harsher, the hunt for scandals has pervaded politics, and investigative journalists and special prosecutors have thrived. In Congress, a combination of younger, more ideologically driven members and the legacy of Watergate produced reforms that enhanced opportunities for a congressional role in shaping domestic policy—sometimes at the expense of presidential influence.

Notes

1 Joan Hoff Wilson, *Nixon Reconsidered* (New York: Basic Books, 1994), 17.
2 Michael A. Genovese, *The Nixon Presidency: Power and Politics in Turbulent Times* (Westport, CT: Greenwood Press, 1990), 10.
3 Zachary Jonathan Jacobson, "The Historical Presidency: The Nixon Act," *Presidential Studies Quarterly* 50, no. 4 (2020): 910–926.
4 Elliot L. Richardson, "Capacity for Greatness," in *Richard M. Nixon: Politician, President, and Administrator*, ed. Leon Friedman and William F. Levantrosser (Westport, CT: Greenwood Press, 1991), 3–4.
5 Tom Wicker, *One of Us: Richard Nixon and the American Dream* (New York: Random House, 1991), 24.
6 Bob Woodward and Carl Bernstein, *The Final Days* (New York: Simon and Schuster, 1976), 455.
7 Wicker, *One of Us*, 389.
8 Fawn Brodie, *Richard Nixon: The Shaping of His Character* (New York: Norton, 1981), 25.
9 Wicker, *One of Us*, 410.
10 Tim Galsworthy, "Carpetbaggers, Confederates, and Richard Nixon: The 1960 Presidential Election, Historical Memory, and the Republican Southern Strategy," *Presidential Studies Quarterly* 52, no. 2 (2022): 260–289.
11 Source: Frank Newport and Joseph Carroll, "Iraq Versus Vietnam: A Comparison of Public Opinion," *Gallup News Service*, August 24, 2005, https://news.gallup.com/poll/18097/iraq-versus-vietnam-comparison-public-opinion.aspx.
12 Michael A. Genovese and Todd L. Belt, *The Post-Heroic Presidency: Leveraged Leadership in an Age of Limits*, 2nd ed. (Santa Barbara, CA: Praeger, 2016).
13 Michael A. Genovese, *The Watergate Crisis*, 2nd ed. (Santa Barbara, CA: ABC-CLIO, 2020).

14 Richard M. Nixon, The *Memoirs of Richard Nixon* (New York: Grossett and Dunlop, 1978); and Wicker, *One of Us*, 412.
15 A. James Reichley, *Conservatives in an Age of Change* (Washington, DC: Brookings Institution, 1981), 58.
16 Rowland Evans Jr. and Robert D. Novak, *Nixon in the White House: The Frustration of Power* (New York: Random House, 1971), 51.
17 Stephen E. Ambrose, *Nixon: The Triumph of a Politician, 1962–1972* (New York: Simon and Schuster, 1989), 236.
18 Wilson, *Nixon Reconsidered*, 53.
19 Ambrose, *Nixon*, 228.
20 John Ehrlichman, *Witness to Power: The Nixon Years* (New York: Simon and Schuster, 1982), 212.
21 Ibid., 207.
22 John H. Kessel, *The Domestic Presidency: Decision-Making in the White House* (North Scituate, MA: Duxbury Press, 1975), 123.
23 John R. Greene, *The Limits of Power: The Nixon and Ford Administrations* (Bloomington: Indiana University Press, 1992), 27.
24 Richard P. Nathan, *The Plot That Failed: Nixon and the Administrative Presidency* (New York: Wiley, 1975); and Richard P. Nathan, *The Administrative Presidency* (New York: Wiley, 1983).
25 H. R. Haldeman, The *Haldeman Diaries: Inside the Nixon White House* (New York: Putnam's Sons, 1994), 6.
26 Greene, *Limits of Power*, 54.
27 Nathan, *Plot That Failed*, ch. 1.
28 Wilson, *Nixon Reconsidered*, 63.
29 Laura Kalman, *The Long Reach of the Sixties: LBJ, Nixon and the Making of the Contemporary Supreme Court* (New York: Oxford University Press, 2017).
30 Ambrose, *Nixon*, 201.
31 Hugh David Graham, *The Civil Rights Era: Origins and Development of National Policy, 1960–1972* (New York: Oxford University Press, 1990), 319.
32 See Herbert Stein, "Discussant Comments," in *Richard M. Nixon: Politician, President, and Administrator*, ed. Leon Friedman and William F. Levantrosser (Westport, CT: Greenwood Press, 1991), 249–254; and Edward R. Tufte, *Political Control of the Economy* (Princeton, NJ: Princeton University Press, 1978).
33 See Todd L. Belt, "Nixon, Watergate, and the Attempt to Sway Public Opinion," in *Watergate Remembered: The Legacy for American Politics*, ed. Michael A. Genovese and Iwan W. Morgan (New York: Palgrave Macmillan, 2012), 147–167.
34 Evans and Novak, *Nixon in the White House*, 103–110.
35 Ehrlichman, *Witness to Power*, 202–203.
36 Jennifer Hora, "'Happy Birthday' and Other Awkward Sentiments: Nixon's Social Interactions as Part of Congressional Relationship Building," *Congress & the Presidency* 46, no. 2 (2019): 380–305.
37 Reichley, *Conservatives in an Age of Change*, 87.
38 Ibid., ch. 5.
39 Ambrose, *Nixon*, 406.
40 Haldeman, *Haldeman Diaries*, 208.
41 Richard A. Watson, *Presidential Vetoes and Public Policy* (Lawrence: University Press of Kansas, 1993), 42. Also see Robert J. Spitzer, *The Presidential Veto* (Albany: State University of New York Press, 1988).
42 *Congressional Quarterly Almanac 1969* (Washington, DC: Congressional Quarterly, 1970), 589.

236 *The Low-Opportunity Presidents*

43 Ibid., 107.

44 John F. Witte, *The Politics and Development of the Federal Income Tax* (Madison: University of Wisconsin Press, 1985), 176.

45 Greene, *Limits of Power*, 62.

46 See in particular Reichley, *Conservatives in an Age of Change*, 143.

47 Haldeman, *Haldeman Diaries*, 32, 181.

48 Martha Derthick, *Policymaking for Social Security* (Washington, DC: Brookings Institution, 1979), 346.

49 William W. Lammers, *Public Policy and the Aging* (Washington, DC: CQ Press, 1984).

50 Haldeman, *Haldeman Diaries*, 246.

51 Christopher J. Bosso, *Pesticides and Politics: The Life Cycle of a Public Issue* (Pittsburgh, PA: University of Pittsburgh Press, 1987), 262.

52 Mark A. Peterson, *Legislating Together: The White House and Capitol Hill from Eisenhower to Reagan* (Cambridge, MA: Harvard University Press, 1993), 247–251.

53 Genovese, *The Watergate Crisis*.

54 Stanley I. Kutler, *The Wars of Watergate* (New York: Knopf, 1992); and Fred Emery, *Watergate: The Corruption of American Politics and the Fall of Richard Nixon* (New York: Touchstone, 1995).

55 Michael Schudson, *Watergate in American Memory* (New York: Basic Books, 1992), 35.

56 Wilson, *Nixon Reconsidered*, 278.

57 See Melissa Graves, *Nixon's FBI: Hoover, Watergate, and a Bureau in Crisis* (Boulder, CO: Lynne Rienner, 2020); and David E. Rosenbaum, "Panel Reportedly Hears Nixon's Aides Tried to Use I.R.S. for His Political Benefit," *New York Times*, June 14, 1974, p. 12.

58 Nixon, *Memoirs*, 521.

59 Wilson, *Nixon Reconsidered*, 113.

60 See Michael A. Genovese and Iwan W. Morgan, eds., *Watergate Remembered: The Legacy for American Politics* (New York: Palgrave Macmillan, 2012).

12 Jimmy Carter
An Outsider's Pursuit of "Trustee" Leadership

In the post-Watergate era, Jimmy Carter (served 1977–1981) assumed office seeking to end the ceremonial trappings and power abuses of the "imperial presidency" while promising the nation a presidency "as good as its people." Despite his promises of positive new directions, his four years in the White House were a continuous struggle.

Carter had sought to govern differently. He liked to pursue policies he viewed to be in the long-term public interest, and he placed less emphasis on bargaining with Congress. His approach featured a zealous pursuit of administrative efficiencies and a desire to have direct, town meeting-style communication with the public. Did this low-opportunity president turn his trustee leadership into success on the domestic front?

Personal Characteristics

James Earl Carter Jr. (1924–) was the first president to have been born and raised in the Deep South since Woodrow Wilson. He also was the most devoutly religious president serving since 1932. Had he been raised in similar circumstances outside of the one-party South, he might have been a Republican.[1]

Jimmy was the son of a prominent peanut farmer and processor in tiny Plains, Georgia. After high school, he left South Georgia to attend college at the US Naval Academy. Upon graduation, as a young officer, he carried out many assignments during his brief naval career, including engineering officer on a nuclear submarine. After the death of his father in 1953, he abruptly left the navy and returned to Plains to run the family business.

Career Path

Jimmy Carter had less experience in significant administrative and elective positions than any other post-1932 president up to that time. After serving on the Sumner County, Georgia, school board and in the state legislature

DOI: 10.4324/9781003426684-15

238 *The Low-Opportunity Presidents*

for four years, he ran unsuccessfully for governor in 1966 and successfully in 1970. Restricted by the state's constitution to a single term, he left office in 1974. While governor, he pushed for reorganization of the state government and budgeting reforms, as well as making progress in the appointments of African Americans. His relationship with the factionally divided legislature was stormy, and it is unlikely he would have been reelected if a second term had been allowed.[2]

Carter emerged victorious in the 1976 primaries as a candidate who appealed to moderate Democrats and many Christian evangelicals. Carter faced a weak incumbent in the fall election. President Gerald Ford had barely survived a close primary contest with Ronald Reagan and was hampered by the lingering issue of his pardon of Richard Nixon. Carter released a lengthy list of issue positions during his campaign but did not give a clear sense of where he was heading. He did, however, frequently assert that his administration would be far more open than Nixon's, and he pledged not to lie or deceive the public. These themes drew some support, but they did not clarify his policy goals. By October 1976, the press had begun to decry the lack of substance in the campaign. Carter was aided in his victory by strong southern support and his ability to hold northern Democratic strongholds such as New York and Massachusetts.

What Manner of Man?

Despite his low-key demeanor, Carter was self-confident and ambitious. During his years in the navy, he had openly aspired to become the chief of naval operations. He was confident enough in his alternative career opportunities to return to Plains after the death of his father. In fact, he was so ambitious that he was willing to embark on campaigns even when experts gave him little chance of victory.[3]

Carter sought vast amounts of information about policy issues. Since he was a "quick read," that information helped him in his campaigning and he often was able to impress observers with his knowledge of national issues. His interest in historical perspectives was limited, as he preferred gathering technical information on specific issues. Some analysts believe this trait contributed to his weaknesses as a broader, strategic thinker.

Staff aide James Fallows, shortly after departing the White House in 1979, stressed Carter's basic fairness and decency. Yet he also found that Carter seemed to conduct a passionless presidency.[4] Others have pointed to Carter's honesty and forthrightness, high degree of self-discipline, and tenacious pursuit of personal goals. Less flattering assessments have pointed to his naïveté about the nature of government, limited creativity, and tendencies toward self-righteousness.

Policy Views

Carter's commitment to government reorganization was unusual. Unlike previous presidential candidates, he made government reorganization a major campaign theme.[5] He also was fond of pointing out that existing policies had been influenced too much by special interests. As a result, in some quarters he was perceived as anti-business.[6]

Carter was fiscally conservative but held liberal views on social and environmental policy issues. Historian Arthur Schlesinger Jr. described Carter as the most conservative Democratic president since Grover Cleveland. Yet, on civil rights, Governor Jimmy Carter had surprised Georgians with the scope of his efforts and his declaration that the era of segregation was over. He continued to support civil rights as president.

Challenges and Opportunities

Carter took office at what observers have described as "not an opportune time"[7] and in "probably a more restrictive atmosphere than any president [had faced] since World War II."[8] The election results and levels of public support were not promising. Carter's margin of victory over Ford in the 1976 election was merely 2.1 percentage points. In terms of popularity, he began with a respectable 61 percent during his first year, but his popularity declined precipitously. Moreover, Carter was an outsider, with little knowledge of the arcane workings of the Washington community.[9]

The situation in Congress was not promising. Party strength looked impressive on the surface, with 292 Democrats in the House and 61 in the Senate. These margins were inflated by the large post-Watergate surge of Democrats in the midterm election of 1974, and Democrats gained only one more House seat in 1976. Post-Watergate reforms aimed at strengthening Congress's role in relation to that of the president had opened the way to Congress hiring more staff to develop proposals and increased the number of subcommittees for ambitious legislators.

In looking forward to some promising issues, Carter also faced expectations within the Democratic Party coalition that would be difficult to meet. Measures such as health care and welfare reform were popular, but the public was shifting away from support for the other spending measures traditionally promoted by the Democratic Party.[10] Environmental issues were the most promising, as Ford had vetoed three environmental bills. Some legislators and citizens also wanted to see the government reduce federal regulation in several areas of the economy.

Unfortunately for Carter, two big problems did not promise easy legislative action.[11] The first was the simultaneous rise in both unemployment and inflation that made it difficult for him to rely on the traditional Keynesian solution of expanded deficit spending. The basic conundrum

240 *The Low-Opportunity Presidents*

for policymakers was that an increase in spending or a reduction in taxes aimed at stimulating the economy might worsen levels of inflation. Further complicating the problem, the budget deficit in the preceding year had been 19.8 percent of total spending. Economist Anthony Campagne was quite blunt about Carter's predicament when he argued that in this situation the economics profession could not offer clear solutions.[12]

Energy policy presented a second tough problem. A wide variety of proposals had been discussed in the wake of the 1973 energy crisis in which an embargo by the Organization of Petroleum Exporting Countries (OPEC) had contributed to a sharp rise in oil prices. Yet consumers and the producers of various energy sources such as coal and oil disagreed on the appropriate remedial policies. A strong environmental movement presented some opportunities for energy conservation, but that approach sparked controversy among its more conservative, antiregulatory political and business opponents. According to political scientist Eric Uslaner, this situation was a "zero-sum game" in which bargaining to develop coalitions was difficult because policy choices created both clear losers and clear winners.[13]

Carter's troubles did not stop there, especially during his last two years in office. A second OPEC oil embargo forced reconsideration of energy policies in the summer of 1979. Then, on November 4, 1979, 52 Americans were taken hostage at the U.S. embassy in Tehran. Carter's popularity rose somewhat as he undertook an extensive, highly publicized effort to gain their release in the months that followed. Yet when no progress was made and an April 1980 rescue attempt had to be aborted, his public approval fell dramatically. The hostage crisis became a major liability in his reelection effort. Further complicating Carter's position in 1980 was the Soviet invasion of Afghanistan. Carter's responses, which included a grain embargo against the Soviets and a boycott of the 1980 Moscow Olympics, proved unpopular.

Leadership Style

Carter brought a distinct leadership style to the White House. He sought to replace the "imperial presidency" with an open administration that was more accessible to the public. He also promoted reforms to improve government efficiencies and to help restore confidence in government. In his overall approach to issues, the president considered himself to be a trustee who looked toward long-range concerns rather than simply cutting political deals on Capitol Hill. As such, he developed a personal dislike for many legislators and interest groups. He had confidence in his ability to develop effective policies and reforms, many of which he had used successfully in Georgia to modernize state government.

The Advisory Process and Approach to Decision-Making

Carter recruited many Georgians and campaign aides for his staff and a variety of prominent figures for his cabinet. Of his top aides, six of the nine had worked for him as governor or during his campaign.[14] Carter sought to increase the legitimacy of his administration and pursue government efficiency by recruiting for his cabinet men and women with extensive Washington experience and strong reputations. Despite the initial "outsider" perspective expressed by Hamilton Jordan that the new administration would not consider Washington establishment figures such as Cyrus Vance, Vance was later asked to serve as secretary of state.

The initial organization of Carter's White House stemmed from his confidence in his own ability to absorb vast amounts of information. It also reflected his desire not to replicate Nixon's strong chief-of-staff model, which Carter associated with abuse of power. He envisioned a White House organization in which aides would have equal access to him in a spokes-in-a-wheel operation. His plan proved unworkable, however. He simply did not have time to soak up information about every single policy issue. Nor did he have time to properly implement the managerial demands of such an approach. By mid-1979, Hamilton Jordan had been named chief of staff.

In his decision-making, Carter intended to fulfill his campaign pledges. Jeff Fishel compared ten issues that Carter had stressed during his campaign and the salience of those issues to Carter's agenda during his first two years in office. Fishel found that Carter failed to maintain a high salience for only one issue—tax policy.[15] In some instances, in keeping with the perspective of a trustee president, Carter was primarily motivated when he thought that an important issue was not being addressed by Congress.

The Carter White House tended to look at policy issues from a technical, engineering perspective and pay little attention to the reasons earlier initiatives had failed. For example, administration officials approached welfare reform by collecting a great deal of current data on systemic problems and seeking solutions in a comprehensive manner, but they paid little attention to political feasibility. This tendency to overlook political feasibility was especially evident in James Schlesinger's rushed effort to put together an energy package in the first three months of the Carter presidency. Carter later recognized that the process had been a mistake, but one dictated by the desire for speed.[16] More generally, Carter encouraged his staff to develop good decisions, telling them to worry about the policy while he worried about the politics. Carter often consulted Hamilton Jordan and First Lady Rosalynn Carter on political feasibility questions. At some points, Carter clearly made political decisions, such as when he had Joseph Califano cut back on an educational campaign against smoking when the tobacco industry lobbied the White House in opposition to

242 *The Low-Opportunity Presidents*

the plan. More often, however, he paid little attention to the political feasibility of an action or decision.

The organization and experience of the Carter White House staff drew criticism, but some observers noted improvement over time. On the negative side, many of Carter's most senior staff had no prior Washington experience. Although the absence of a more hierarchical staff at the outset seemed to prevent timely decisions, some significant improvements were noted. For example, over time fewer special task forces were used to develop proposals. Along the way, former Georgia lawyer Stuart Eizenstat, chairman of the Domestic Policy Staff, became one of the most powerful men in Washington.[17]

Carter's relationships with his cabinet did not show a comparable improvement over time.[18] His cabinet members were generally quite capable of taking strong roles in developing and promoting policies. Nevertheless, they possessed little personal loyalty to Carter, and, because they often received little direction, they usually went their own way. Controversies over specific policies erupted periodically, however. HEW Secretary Joseph Califano, for example, objected to Carter's cautious approach to several policy issues.[19]

In July 1979, Carter took the unprecedented step of removing no fewer than five of his cabinet officers, including some of the more prominent figures such as Michael Blumenthal, Joseph Califano, and James Schlesinger. He had become increasingly frustrated with press leaks and signs of disloyalty, and some leading Democratic Party officials advised him that to reorient his administration, he would have to seek several resignations. The firings, though, produced considerable uncertainty about the stability of the administration and led to a decline in public support.

Administrative Strategies

As noted, Carter was unusually interested in "good government."[20] In keeping with that interest and his desire to streamline White House operations, he successfully sought legislation that would restore the president's reorganization authority, which had expired in 1973. Carter also succeeded in creating two new departments. One was the Department of Energy, an idea that had surfaced in the Ford administration and in Congress. Carter had to compromise significantly on his initial proposal in the face of pressures from various energy interests, but with the aid of several key legislators, the measure passed in 1977.[21] Carter also led a fight to establish the second new department, the Department of Education. Passage of this legislation in 1979 was strongly supported by the National Education Association, which had backed Carter in the 1976 election.

Civil service reform was high on Carter's agenda as well. His strong efforts to gain legislative support included convening a task force, headed by Les Francis of the legislative liaison staff. Francis coordinated legislative lobbying, orchestrated calls by cabinet secretaries to key legislators, and made his own phone calls to designated legislators.[22] By pushing an issue that Congress otherwise would not have pursued, Carter was able to see enactment of the most extensive civil service reform since the system was founded in 1883.

Carter's commitment to good government drew mixed assessments. Two public administration specialists found civil service reform "the most impressive achievement of Jimmy Carter's presidency."[23] Yet by 1981, top aide Jack Watson was pondering Carter's efforts: "I think we spent an undue amount of emphasis, time, political capital, and energy on governmental reorganization too much as an end in itself rather than as a means to an end."[24]

Carter staffed administrative roles dealing with civil rights with more African Americans than any president to that time. On affirmative action, he sought to manage conflicts rather than take strong positions and generally subscribed to a position of defending affirmative action but not quotas.[25] On abortion, he made little effort to support the opposing sides by either legitimizing the 1973 *Roe v. Wade* decision or working against it.[26] That lack of decisive action, according to Barbara Craig and David O'Brien, was reflected in Carter's appointments, which sent mixed signals on various abortion rights matters.

Public Leadership

Carter was a firm believer in the importance of how a president related to the public. In his view, presidents should set a high moral tone while also communicating directly with the public to circumvent the concerns of special interests.

The results of Carter's efforts were mixed. His public approval fell in his first year, and he periodically received ratings under 30 percent during his last two years in office. Some of Carter's problems stemmed from his poor choice of persona. He campaigned as an "outsider" and proceeded to dramatically de-emphasize presidential symbols such as the anthem "Hail to the Chief." Yet over time it became apparent that the removal of the trappings of office had gone too far, as the public seemed unmoved by his attempt to present himself as a rather unassuming "nice guy" and an "average American."[27]

Carter also had problems in gaining favorable press coverage. Especially in the beginning, he did not go out of his way to court the press. In the aftermath of Watergate, when reporters played a key role in the investigation, some journalists seemed eager to show that they could take a critical

244   *The Low-Opportunity Presidents*

stance toward a Democratic president. In an examination of the content of leading newspapers, Mark Rozell found that views of Carter in these newspapers were more negative than the public's views.[28]

Overall, Carter's public leadership reflected his preferences for less traditional public relations activities. He held fewer press conferences than most presidents, and he was not particularly skilled at focusing on issues or at presenting his administration in a favorable light. He gave only 1.5 televised domestic addresses per year—slightly below average. Because Carter preferred to seek direct contact with the electorate, he gravitated toward the use of town meetings. The town meetings, however, proved to be less effective for him, as the public seemed more interested in a president who had proposals to present rather than one who simply wanted to listen to the public. Moreover, Carter was unable to get the town meetings on the air, and so they rarely changed anything.[29]

Finally, there was the matter of Carter's speaking style. Because he viewed public addresses as more of a burden than an opportunity, he only achieved mixed results. One problem was his preference for a somber, moralistic tone. As one staffer saw it, "If Carter had delivered FDR's 'nothing to fear' speech, the Depression would still be going on."[30]

Congressional Leadership

Carter's relationships with members of Congress were marked by considerable tension and widespread criticism. Frank Moore, Carter's one-time liaison with the Georgia state legislature, handled the day-to-day interactions with Congress from the unusually small Office of Legislative Liaison. Moore drew widespread criticism for his lack of experience and Washington savvy. No other top aide had a strong role. Carter's staff of Washington outsiders were ignorant of the ways of Congress and failed to engage in the expected care and feeding of members of Congress. Chief of Staff Hamilton Jordan, who enjoyed campaign politics more than legislative tactics, maintained no direct contact with Speaker Tip O'Neill.

Carter's own relationship with Congress was shaped not only by his dislike of bargaining and patronage but also by his tenacity in trying to get things done. He continued the traditional morning breakfasts with legislative leaders and maintained a concerted effort to enlist their aid. Frequently, he tried to achieve influence with members of Congress by presenting information rather than direct bargaining. This is because Carter believed bargaining produced short-term, wasteful policy results, and thus he avoided it.[31] One staff aide was vehement on the subject: "[Carter] doesn't like politicians.... He knows there are good ones and bad ones and so on, but he really does not like them. He's anti-politician."[32]

Carter's approach changed over time. During his first year, he made energy policy a top priority and decided to wait on health care until 1978.

Yet, he was reluctant to choose among other issues and would even comment that he had "over a hundred priorities." As a result, by March 1977, too many bills were heading for the House Ways and Means Committee. Carter did not force himself to focus his energy on specific issues. As his term progressed, however, he began to set priorities, including civil service reform to hospital cost containment. Efforts to build public support improved when Anne Wexler took over the public liaison responsibilities and placed greater emphasis on possible interest group coalitions than on the bland advocacy of "good government."

Legislative Enactments

No landmark legislation emerged during Carter's four years in office. He attempted a fast-start strategy in 1977 and was able to chalk up several easy victories because of previous Ford vetoes, but he suffered a crushing defeat in the rejection of his energy initiative. In his second year, he was able to produce several important new enactments, including some in which he played a significant role. During his final two years, Carter clashed intensely with liberals in his own party and saw frequent stalemates, but he also achieved a few legislative victories.[33] His levels of influence and success differed among policy areas.

Energy Policies

In 1977, Congress had two topics on the table: Energy and everything else, as Carter had pushed energy to the top of the agenda.[34] Although there had been some (largely unsuccessful) efforts to decrease America's dependence on foreign oil between 1973 and 1976 and a considerable amount of public discussion, neither the public nor Congress anticipated that President Carter would present Congress with a major energy initiative. This was particularly the case since Carter had said little on the subject during the 1976 campaign.

Carter made his commitment to focus on energy for several reasons. Assessments by the Central Intelligence Agency regarding OPEC and the international oil market were sobering. A record-setting cold wave in January had underscored the nation's energy problems. In addition, the many issues involved in devising an energy policy appealed to Carter's desire to develop a comprehensive policy approach.[35]

The policy proposal submitted to Congress in April was a complex, controversial document containing over 100 separate initiatives.[36] It emphasized conservation and the development of alternative energy sources more than efforts to expand production. Major initiatives in the proposal called for maintaining price and production controls on natural gas in interstate commerce, taxing foreign crude oil to encourage American production,

246 *The Low-Opportunity Presidents*

imposing a "gas guzzler" tax on automobiles, and boosting gasoline taxes dramatically. Conservation measures included mandatory energy efficiency standards for home appliances, reform of electric utility rates, and tax credits for home insulation.

Although Carter tried to rally public support for his proposal, he largely failed. In a period of considerable public skepticism about oil company operations, he was unable to convince a majority of the electorate that the energy crisis was real. Also, the public could not bring itself to applaud gas taxes and other measures requiring greater pain for consumers. The president was able to generate some public support for the less costly conservation measures, however.

Entries in Carter's own diary describe his coalition-building efforts. He noted he had held meetings several times a week with leaders from "business, agriculture, finance, transportation, the elderly, international trade, local and state government, the news media, consumer affairs, electric utilities, mining, and oil and gas industries for briefings and appeals from me ... and others."[37] Quite strikingly, this list did not include segments of the liberal Democratic coalition such as labor and representatives of minority groups. In a similar fashion, the Office of Public Liaison sought an educational role and eagerly pursued individual suggestions, but it did little in the way of systematically seeking to organize coalition support.

The defeat of the energy bill can be traced in part to the intense lobbying efforts of the oil and natural gas producers and their allies in Congress. But Carter's efforts also were ineffective. He had taken on a difficult problem and proposed a solution, but had paid little attention to its political feasibility. Moreover, his approach to building public support was flawed. He phoned legislators when the energy bill became bogged down in the Senate, but he had little success with key opponents such as oil industry supporter Russell Long (D-LA). It is not surprising that a flawed leadership effort on behalf of an extremely ambitious and difficult policy proposal ended in defeat.

Carter took a very different and more skillful approach to energy policy in 1978. Most importantly, he decided to return to the position he had originally taken during the 1976 campaign and support phased decontrol of natural gas prices. That step, plus the elimination of the proposed gasoline tax, substantially improved prospects for passage of the energy bill. Moreover, the Carter administration, which had learned from past mistakes, launched a very impressive executive lobbying effort on behalf of the natural gas compromise. According to Elizabeth Sanders, the White House employed all of the tools of presidential persuasion:

> pragmatic bargains involving tangible *quid pro quos* were struck with individual congressmen; grassroots support was marshaled by lectures to visiting community opinion leaders and high-level

conferences with banking and business executives who were subtly reminded of the many ways in which executive prerogatives could be used to help or hurt them.[38]

In addition, legislators who supported the measure lobbied those who were undecided.

Despite Carter's distaste for repeatedly dealing with energy policy, a 1979 Iranian boycott of oil sales to the United States forced additional action in 1980. This occurred as motorists were becoming increasingly angry with a new surge in prices and long lines at gas stations. Carter's response to the situation came in two different steps. In an attempt to appeal to the more liberal segments of his coalition, he successfully promoted the establishment of a windfall profits tax. He also used his administrative discretion to deregulate oil prices. Carter sought to have the revenue from the windfall profits tax placed in trust funds for designated programs such as mass transit and assistance for low-income energy consumers. Congress at first resisted the promotion of trust funds, but later overcame an intense lobbying effort by the oil industry and established a modified trust fund approach. Declining oil prices in 1980 and actions by the Reagan administration eliminated that revenue source.

In an attempt to pursue new energy sources, Carter successfully promoted an initiative seeking to extract oil from shale, which passed the House in 1979. Carter embraced proposals for synfuel development as part of his July 1979 address that called for both new energy policy initiatives and other steps to overcome a seeming "crisis of confidence."[39] As the battles over the initiatives began in key legislative committees, the Carter administration limited its involvement.[40] The omnibus energy measure finally produced called for $88 billion in new spending. It had a relatively short life, however. A combination of fewer energy shortages in the 1980s and the desire for fiscal constraint in the Reagan administration led to a sharp reduction in, and ultimately the dismantling of, this policy initiative.

Environmental Policies

The struggle over environmental policy began early in Carter's first year as he sought to reduce the number of water projects being built by the U.S. Army Corps of Engineers. For Carter, unnecessary dams and water projects were the "worst examples" of pork barrel politics.[41] After a veto of some of these projects, Carter agreed to a compromise arranged by House Speaker Tip O'Neill and got a reduction of about half of what he had hoped to achieve.

In 1977, Congress passed three environmental measures that had been vetoed by Gerald Ford or Richard Nixon or both. The Carter administration supported the measures, but interaction with Congress often occurred

248 *The Low-Opportunity Presidents*

at the departmental level, and none of these issues achieved the importance the Carter administration attached to energy policy. The most far-reaching bill amended the Clean Air Act by both expanding and reducing the standards being applied. The other two measures established strip mine regulations for surface and underground mining and modified segments of the Clean Water Act.

Other important legislation came at the end of Carter's four years in office. Despite his languishing position in the polls, he was able to help gain passage of two major environmental measures in 1980. A proposal for a "superfund" had been in the works for over two years. The fund would address problems such as the dramatic toxic waste episode at Love Canal, New York, in 1977. Because Carter and the environmentalists had to compromise considerably in 1980, the final measure covered only toxic chemical cleanup sites and not oil spills. Nevertheless, a major new effort had been launched.

The environmental measure on which Carter had the strongest impact came a week after his 1980 reelection defeat when Congress passed a bill that more than doubled the size of the country's national parks and almost tripled the area of land designated as wilderness. Carter worked with key legislators such as Democratic House member Morris Udall of Arizona and encouraged the mobilization of interest groups by orchestrating a White House kickoff in July to help build support for the proposed legislation. Carter also watched attentively as on Capitol Hill the inevitable compromises were pursued prior to the final passage of the bill.

Taxes, Jobs, and the Minimum Wage

Carter and Congress engaged in repeated conflicts over how to address the problems of a stagnant economy. He had started off badly in 1977. In the wake of his criticism of Ford and 8 percent unemployment, he had proposed a $50 per person tax rebate. He then infuriated supporters a mere two months later when he concluded that signs of an economic upswing made the rebate unnecessary. In the halls of Congress, members and staff bantered about the line that the president had invented a new "Carter bomb" that killed its friends and left its enemies standing.

In 1978, the administration produced another tax reform proposal calling for simplification, greater equity in taxation, and an effort to promote greater incentives for investment. The proposal stalled, however, and for a time was judged to be dead in the House Ways and Means Committee. Earlier, in June 1977, California voters had approved a massive tax reduction initiative (Proposition 13) that served as a catalyst for further action in Congress. But the Carter administration did not join in support until a compromise bill was about to reach the House floor. The measure that finally emerged was significantly different from the original administration proposal. Its major provisions called for reducing the capital gains tax from 30 percent to 28 percent, expanding opportunities for uses of individual retirement accounts (IRAs), and increasing the earned income tax credit. Ultimately, the tax measures that passed in 1977 and 1978 bore almost no resemblance to the legislation proposed by Jimmy Carter.[42]

The 1977 increase in the minimum wage was achieved through bargaining between the White House and the other players. The Carter administration bargained with AFL-CIO president George Meany and Democratic members of Congress over the size of the increase. Meany was angered by the administration's initial proposal of a $0.20 increase to $2.50 an hour along with future indexing for inflation. They finally agreed on $2.65 an hour, plus indexing. The ultimate legislative compromise produced a bill with no indexing, but a gradual increase to $3.35 an hour.

Carter's proposal to broaden the government's job creation efforts revealed the sharp tensions between himself and many Democratic liberals. In 1977, the president successfully promoted an expanded jobs program with a multiyear increase of $5.5 billion in funding for the Comprehensive Employment Training Act (CETA).[43] Liberals sought a broader program, including a national policy of full employment, increased real income, economic growth, greater productivity, stable prices, and a balanced budget. Carter was lukewarm to their proposal—and many of his aides were opposed—so he gave only reluctant support, bowing to heavy pressure from the Black Caucus and organized labor. Final passage of a bill, stripped of its automatic trigger mechanism for new jobs, proved to be largely.[44]

Economic Deregulation

Between 1977 and 1980, the Carter administration joined some liberal and conservative advocates in Congress in promoting deregulation as an anti-inflation strategy. The passage of a bill in 1978 deregulating the airline industry was the first of four important measures. The Carter administration was an important player in the passage of the bill, which was eased by the major divisions within the airline industry itself.[45] With that victory, the government took the relatively rare step of eliminating the Civil Aeronautics Board and its role in regulating the price of airline tickets.

Carter and his administration played an even bigger role in the deregulation of the trucking industry. The initial impetus for reducing the role of the Interstate Commerce Commission came from commission members themselves. Carter then joined that effort and surprised members of Congress by making trucking deregulation a high-priority issue. In pushing for a strong measure, he called and met with key legislators. He may have compromised a bit too early, but there was widespread agreement that a strong measure emerged because of his leadership role. A top staff

250 *The Low-Opportunity Presidents*

member, perhaps forgetting the time constraints Carter faced, praised his effort and suggested that if Carter had made a comparable effort on other legislation, he would still be president.[46]

Deregulation of the savings and loan industry also began during the Carter years. Legislators and others, responding to the adverse impact of inflation on this industry together with the technological changes occurring in the nation's financial institutions, had been calling for action to modify regulations.[47] Congress acted in 1978 by lifting the ceilings on the interest rates savings and loan institutions could offer. This and the 1982 Garn-St. Germain Depository Institutions Act (which increased deposit guarantees from $40,000 to $100,000) were major factors leading to the 1989 federal bailout of the ailing savings and loan associations.

Social Security, Welfare, and Health

Carter had one success and two losses in his efforts to change Social Security, welfare, and health policies. Social Security provided Carter's success in 1977 as Congress moved to expand the Social Security tax amid projections that a tax increase was needed to maintain the solvency of the Social Security trust fund.[48] This problem arose largely because far higher-than-expected inflation rates had sharply increased benefit levels with the application of the 1972 cost of living adjustment. Carter initially responded to the projected shortfall with a proposal calling for an increase in employer taxes but not employee taxes. Congress then modified his proposal by increasing the taxes on both employees and employers. Carter thus contributed to this enactment, but the impetus had come from the projections of the Social Security Administration, and Congress significantly modified his initial proposals.

Carter also tackled welfare reform in his first year, in part because of his experiences in dealing with federal-state relations on welfare policy while serving as governor of Georgia. As a first step, he asked Joseph Califano to head a task force charged with developing a comprehensive reform proposal. However, the planning process suffered from Carter's lack of a clear direction and difficulties in meeting his desire for a comprehensive policy that included both welfare reform and an overhaul of manpower programs.[49]

Despite indications of public approval of the plan that emerged from the task force, Carter was handicapped by two factors in his dealings with Congress. He had reluctantly agreed to an increase of $2.8 billion in his proposal, but the recently created Congressional Budget Office (CBO) projected that the actual cost would be $14 billion. These cost concerns increased resistance to the plan. Senator Russell Long, chairman of the Senate Finance Committee, and Al Ullman (D-OH), chairman of the House Ways and Means Committee, already had a plan they regarded as far too ambitious. Thus, neither of their committees reported out a bill in 1977, and the administration's later attempts to push smaller bills were unsuccessful.

Carter found health policy issues no easier to tackle.[50] Health care costs were rising rapidly. In fact, once Nixon's cost controls were removed in 1974, hospital costs and health care costs generally began to increase at unprecedented double-digit rates. For labor unions, consumers, and legislative allies such as Senator Edward Kennedy, the lack of health insurance for the uninsured and the inefficiencies in the system cried out for a national health insurance plan.

In response to pleas from Senator Kennedy and nudges from HEW Secretary Califano, Carter chose in 1978 to move toward a system of national health insurance while focusing on policies aimed at containing hospital cost increases. Carter submitted a complex cost control proposal to Congress and immediately faced opposition not only from hospitals but also from other groups that feared the precedent of expanded federal regulation. In this instance, Carter fought hard for his proposal, including direct appeals to committee members, but he lost by a single vote in a key committee, and the proposed legislation did not move forward. Carter persisted in 1979 with a less ambitious proposal that sought to address criticisms made of his previous one. Eventually, both Carter and members of Congress began to lose interest in the issue, and the ultimate result was passage of a measure calling only for voluntary efforts at hospital cost containment.

The notion of health insurance for the uninsured produced a stalemate as well. Liberals, led by Senator Kennedy, vehemently criticized Carter's unwillingness to introduce and promote a major federal commitment. After a tense meeting between Kennedy and Carter in mid-1978, the falling-out was complete. Kennedy then proceeded with an unsuccessful initiative of his own and moved toward his decision to challenge Carter for the Democratic presidential nomination in 1980. Subsequent limited efforts by Carter also did not succeed. Health policy specialist Paul Starr attributed the stalemate to the combination of a large deficit, concerns about inflation, and a public that was growing skeptical of new government initiatives. Thus, Carter had no realistic opportunity to succeed in passing a broad system of national health insurance.[51]

Carter and Congress

Carter clearly had difficulty in his relationships with Congress. His effort to undertake a fast start in 1977 was handicapped by his overly large agenda, and he had no clear wins in his efforts to "go public" on major pending legislation. He also underachieved in his ability to obtain smaller measures in some policy areas. He was particularly unsuccessful in the

252 *The Low-Opportunity Presidents*

extent to which he was able to successfully push his perspectives into legislation that often was developed with little influence from the White House. Despite his reputation for disliking legislative affairs, he tenaciously and successfully pursued some measures such as civil service reform and his scaled-back energy package in 1978.

An Assessment

Despite his frequent policy failures, President Jimmy Carter helped to create some domestic policy legacies—notably, energy and environmental policies as well as steps toward deregulation. With help from world market forces, the highly controversial natural gas deregulation had a "soft landing" in the early 1980s without the disruptive higher prices some had feared. The country also made some progress on conservation issues. Tough measures, such as a major gasoline tax to reduce consumption, failed. But steps taken by industry led to considerably more efficient energy use. Although the synfuels program was ultimately abandoned as energy prices dropped in the 1980s, some efforts to develop alternative sources of energy continued.

Economic deregulation, which the Carter administration had initiated in several areas of the economy, picked up speed in the Reagan administration and, along the way, quashed regulatory efforts begun during the Roosevelt administration.[52] The two most prominent acts of deregulation produced different legacies. Airline deregulation, criticized by some for its effects on safety and the possibility that it might lead to a cartel, was hailed for its impacts on ticket prices. Conversely, the move to reduce regulations on the nation's savings and loan associations—while also increasing federal insurance coverage of deposits—proved to be a disaster, necessitating a costly government bailout.

How well, then, did Carter use his opportunities? Presidential scholar Erwin Hargrove found him to be "a good president who made the most of his opportunities, which however were not great."[53] Granted, the areas in which he failed—health and welfare reform—were extremely difficult to address during a time of intense budgetary pressures. Other observers, however, have argued that a president with greater legislative skills would have been able to make at least some progress in these areas. Moreover, Carter could have achieved more goals if he had assigned priorities to his efforts and sought more effectively to build supportive coalitions among key interests and members of Congress.

But Carter's greatest failing was his ineffective public leadership. His first year was especially damaging, as he projected the image of a struggling and ineffective president. The image was difficult to change. For a "trustee" president seeking to mobilize public support with direct appeals, he displayed remarkably little interest in improving his modest rhetorical skills. As he followed public opinion away from traditional Democratic Party positions during his final two years in office, he was again quite ineffective in developing support for centrist positions. Ironically, the derisive epithet "Jimmy Hoover" used by some liberal Democrats was, in one sense, appropriate. Jimmy Carter was an underachiever.

Notes

1 For a discussion of Carter's southern roots, see Betty Glad, *Jimmy Carter: In Search of the Great White House* (New York: Doubleday, 1980).

2 For a discussion of Carter's experiences as governor, see Gary Fink, *Prelude to the Presidency: The Political Character and Leadership Style of Jimmy Carter* (Westport, CT: Greenwood Press, 1980).

3 In 1970, for example, Carter vowed that he would openly seek the support of those opposing integration rather than give up that segment of the electorate to his opponent, despite the fact that he was not espousing his personal views.

4 James Fallows, "The Passionless President," *Atlantic Monthly*, May 1979, 33–48.

5 Peri E. Arnold, *Making the Managerial Presidency: Comprehensive Reorganization Planning, 1905–1980* (Princeton, NJ: Princeton University Press, 1986), 301.

6 Bert Lance, *The Truth of the Matter: My Life In and Out of Politics* (New York: Summit Books, 1991).

7 Anthony S. Campagne, *Economic Policy in the Carter Administration* (Westport, CT: Greenwood Press, 1995), xi.

8 Dilys M. Hill and Phil Williams, introduction to *The Carter Years: The President and Policymaking*, ed. M. Glenn Abernathy, Dilys M. Hill, and Phil Williams (New York: St. Martin's Press, 1994).

9 See Jonathan Alter, *His Very Best: Jimmy Carter, a Life* (New York: Simon & Schuster, 2020), chs. 20–24.

10 On this issue, it can be argued that some measures of liberalism and conservatism in the electorate did not show a major shift either as of 1976 or as of Reagan's win in 1980. Indications of a sea change could be found in various indicators, however. In California, the property tax protest culminated in the passage of Proposition 13 in 1978. A perhaps more telling indication of the change was that Michael Pertschuk, chairman of the Federal Trade Commission, was astonished to find in March 1978 that his proposed new regulation of advertising that targeted children was being strongly criticized by a most surprising source—the *Washington Post*. See Michael Pertschuk, *Revolt against Regulation: The Rise and Pause of the Consumer Movement* (Berkeley: University of California Press, 1982), 69.

11 Carter's problems nicely fit Skowronek's analysis of the problems a "president of disjunction" faces when his party no longer limits policy ideas that can be used to address changing circumstances. See Stephen Skowronek, *The Politics Presidents Make: Presidential Leadership from John Adams to George Bush* (New Haven, CT: Yale University Press, 1993), ch. 7.

12 Campagne, *Economic Policy in the Carter Administration*, xi.

13 Eric M. Uslaner, *Shale Barrel Politics: Energy and Legislative Leadership* (Palo Alto, CA: Stanford University Press, 1989).

14 Bert Lance, Carter's original head of the Office of Management and Budget, was a Georgian and a potentially valuable adviser who emphasized political

254 *The Low-Opportunity Presidents*

feasibility in many of his assessments. His resignation on September 21, 1977, was a serious loss. The charges leading to his resignation stemmed from his practices as head of a small-town Georgia bank. In 1980, however, he was acquitted of those charges. See Lance, *Truth of the Matter*, 16, ch. 8.

15 Jeff Fishel, *Presidents and Promises: From Campaign Pledge to Presidential Performance* (Washington, DC: CQ Press, 1985), 91.

16 This emphasis is drawn from Barbara Kellerman, *The Political Presidency: Practice of Leadership* (New York: Oxford University Press, 1984), ch. 10.

17 The growth in Eizenstat's role is emphasized in Walter Williams, *Mismanaging America: The Rise of the Anti-Analytic Presidency* (Lawrence: University Press of Kansas, 1990), 57–60.

18 On staff problems, see ibid., ch. 9; and Colin Campbell, *Managing the Presidency: Carter, Reagan, and the Search for Executive Harmony* (Pittsburgh, PA: University of Pittsburgh Press, 1986).

19 See Joseph A. Califano Jr., *Governing America: An Insider's Report from the White House and the Cabinet* (New York: Simon and Schuster, 1981).

20 Arnold, *Making the Managerial Presidency*, 303.

21 This measure was not included in Mayhew's initial list but nicely reflects Carter's organizational interests. For details, see James E. Katz, *Congress and National Energy Policy* (New Brunswick, NJ: Transaction Books, 1984), chap. 5.

22 Charles O. Jones, *The Trusteeship Presidency: Jimmy Carter and the United States Congress* (Baton Rouge: Louisiana State University Press, 1988), 161.

23 P. W. Colby and P. W. Ingraham, "Civil Service Reform: The Views of the Senior Executive Service," *Review of Public Personnel Administration* 1 (1980): 75.

24 Jack Watson interview, 17 April 1981, Miller Center interviews, transcript, 30, Jimmy Carter Library, Atlanta.

25 Kenneth O'Reilly, *Nixon's Piano: Presidents and Racial Politics from Washington to Clinton* (New York: Free Press, 1995), 344.

26 Barbara H. Craig and David M. O'Brien, *Abortion and American Politics* (Chatham, NJ: Chatham House, 1993), 162.

27 Mary E. Stuckey, *The President as Interpreter-in-Chief* (Chatham, NJ: Chatham House, 1991), 102.

28 Mark Rozell, *The Press and the Carter Presidency* (Boulder, CO: Westview Press, 1989), 18, 62–63.

29 Robert S. Littlefield, "Carter and the Media: An Analysis of Selected Strategies Used to Manage the Public Communication of the Administration," in *The Presidency and Domestic Policies of Jimmy Carter*, ed. Herbert D. Rosenbaum and Alexej Ugrinsky (Westport, CT: Greenwood Press, 1994), 429.

30 Milton Gwirtzman quoted in Robert Shogan, *The Fate of the Union* (Boulder, CO: Westview Press, 1998), 50.

31 Matthew R. Kerbel, *Beyond Persuasion: Organizational Efficiency and Presidential Power* (Albany: State University of New York Press, 1991), 60.

32 Thomas E. Cronin, *The State of the Presidency*, 2nd ed. (Boston: Little, Brown, 1980), 216.

33 See Kai Bird, *The Outlier: The Unfinished Presidency of Jimmy Carter* (New York: Crown, 2021), ch. 12.

34 See Jay Hakes Norman, *Energy Crises: Nixon, Ford, Carter and Hard Choices in the 1970s* (Norman, OK: University of Oklahoma Press, 2021), ch. 17.

35 On Carter's motivations, see Jimmy Carter, *Keeping Faith: Memoirs of a President* (New York: Bantam Books, 1982), 91–93.

36 The story of Carter's failed energy policy initiative has been told in numerous sources. This case study is drawn in particular from Jones, *Trusteeship Presidency*, 135–144; Kerbel, *Beyond Persuasion*; and Kellerman, *Political Presidency*, ch. 10.
37 Carter, *Keeping Faith*, 103.
38 M. Elizabeth Sanders, *The Regulation of Natural Gas: Policy and Politics, 1938–1978* (Philadelphia, PA: Temple University Press, 1981), 187.
39 This speech was originally planned as an energy address, but Carter decided to take a broad approach to what he saw as a national crisis of confidence. The speech was received with moderate favor, but the subsequent firing of five cabinet members raised concerns about the stability of the Carter administration. While Carter did not use the phrase, this address is often known as his "malaise" speech.
40 See Uslaner, *Shale Barrel Politics*, ch. 4.
41 For a review of the water projects fight, see Jones, *Trusteeship Presidency*, 143–149.
42 John F. Witte, *The Politics and Development of the Federal Income Tax* (Madison: University of Wisconsin Press, 1985), 199.
43 For a review of CETA's enactment and economic impact, see Campagne, *Economic Policy in the Carter Administration*, 57–60. In a related measure, Carter resisted pressures from liberals in Congress, the Black Caucus, and organized labor for a sweeping commitment to new federal jobs as a last resort and then acquiesced as Congress passed the Humphrey-Hawkins Act, which had symbolic importance but few specific provisions requiring action.
44 Lance T. LeLoup and Steven A. Shull, *Congress and the President: The Policy Connection* (Belmont, CA: Wadsworth, 1993), 188.
45 This interpretation draws from Martha Derthick and Paul J. Quirk, *The Politics of Deregulation* (Washington, DC: Brookings Institution, 1985).
46 The interpretation of this case study is based on Dorothy Robyn, *Braking the Special Interests: Trucking Deregulation and the Politics of Policy Reform* (Chicago: University of Chicago Press, 1987), ch. 7.
47 For details on this role, see James R. Adams, *The Big Fix: Inside the S and L Scandal: How an Unholy Alliance of Politics and Money Destroyed America's Banking System* (New York: Wiley, 1990).
48 See Edward Berkowitz, *Mr. Social Security: The Life of Wilbur J. Cohen* (Lawrence: University Press of Kansas, 1995); and William W. Lammers, *Public Policy and the Aging* (Washington, DC: CQ Press, 1983).
49 For a review of differing views of Carter's failure, see Laurence E. Lynn Jr. and David Whitman, *The President as Policymaker: Jimmy Carter and Welfare Reform* (Philadelphia, PA: Temple University Press, 1981), chs. 10–11.
50 This account is drawn from William W. Lammers, "Presidential Leadership and Health Policy," in *Health Politics and Policy*, ed. Theodore Litman and Leonard Robbins, 2nd ed. (Albany, NY: Delmar Publishers, 1991), ch. 5.
51 Paul Starr, *The Social Transformation of American Medicine* (New York: Basic Books, 1982), 405–410.
52 This discussion is drawn from Larry N. Gerston, Cynthia Fraleigh, and Robert Schwab, *The Deregulated Society* (Pacific Grove, CA: Brooks/Cole, 1988), chs. 4 and 5.
53 Erwin C. Hargrove, *Jimmy Carter as President: Leadership and the Politics of the Public Good* (Baton Rouge: Louisiana State University Press, 1988), 19.

13 George H. W. Bush
A Reluctant Guardian

George H. W. Bush (served 1989–1993) entered the White House in 1989 with a résumé documenting many years of public service. For over two years of his tenure as president, he garnered unusually high public approval ratings, yet when he ran for reelection, he suffered a crushing defeat as 62 percent of the electorate, throwing their support toward either Democrat Bill Clinton or independent candidate Ross Perot, concluded that he was poorly equipped to serve a second term. In 1992, Bush had been stymied by a weak economy and a well-run Clinton campaign. Yet, critics have wondered whether he, in his leadership endeavors, had actually made this difficult situation worse.

Personal Characteristics

Like Presidents Franklin Roosevelt and John Kennedy, George Herbert Walker Bush (1924–) was born to wealth. In fact, he was lampooned at the 1988 Democratic National Convention by Texas State Treasurer Ann Richards for having been born with a silver foot in his mouth. Although he was born in Milton, Massachusetts, George grew up in Greenwich, Connecticut. Bush's father, Prescott Bush, was far less wealthy than Joseph Kennedy, and the family ancestry was less distinguished than Roosevelt's, but he enjoyed the upper-class status of elite schools as well as vacations at the family's spacious Kennebunkport summer home on the Maine coast. He also was the only president in the twentieth century whose father had held national elective office. Prescott Bush manifested some of the sense of service he sought to instill in his sons and daughters when he spent the last ten years of his active career as a moderate Republican senator from Connecticut.[1]

Bush's background also includes distinguished military service. He enlisted in the navy in 1942 at only 18 years of age, and rules were waived to allow him to become the navy's youngest commissioned pilot. In September 1944, 1 of the 58 missions he flew in the Pacific during World War II produced a life-threatening situation. While he was on a bombing run, a Japanese shell hit his plane. He was able to deliver his bombs on

DOI: 10.4324/9781003426684-16

target but soon thereafter had to parachute from his plane. After several hours at sea, he and members of his crew were rescued by a U.S. submarine. His crew praised his leadership, and the navy awarded him with a Distinguished Flying Cross.

Like many veterans after the war, Bush seemed to be a man in a hurry. He entered Yale University in 1945 shortly after marrying his high school sweetheart, Barbara Pierce. At Yale, he majored in economics and earned a Phi Beta Kappa key. Bush played first base and served as captain of Yale's baseball team. After graduation, he chose a business career, and making a break with his family, he and Barbara moved to Texas. Bush started at the bottom of the Texas oil business with a few sales jobs. Then, with financial assistance from his uncle, Herbert Walker, he established an independent offshore oil drilling firm in 1953. Over the next decade, he made a fair amount of money, raised a large family, sold his firm, and began eyeing a political career.

Career Path

Bush's lengthy political experience began with an unsuccessful effort to win a Houston congressional seat as a highly conservative candidate in 1964. He was successful, though, in the 1966 and 1968 races. In 1970 he responded in part to Richard Nixon's encouragement as he sought election to the Senate. He won the Republican primary but lost to moderate Democrat Lloyd Bentsen in the general election. Later, he served for brief periods in four different roles that included two years as U.S. ambassador to the United Nations, over a year as chairman of the Republican National Committee (where he was a Nixon defender until a few weeks before Nixon's resignation), and two years as U.S. envoy (ambassador) to China. It was with some reluctance that he also served as director of the Central Intelligence Agency for a year (he feared the position would not help his presidential aspirations). When Jimmy Carter assumed the presidency in 1977, he did not accept Bush's offer to remain as director, so Bush and his family headed back to Texas.

Bush's pursuit of the 1980 Republican nomination began in May 1979 as he announced his candidacy with a statement characterized by biographer Fitzhugh Green as "honorable but bland and without ... originality."[2] He was elated with a surprise victory in the Iowa caucuses, but his defeat by Reagan in New Hampshire and his difficulty in rebounding as Reagan made a strong showing in the South ended his campaign. Bush then eagerly accepted Reagan's offer of the number two spot on the Republican ticket and ended up serving as Reagan's "understudy" for eight years. During that time, he played the role of a loyal vice president who made few waves.

258   *The Low-Opportunity Presidents*

The fall 1988 general election campaign against Governor Michael Dukakis of Massachusetts was widely criticized as being highly negative and remarkably lacking in a serious discussion of the issues.[3] Neither Bush nor Dukakis was eager to talk about the mounting financial costs accruing from federal insurance obligations to cover soaring investor losses in the savings and loan crisis. On the issue of the federal deficit, Bush talked vaguely about savings in spending and "no new taxes." Dukakis, by stressing the monies to be saved by a taxpayer amnesty (allowing those who had failed to file tax returns in the past to file without penalty), tried to avoid the problems Democratic nominee Walter Mondale had encountered in 1984 with his commitment to a tax increase.

Undoubtedly, the most widely debated aspect of the 1988 campaign was the emphasis Bush and his campaign staff placed on "wedge" issues.[4] In a successful effort to depict Dukakis as an ultra-liberal, Bush attacked the governor for vetoing a Massachusetts law requiring that school classes begin with the recitation of the Pledge of Allegiance (Dukakis's attorney general had advised him the law was unconstitutional). Bush also attacked Dukakis for his state's prison furlough program. In the so-called Willie Horton commercial run by an independent Bush support committee, many viewers and analysts felt the Bush campaign was trying to unfairly play on white fears of black-on-white violence.[5]

Bush was fortunate in his election bid in two respects. First, the strong economy provided an easy basis for promising a continuation of good economic conditions. Second, Dukakis proved to be a disappointing candidate. He made little attempt early in the race to respond to Bush's television advertisements painting him as a "card carrying member of the American Civil Liberties Union" and an extreme liberal. He also proceeded rather clumsily with his own campaign and never developed an effective electoral college strategy. He thus saw an early 17 percentage point advantage over Bush and a much more favorable candidate perception turn into an 8 percentage point loss. By election day, however, both candidates were perceived quite negatively by the voters.

What Manner of Man?

With the exception of his approach to election campaigns, Bush was widely regarded as a thoughtful, kindly person. He was well known for his good manners, which included writing many gracious notes. As president, he extended his thoughtfulness by inviting Senator Edward Kennedy to visit the private quarters of the White House for the first time since the death of his brother John Kennedy. Putting these characteristics in a broader context, *Time* magazine's veteran president watcher Hugh Sidey stated as of 1989 that Bush "may be the mildest, the most unassuming, the least self-centered of the modern presidents."[6]

Yet Bush also was intensely competitive. He pushed hard for any possible advantage in his athletic endeavors, and in his business career he was willing to take risks to succeed. In running for public office, he seemed to take the attitude that whatever was needed to win was an acceptable strategy. This mind-set was most evident in the presidential campaigns of 1988 and 1992 as he aggressively attacked his opponents' character.

Intense energy flowed from Bush's competitiveness. During his business career, his hectic schedule and stress had led to sleeplessness and ultimately stomach ulcers. As for his physical activities, he entered the White House at age 64 and continued a round of physical activities that included jogging, golf, and tennis. He undertook foreign travel with a zealousness that both awed and concerned the aides responsible for implementing his schedule. In his first two years, for example, he traveled abroad more than Reagan did in his entire eight years in office.

Policy Views

Bush's policy goals often have been characterized as frequently changing and lightly held. For example, he opposed the Civil Rights Act of 1964 but supported housing desegregation legislation in 1968, and then resisted civil rights legislation as president. On abortion, he shifted from pro-choice to pro-life. In much the same way, he branded Reagan's economic proposals in the 1980 campaign as "voodoo economics" and then loyally supported the same ideas when he served as Reagan's vice president. His most noted reversal occurred in 1990 when he reneged on his 1988 "no new taxes" campaign pledge.

Journalist Gail Sheehy suggested that even before he entered the White House, Bush held his views lightly and that even his closest associates would be unable to uncover many strongly held views other than general values such as fairness.[7] Similarly, conservative staffer Charles Kolb noted that, in contrast to Reagan, not even Bush's closest advisers knew where he really stood on domestic issues.[8] Bush was certainly not alone among recent presidents in changing positions over the years, but he seemed to stand out for both his casual shifts and his lack of personal intensity about those positions.

Despite the frequent criticism he received for lacking a policy agenda, Bush formulated and promoted some policy goals. His primary economic interest was a reduction in the capital gains tax. In the 1988 campaign, Bush hinted that he wanted to differ from Reagan's more strident conservatism and stand at the helm of a "kinder, gentler nation." To that end, he promoted passage of the Americans with Disabilities Act, steps toward improving the nation's school system, a greater national concern about some environmental issues, a greater emphasis on voluntarism (labeled "a thousand points of light"), and full funding of Head Start (a preschool

260   *The Low-Opportunity Presidents*

education program for disadvantaged children). Given his election promises, Bush came to office as a president with a limited agenda oriented toward modest changes in the policies Reagan had initiated.[9] Bush was quite aptly viewed as being more interested in serving his country than in changing or leading it.

Challenges and Opportunities

President Bush faced several challenges during his four years in office. Continued upheavals in the Soviet Union and the collapse of Soviet control of Eastern Europe forced him to manage an end to the Cold War. This challenge was addressed cautiously and without loud proclamations of victory, which might have made the process more difficult. In August 1990, Bush faced his biggest foreign policy crisis yet. Iraqi military troops, led by Iraqi dictator Saddam Hussein, moved into neighboring Kuwait. Using what some called "Rolodex diplomacy," the president put together an impressive coalition of North American, European, and Middle Eastern countries. Together, these nations launched a successful military operation that forced Iraq's forces out of Kuwait.

Domestically, the savings and loan bailout could no longer be delayed, and neither could the mounting deficit. Thus, the domestic scene contained more constraints than opportunities for new initiatives.[10] Eight years earlier, Reagan had entered the presidency arguing that he had a mandate for change and held the advantage of confronting a demoralized Democratic Party in Congress. Bush, by contrast, entered after an election that had done little to produce support for new policy initiatives and faced a Democratic Party that had been emboldened by its increased strength in Congress.

The economic conditions in the late 1980s had various impacts on Bush's opportunities. In view of the economic growth and job creation that had begun in 1983, Bush found it hard to argue for the necessity of a cut in the capital gains tax. Yet when the economy slid into recession in 1991, he was still in a relatively poor position to take strong action. Moreover, this recession differed from the earlier, post-World War II recessions—the downturn was affecting the service sector more than the manufacturing sector. Thus, public anxiety (especially among likely middle-class voters) was higher than might be expected from a simple reading of unemployment statistics.

Two other factors offered some possible advantages. To his surprise and delight, Bush was (at least at first) unusually popular. He seemed somewhat skeptical about the value of polls, however, as he liked to point out that high numbers simply meant that the big story would be his loss of popularity when the numbers inevitably fell. Nevertheless, his popularity did create an opportunity for an agenda that some aides promoted in the wake of his high support after the Gulf War in 1991. Also on the positive

George H. W. Bush   261

side, there was some indication that Democratic leaders in Congress looked forward to working with Bush after eight years of dealing with Reagan.

Leadership Style

Bush's leadership style has been characterized as that of a "guardian."[11] He professed an admiration for Theodore Roosevelt, but more for his commitment to public service than his activist bully pulpit presidency. Bush was deeply skeptical that government policies could provide positive change and generally saw his role as one of defending the status quo. As a guardian, especially in the foreign policy arena, he preferred to be ready to meet new challenges as they might arise. A desire to subtly differentiate himself from Reagan also was evident as he sought to downplay the rhetorical aspects of the president's role (Reagan's strong suit) while demonstrating that he was a hard worker who was mastering the details of government.

The Advisory Process and Approach to Decision-Making

Unlike most presidents, Bush recruited several of his closest friends and campaign aides for his cabinet rather than for top staff positions. He knew ten cabinet members personally.[12] Campaign manager James Baker became secretary of state, and fellow Texans Nicholas Brady and Robert Mosbacher were chosen to head, respectively, the Treasury Department and the Department of Commerce. Other appointees were drawn from Congress, such as Jack Kemp as secretary of housing and urban development, and from prior Republican administrations, such as Elizabeth Dole as secretary of labor. Bush sought diversity in his cabinet, and appointed African American physician Louis Sullivan as secretary of health and human services and two Hispanics, Reagan administration holdover Lauro Cavazos as secretary of education and Manuel Lujan Jr. as secretary of the interior.

The organization of the Bush presidency reflected his preference for dealing with a limited number of top cabinet and staff members and a strong chief of staff. James Baker promoted the use of a troika (as in Reagan's first term), but this suggestion was rejected. Chief of Staff John Sununu played a strong but sometimes negative role in the Bush White House until his forced departure in late 1991. As the former governor of New Hampshire, he had been instrumental in Bush's key primary win in that state the previous year. His selection was seen as a signal to conservative Republicans that "one of them" would have an important voice in the Bush administration. Sununu was quick to display his high intelligence—but equally quick to take exception to views and people he did not like. More than many chiefs of staff, he also sought to promote his own views.[13] With his gruff personal style, Sununu made more enemies than friends. It did not endear

262 *The Low-Opportunity Presidents*

him to members of Congress, for example, when the report filtered back to them that he had told a conservative group in late 1990 that Congress could go home until after the 1992 election—nothing else really needed to be done.[14] When Sununu's use of government planes for personal purposes, such as visiting a dentist in Boston, became known in 1991, criticism quickly mounted. Bush asked Sununu to resign, and Transportation Secretary Samuel Skinner assumed the chief of staff role for the first half of 1992, followed by James Baker, who reluctantly gave up his position of secretary of state so he could revive Bush's faltering reelection campaign.

The most dominant adviser in shaping Bush's domestic policy was Office of Management and Budget (OMB) Director Richard Darman. Darman was an experienced Washingtonian who had served in a low-level position in the Nixon administration and then as Chief of Staff James Baker's deputy during the Reagan administration. He brought to his role substantial knowledge of domestic policy and a reputation for being a cunning schemer in pursuing elaborate scenarios in the policymaking process. In fact, the term *Darmanesque* was used to refer to his complex schemes. Darman's budget analyses were central to Bush's budgetary strategies. Darman, along with John Sununu, was the major negotiator in the top-level deficit-reduction negotiations in 1990. In addition, he had a big hand in developing some of Bush's domestic policy speeches.

In his decision-making, Bush sought to avoid mistakes and to soften some aspects of Reagan's domestic policy choices in keeping with the theme of a "kinder, gentler" America. Yet conversely, he sought to make decisions that would sustain the support of conservatives who viewed him suspiciously as a "closet moderate." Finally, in part because of budgetary constraints, Bush preferred to take many small steps rather than commit to one or two major initiatives. On pressing decisions, he was guided by political feasibility, and he used polls to determine the content of his January 1992 State of the Union address as he tried to reassert his domestic agenda.

The process Bush created reflected his own preferences. His cautiousness led to an "in box" approach—he would deal with problems as they arose but would not seek new ideas with his own "out box" requests. His disinterest plainly showed at points, and he became visibly bored in a variety of meetings dealing with domestic policy. Just as with foreign policy, he preferred to deal with a fairly small group of people.

Overall marks for Bush's decision-making process have not been very high. He generally gets credit for operating an orderly process, but some critics believe he relied too heavily on a very few top aides and cabinet members rather than pursuing a more open process. Shirley Anne Warshaw, who looked at Bush's cabinet process, concluded that the White House needed to establish a structure that guided the cabinet's development of domestic policies but in a way that satisfied the campaign agenda without significant increases in funding.[15] This structure, however, was not created until Samuel Skinner took over as chief of staff in 1992.

Administrative Strategies

Administrative strategies were periodically important for Bush. At the outset of his administration, he made his belief in government the focal point of an address to top federal officials: "We're all wise in the ways of Washington," he said, "especially you who have served your country with such distinction."[16] Later, however, he showed little interest in reorganization of government to achieve greater efficiency or a sustained interest in implementation issues in specific policy areas. He paid little attention to regulatory policy reform, for example, until late 1991 when a *National Journal* article referred to him as a "re-regulation president" and asserted that he had presided over the greatest expansion in regulatory policies since the early 1970s.

The Bush administration made its most visible effort to leverage policy impact in the area of education. Bush followed up on his campaign promise to be "the education president" with an early initiative, introduced at a well-publicized meeting of the nation's governors. The actual implementation of the proposed guidelines for the resulting Goals 2000 project did not occur until 1991, however, and the administration made little effort to support the initiative over the long term.

Bush's arsenal of administrative strategies was most manifested in his efforts to please segments of the divisive Republican coalition. On abortion, Bush followed Reagan's rhetoric and tactics as he made a modest effort to push new legislation while looking to the courts to provide additional limits.[17] In the wake of criticism of National Endowment for the Arts (NEA) chief John Frohnmayer by Pat Buchanan in his primary challenge in 1992, Bush dismissed Frohnmayer from office. On enforcement of civil rights legislation, Bush urged a cautious approach.

Bush took one of his most controversial administrative actions in 1991 when he nominated Clarence Thomas, an African American who was serving as chairman of the Federal Employment Practices Commission (FEPC), to replace retiring Supreme Court justice Thurgood Marshall, the first African American to serve on the Court. With this step, he could not only continue the tradition of having an African American on the Supreme Court but also gain a conservative voice since Thomas's skeptical views of many liberal policies were well known. Thomas was confirmed by the Senate, but only narrowly (52-48) and after an exceedingly acrimonious proceeding. Some opponents, including many African Americans, argued that a person with Thomas's views of civil rights was not a worthy successor to Thurgood Marshall. Others pointed to his lack of judicial

264 *The Low-Opportunity Presidents*

experience. The conflict intensified with charges of sexual harassment by Anita Hill, a former employee at the FEPC.

Finally, the Bush administration decided to take a closer look at economic and environmental regulations with an eye toward modifying implementation of recently enacted legislation. The central mechanism was the Council on Competitiveness, chaired by Vice President Dan Quayle. This essentially pro-business council met in 1991 and 1992 to secretly review controversial regulatory issues. This strategy had some policy consequences but also produced considerable disagreement. The council decided to recommend about 50 regulatory changes, including a highly controversial one that would have allowed modifications in the implementation decisions for the Clean Air Act without public comment.[18] While some were pleased with the council's decisions, others were somewhat reluctant to be involved in a process that was widely criticized in Congress and in some press commentary as lacking legitimacy. According to political scientists Richard Harris and Sidney Milkis, the process suffered from the limitations of pragmatism without a reasoned defense.[19] In short, the council's penchant for secrecy and avoidance of public discourse further reduced Bush's potential effectiveness.

Public Leadership

Bush's media strategies were designed carefully. He recognized his constraints in his ability to deviate from Reagan's policy positions but felt he could show his independence with a different political style.[20] That style, in turn, reflected Bush's desire to lower the public's expectations, his genuine skepticism about the ability of public addresses to change opinion, his personal dislike of public speaking, and his limited interest in promoting new programs.

Reagan staffer Marlin Fitzwater stayed on as press secretary in the Bush administration. But in one of several changes, speechwriters and public liaison officials found themselves reduced in number and status. The Reagan Administration had used a "theme for the day" technique and strategized to ensure frequent news coverage, but Bush did not continue these efforts, and it showed. In his first 22 months in office, Bush was on the evening news only one-third as often as Reagan in the same time period.[21] The number of press conferences skyrocketed, however, as Bush sought to publicly demonstrate his level of involvement, knowledge of issues, and enjoyment of his job. He used the presidential bully pulpit from time to time, but in his public speeches his average of one voluntary domestic policy address a year was exceedingly low. Additionally, Bush seldom used his State of the Union addresses to assert legislative leadership.[22]

Bush seldom tried to change the opinion or behavior of others, but when he did, it was in conjunction with major policy initiatives. His first specially televised address to the nation dealt with drug use. He paid increasing attention to the issue at first, but eventually his attention level returned to normal.

Other speaking opportunities were used sparingly or skipped altogether. In 1990, for example, he waited over three months after the decision had been made to explain why he abandoned his pledge not to raise taxes. After the Gulf War, he gave no major speeches to promote domestic policies, despite the encouragement of some of his aides. In April 1992, in a speech made in the wake of the Los Angeles riots, he largely criticized past policies rather than promoting new initiatives or addressing urban issues.

Bush reserved his most extensive use of the bully pulpit for his voluntarism initiative called "a thousand points of light." He devoted many speeches to this initiative and organized a modest-sized staff to promote and recognize volunteer efforts. Staffers worked to change people's attitudes, discover and encourage leaders, establish supporting institutions, and reduce the vulnerability of volunteers to legal liability.[23]

In implementing his media strategies, Bush was quite successful initially in differentiating himself from Reagan and in creating public perceptions of a "nice, hard working president who was enjoying his job." As a result, he was unusually popular.[24] His problems came with his inability to reassure the public as the economy soured. Some observers wondered, for example, what might have happened if the well-received address he gave on economic issues in September 1992 had been given months earlier.[25] Staffer Charles Kolb also has pointed to Bush's inability to coordinate the actions of his administration. According to Kolb, Bush and others made virtually no effort to connect legislative priorities, speechwriting, and communication outreach through the Office of Public Liaison.[26]

Congressional Leadership

Bush's legislative relationships were defined by a moderate use of the traditional legislative liaison role along with a strong role for his first chief of staff, John Sununu. Bush recruited Fred McClure to head his Office of Legislative Liaison. A former staff aide to Senator John Tower (R-TX), McClure was the first African American to hold that office.

Bush's preference for dealing with individuals directly was evident in his approach to Congress. He sought to utilize his friendship dating back to his own days in Congress with House Ways and Means Chairman Daniel Rostenkowski (D-IL), and the associations he had made with other legislators in more recent years. At the beginning, he sought good relationships with leaders through informal meetings. And periodically he worked the phones for, among other things, the capital gains tax cut in 1989.

266   *The Low-Opportunity Presidents*

Bush took a limited approach to his agenda-setting role in both scope and depth. In 1989 he mentioned some attractive proposals in his initial speeches and messages but left the all-important question of funding mechanisms to Congress. Pundits commented that Bush had "hit the ground strolling" rather than running and called him the president who had created an "agenda gap."

Bush employed other strategies and tactics more extensively. Until the bitter fight over deficit reduction in 1990, he often was quite conciliatory. The same pattern of top-level negotiation he favored on foreign policy matters was used on the key issue of deficit reduction. Throughout his four years, he also brandished both vetoes and veto threats as an effective source of influence. He was proud of his unbroken record of 41 successful vetoes, which held until a congressional override of a cable television deregulation bill on October 3, 1992. Bush owed his success rate to his unwillingness, unlike Reagan, to veto a bill when there was a good possibility of a congressional override. Nevertheless, both threats and uses of vetoes were an important part of his legislative strategy, as both were often in line with his preferences for preventing domestic policy action.

Legislative Enactments

President Bush had ups and downs in dealing with Congress over his four years in office. The most far-reaching enactment in 1989 addressed the savings and loan crisis. In 1990, Bush had his most significant impact on policy with the passage of the Clean Air Act Amendments and the Americans with Disabilities Act (ADA). That year also produced landmark deficit-reduction legislation, but with Bush as a virtual bystander in the final deliberations. The next two years featured some new legislation but increased animosity between Bush and Congress.

Early Efforts

By 1989, the solvency of government programs designed to insure deposits was threatened by the savings and loan crisis. The cause was a combination of overly zealous deregulation in Washington and in some states, the reckless and corrupt actions of individuals in the savings and loan industry, and the reluctance of Congress to re-address the issue. Bush did not have to engage in a significant public role in the savings and loan bailout, because Congress was well aware that action could no longer be avoided. The president did, though, have Treasury Secretary Nicholas Brady quickly develop a new proposal. The Bush administration entered the fray primarily on the accounting issue associated with the legislation—it opposed direct financing—but it did not have a strong bargaining role as the final bill compromised on the accounting issue.

George H. W. Bush   267

Successful passage of the savings and loan bailout did not carry over to Bush's efforts to achieve his personal pet project—a cut in the capital gains tax. He succeeded in the House but failed in the Senate. At first, Bush and House Ways and Means Committee Chairman Rostenkowski pursued a possible compromise. Rostenkowski would seek support of a temporary capital gains tax reduction, and Bush would agree to support, among other things, an expanded earned income tax credit, efforts to block cuts in Medicare payments to inner-city hospitals, and a deficit-reduction package in 1990 that would include a sizable tax hike.[27] This bargain, however, did not materialize. Despite Rostenkowski's shift into opposition, conservative Democrats and many Republicans on the Ways and Means Committee began to see greater legitimacy for a capital gains cut. The committee passed a measure calling for a temporary reduction and then sent it to the full House for a vote. Bush worked the phones in an all-out effort for the capital gains reduction. In the end, then, Bush's strong campaign produced a decisive 239-190 win in the House for a temporary capital gains tax cut.

Leadership actions in the Senate produced a very different result. Majority Leader George Mitchell (D-ME), who wanted to chalk up some successes in his first year as leader, worked very hard to mobilize Democrats around the proposition that it was important for their party leader to win rather than the president. Because of procedural rules associated with some provisions, Mitchell had a major advantage: 60, not 51, votes would be needed for the capital gains measure to carry. Ultimately, Bush was able to marshal fifty-one votes, but because of the prevailing rule, the measure failed.

Clean Air Act Amendments of 1990

The passage of the first new legislation in the area of air quality control since 1977 was a major policy achievement. Some opportunities existed in this area because of the stalemate that had occurred during the Reagan years and growing support within Congress for a variety of proposals seeking to address air pollution problems. Provisions of the sweeping final legislation included expanded efforts to reduce automobile tailpipe emissions; detailed steps to improve air quality, especially in smog-ridden urban centers like Houston and Los Angeles; the first major restrictions on midwestern industrial pollution from coal-fired burners that had been contributing to the formation of acid rain; and a listing of 189 toxic chemicals for which the Environmental Protection Agency must set public health standards. The bill also included the first steps to deal with issues such as global warming and the growing hazard of high-altitude ozone depletion—problems that were unknown, even by scientists, when Congress passed the original Clean Air Act of 1977.

268 *The Low-Opportunity Presidents*

Bush had made air pollution policy a top priority for Congress. In fact, his actions made it virtually certain that some air pollution control legislation would be passed by 1990.[28] Bush had noted the issue during the 1988 campaign, stressed it in his first State of the Union address, and unveiled his proposal with a widely publicized gathering in the East Room of the White House. Although he made no major addresses on the issue while the bill made its way through Congress, he continued to emphasize the importance of this legislation in a variety of secondary speeches. Congress recognized the president's significant role. Key legislative promoter Senator Max Baucus (D-MT) echoed that recognition when he stated, "The Reagan administration was very much opposed to clean air. The Bush administration is very much in favor of clean air legislation. George Bush deserves major credit."[29]

Americans with Disabilities Act (ADA, 1990)

During the 1988 campaign, Bush had spoken favorably of the ADA, which had been under consideration in Congress for several years. In a speech at the Department of Health and Human Services two days before his inauguration, he again spoke very glowingly in favor of the bill. With the help of the Bush administration and an alliance of supporters that included the disability movement, civil rights groups, and liberals, the legislation passed in the Senate and one of the necessary four House committees in 1989. The bill sought to add the disabled to the groups protected against discrimination by the landmark Civil Rights Act of 1964.

As it did for the Clean Air Act Amendments, the Bush administration articulated the concerns of the business community about specific provisions of the ADA. The issue was whether aggrieved parties would be allowed to sue for damages. Attorney General Richard Thornburgh pointed out that legislators had agreed in 1989 to a compromise in which the administration would broaden the public accommodations provision of the act in exchange for language that would indicate an agreement that individuals would not be able to sue for damages. When the language used in the 1964 civil rights legislation was modified in response to a Supreme Court decision, however, Democrats argued that the language used for ADA also should be changed. The Bush administration lost in committee votes on this issue.

The ADA legislation that emerged from Congress in 1990 included major provisions outlining the rights of the disabled vis-à-vis public accommodation and prohibitions against discrimination in employment. Although Bush helped to make this an issue of top legislative concern, he did not engage in any significant personal advocacy once congressional hearings had begun. In shaping the final legislative result, he also failed to reduce the scope of protection provided in the ADA, as he had originally intended.

Landmark Deficit Reduction

The Omnibus Budget Reconciliation Act of 1990 (OBRA 90), the most significant domestic policy of Bush's years in office, was a strong measure that reduced the projected budget deficit by some $482 billion over five years. The measure cut about two dollars in spending for every dollar in tax increases. It also helped to constrain future spending through its "pay as you go" (PAYGO) provisions—future lawmakers would have to find budget savings or new revenue for the additional expenditures they imposed. As Congressional Budget Office (CBO) Director Robert Reischauer saw it, this measure would have a forceful impact on the ability of the federal government to reduce deficits in the 1990s.[30] In the short run, however, its impact was not readily apparent. The federal budget in the next two years reflected the costs of the savings and loan bailout and the reduced revenues and increased spending caused by the recession of 1991-1992. These developments, and the manner in which Bush handled his role, eliminated any possibility that Bush would receive significant credit for the measure in the 1992 election.

The pathway to deficit reduction included top-level negotiation, multiple players, and a series of questionable moves by Bush.[31] In 1989, the Bush administration, especially OMB Director Richard Darman, showed some interest in negotiating a deficit-reduction package. But suspicions about the motivations and possible actions of the other side, coupled with the divisive fight over capital gains, produced only a limited effort. As 1990 began, it was increasingly apparent that policymakers faced one of two choices: they had to either negotiate a substantial deficit-reduction package or see sequestration (deep spending cuts) imposed by the provisions of the Gramm-Rudman Act.

Bush's initial budget was essentially a bargaining position for his negotiations with Congress. He proposed substantial spending cuts for Medicare and other programs favored by Democrats, small defense cuts, no tax increase, and a new version of the capital gains tax reduction. Using optimistic economic estimates, the program promised a deficit reduction of $36 billion—a figure well below the $64 billion reduction required by Gramm-Rudman. In part because of the additional spending required for the savings and loan bailout, the mandatory Gramm-Rudman deficit-reduction targets quickly escalated. In that context, some observers in both Congress and the Bush administration grew concerned that an effort to meet the Gramm-Rudman deficit reduction might send the economy into a tailspin. Thus, a consensus was formed on a revised goal of a long-term

270　*The Low-Opportunity Presidents*

measure that would cut the deficit by $50 billion in 1991 and $500 billion over a five-year period.

Politically, Bush was widely viewed as the big loser in the budget battle—and in ways for which he was at least partly to blame. In the final stages his administration had not played the inside bargain game well. More centrally, however, Bush's efforts at public leadership had been remarkably limited. He neglected to explain his reasons for abandoning his "no new taxes" promise. His lack of effectiveness was evident in public opinion polls as his popularity dropped from 74 percent in late August 1990 to 59 percent in early October. According to David Mervin, "The President's conduct during the budget crisis severely damaged his credibility as a leader and eroded respect for his competence in economic policy."[32]

Civil Rights

In 1989, the Supreme Court handed down a decision, *Wards Cove Packing Co. v. Antonio*, that made it more difficult for civil rights claims to be pursued through legal channels.[33] In its ruling, the Court rejected the use of affirmative action suits brought on the basis of statistical underrepresentation of minorities in a specific company. Congress then sought in 1990 to reinterpret congressional intent in ways that would restore the previous understanding and thereby allow the broader use of legal action against claims of civil rights violations. Bush responded with a veto, saying (despite congressional denials) that the new legislation would establish a system of quotas for job hiring. Because Congress was unable to override Bush's veto in 1990, the issue was open to possible action in 1991 when Congress enacted similar legislation. Bush chose to interpret this legislation as enough of a change from the measure he had vetoed in 1990 that he could sign it. Bush's acquiescence was widely attributed to election concerns, the tensions surrounding the rise of overt racists such as former Ku Klux Klan leader David Duke in the Republican Party, and the fallout from his successful elevation of African American Clarence Thomas to the Supreme Court.

Bush and Congress

Bush's limited circumstances were not conducive to a highly productive legislative record. He could rightly take credit for his helpful roles in some major legislation such as the savings and loan bailout, Clean Air Act Amendments, and the ADA, and his defensive use of vetoes shaped some legislation as well. Yet few observers have given him high marks for legislative leadership. After his most productive first two years, Paul Quirk observed that "it is not difficult to suppose that another president who had set out to attempt cooperative leadership could have accomplished more

George H. W. Bush   271

than Bush did."[34] Looking back after four years, Barbara Sinclair concluded, "He didn't seem to have much he wanted to do. I'm not sure there is much more he could have done. But he didn't really try."[35]

An Assessment

George H. W. Bush was ultimately an unlucky president. As the understudy, he faced the difficult task of differentiating himself from his predecessor, Ronald Reagan, while maintaining the appearance of loyalty to Reagan's agenda. After adopting a leadership style that fit his circumstances fairly well, Bush confronted a stubborn recession in his reelection year. Furthermore, voter concerns about job security in the face of the new global pressures affecting the nation's economy were a growing problem. The onset of the recession also robbed him of an opportunity to take credit for the lower deficit that was supposed to stem from the deficit-reduction package passed in 1990. In those circumstances, how well did he do?

Bush's policy legacies include most centrally the deficit-reduction measure of 1990, which stands up quite well when compared with some of the more recent deficit-reduction packages. According to Robert Reischauer, onetime director of the CBO, Bush's measure contributed significantly to the movement toward very low deficits by 1997 and the eventual achievement of a balanced budget agreement.[36] Yet while Bush's willingness to accept a tax increase was central to passage of the legislation, his leadership contributions were quite limited. For that reason, the Clean Air Act Amendments stands out as the most important legacy in which President Bush fulfilled a variety of leadership roles. While the Americans with Disabilities Act was another monumental piece of legislation, Bush's role was much more limited.

In his overall performance, Bush seemed to have difficulty putting the various pieces of his presidency together. Members of his administration took various actions, but not necessarily with a coordinated sense of purpose or direction. Bush gave some indications of ways in which a president could sustain personal support with a less-glorified public view of the presidency, but even this more modest approach to dealing with the public was never effectively developed. His greatest failing, however, was in his public leadership. His inept handling of the deficit-reduction struggle and the credibility he lost as a domestic policy leader during his last two years in office were arguably the clearest indication of a lack of skill. His difficult circumstances combined with his limited domestic agenda affected his accomplishments in office—and his reelection prospects.

George H. W. Bush, then, like Jimmy Carter, proved to be an underachiever. On the domestic front, his decision to be a guardian-type leader may have been a poor one. In the modern era, can a president assume a

272   The Low-Opportunity Presidents

more diminished role in agenda-setting and leadership? The George H. W. Bush presidency suggests the answer may be no.

Notes

1 See Fitzhugh Green, *George Bush: An Intimate Portrait* (New York: Hippocrene Books, 1989), 65.
2 Ibid., 169.
3 Sidney Blumenthal, *Pledging Allegiance: The Last Campaign of the Cold War* (New York: HarperCollins, 1990).
4 John J. Pitney, *After Reagan: Bush, Dukakis, and the 1988 Election* (Lawrence, KS: University of Kansas Press, 2019).
5 Craig Allen Smith and Kathy B. Smith, *The White House Speaks: Presidential Leadership as Persuasion* (Westport, CT: Praeger, 1994), 83.
6 Green, *George Bush*, XII.
7 Gail Sheehy, *Character: America's Search for Leadership* (New York: Morrow, 1988), 160.
8 Charles Kolb, *White House Daze: The Unmaking of Domestic Policy in the Bush Years* (New York: Free Press, 1994), 241.
9 John Robert Greene, *The Presidency of George Bush* (Lawrence, KS: University of Kansas Press, 2000), ch. 5.
10 Paul J. Quirk, "Domestic Policy: Divided Government and Cooperative Presidential Leadership," in *The Bush Presidency: First Appraisals*, ed. Colin Campbell and Bert A. Rockman (Chatham, NJ: Chatham House, 1991), 73.
11 David Mervin, *George Bush and the Guardianship Presidency* (New York: St. Martin's Press, 1996).
12 Shirley A. Warshaw, *Powersharing: White House-Cabinet Relationships in the Modern Presidency* (Albany: State University of New York Press, 1996), chap. 7.
13 Michael Duffy and Dan Goodgame, *Marching in Place: The Status Quo Presidency of George Bush* (New York: Simon and Schuster, 1992), 125.
14 Ibid., 123.
15 Warshaw, *Powersharing*.
16 *Public Papers of the Presidents of the United States: George H. W. Bush, 1989*, vol. 1 (Washington, DC: Government Printing Office, 1989).
17 Barbara H. Craig and David M. O'Brien, *Abortion and American Politics* (Chatham, NJ: Chatham House, 1993), 191.
18 Barry D. Friedman, *Regulation in the Reagan-Bush Era: The Eruption of Presidential Influence* (Pittsburgh, PA: University of Pittsburgh Press, 1995).
19 Richard A. Harris and Sidney M. Milkis, *The Politics of Regulatory Change: A Tale of Two Agencies* (New York: Oxford University Press, 1996).
20 Mary E. Stuckey, *The President as Interpreter-in-Chief* (Chatham, NJ: Chatham House, 1991), 128.
21 Duffy and Goodgame, *Marching in Place*, 46.
22 Iwona Świątczak-Wasilewska, "The Failure of Legislative Leadership: A Retrospective Study of Crafting the State of the Unions in the George H. W. Bush White House," *Res Rhetorica* 7, no. 2 (2020): 83–103.
23 Mervin, *George Bush and the Guardianship Presidency*, 106.
24 On the factors producing Bush's early popularity, see in particular George C. Edwards III, "George Bush and the Public Presidency: The Politics of Inclusion," in *The Bush Presidency: First Appraisals*, ed. Colin Campbell and Bert A. Rockman (Chatham, NJ: Chatham House, 1991), 129–154.

25 Smith and Smith, *White House Speaks*, 82–90.

26 Kolb, *White House Daze*, 41.

27 Quirk, "Domestic Policy," 69–91.

28 *Congressional Quarterly Weekly Report*, June 17, 1989, 1460.

29 Steven V. Roberts and Kenneth T. Walsh, "Is Bush in Nature's Way?" *U.S. News and World Report*, March 19, 1990, 20.

30 Robert D. Reischauer, *Setting National Priorities: Budget Choices for the Next Century* (Washington, DC: Brookings Institution, 1996).

31 For helpful case studies of these events, see Richard Darman, *Who's in Control: Polar Politics and the Sensible Center* (New York: Simon and Schuster, 1996); George Hager and Eric Pianin, *Mirage* (New York: Random House, 1997); and Quirk, "Domestic Policy."

32 Mervin, *George Bush and the Guardianship Presidency*, 155.

33 *Wards Cove Packing Co. v. Antonio*, 490 U.S. 642 (1989).

34 Quirk, "Domestic Policy," 88.

35 Barbara Sinclair, "How Will George Bush Go Down in History?" *Los Angeles Times*, November 1, 1992, 13.

36 Reischauer, *Setting National Priorities*, 13.

14 Bill Clinton
A Perpetual Campaigner under Siege

The presidency of Bill Clinton (served 1993–2001) resembled a roller-coaster ride. In his first year, he suffered a rapid three-month loss of popularity, and yet the same year, he achieved passage of a landmark deficit-reduction package and other new legislation, earning him an 86 percent legislative success score for 1993–1994. In his second year, he suffered the resounding defeat of his health care package and damaging charges of a White House cover-up. He and his party bore a stunning rebuke in 1994 as the Republicans gained control of both the Senate and House of Representatives for the first time since 1954.

And the shifting fortunes continued. In 1995, Clinton outmaneuvered Republican leaders in Congress on budget politics when they incorrectly assumed he would cave in to their demands. Only a year later, against the predictions of all the pundits, he became the first Democratic president to attain reelection since FDR. In the fall of 1997, a sex scandal involving a young White House intern dominated the headlines, followed in 1998 by impeachment in the House of Representatives and a trial, but not a conviction, in the Senate in 1999. In the aftermath of the 1998 midterm elections—which went surprisingly well for the Democrats—people's views of the president continued to vary. Some were awed by a politically skilled chief executive who, holding office during a transitional period, was remarkably able to land on his feet. Others argued that his personal limitations were producing underachievement. What was the real story of Bill Clinton in terms of how he performed given his low level of opportunity?

Personal Characteristics

William Jefferson Clinton (1946–) was the first of the baby-boom generation to attain the White House. Virtually all of his predecessors had gained at least some credit for having served in the military. A question plagued him: How did he avoid serving in the Vietnam War? His answer regarding marijuana use—"I did not inhale," he said—became a campaign issue for a time. The young president's strong rejection of hierarchical structures in

DOI: 10.4324/9781003426684-17

organizing his administration also was viewed as a reflection of the attitudes of many baby boomers.[1] The presidency was undergoing a profound generational passage, and this made for some harsh intergenerational criticism of the president.

Clinton's early family experiences gave little indication he would become the first member of his generation to occupy the presidency.[2] His father died before he was born, and his mother returned to school to train as a nurse anesthetist, leaving Bill living for a time with his grandparents in Hope, Arkansas, before his mother moved the family to Hot Springs. After her remarriage to the alcoholic and sometimes abusive Roger Clinton, young Bill Clinton at times found himself having to aggressively defend his mother. When the family's economic situation improved, Bill was raised as part of a growing middle class as he proceeded through his school days in Hot Springs.

Following a strong high school performance in which he graduated fourth in a class of 363, he pursued his undergraduate degree, with a major in international relations, at Georgetown University. After graduation, he left the country for England and two years of study as a Rhodes scholar at Oxford University. He returned to complete his legal studies at Yale Law School.

Career Path

Bill Clinton was involved in more major political campaigns than any of the other post-1932 presidents. In high school and college, he frequently ran for office, and to help pay his college tuition, he worked in the office of Senator William Fulbright (D-AR). Clinton loved campaigns. He had worked on races in Arkansas, Connecticut, and Texas (as co-chair of the George McGovern presidential campaign in 1972) before his own surprisingly close but unsuccessful bid for a congressional seat in Arkansas in 1974. By the time he ran for the presidency in 1992, he had run in no fewer than eight Arkansas elections.

Clinton's career path to the presidency included ten years as governor of Arkansas. He was elected in 1978, was defeated in 1980, and won enough reelection bids to serve from 1983 until his resignation after winning the presidency in 1992. The early defeat produced a change in his leadership style—he abandoned some of his more ambitious programs, recruited a staff who appeared less Ivy League, and proceeded more cautiously. The one exception to his cautious approach was his strong and largely successful promotion of education reform in 1983. In fact, during his ten years in the governor's office, Clinton often showed interest in innovative programs, such as efforts to combat adult illiteracy and different ways of delivering home services to the elderly. He also was highly successful in building support within the state's African American community.

276 The Low-Opportunity Presidents

Clinton tended to rely on personal persuasiveness in dealing with members of his state legislature. It was nominally controlled by the Democratic Party, but in fact it included diverse factions, some of whom were hesitant about significant political reform. As governor, he gained the attention of the national media, which pronounced him a rising star as one of the "most effective" governors. But, like all politicians, he also came in for his share of criticism: his tendency to shift according to changing political winds, the limited attention he paid to the administration of new programs, and his coziness with economic elites, which was at variance with his populist political rhetoric.[3]

Clinton's emergence as the Democratic nominee in 1992 occurred despite two personal issues that might have torpedoed his candidacy. The first was his account of how he avoided serving in the Vietnam War. His initial explanation that he had received a low draft number omitted the fact that he had achieved and later declined an ROTC (Reserve Officers' Training Corps) appointment at the University of Arkansas before receiving the low lottery number. The second issue was Gennifer Flowers, a nightclub singer in Little Rock who claimed she had had a 12-year affair with Clinton. Clinton helped defuse this issue when he appeared with Hillary on the television program *Sixty Minutes*. He confessed to having caused "pain in our marriage," and they both spoke of the renewed strength of their relationship.

Clinton displayed considerable energy and political skill as he fought for the nomination, despite public skepticism about his past behavior. He was helped in the crucial New Hampshire primary by a large network of personal friends who joined his effort. As the campaign progressed, he realized he had an advantage over most of the other Democratic candidates: his years of work with policy issues in Arkansas had given him a good grasp of policy and an ability to articulate an agenda as a "New Democrat."

As the Democratic nominee, Clinton was both fortunate and effective in the fall campaign. The economy continued to slump, and the reminder "It's the economy, stupid," posted on the wall of his Little Rock campaign office, became his central theme. Clinton was able to capitalize on and articulate voters' concerns about issues such as health care and the need for fundamental welfare reform. By comparison, President Bush ran a surprisingly ineffective campaign, poorly organized and lacking focus. In the end, Clinton was able to put together an electoral college coalition that included some traditionally liberal states, California, some swing states, and four southern states.

What Manner of Man?

Few have doubted Clinton's intelligence, ambition, and high energy level.[4] His ambition for political office was manifested as early as his high school days, when he turned away from other possible career choices such as music or medicine. A high school trip to Washington as part of the American Legion's Boys Nation in 1963 and a handshake from President John Kennedy probably helped to kindle that ambition.

Clinton's late-night calls to friends and staff both before and after his election were one indication of his high energy level. In fact, his energy was often highest when he was focused on a particular task. Later, after he moved into the White House, his efforts to overcome early problems produced similar bursts of energy and a White House that was rumored to be suffering from sleep deprivation.

Clinton possessed a high level of self-confidence, but he required validation. Toward that end, he sometimes seemed to display his extensive knowledge of issues more to impress listeners than to marshal effective, persuasive arguments. His confidence was shaken at low points during his presidency, such as his first months in office and in the aftermath of the Republican triumph in the 1994 elections. When in one of his low moods, he often blamed others, such as staffers or the press, for his problems, and on occasion he would lose his temper.

As president, he continued to read many books as well as a variety of assessments of policy issues. In this way, he developed an understanding of budgetary issues that rivaled the knowledge of longtime committee members in Congress and gave him a major advantage in top-level negotiations with rivals such as Speaker Newt Gingrich (R-GA). Yet, at times Clinton's ability to absorb detail was not an advantage. Like Jimmy Carter, he sometimes spent too much time on unnecessary information.

As for his relationships with friends and constituents, Clinton seemed to have a genuine interest in people and an unusually high degree of empathy. Indeed, from an early age, he liked to help others who were in trouble. Clinton found he could use his empathetic qualities very effectively in town hall-style meetings, including presidential debates conducted in that manner. His empathy was also manifested in some of his presidential roles, such as expressing the nation's grief after the terrorist bombing in Oklahoma City in April 1995.

In dealing with others, Clinton often seemed reluctant to openly reveal his opposition to various ideas and suggestions. At times, he even used this trait to see how others would handle an issue, causing confusion among subordinates and other political figures because his noncommittal response was taken inappropriately as an indication of his approval of their ideas. It is not surprising, then, that the epithet "Slick Willie" clung to Clinton from his Arkansas days.

The personal quality that produced the most intense debate about Clinton was his tendency to shade the truth, or dissemble, when it came to personal matters. He faced questions early on in his presidential bid about his draft status during the Vietnam War. Later, when he was in the White

278   *The Low-Opportunity Presidents*

House, he drew criticism for his interpretations of suspicious White House operations such as the abrupt dismissal of travel agents, his reasons why FBI files of Republicans came into the hands of White House staffers, and his explanation of the extent to which guest stays in the Lincoln Bedroom were used for fund-raising. According to political scientist Stanley Renshon, Clinton tended to dissemble because of a somewhat idealized self-view and thus his difficulty in accurately interpreting his own behavior.[5]

Policy Views

Clinton came to the presidency from a state lacking a liberal tradition. From his childhood experiences and years as governor, he brought to the White House his supportive views on civil rights and the death penalty and a moderate orientation on many issues. As a product of one of the nation's poorest states, he wanted to see government help people improve their economic well-being. Thus, in his presidential campaign he called for investments in educational training to improve a worker's job prospects. In fact, in the 1992 campaign he touted programs to create new jobs far more than his commitment to cutting the deficit by 50 percent. He spoke often of the need to help average Americans who were living by the rules and having a hard time. And he spoke of a New Covenant, but with an emphasis on individual responsibility.

The need to find a "third way" to address policy issues was central to Clinton's views. As one of the founders of the Democratic Leadership Council—a group supported by the more conservative figures in the Democratic Party—he sought policy approaches that would be more mainstream than the traditional liberal views.[6] In health care, for example, his 1993 proposal ended up being highly regulatory because he wished to avoid a Canadian-style system of direct government financing while also providing universal coverage rather than more limited reforms. More broadly, he wanted to use government to address economic and social problems, yet he wanted to rely largely on market mechanisms and individual initiative. He believed in a smaller—but still active—government.

Challenges and Opportunities

When Clinton assumed the presidency, he faced the challenge of addressing the concerns of an angry public. It wanted action on health care and the economy but was skeptical about the effectiveness of many federal policies and uncertain about the intentions of the political parties. This gave Clinton an opportunity to build a new coalition. However, the task was difficult considering he had won the election with only a plurality in a three-person race.

Several aspects of Clinton's position were not overly promising. In terms of election results, his 5.6 percentage-point winning margin over George H. W. Bush ranked in the middle of the pack (7th) among the post-1932 presidents, and his 43.0 percent of the total vote ranks him last in electoral support (see Table 1.1). As for his personal approval ratings, he started with a respectable 58 percent, which dropped to only 38 percent after three months. In addition, Clinton was confronting an increasingly skeptical electorate; only 22 percent agreed with the proposition that one could trust the government in Washington to do the right thing most of the time (see Figure 1.1).

In Congress, the Democratic majorities in the House and Senate were smaller than those of other newly elected Democratic presidents, but they included fewer conservative southern Democrats. Less promising for Clinton was the growing trend toward partisan voting in Congress and the increased use of filibusters in the Senate to block presidential initiatives.

In view of the economic recession of 1991–1992 and his concentration on creating jobs, Clinton appeared to have a big opportunity to move on his job creation agenda early in his administration. Several factors served to reduce that opportunity, however. Improved economic figures for the fourth quarter of 1992 and improved projections for 1993 lessened the sense of urgency about creating new jobs. At the same time, higher deficit projections reduced support for new spending programs. But therein lay another opportunity for Clinton. The growing demands for deficit reduction may have made it more difficult for him to promote job creation programs with the public and with Congress, but they gave the new president a better opportunity to promote a deficit-reduction plan.

At first, health reform seemed to be a promising opportunity as opinion polls showed majority support for major changes in the health care system. The difficulty lay in obtaining any kind of agreement on a specific policy design. When the public envisioned health care reform, it most often had in mind reducing waste and fraud. But as the intense debate over health policy developed, those responsible for developing specific plans underscored the importance of containing costs and helping those who lacked coverage acquire health insurance.

Clinton's opportunities changed dramatically in the wake of the Republican takeover of the House and Senate in the 1994 midterm elections. Fundamentally, however, the Republican move to the right on a variety of issues created a new opportunity for Clinton to establish a centrist position and successfully appeal to voters' apprehensions about the more extremist policies of the Republicans in Congress.

Foreign policy concerns provided some distractions and difficulties but no major disruptions to Clinton's domestic policy roles. In October 1993, the nation was shocked by the slaying of American soldiers stationed

280　*The Low-Opportunity Presidents*

in Somalia as part of a humanitarian mission and television pictures of the body of a pilot being dragged through the streets of Mogadishu. In response to the situation, Clinton swung his attention to devising strategies for ending that mission during a time he had hoped to focus on promoting his health policy initiative.[7] Clinton also had to struggle during most of his first term with the civil war in the former Yugoslavia. Ultimately, he decided against direct involvement and contributed to the development of plans that, in effect, called for partitioning the country.

Clinton's second term began with more limitations than advantages. He was reelected by a far smaller-than-average margin, and he had to muster bipartisan support for any new policies since both houses of Congress remained under Republican control. His campaign had featured many minor proposals, but it was primarily a defense of existing programs. Continuing economic growth, however, meant that the opportunities for congressional passage of a multiyear balanced budget agreement had increased dramatically.

Leadership Style

At various points during administration, Clinton expressed admiration for Presidents Franklin Roosevelt, Harry Truman, John Kennedy, and Ronald Reagan (for his effective use of the fast-start strategy). Clinton's early difficulties and the Republican victories in 1994 prompted his search for a better leadership style. In improving his leadership efforts, the president sought to respond better to drastic changes and to adjust based on lessons learned from his earlier career experiences. As the president with the most extensive experience in major campaigns prior to his election, he often seemed to be a perpetual campaigner. He studied the public opinion polls incessantly and diligently sought to sell himself and his administration to the public.

The Advisory Process and Approach to Decision-Making

As he organized his administration, Clinton tried to keep his campaign commitment to filling his cabinet with Americans from diverse backgrounds—"a Cabinet that looks like America."[8] As a result, the top 23 positions included six women, four African Americans, and two Hispanics. It was the most diverse cabinet up to that point. Key domestic policy positions were filled by deficit-reduction "hawks" and former senator Lloyd Bentsen as Treasury secretary. The more liberal voices were those of university president Donna Shalala as secretary of health and human services and Clinton's fellow Rhodes scholar Robert Reich as secretary of labor.

Bill Clinton 281

Also occupying important positions of power in the Clinton White House were Vice President Al Gore and First Lady Hillary Rodham Clinton. Gore, according to some analysts, was the most influential vice president in the nation's history up to that time. And he had a very close relationship with Clinton.[9] The vice president's most public domestic role was aimed at reviewing and then cutting, consolidating, and reshaping the federal government. It was known as the National Performance Review and later renamed the National Partnership for Reinventing Government.

The significant influence of the first lady on the president was indicated in part by her large staff and prominent West Wing office. During the first two years, she led the administration's health care reform effort. In the early days of the administration, she was present at a wide variety of meetings and was viewed by staff and cabinet members as an important channel of influence on presidential decisions.

Clinton's decision-making process was characterized by his extensive involvement (perhaps too much) in policy details. And, as noted, he also tended to seek a "third way" in policy disputes. Consultant Dick Morris liked to call this tendency "triangulation," but the president's fondness for hybrid solutions was well established before Morris arrived on the scene in late 1994. Clinton also paid a great deal of attention to opinion polls, and political consultants armed with polling data and the results of focus groups had greater access in the Clinton White House than in any previous administration.[10] Political feasibility was tested as well through personal contact with many members of Congress.

During his first term, Clinton was criticized by the media and others for his rather chaotic staff processes and inexperienced media relations personnel. Because the president tended to immerse himself in one or a few issues and because he disliked hierarchies, the White House sometimes seemed to lack coordinated direction. In fact, in the beginning, Clinton and his staff seemed to have few plans for how the presidency should proceed. According to journalist Elizabeth Drew, plans existed for only the first two weeks.[11]

But things did improve with experience and a few staff changes. In 1994, Chief of Staff Mack McLarty was replaced by Leon Panetta, who imposed greater discipline on staff operations. By 1997, Erskine Bowles brought his experience to bear on the White House organization, and the administration ran more smoothly.

Administrative Strategies

Clinton used administrative strategies freely. As noted, in 1993–1994, Vice President Al Gore led an effort to make the federal government leaner and more efficient, and he succeeded in achieving substantial changes.

282 *The Low-Opportunity Presidents*

After the Republican victories in the 1994 midterm election, the reform movement took on new urgency as a strategy for avoiding more sweeping Republican-led changes in some agencies.[12] Several observers credited these reform efforts and a tendency toward greater caution in creating new regulations with serving to mute initial Republican efforts to dismantle some agencies and departments.

Clinton's attempts to use administrative strategies to please segments of his electoral coalition produced some modest successes and at least one highly visible failure. Although some supporters felt his quick action on abortion rights conflicted with his image as a "New Democrat," other supporters applauded his actions, such as his reversal of the "gag rule" applied during the Bush years, forbidding doctors at federally funded clinics from furnishing any information on the option of requesting an abortion. But when Clinton tried to modify the policies on gays in the military, he unleashed a torrent of criticism. During his first week in office, the president sought to make good on a campaign promise to eliminate prohibitions against homosexuals serving in the military. This move, however, triggered an intense protest from Congress, including some leading Democrats. The political costs to the president on this issue were immense. By looking weak and indecisive at the outset of his administration, he diminished his "honeymoon" period. In the end, he did not achieve a significant change in policy.

Administrative strategies were also in considerable evidence during 1995–1996 when, to keep his presidency in the news, Clinton used a wide variety of executive orders and pursued administrative actions. Consultant Dick Morris played a role in promoting these steps, which included pushing development of the V-chip as an aid for parents trying to select suitable television programming for their children. Clinton also issued an executive order requiring teenage mothers on welfare to work or to attend school and live at home.

Public Leadership

Although several of Clinton's early major and secondary speeches were well received—especially his thoughtful and candid remarks on race relations in October 1993.[13] His "honeymoon period" seemed unusually short, leading to talk of a failed presidency. Some of his support-building efforts drew skeptical reviews, and he struggled with harsh assessments by the media. In fact, in his first three months in office, only 21 percent of comments by TV reporters were favorable—in stark contrast to George H. W. Bush's figure of 74 percent. Clinton also found himself receiving four times as many references in the humor segments of late-night TV show hosts as Bush received during his first hundred days in office.[14]

Clinton contributed to these problems by adopting an unusual media strategy of largely bypassing the Washington media and relying on local news outlets and alternative news sources. The results were mixed—while he was able to go directly to the public, he also generated resentment from the Beltway pundits.

Although some improvements were made, media relationships proved difficult for Clinton. After three months, David Gergen, a veteran media specialist from the Reagan administration, was recruited (to the dismay of some Clinton staffers) to improve press relations. He arranged social events such as a barbecue to bring the president and the press together and scheduled an unusually late first formal press conference. The press conference proved to be a brief exception to Clinton's pattern of avoiding such gatherings. Then, as the Clinton real estate scandal known as "Whitewater" broke, media-White House relations became tense once again.

Clinton's quest for personal popularity showed some improvement over time. His 34 percent disapproval rating after only a month in office and his June 1993 approval figure of only 37 percent had given way by 1996 to approval ratings above 50 percent. According to George Edwards III, Clinton's figures were particularly low for a president holding office with a strong economy.[15] Contributing to his popularity in 1996 were his January 1996 State of the Union address and his successful resistance to unpopular Republican proposals. Even during the tense days of impeachment in 1998, Clinton maintained surprisingly high approval ratings.

Despite his attempts to improve his public leadership, Clinton was handicapped in several ways. From the start, he was confronted with greater hostility from segments of the media and the electorate than any president since Richard Nixon. Conservative talk show hosts such as Rush Limbaugh subjected their audiences to an ongoing barrage of character attacks on Clinton and his family. Mainstream newspapers, including the *New York Times*, seemed to be slanting their coverage of Whitewater stories beyond the factual merit of the story.[16]

Congressional Leadership

In addition to the traditional legislative liaison structure, Clinton enlisted his chiefs of staff, especially Leon Panetta, in paving the way for congressional passage of favored bills. The administration's most innovative device was the "war room," which coordinated actions between its legislative liaison and public liaison segments. This arrangement was modeled in part on the Clinton campaign's effective swift response mechanism. The war room was used most notably in the deficit-reduction fight and the battle over NAFTA in 1993 and the campaign for health care reform in 1994.

For Clinton, congressional relations consumed considerable time and energy. Shortly after his election, he initiated a series of meetings with legislators, and, in preparation, he learned the names of many of them.

284   *The Low-Opportunity Presidents*

In setting up routine leadership meetings, he was surprised to learn how seldom President Jimmy Carter had met with members of Congress. He was also a frequent visitor to Capitol Hill and called individual legislators often. Treasury Secretary Lloyd Bentsen judged Clinton to be the most legislatively active of the eight presidents he had observed during his lengthy career in Washington.

Acting on the assurances of widespread party support he had received from Democratic leaders in early meetings held in Little Rock, the president sought partisan coalitions in 1993 in order to achieve a Reagan-like first year. But he faced an uphill struggle. Congress was increasingly partisan, and the Republican minority leader had cautioned him that there would be no Republican support for a deficit-reduction package that included a tax increase. Clinton was able, however, to put together a bipartisan coalition—the first of several—to achieve passage of NAFTA.

After the midterm election losses, Clinton changed his position, moving to the right on several issues while periodically holding firm. This helped him to highlight differences between his positions and those of the Republican-controlled Congress during his reelection effort. After surviving reelection, he used top-level negotiations to achieve a five-year agreement for a balanced budget.

Legislative Enactments

In his first term, Clinton produced surprisingly big, fundamental changes in domestic policy. Despite cries of gridlock and the dramatic three-week government shutdown in late 1995, Congress passed a higher-than-average amount of major legislation, along with landmark deficit reduction in 1993 and welfare reform and telecommunications reform in 1996. According to David Mayhew, 1996 saw the passage of prominent changes in economic regulation policies, including those for agriculture, pesticides, and drinking water.[17] Conspicuously absent, however, was a health reform package bearing any resemblance to Clinton's initial proposal.

First-Year Successes and Failures

Of the issues Clinton had strongly promoted during the fall campaign, he enjoyed one partial success and one high-profile failure in his first year. The failure came with his inability to achieve passage of an economic stimulus package in March 1993. The measure that Congress debated was a scaled-back version of his proposed "investments" to put people back to work. It passed in the House but ran into a Republican filibuster threat in the Senate.

Observers chalked up the defeat to a changing economy, a difficult-to-defend package, and a poor selling job by Clinton, as well as problems with legislative tactics. Economically, the stronger-than-expected performance in the last three months of 1992 weakened the "dire need" argument for the program. The program itself was a catchall of favorite spending ideas rather than a few, more easily defensible commitments.[18] Clinton talked about his program in some settings but made no focused effort to sell it. With the Republicans sensing that they could successfully oppose a president with sagging public support, the scene was set for an embarrassing presidential defeat. Minority Leader Robert Dole of Kansas mobilized the entire Republican delegation behind a filibuster threat, and Clinton had to retreat.

The first of Clinton's dramatic successes came with the narrow passage of a landmark deficit-reduction package in August. The package was central to Clinton's first-year performance as well as to the economy's subsequent upturn, perhaps explaining why, after a considerable internal struggle, the Clinton administration made deficit reduction its primary domestic policy effort in 1993. As the bill wound its way through the House, it encountered a tortured process of narrow votes with Republicans often in unanimous opposition. The bill that finally emerged reduced the deficit by one-third over a five-year period through deficit-reduction steps quite similar to the plan a Democratic-controlled Congress had forced on Bush in 1990. Major provisions of the 1993 plan included tax increases to a top rate of 36 percent for individuals with incomes over $140,000, a top corporate rate of 35 percent, a $20.8 billion expansion of the earned income tax credit to help the working poor, a $3.5 billion provision for empowerment zones, and $55.8 billion in Medicare cuts.

When the measure reached the Senate, Clinton had to make a series of retreats from his original proposal. The most controversial item was his proposed BTU tax, opposed by senators representing the high-energy-producing states. Ultimately, a simpler-to-calculate increase in the gasoline tax was imposed.

The final votes in each house were much closer and more partisan than those normally associated with landmark legislation. In trying to marshal the necessary votes, Clinton increased pressure on Congress through a major address. When that approach failed, Clinton turned to an insider game. In dealing with legislators directly, Clinton spent considerable personal time and mobilized key figures in his administration, including Chief of Staff Mack McLarty. After convincing a few key legislators, Clinton was able to narrowly avoid what many felt would have been a devastating defeat for a first-year president.[19]

Clinton enjoyed considerable success with measures that had languished on the congressional agenda. Passage of the Family and Medical Leave Act during Clinton's first weeks in office nicely illustrated the advantages of a promising measure.[20] This legislation required employers to provide leave (but not pay) for new mothers and any employees facing demanding family

286 *The Low-Opportunity Presidents*

medical matters. After an acrimonious few years, the measure was passed in 1990 but vetoed by George H. W. Bush. A resounding 390-vote veto override in the House proved the measure's popularity there, but it fell four votes short of the two-thirds override requirement in the Senate. A similar pattern of successful presidential vetoes followed in the next two sessions of Congress.

From the earliest days of his primary campaign, Clinton had spoken out forcefully about the family medical leave legislation. Clinton had emphasized that he, in contrast to George H. W. Bush, would be willing to sign the new legislation promptly once in office. This was an easy bill for him to support and helped to strengthen his ties with a supporting coalition.

The "motor voter" bill, which allowed citizens to register to vote at state motor vehicle departments, proved to be a considerably more difficult measure to push than medical leave legislation. It had also been debated for several years, but with considerable Republican resistance. Yet, the Clinton administration pushed quite hard for this measure and was instrumental in engineering final compromises that allayed some Republican fears and facilitated passage.

Clinton played his strongest role in successfully promoting legislation providing for a new system of national service known as AmeriCorps.[21] Clinton's emphasis on a service program in his first year paralleled FDR's promotion of the Civilian Conservation Corps and John Kennedy's success in establishing the Peace Corps. Clinton found the concept of a national service program appealing and highly popular on the campaign trail, crossing racial and class lines. Once in office, he recruited two legislative staffers to write the legislation and placed veteran staffer Eli Segal in charge of promotion. The president also helped search for votes when the program ran into resistance in Congress. The program that finally emerged was far smaller than Clinton had originally envisioned but kept its basic philosophy: Participants (17 years and older with a high school or equivalent degree) would receive education awards for their part-time or full-time work in community programs. The legislation called for an allocation of $300 million in 1994 and $700 million by 1996, with participants receiving awards of slightly under $5,000 a year.

Mounting Difficulties in 1994

Clinton's relationship with Congress soured in 1994 as he suffered from an embarrassing near-defeat and then the total collapse of his health policy initiative. The near-defeat came on a crime bill designed to show he was a "New Democrat" devoted to law enforcement. It called for, among other things, funding to hire 100,000 new police officers. In the House, there were underlying cleavages on issues such as an assault weapons ban and differing views of prevention programs. Coalitions formed on the left and on the right, effectively preventing final consideration of the bill. Chief of Staff Leon Panetta worked virtually around the clock to find solutions that would keep enough factions happy to produce majority support. In the end, the measure passed as legislators were attracted to the idea of passing a crime bill in an election year.

The defining event of Clinton's second year in office was the total defeat of his proposed Health Security Act,[22] which has been attributed to many different factors.[23] Prior to his election, Clinton had committed himself to a new approach to health care reform called "managed competition." He felt that his approach—an effort to control market pressures in the health field—along with employer mandates, would achieve universal coverage while also dealing with the rapidly escalating cost of the nation's health care. Although he was later criticized for a plan to "take over one-seventh of the nation's economy," he was in fact seeking a middle way that avoided the taxation and control mechanisms found in the Canadian health care system, which some were advocating. Given these concerns, what was produced was an overly elaborate plan that was difficult to explain.

In early 1993, the Task Force on National Health Reform, under the leadership of Hillary Rodham Clinton and Ira Magaziner, began its work. Its elaborate system of consultation, involving over five hundred experts in various fields, drew criticism. The task force contacted various interest groups and members of Congress, but many of those contacted felt they should be more centrally involved. The task force tried to have the outlines of a plan approved in the budget reconciliation process, but key members of Congress objected. In retrospect, as Jimmy Carter had found in 1977, it was a risky strategy to try to seek a new policy for health care combined with a fast start. The repeated deadlocks in Congress and the lack of willingness on the part of key committee members to proceed from a skeleton proposal meant the administration needed to develop a new approach.

Another factor contributing to the defeat of the Health Security Act was ineffective public promotion by the White House. Clinton was distracted in the fall of 1993, first with NAFTA and then with foreign policy issues. His White House was poorly organized to develop the support campaign outlined by the task force. In seeking a message to support the campaign, the White House relied on marketing approaches and simple slogans. Staffers decided from polling results, for example, that "managed competition" sounded too much like the often unpopular "managed care" approach using health maintenance organizations, and the phrase was dropped. Promotions emphasized benefits but did little to explain the mechanisms involved.

With the public unable to understand exactly what changes were being proposed, the Health Security Act became vulnerable to the well-orchestrated opposition campaign, which included the infamous "Harry and Louise" ads funded by the health insurance lobby. Republicans joined the

288   *The Low-Opportunity Presidents*

cause through legislative channels. Representative Dick Armey (R-TX) displayed a diagram of the Clinton plan that consisted of a large, unintelligible maze of boxes and arrows. By early December, Republican strategist William Kristol had begun to urge party members to speak out against a plan that could become a major new entitlement and fundamentally expand support for the Democratic Party.

The uneven public relations battle was won by opponents of the Health Security Act. From strong majority support in the early fall of 1993, support fell to 52 percent by January 1994 and the negatives were up sharply. By March, for the first time, more people opposed the plan than supported it. By July, only 43 percent supported Clinton's proposal; 47 percent opposed it. Along with his weak public relations effort, Clinton was hurt by his own falling popularity as the controversial Whitewater land deal became a hot political topic.

Clinton also faced defeats in the areas of campaign finance reform and welfare reform. Campaign finance reform was subjected to the traditional partisan divisions and did not appear to be high on the president's wish list. An interagency task force that included several highly regarded students of welfare policy developed Clinton's welfare reform proposals. The task force struggled, however. While the goal of moving recipients off the welfare rolls and into the ranks of the employed was laudable, the associated costs of child support and additional job training could make those efforts more expensive than simply leaving people on welfare. In the face of these underlying conflicts, the task force produced no legislation in 1994.

1995–1996

The 104th Congress began with an unprecedented effort by Republicans and House Speaker Newt Gingrich to control the congressional agenda by pushing a series of measures popularized during the fall campaign—the "Contract with America." A majority of the ten Republican measures were passed by the House, but they faced difficulty in the Senate. Major legislation that succeeded included the Congressional Responsibility Act requiring that laws applying elsewhere also apply to Congress, a curb on unfunded mandates to the states, and restrictions on stockholder lawsuits against securities firms.

However, the central battle shaping relations between Clinton and the 104th Congress came over Republican plans for a balanced budget to be achieved in seven years.[24] The Republican proposals called for cuts in both taxes and spending, thereby fulfilling Republican desires to reduce the size of the federal government. Because the GOP also wanted to see a moderate increase in defense spending and sought to avoid addressing Social Security issues, the proposed cuts centered on discretionary programs and two rapidly growing health care entitlement programs—Medicare and Medicaid.

Of the proposed cuts of between $900 billion and $1 trillion over seven years, between $250 billion and $300 billion were to come from reductions in projected Medicare spending.

Clinton refused to accept Republican proposals even as the government shut down twice for lack of appropriations, including a 17-day period from mid-December 1995 to early January 1996. Clinton's defense of his opposition to the Republican plan was that the proposed tax cuts rewarded the wealthiest Americans while taking excessive amounts out of Medicare, Medicaid, and environmental programs. The similarity between the size of the tax cut and the reductions in future Medicare spending exposed an obvious vulnerability in the plan: One could argue that Medicare was being cut to give tax breaks to the wealthy. As top-level negotiations proceeded at length, Clinton and his aides continued to resist Republican overtures as Republican leaders realized they were losing the battle for public opinion. After negotiations on a seven-year agreement collapsed in January 1996, single-year appropriations to restore government operations were approved. Then, in an effort to strengthen his bargaining position for decisions on the 1997 budget, Clinton put forward his own plan for a balanced budget to be achieved within seven years. This proposal made smaller cuts in Medicare and Medicaid and contained fewer tax cuts.

Republican forces in Congress had greater success with the enactment of landmark welfare reform legislation. In 1992, while campaigning, Clinton had articulated widespread public disapproval of the existing Aid to Families with Dependent Children (AFDC) program with a pledge to "end welfare as we know it." The presidential task force that had looked at welfare reform in 1993 had stressed job training and child care along with time limits for receiving AFDC benefits. But it had failed to bring forth any concrete proposals in 1994 as relations between Clinton and Congress deteriorated.

The Republican proposals that emerged in the 104th Congress paid less attention to transitional support and placed a greater emphasis on time limits. One version also eliminated Medicaid in favor of less comprehensive, state-determined programs. Two Clinton vetoes, however, succeeded in derailing those Republican initiatives.

Republican strategists then designed a welfare reform bill that presented Clinton with a difficult choice. In part because federal AFDC costs were minor, the next welfare reform bill focused substantially on eliminating aid to legal immigrants to achieve the projected savings of $54 billion over five years (the other major savings was in tighter eligibility requirements for food stamps). As for AFDC, it was eliminated, and states were to receive funds to design their own programs for moving people from welfare to the workforce. Other provisions called for penalizing states unable to meet targets and for moving welfare recipients off the welfare rolls within two years.

290 *The Low-Opportunity Presidents*

This bill emerged as Congress was getting ready for its August recess. The Clinton administration was split in its views. Secretary of Labor Robert Reich, Treasury Secretary Robert Rubin, and some aides who had worked on Clinton's earlier proposals favored a veto. Political adviser Dick Morris and others strongly opposed a veto. In the end, Clinton indicated his displeasure with the bill, especially with the provisions pertaining to legal immigrants, but signaled his willingness to sign the measure. It then passed easily in both houses when Democrats in each body split evenly in their support or opposition. While not what he had originally envisioned, Clinton could claim that he had kept his 1992 campaign promise on welfare as he campaigned for reelection.[25]

Other major legislation included the passage of an increase in the minimum wage. Clinton had promoted an adjustment in the minimum wage in his State of the Union address, and Senate Democrats had managed to keep the issue on the agenda. When Senator Trent Lott (R-MS) replaced Robert Dole as majority leader in 1996, he decided to facilitate passage in return for opportunities to move legislation in other areas. Republicans in the House were able to add a lower training wage, but many were reluctant to stand against the minimum wage in an election year.

The 1997 Balanced Budget Agreement

In the spring of 1997, top-level negotiators finally met the elusive goal of a five-year balanced budget agreement. Several factors figured prominently in this achievement. First, a booming economy had eased budget pressures enormously. Second, each side realized that with the continuation of divided government, it could not achieve a more complete victory in the foreseeable future. Third, Republicans were less eager to pursue fundamental changes in Medicare, and the White House was willing to go along with reductions in expenditures that were focused primarily on providers such as hospitals and physicians. Republicans were delighted with the projected tax cuts, and Clinton was pleased to see opportunities for some new spending.

Clinton and Congress

In his first term, Clinton was able to exert some influence in shaping and promoting domestic legislation such as deficit reduction, a national service program, and the Family and Medical Leave Act. With the onset of the 104th Congress, he successfully resisted aspects of the seven-year balanced budget agreement passed by Republican majorities and made some contributions to the productive session in 1996. To some extent, the perceptions of failure in areas such as health care and campaign finance reform were the result of his large agenda. Perhaps the most surprising aspect of

Clinton's first term was the scope of legislation that did emerge despite divided government and complaints of gridlock.

An Assessment

Clinton could claim some credit for the booming economy and the reduction in federal deficits during his time in office. On deficit reduction, he changed course in 1993 and made reducing the deficit his primary emphasis. The strong economy stemmed in part from Clinton's efforts, using policy tools that differed from those stressed in his 1992 campaign. Deficit reduction was central because lower deficits created greater confidence in the bond markets and lower interest rates. The lower rates, in turn, helped generate additional demand in the economy without reigniting inflationary pressures. The results were impressive, with unemployment at just under 5 percent (the lowest level in 25 years), growth figures consistently in the 3 percent range, and inflation rates also in the 3 percent range.

Federal Reserve Board Chairman Alan Greenspan was hailed by many critics for his astute leadership on monetary policy. Some also pointed out that Greenspan's willingness to reduce interest rates was closely related to the fact that deficit reduction was making inflation a less likely problem. The bond market similarly reflected that confidence. Economic forces were at work as well, including the impact of corporate downsizing. While painful to individuals in previous years, those steps nonetheless made American corporations more competitive in the global economy during Clinton's years in the White House.

Of the surprisingly large number of landmark measures enacted on Clinton's watch, arguably the most dramatic was welfare reform, but Clinton could claim some credit for other measures as well. Perhaps the most popular major new legislation was the Family and Medical Leave Act. After 1993, as the political climate changed, Clinton began to pursue small-scale efforts that used federal initiatives in an attempt to leverage efforts by others. This emphasis was evident in his approaches to education policy, where little chance of new spending led the president to promote standards and other small initiatives.

Overall, President Clinton's performance in relation to his circumstances warrants both credit and criticism. Given the constraints on domestic initiatives he inherited, he did not miss an opportunity for passing bold new programs, relying on a strong role for the federal government. And, given the Republican surge in 1994, he can also be credited with preserving many service programs that Republicans had hoped to cut or eliminate. A less skilled president or one who refused to modify positions would have had less success.

292　*The Low-Opportunity Presidents*

In several other respects, however, Clinton's performance was less impressive. His stormy first two years contributed to the Republican surge in the midterm elections. In fact, his Health Security Act became an easy target.[26] Critics such as former welfare policy analyst Peter Edelman argue that on issues such as welfare reform, Clinton undercut progressive policy positions by being too willing to move toward Republican positions. On welfare reform, Clinton acted despite opinion polls showing that a decision for or against the proposed revision would have little impact on his support in the fall election.[27] Clinton also suffered from personal flaws that called his character into question.[28]

As for presidential leadership, Clinton left a mixed legacy. His use of top-level negotiation, the bully pulpit, and the pursuit of objectives through administrative strategies and the leveraging of small programs produced significant results. Yet, Clinton's tendency to dissemble in the face of accusations also contributed to a climate of distrust. Sadly, the result of that combustible mixture was a decline in the stature of the presidency itself. Clinton demeaned himself and diminished the presidency. In this context, his policy successes seem even more surprising.

Notes

1 Mark White, "Son of the Sixties: The Controversial Image of Bill Clinton," *History* 103, no. 354 (2018): 100–123.
2 On Clinton's early life, see David Maraniss, *First in His Class: A Biography of Bill Clinton* (New York: Simon and Schuster, 1995); and Martin Walker, *The President We Deserve: Bill Clinton, His Rise, Falls, and Comebacks* (New York: Crown, 1996).
3 On Clinton as governor, see John Brummett, *Highwire: From the Backroads to the Beltway—The Education of Bill Clinton* (New York: Hyperion, 1994); Diane D. Blair, *Arkansas Government and Politics: Do the People Rule?* (Lincoln: University of Nebraska Press, 1988); and Meredith L. Oakley, *On the Make: The Rise of Bill Clinton* (Washington, DC: Regnery Publishing, 1994).
4 On psychological characteristics, see Stanley A. Renshon, *High Hopes: The Clinton Presidency and the Politics of Ambition* (New York: New York University Press, 1996); and, by the same author, *The Psychological Assessment of Presidential Candidates* (New York: New York University Press, 1996).
5 Renshon, *Psychological Assessment*, 261–262.
6 Patrick J. Maney, *Bill Clinton: New Gilded Age President* (Lawrence, KS: University Press of Kansas, 2016).
7 Theda Skocpol, *Boomerang: Clinton's Health Security Effort and the Turn against Government in U.S. Politics* (New York: Norton, 1996), 78.
8 Shirley Anne Warshaw, *Powersharing: White House-Cabinet Relations in the Modern Presidency* (Albany: State University of New York Press, 1996), 205–206.
9 Thomas E. Cronin, Michael A. Genovese, and Meena Bose, *The Paradoxes of the American Presidency*, 6th ed. (New York: Oxford University Press, 2022), chap. 10; and James W. Davis, *The American Presidency*, 2nd ed. (Westport, CT: Praeger, 1995).

10 George Edwards III, "Frustration and Folly: Bill Clinton and the Public Presidency," in *The Clinton Presidency: First Appraisals*, ed. Colin Campbell and Bert A. Rockman (Chatham, NJ: Chatham House, 1996), 234.

11 Elizabeth Drew, *On the Edge: The Clinton Presidency* (New York: Simon & Schuster, 1994), 34.

12 Jonathan Weisman, "True Impact of GOP Congress Reaches Well Beyond Bill," *Congressional Quarterly Weekly Report*, September 7, 1996, 2515–2520.

13 For more on this aspect of Clinton's public leadership, see Charles M. Lamb, Joshua Boston, and Jacob R. Neiheisel, "Presidential Rhetoric and Bureaucratic Enforcement: The Clinton Administration and Civil Rights," *Political Science Quarterly* 135, no. 2 (2019): 277–302.

14 Walker, *President We Deserve*, 202.

15 Edwards, "Frustration and Folly," 239.

16 Gene Lyons, *Fools for Scandal: How the Media Invented Whitewater* (New York: Franklin Square Press, 1996).

17 David Mayhew, personal communication, January 9, 1997.

18 Robert B. Reich, *Locked in the Cabinet* (New York: Knopf, 1997).

19 Richard Cohen, *Changing Courses in Washington: Clinton and the New Congress* (New York: Macmillan, 1992).

20 The long gestation of this legislation is effectively traced in Ronald D. Elving, *Conflict and Compromise: How Congress Makes the Law* (New York: Simon and Schuster, 1996).

21 Steven Waldman, *The Bill* (New York: Viking, 1996).

22 Useful studies on this legislative failure include Haynes Johnson and David S. Broder, *The System: The American Way of Politics at the Breaking Point* (Boston: Little, Brown, 1996); and Skocpol, *Boomerang*.

23 For a longer review of these issues, see William W. Lammers, "Presidential Leadership and Policy," in *Health Politics and Policy*, ed. Theodore J. Litman and Leonard Robins, 3rd ed. (Albany, NY: Delmar Publishers, 1997), chap. 5.

24 On this controversy, see Elizabeth Drew, *Showdown: The Struggle between the Gingrich Congress and the Clinton White House* (New York: Simon and Schuster, 1997); and George Hager and Eric Pianin, *Mirage: Why Neither Democrats nor Republicans Can Balance the Budget, End the Deficit, and Satisfy the Public* (New York: Random House, 1997).

25 Michael Nelson, *Clinton's Elections: 1992, 1996, and the Birth of a New Era of Governance* (Lawrence, KS: University Press of Kansas, 2020).

26 Skocpol, *Boomerang*, xiv.

27 Peter Edelman, "The Worst Thing Bill Clinton Has Done," *Atlantic Monthly*, March 1997, 44.

28 Thomas E. Cronin and Michael A. Genovese, "President Clinton and Character Questions," *Presidential Studies Quarterly* 28 (Fall 1998): 892–897.

15 Joe Biden
Cleaning the Augean Stables

Donald Trump's bold, blustering style, his shoot-from-the-hip position taking, serial insults, big promises (but weak delivery), stoking of his populist base, and debasement of presidential norms and traditions made him a different sort of president. In the 2020 election, American voters made it known that they had had enough of his style of leadership and favored a return to a more traditional type of presidency. Joe Biden, a man in the public eye for virtually all his adult life, a known quantity and a safe choice, fit the bill.[1]

How would Biden's personality, programs, process, and agenda differ from his predecessor? Would a more traditional style work in a post-Trump age? Biden, who served as President Barack Obama's vice president for eight years, defended the Obama policies that Trump attempted to eviscerate. Would the COVID pandemic he inherited cause him to hit the ground stumbling rather than running? And how could he clean up the chaos he inherited from his predecessor in order to restore the normalcy of governance he promised?

Personal Characteristics

Joe Biden (1942–) was born into a blue-collar family in a blue-collar city, Scranton, Pennsylvania. The values of his upbringing are a source of both pride and political identity for him. Biden feels like a part of middle-class America, speaks their language, and promotes their interests and values. His father worked cleaning furnaces and selling used cars. A lifelong Catholic, Biden attended St. Paul's Elementary School. When he was 13, his family moved to Mayfield, Delaware. As a child, Biden had a pronounced stuttering problem and was the subject of considerable mocking. To overcome this speech impediment, Biden would memorize long passages of poetry and recite them aloud in front of a mirror.[2]

Biden attended the Archmere Academy where he was a star receiver on the football team. He graduated in 1961, and then attended the University of Delaware, where he majored in History and Political Science, and also

DOI: 10.4324/9781003426684-18

Joe Biden   295

played football. On a spring break vacation to the Bahamas, Biden met a student from Syracuse University, Neilia Hunter, who would later become his wife. After graduating from the University of Delaware, Biden attended Syracuse University Law School, graduating in 1965. In 1966, he and Neilia were wed, and they moved to Wilmington, Delaware. He began to practice law but was drawn to politics. In 1970, he was elected to the New Castle County Council, and in the following year, he started his own law firm. The Bidens had three children, Joseph (Beau), Hunter, and Amy.

Career Path

In 1972, at the age of 29, Biden ran for a Senate seat in Delaware against incumbent Republican J. Caleb Boggs. Biden shocked the state (and the nation) by upsetting Boggs. But before he took the oath of office, tragedy struck. A week before Christmas in 1972, Neilia and the three children were in a terrible car accident. Neilia and Amy were killed, and Beau and Hunter were seriously injured. Joe Biden was understandably devastated and considered resigning to tend to his sons' injuries. Biden was persuaded by Senate Majority Leader Mike Mansfield not to resign, and he took the oath of office at age 30, making him the sixth youngest U.S. senator in history.

While a Senator, Biden met Jill Jacobs in 1975 on a blind date. They were married in 1977, and had a daughter, Ashley. Biden sought the Democratic Party nomination in 1987 and, after a lackluster campaign, dropped out early in the race. He attempted to win the party's nomination 20 years later in 2007, but his campaign flagged behind the history-making contest between Hillary Clinton and Barack Obama.

In 2007, Barack Obama selected Biden as his vice president, helping to balance the ticket with Biden's age and experience. He served under Obama for two terms, and after Obama's second term many thought Biden would run for president himself. But in 2015, another tragedy struck when Biden's son, Beau, died of cancer. Biden was too distraught to go through the rigors of a long campaign and decided to forgo the race.

But at age 77, Biden decided to go after the nomination of his party, spurred on by a sense of duty and his reaction to the rise of white supremacists during Trump's presidency. After a slow start, Biden gained momentum by winning the South Carolina primary (thanks to the endorsement of Congressman Jim Clyburn), and cruised to victory in subsequent contests. Biden was also buoyed by notions that he seemed to have the strongest chance of defeating Donald Trump. During the general election, Biden cast the stakes of the election as a "battle for the soul of America."[3] Determined to avoid a repeat of the divisions in 2016, Democrats united behind Biden.[4] Biden's campaign was somewhat hampered by his decision to forego

296   *The Low-Opportunity Presidents*

standard campaign tactics such as canvassing and large events due to the COVID pandemic (the Trump campaign continued these tactics).[5] Biden emerged victorious in the highest turnout election in U.S. history, beating Trump by a margin of 306-232 electoral votes (and by over seven million in the popular vote).

But Trump refused to concede, claiming that the election was stolen from him. Trump pressed to have the results of the election overturned, but to no avail. On January 6, the day the Vice President and Congress were to certify the results of the election, Trump held a rally in Washington, DC, and encouraged his followers to march to the Capitol, fight, and take back their government. They did so, and a violent insurrection ensued. Several people, including law enforcement officers, were killed. After several hours of overrunning the Capitol, breaking in, and causing material damage, the Capitol was finally reclaimed by law enforcement and official proceedings to certify Biden's election ensued. Biden would take over the presidency with millions of Americans mistakenly believing his election was the result of fraud and corruption.

What Manner of Man?

At age 78 when he took the oath of office, Biden was the oldest president ever to serve. Much of Biden's political personality derives from the series of deep personal tragedies he faced. The tragic loss of his first wife and their daughter in a car accident, the loss of his son Beau to cancer, and his own failure to attain his party's nomination for president twice, all weighed heavily on Biden. But they also shaped his outlook and personality, making him more sensitive and more empathetic. Biden particularly excelled in the role of "consoler-in-chief."[6]

Biden is outgoing and personable. He loves the retail end of politics. He exudes confidence and a positive attitude. Over many years in the cutthroat atmosphere of hyper-partisan politics that Washington, DC, has become, Biden stands out as being friendly and welcoming to Democrats and Republicans alike. He repeatedly reached across the aisle to Republicans, looking for common ground, trying to bring disparate sides together. His ability as vice president to assist Obama's legislative strategies earned him the moniker "The McConnell Whisperer" (for his ability to get deals done with Republican Majority Leader Mitch McConnell).[7]

Early in his career, Biden seemed to be too ambitious—moving too fast and looking to rise for the sake of rising in the political world. But over the years, Biden, again, partly due to facing such deep personal tragedies, matured. He became less personally ambitious and more attuned to others. He represented the antithesis of Trump's personality.

Policy Views

For most of his career, Joe Biden has been a left-of-center, liberal Democrat, somewhere in the middle of the Democratic Party. In the Senate, he served for many years as chair of the Foreign Relations Committee and the Judiciary Committee. Over his career and as a candidate for president, Biden has championed the causes of strengthening voting rights, expanding job opportunities, criminal justice reform, environmental protection (including climate change policies), student debt forgiveness, universal pre-school, and re-tooling the United States to compete in the changing world economy.

During the 2020 presidential primary campaign, some progressives in the Party attacked Biden as being too moderate. In fact, during the primaries, Biden presented himself as a "safe" liberal, someone not captured by the left-wing of the party. As President, however, Biden seemed more willing to promote dramatic changes such as a huge economic relief program, a strong response to climate change, and a massive infrastructure reform law. And while some progressives in the Democratic Party were dissatisfied, Biden governed from a more liberal orientation than he had campaigned.

Challenges and Opportunities

As president, Joe Biden inherited a series of difficult problems. The nation was plagued with by the Coronavirus pandemic and a death toll of over 400,000 Americans at the time of Biden's inauguration. A significant portion of the population did not believe in vaccinations or exercising responsible protective measures. The economy was in a state of recession. Donald Trump continued to erroneously assert to his voters that Biden's presidency was illegitimate, stoking partisan animosity. The frequency of climate change-related catastrophes had spiked. Russia was actively interfering in elections in the United States and elsewhere. China was rising to challenge U.S. global economic and political leadership in the void left by Trump's incoherent foreign policy. And finally, the longest war in U.S. history was still being waged in Afghanistan.

The challenges were enormous, and the opportunities seemed limited. Democrats achieved a 50-50 split in the Senate after picking up three seats, but lost 13 House seats, yielding a razor-thin 222-213 majority as Biden began his term.

While personally hopeful and optimistic, Biden entered office as a low-opportunity president. Although the Coronavirus pandemic and ensuing recession created a groundswell of support for economic stimulus, Republicans would quickly become concerned about spending on any new initiatives as deficits mounted. Some good news arrived in August of 2021

298 *The Low-Opportunity Presidents*

when COVID vaccines became available, helping the economy and government services to further reopen.

Inflation was a problem for much of the first three years of Biden's term, and violent crime in the cities was also a salient issue for voters ahead of the 2022 midterm elections. But in June of 2022, the Supreme Court issued the *Dobbs* decision, which struck down abortion protections afforded to women in the *Roe v. Wade* decision (1973). What might have been an overwhelming "red wave" victory for Republicans turned out to be underwhelming.[8] Republicans took control of the House by flipping nine seats, securing a meager 222-213 majority. Democrats actually picked up one seat in the Senate. While the *Dobbs* decision was clearly a factor,[9] other factors included Republicans' defense of the January 6th attack on the Capitol as well as a number of uninspiring Trump-endorsed candidates (required to repeat his lies about election fraud), who Senate Minority Leader Mitch McConnell (R-KY) credited for losing a "candidate quality test."[10] Kevin McCarthy (R-CA) would become Speaker (after 15 ballots), but doing so would mean cutting deals with the hard-right fringe of the party that would increase their clout and eventually topple his speakership.[11] Divided government would be a problem for Biden, but a weak Speaker who could not deliver the votes of his own party, would be quite another.

Leadership Style

Joe Biden has always been confident in his ability to broker compromise in the Senate, and he brought that "bridge-builder" mentality with him to the presidency. In his inaugural address, he asserted that his goal was to unite Americans who had been divided by an "uncivil war."[12] However, he would find the divisions plaguing the nation nearly insurmountable.

The Advisory Process and Approach to Decision-Making

Biden assembled his cabinet with specific goals in mind: to signal a return to competent, stable leadership, to achieve gender parity, and to have a majority of people of color.[13] His cabinet reflected those priorities.[14] For Chief of Staff, Biden selected Ron Klain, a senior advisor from his campaign. Klain stayed through Biden's 2023 State of the Union speech, and was replaced by Jeff Zients, who was co-chair of Biden's transition team and served as his COVID czar during the first few years of the administration. Both Chiefs had extensive Washington experience and brought a level of normalcy back to the White House.

While Klain was credited for ensuring low turnover and little drama in the White House, he was sometimes criticized for being a micromanager.[15] Klain led the White House through its big, and often progressive, initial

Joe Biden 299

legislative victories, executive actions, and left-of-center administrative appointments. Zients moved the White House's positioning back to more moderate stances[16] both to deal with the newly Republican House after the midterm elections, and to prepare for Biden's reelection run. Presidential scholar Lindsay Chervinsky rated the performance of the Biden cabinet in the first year as "above average" along four performance dimensions.[17] Additionally, the complete lack of department head turnover through two years into Biden's term was remarkable.[18] Staff turnover was historically low during the first year, but ticked up significantly in the second year, as is often the case, as the administration moves into reelection mode.[19]

In consulting with his staff, Biden was known for always wanting more details and for taking time to deliberate over decisions in a thoughtful and non-impulsive way.[20] Nonetheless, Biden's advisory process led to several unforced errors. These came in the form of the Afghanistan withdrawal and his staff's strained dealings with Democratic Senator Joe Manchin (WV). Additionally, Biden's student debt forgiveness plan (overturned by the Supreme Court) and reversals on drilling on public lands caused lingering doubts among his supporters about his ability to deliver on his promises. However, for the most part, Biden received advice that helped him squeeze as much out of the circumstances as opportunity offered.

Administrative Strategies

Following the 2020 election, Donald Trump actively worked to delegitimize Biden's victory, and would not concede defeat. Emily Murphy, the head of the General Services Agency under Trump, delayed designating Biden the winner for 16 days, forestalling resources ($7 million in funds and access to federal agencies) that could be used for the presidential transition.[21] The delay didn't handicap Biden's transition much, as his team had begun preparations early and was composed of individuals with significant managerial and governmental experience.[22] As a result, key staffing and appointment decisions were already in place when he took office.

Biden promised a diverse administration, and he delivered one through his appointment process. Record numbers of women and minorities were appointed,[23] and the judicial bench was diversified in terms of professional background, with more public defenders and fewer prosecutors appointed than in previous administrations.[24] However, nominations requiring Senate confirmation were significantly delayed due to the ongoing COVID pandemic, and the Senate trial for Donald Trump's second impeachment, as well as delay tactics employed by Senate Republicans.[25]

As with previous administrations, Biden instituted quick reversals of his predecessor's policies through executive orders. In their first 100 days, Obama issued 19 executive orders, Trump issued 33, and Biden issued 42.[26] The increase is a reflection of both the pendulum-like reversals of

300 *The Low-Opportunity Presidents*

partisan policies, as well as the desire to move quickly in the face of a slow-moving Congress (especially to signal action to the new president's electoral coalition). First-day reversals of Trump policies included Biden's directives and orders on halting the construction of the border wall, ending the Muslim immigration ban, reinstating ties with the World Health Organization, re-entering the Paris Climate Accord, and freezing all late-issued Trump orders.[27]

As with Trump, in some areas, the courts found that Biden had gone too far, and overruled his orders. For example, as Biden used orders to mandate COVID vaccinations, an appellate court overturned his federal employee vaccine mandate,[28] and the Supreme Court overruled his vaccine-or-test mandate for large private companies.[29] Additionally, the Supreme Court overturned Biden's plan for a degree of college student loan forgiveness.[30]

Public Leadership

In his first year, Biden kept media appearances to a minimum, avoiding the constantly-in-your-face aspects of the Trump presidency for a more low-key approach.[31] While this strategy communicated a level of decorum during the COVID pandemic, it left the president's supporters worried he was being overly cautious as his approval ratings began to slide.[32] While the public continued to view Biden as likeable and intelligent, they had begun to sour on his competence and effectiveness a year into his term.[33] At this point, many labeled his presidency a failure.[34]

Biden's second year brought a flurry of legislative successes and some popular executive orders. However, the president was unable to convert these successes into positive public approval. Analysts noted that, at a time of intense hyper-partisanship, Biden was faced with (as perhaps any president would be) a high floor and low ceiling to his approval rating.[35] There was simply a large group of Americans that he could not and would never reach.

Biden could be friendly and gregarious at times, while combative at others. Biden often displayed a friendly uncle or grandfatherly persona, with a fondness for aviator glasses and ice cream. His folksy demeanor concealed a temper that occasionally burst out against underprepared staffers[36] and reporters.[37] At times he lambasted his opponents and members of the press. Following a year's worth of inability to pass voting rights legislation, Biden made an angry speech on Martin Luther King Day (ostensibly designed to shame Republicans). Prior to the 2022 midterms, he made a speech in Philadelphia in front of Constitution Hall, warning against the threat to freedom posed by "Ultra-MAGA" Republicans. At times, when a reporter would ask a question as he was leaving a speech or press conference, he would scold them for the implications of the question.

Biden's first press secretary, Jen Psaki, also displayed a combative nature in dealing with unfriendly reporters, particularly those from FOX news. After Psaki left, her successor, Karine Jean-Pierre, took a less antagonistic approach to the position. For the most part, the administration's messaging was disciplined, with the exception of Ron Klain tweeting glowingly about falling gas prices as the administration was trying to stress the president's limited ability to affect them.[38]

A significant stumble for the president's communications team was how they handled messaging on inflation. As prices began to rise, the administration assured Americans that the problem was a "transitory" one that would be relieved once supply chains were restored following the economic upheaval associated with the COVID pandemic.[39] The administration gave Americans false hope that the prices would decline quickly, and resentment against the president and his programs built as inflation remained problematic into his third year.[40]

Congressional Leadership

Though majorities were slim, Biden was aided by his allies in Congressional leadership. Speaker Pelosi (D-CA) delivered the highest level of party unity in floor votes ever.[41] Senate Majority Leader Chuck Schumer (D-NY) stepped in to finalize deals with recalcitrant senators when Biden had done as much as he could. For the most part, the two Democratic leaders and Biden were in agreement on the issues, and were more than willing to lend their support to the president.

Meetings with principal congressional members on key pieces of legislation were common. Biden was confident that his years of experience in the Senate gave him the necessary background to bargain with anyone. He found a difficult partner in Senator Joe Manchin, who held up some key pieces of legislation. At one point, Biden dispatched Ron Klain to meet with the senator on his houseboat to woo and cajole him for his vote.[42] Although the president was confident in his abilities, he also knew when to step back and let others finalize a deal.

Upon losing control of the House in the 2022 election, Biden prepared for an uphill battle in dealing with new Speaker Kevin McCarthy (D-CA). To secure his speakership, McCarthy had to promise far-right Republicans that he would take a hard line on future spending in his negotiations with the president (a promise that would cost McCarthy his speakership). Anticipating this, the president used his 2023 State of the Union Address to lure Republicans into booing the statement that some Republicans would be willing to cut Social Security and Medicare to achieve their goals. Biden effectively painted these legislators into a corner by having them go on record during a nationally televised address registering their opposition to

302 *The Low-Opportunity Presidents*

such cuts.[43] This rhetorical masterstroke strengthened the president's position in subsequent negotiations.

Legislative Enactments

Joe Biden labeled his economic agenda "Build Back Better." Programs focused on the middle class, and included not only economic recovery from the COVID-instigated recession but plans to re-shape the U.S. economy to be more productive, environmentally sustainable, and less dependent on foreign production. The three main legislative initiatives included the American Rescue Plan, the American Jobs Plan, and the American Families Plan. The proposals were so enormous in size and vast in scope that many likened them to the New Deal.[44]

While the Coronavirus pandemic and ensuing recession created a groundswell of support for economic stimulus, Republicans would quickly become concerned about spending on any new initiatives as deficits mounted, particularly after Trump left office. Biden got no help from Republicans in passing these pieces of legislation, and had to significantly pare down the Jobs and Families plans and rework them into different bills in order to retain thin Democratic majorities for passage.

American Rescue Plan Act of 2021

The American Rescue Plan (ARP) was the third effort to provide economic relief and medical assistance to the nation as it dealt with the ongoing COVID pandemic. The ARP followed the CARES Act ($2.2 trillion in March 2020) and the Consolidated Appropriations Act, an omnibus appropriations bill that added $900 billion in stimulus relief into a fiscal spending bill (passed in December 2020). Unlike the preceding bills, which passed overwhelmingly, the ARP faced stiff resistance from Republicans in Congress.

During the first year of Biden's presidency, legislation proceeded against the backdrop of Donald Trump's second impeachment trial. While many top congressional Republicans were quick to condemn Trump's role in the January 6 insurrection, most rallied behind him during and after the second impeachment proceedings. Divisions between the parties spilled over into the legislative process. Ten moderate senate Republicans (some of whom voted to convict Trump) put forth an alternative relief package tagged at $600 billion, but the proposal went nowhere. Republicans criticized Democrats for adding seemingly tangential "wish list" items, such as support for broadband, cybersecurity, transportation, an increase in the minimum wage, and an extension of the child tax credit in addition to the usual relief elements of unemployment and direct payments to individuals.[45] Once Democrats realized they would not get Republican support in the Senate, they moved to use the budget reconciliation process to pass the bill. The senate parliamentarian ruled against the inclusion of the minimum wage provision in the reconciliation bill.[46]

The bill passed the Senate along party lines and narrowly passed the House 220-211 with one Democrat voting against the bill. The act provided $1.9 trillion in aid to the country. In addition to the programs mentioned above, the bill included $1,400 direct payments to individuals, $350 billion in aid to state and local governments, funding for vaccine distribution, and funding for the safe reopening of schools.[47] Finally, the act provided continued funding for the Paycheck Protection Program, which provided support to businesses (and would turn out to be widely abused by users).

Infrastructure Investment and Jobs Act (2021)

Aspects of Biden's American Jobs Plan were eventually reworked into a bipartisan infrastructure bill. Biden attempted to combine his desired climate and jobs plans with desires in Congress for a comprehensive infrastructure bill (something the Trump administration failed to deliver).[48] The original proposal, tagged at $2.2 trillion, was strongly opposed by Republicans. In the Senate, Republicans offered counter-proposals, which were far less than what Biden wanted. Eventually, a bipartisan group of senators negotiated a compromise bill that would call for $974 billion in spending over five years.[49] In addition to Senate Minority Leader Mitch McConnell (R-KY), key Senate Republicans who helped move the bill along included Rob Portman (R-OH), Mitt Romney (R-UT), Bill Cassidy (R-LA), and Susan Collins (R-ME). Since he was planning to retire, Portman was immune to the wrath of Republican voters ginnedup by Trump, who was a vocal critic of the bill.[50] The bill gained strong bipartisan support in the Senate, passing 69-30 in August 2021.

Progressives in the House of Representatives said they would not vote for it unless it was passed simultaneously as the Biden's social and climate policy bill (titled the "Build Back Better Act" at that time), tagged at around $3.5 trillion.[51] Biden invited key progressives and moderates to the White House for a series of meetings to get the sides closer together.[52] Top White House staff worked the phones relentlessly to bring the Democrats on board, but Representative Pramila Jayapal (D-WA), the leader of the progressive caucus, continued to hold out.[53] Biden organized a conference call with the progressive caucus, urging the progressives to pass the bill because "the people want to see us deliver."[54] Eventually, the two sides brokered a deal in which the moderates agreed to support Build Back Better if the Congressional Budget Office determined it would not contribute to the debt.[55] Eventually, 13 Republican House members voted for the infrastructure bill while six Democratic members voted against it, permitting it

304   *The Low-Opportunity Presidents*

to pass 228-206 in early November of 2021. Biden signed it in a bipartisan ceremony on November 15, 2021.

Ultimately, the $1.2 trillion bill provided $550 billion in new spending beyond what had already been planned in regular appropriations bills.[56] The act added only $256 billion to the debt, since much of it was paid for through unspent coronavirus relief funds and increased enforcement of taxpayers reporting investment gains from cryptocurrency.[57] Major investments included repairs for roads and bridges, upgrades to railroads and the power grid, expansion of internet broadband, lead pipe replacement, electric vehicle charging stations, public transit, airport upgrades, and other efforts to modernize the nation's infrastructure and to make it more resilient to the effects of climate change.[58]

CHIPS and Science Act (2022)

The COVID-19 pandemic and ensuing supply chain disruptions illustrated the problem of the United States' dependency on foreign manufacturing. Inflation soared as manufacturing in China slowed down and deliveries piled up at understaffed ports, causing a backup of container ships. Particularly affected were any industries creating products relying on computer chips (such as automobiles).

Electoral politics was also a motivating force, since many Democrats interpreted their off-year loss of the Virginia Governorship in 2021 to voters' perception of a lack of progress from the Biden Administration. Democrats were eager to deliver on Biden's agenda so they could tout legislative victories ahead of the 2022 midterm elections.

In one sense, the CHIPs Act was a ripe issue for Biden—one that the Congress had put significant effort into, but had not yet passed. In another sense, it wasn't an "easy win," since it took some significant retooling and the combination of existing legislation so that it matched the needs of the day.

Efforts to promote U.S. competitiveness in the market for semiconductors began prior to the COVID pandemic under the Trump administration. In 2019, Trump officials presented Congress with a bill called the Endless Frontiers Act, which was designed to stimulate investment in high-tech research, paid for by a public/private matching partnership. The bill was first introduced in 2020, co-sponsored by Chuck Schumer and Todd Young (R-IN), but failed to progress out of committee.[59] In 2021, the bill was renamed the United States Innovation and Competition Act (USICA) and had become more focused on specific technological areas such as semiconductors, artificial intelligence, and quantum computing.[60]

A separate bill, the CHIPS for America Act, was introduced in June of 2020.[61] This bill was designed to stimulate education in semiconductor engineering at U.S. universities, as part of an effort to incentivize manufacturers such as the Taiwan Semiconductor Manufacturing Company to move production to the United States.[62] Both bills were merged into the USICA in the Senate, which passed the bill in June of 2021. The companion bill in the House, titled the America COMPETES Act, was passed in February of 2022. The bills were significantly different, and it took the Congress several months to negotiate a compromise piece of legislation, which finally bore the name the CHIPS and Science Act. The bill passed with strong bipartisan support, and was signed by Joe Biden in August of 2022.

The CHIPS and Science Act provided $280 billion over ten years to boost research and production of semiconductors.[63] The act included $52.7 billion in incentives and tax credits to build and modernize U.S. semiconductor manufacturing facilities and equipment.[64] Other provisions included $170 billion for research on energy and space exploration,[65] as well as significant investment in research on advanced computing and climate change.[66]

Inflation Reduction Act of 2022

Biden's Jobs Plan and Families Plan were together tagged at around $4 trillion in spending. Progressives "trimmed the tree" with pet projects to the tune of $6 trillion.[67] While some of the proposals from Biden's Jobs Plan were integrated into the Infrastructure bill, many of the environmental policy programs needed a legislative vehicle. These programs were combined with the American Families Plan into the Build Back Better bill.

While the CHIPS Act gave the Biden Administration another bipartisan victory ahead of the 2022 midterm elections, many progressives felt slighted in that their priorities in the Build Back Better bill had not been passed in tandem with the CHIPS Act. Further complications arose due to the compromise between progressives and moderates that required the bill not contribute to the debt (e.g., be "revenue neutral"). Since the Senate was split 50-50, Democrats needed every single vote to pass a measure through the reconciliation process. This gave the most moderate Democratic senator, Joe Manchin, tremendous leverage in crafting the bill.[68] Negotiations between Biden and Manchin at times proceeded in fits and starts over more than a year, at one point with Manchin proclaiming the need to start from scratch.[69] Manchin's reservations stemmed from a number of concerns, primarily how the energy sector of his state would be affected and increasing economic inflation. Kirsten Sinema (D-AZ), another moderate Senator with reservations about taxing and spending, would also prove to be a key player in negotiations.

Following the passage of the infrastructure bill, Biden floated a $1.75 trillion plan to pass Build Back Better through the reconciliation process.[70] The plan was drafted as a result of weeks of negotiations among Biden, Sinema, and Manchin.[71] Democrats in the House added more programs to

306 *The Low-Opportunity Presidents*

Biden's plan, including four weeks of paid medical and family leave, bringing the price tag to $2.2 trillion.[72] The bill passed the House in November 2021, along a party-line vote of 220-213.

In early December of 2021, Manchin called for a "strategic pause" in considering the bill due to rising inflation.[73] Manchin's concern was that the House Bill kept many of the progressives' pet programs, but shortened the timeline of provision in the hope that those programs would become popular and get reauthorized.[74] Biden held one-on-one meetings with Manchin to close the gap, with the sides appearing to be making progress.[75] Then, just before Christmas, Manchin made an appearance on FOX News saying that "I cannot vote to continue with this piece of legislation. I just can't. I tried everything humanly possible. I can't get there," seemingly closing out negotiations.[76] The dramatic change of heart from Manchin as negotiations progressed was perplexing. What had caused Manchin's reversal was a statement issued by the White House naming him as the focus of the negotiations (Manchin's team asked either to have his name removed or Sinema's added).[77] Manchin felt that the move had unnecessarily singled him out at a time when he and his family were targets of protests from progressives.[78] Biden left a frustrated voicemail on Manchin's phone and White House Press Secretary Jen Psaki accused Manchin of "a sudden and inexplicable reversal in his position, and a breach of his commitments to the President and the Senator's colleagues in the House and Senate."[79]

The diplomatic misstep required healing. Biden and Manchin spoke at the end of the year, and agreed to a cooling-off period. In the summer of 2022, Manchin began negotiating on a bill framework with Senate Majority Leader Chuck Schumer.[80] The bill was scaled back significantly and renamed the Inflation Reduction Act, making it more saleable for members' reelection concerns. Schumer then turned his attention to Sinema, who remained the only Democratic holdout in the Senate. Sinema demanded a restructuring of the minimum corporate tax, eliminating a tax increase on hedge fund managers, and drought relief funding for her home state of Arizona.[81] The bill passed the Senate 51-50 (with Vice President Harris as the tiebreaker) and passed the House 220-207. The bill was signed by Biden on August 16, 2022.

The Inflation Reduction Act raised $737 billion in revenue with $433 billion in spending (the $300 billion balance going toward deficit reduction). It was a far cry from the major "human infrastructure" investments that many progressives had wanted. Other than $64 billion in extending the Affordable Care Act and a cap on insulin prices for those on Medicare, the overwhelming majority of the spending in the bill went to energy security and climate change.[82] The act also failed to extend the child tax credit, which had been lauded for reducing childhood poverty.[83] While the law provided real benefits and savings to many Americans, economists predicted it would only reduce inflation by 0.1 percent over five years, in spite of its aspirational moniker.[84]

Biden and Congress

Biden's four pieces of major legislation within his first two years in office are impressive for any president. They are even more impressive considering the difficulty he had in working with Republicans, most of whom remained under the sway of former President Trump, who actively sought to thwart Biden's agenda. Some likened Biden's initiatives to being as monumental as the New Deal, and many Democrats lamented his inability to gain credit for the magnitude of the rebuilding effort.[85]

In addition to these landmark pieces of legislation, Biden was successful in getting other significant measures passed either as a vocal proponent or an active participant in negotiations. The first was the COVID-19 Hate Crimes Act, which made the reporting of hate crimes (which spiked against Asian Americans during the COVID pandemic) more accessible, directed the Department of Justice to provide personnel to expedite review of accusations, and provided grants to state and localities for hate crime reduction programs.[86] As mass shootings continued to plague the country, Congress passed the Bipartisan Safer Communities Act. While the bill did not go as far as Biden would have liked, the bill provided the first piece of gun control legislation in nearly 30 years.[87] Another bipartisan piece of legislation, the Honoring our PACT Act, was also passed, improving access to healthcare for veterans exposed to toxic substances while serving.

Biden was not without legislative failures, particularly in the areas of immigration and voting rights.[88] Given the tremendous divisions in the country, it was impossible for Biden to be a unifier for both sides to rally behind. But Biden seemed the right person with the right experience to wrest what little he could out of the deeply partisan Congress. His skills were particularly on display when negotiating a compromise with Speaker McCarthy in 2023 on the debt ceiling, a deal that many Republicans felt gave away too much.[89] Biden worked individually when he could (particularly with respect to Republicans) and through his party's Congressional leadership (particularly to keep the party in line) when he needed to. The result was an impressive legislative record given the severe limitations.

An Assessment

Joe Biden came to office facing tremendous challenges. Although he had narrow margins in Congress, resistance from a couple of pivotal members in his party caused significant difficulty. The economy was in a state of shambles as COVID lockdowns continued. There seemed little appetite in Congress for the sweeping build-back the president envisioned. The

308 *The Low-Opportunity Presidents*

president's predecessor had attempted to overturn his election, further dividing an already polarized nation. It was definitely a low-opportunity situation for the newly elected president.

In August of 2021 when COVID vaccines became available, the economy and government services were able to more fuly reopen. As people went back to work, inflation remained a problem. Enthusiasm for Biden's bold Build Back Better agenda further waned as the need seemed to be disappearing and concerns over government spending contributing to inflation mounted.

It should also be noted that Biden faced another impediment that no other predecessor faced—a former president actively working to thwart him at every turn. Republicans in Congress and in governor's mansions across the country remained cowed by the former president. Trump continually berated the president, his policies, his appointees, and particularly any Republicans who worked with the president. Biden's efforts to mitigate COVID-19 and subsequent variants were hampered by Trump and his followers politicizing an ostensibly public safety issue.

A key to Biden's success was his ability to cultivate personal relationships with key political figures, and he had long been a crusader for the restoration of this type of traditional politics. Biden brought to the presidency the deal-making prowess he honed as a senator and vice president.[90] But he was also been keenly attuned to pushing too far and imperiling his relationships with legislators. In these cases, he stepped back and lalowed others, such as Chuck Schumer, Ron Klain, and Shalanda Young,[91] to take the lead in legislative negotiations.

In addition to Biden's legislative successes, he issued many directives and orders on issues such as marijuana enforcement, student loans, voting rights, and the environment, fulfiling campaign promises. The president even intervened to help avert a potentially crippling rail strike as the economy was reopening after the COVID shutdown. While not all of Biden's efforts would withstand judicial scrutiny, significant administrative changes were achieved in many areas. He also diversified the federal bench (in terms of gender, ethnicity, and occupational background) and appointed the first black woman, Ketanji Brown-Jackson, to the Supreme Court.

Considering all of the difficulties facing him, it is remarkable that Biden was able to achieve the victories he did. While neither he nor his party got everything they wanted out of his landmark pieces of legislation, Biden seemed to get everything he could. We rate him as an overachiever considering the forces arrayed against him (though certainly not in the league of FDR as some acolytes have maintained).

Notes

1 For a general introduction to Joe Biden, see: Evan Osnos, *Joe Biden: The Life, The Run, and What Matters Now* (New York: Simon & Schuster, 2020); and

Jules Whitcover, *Joe Biden: A Life of Trial and Redemption* (New York: William Morrow, 2019).

2 Janet Hook, "Joe Biden's Childhood Struggle with a Stutter: How He Overcame It and How It Shaped Him," September 16, 2019, https://www.latimes.com/politics/story/2019-09-15/joe-bidens-childhood-struggle-with-a-stutter.

3 Steve Holland, Jarrett Renshaw, and Heather Timmons, "Biden, 80, Makes 2024 Presidential Run Official as Trump Fight Looms," *Reuters*, April 29, 2023, https://www.reuters.com/world/us/biden-80-makes-2024-presidential-run-official-lets-finish-this-job-2023-04-25/.

4 See Todd Belt, "Social Media Activism and Polarization: Did Democratic Social Media Activists Influence the Outcome of the 2020 Presidential Election?" in *Polarization and Political Party Factions in the 2020 Election*, ed. Jennifer C. Lucas, Tauna S. Sisco, and Christopher J. Galdieri (New York: Lexington Books, 2022), 9–24; and Seth Masket, *Learning from Loss: The Democrats, 2016–2020* (New York: Cambridge University Press, 2020).

5 Alex Thompson, "Trump's Campaign Knocks on a Million Doors a Week. Biden's Knocks on Zero," *Politico*, August 4, 2020, https://www.politico.com/news/2020/08/04/trump-joe-biden-campaign-door-knockers-391454.

6 Alex Seitz-Wald and Mike Memoli, "'Grief Must Be Witnessed': Joe Biden's First 100 Days as Consoler-in-Chief," *NBCNews.com*, April 28, 2021, https://www.nbcnews.com/politics/white-house/grief-must-be-witnessed-joe-biden-s-first-100-days-n1265167.

7 David Hawkings, "This Democrat Could Be the McConnell Whisperer," *Roll Call*, November 17, 2014, https://rollcall.com/2014/11/17/this-democrat-could-be-the-mcconnell-whisperer/.

8 Gary C. Jacobson, "The 2022 Elections: A Test of Democracy's Resilience and the Referendum Theory of Midterms," *Political Science Quarterly* 138, no. 1 (2023): 1–22.

9 Barbara Norrander and Clyde Wilcox, "Trends in Abortion Attitudes: From Roe to Dobbs," *Public Opinion Quarterly* (2023), nfad014, https://doi.org/10.1093/poq/nfad014.

10 Sahil Kapur, "McConnell Says Trump Fueled 'Candidate Quality' Problems in the Midterms," *NBCNews.com*, December 13, 2022, https://www.nbcnews.com/politics/2022-election/mcconnell-says-trump-fueled-candidate-quality-problems-2022-rcna61572.

11 Anthony Adragna, Nicholas Wu, Meredith Lee Hill, and Marianne Levine, "McCarthy Claims Speakership on 15th Ballot," *Politico*, January 7, 2023, https://www.politico.com/news/2023/01/07/mccarthy-claims-speakership-on-15th-ballot-00076882.

12 Aaron Blake, "4 Takeaways from Joe Biden's Inaugural Address," *Washington Post*, January 20, 2021, https://www.washingtonpost.com/politics/2021/01/20/takeaway-biden-harris-inauguration/.

13 Alexandra Jaffe, "What Biden's Cabinet Picks Say About How He Plans to Govern," *Associated Press*, January 10, 2021, https://apnews.com/article/joe-biden-donald-trump-race-and-ethnicity-cabinets-coronavirus-pandemic-2da5b94270676e9a42643b9b2d67d2db.

14 Alana Wise, "Biden Pledged Historic Cabinet Diversity. Here's How His Nominees Stack Up," *NPR.com*, February 5, 2021, https://www.npr.org/sections/president-biden-takes-office/2021/02/05/963837953/biden-pledged-historic-cabinet-diversity-heres-how-his-nominees-stack-up.

310 *The Low-Opportunity Presidents*

15 Eli Stokols, "Staff Changes Are Coming to the White House. Will Klain Be Part of Them?" *Politico*, November 8, 2022, https://www.politico.com/news/2022/11/08/biden-team-shakeup-klain-00065716.

16 Alexander Sammon, "What the Heck Is Joe Biden Thinking Lately?" *Slate.com*, March 27, 2023, https://slate.com/news-and-politics/2023/03/biden-zients-willow-drilling-family-separation-right-lean.html.

17 Lindsay Chervinsky, "President Biden's Cabinet One Year Later," *DividedWeFall.com*, February 3, 2022, https://dividedwefall.org/president-bidens-cabinet/.

18 Peter Nicholas and Carol E. Lee, "Biden's Cabinet Is Sticking Around, Bucking the Turnover Trend of His Predecessors," *NBCNews.com*, January 23, 2021, https://www.nbcnews.com/politics/white-house/bidens-cabinet-sticking-bucking-turnover-trend-predecessors-rcna66912.

19 Kathryn Dunn Tenpas, "The Biden 'A-Team' after 24 Months: A Significant Uptick in Year Two Departures," *Brookings.com*, January 20, 2023, https://www.brookings.edu/articles/the-biden-a-team-after-24-months-a-significant-uptick-in-year-2-departures/.

20 James P. Pfiffner, "Organizing the Biden Presidency," *Presidential Studies Quarterly* 51, no. 4 (2021): 824.

21 Lisa Rein, "Under Pressure, Trump Appointee Emily Murphy Approves Transition in Unusually Personal Letter to Biden," *Washington Post*, November 23, 2020, https://www.washingtonpost.com/politics/gsa-emily-murphy-transition-biden/2020/11/23/c0f43e84-2de0-11eb-96c2-aac3f162215d_story.html.

22 Martha Joynt Kumar, "Joseph Biden's Effective Presidential Transition: 'Started Early, Went Big,'" *Presidential Studies Quarterly* 51, no. 3 (2021): 582–608.

23 See Wise, "Biden Pledged Historic Cabinet Diversity"; and Robert C. Smith, "The First Since Benjamin Harrison: The Biden Administration and Policy Responsiveness to the Black Vote," *Presidential Studies Quarterly* 52, no. 3 (2022): 662.

24 Coleen Long, "Biden Seeking Professional Diversity in his Judicial Picks," *Associated Press*, February 10, 2022, https://apnews.com/article/joe-biden-us-supreme-court-business-congress-race-and-ethnicity-e775b084ed2943c9c328a4726b21b579.

25 Kathryn Dunn Tenpas, "Waiting for Advice and Consent: Record-level Diversity Amidst an Exceedingly Slow Confirmation Pace During the First 300 Days of the Biden Administration," *Presidential Studies Quarterly* 52, no. 3 (2022): 709–717.

26 Terri Bimes, Casey B. K. Dominguez, and Dan Grushkevich, "Hyperpartisanship and the First Hundred Days," *Congress & the Presidency* 50, no. 1 (2023): 67.

27 Aishvarya Kavi, "Biden's 17 Executive Orders and Other Directives in Detail," *The New York* Times, January 20, 2021, https://www.nytimes.com/2021/01/20/us/biden-executive-orders.html.

28 Kevin McGill, "Court Blocks COVID-19 Vaccine Mandate for US Gov't Workers," *Associated Press*, March 24, 2023, https://apnews.com/article/vaccine-requirement-biden-covid-fifth-circuit-74ae504966aaf5239a42cc3e677182b4.

29 Nina Totenberg, "Supreme Court Blocks Biden's Vaccine-or-test Mandate for Large Private Companies," *NPR.com*, January 13, 2023, https://www.npr.org/2022/01/13/1072165393/supreme-court-blocks-bidens-vaccine-or-test-mandate-for-large-private-companies.

30 Lawrence Hurley, "Supreme Court Kills Biden Student Loan Relief Plan," *NBCNews.com*, June 30, 2023, https://www.nbcnews.com/politics/supreme

-court/supreme-court-rule-bidens-student-loan-forgiveness-plan-friday
-rcna76874.

31 Eugene Daniels, "The Biden White House Media Doctrine: Less Can Be More," *Politico*, April 12, 2021, https://www.politico.com/news/2021/04/12/biden -white-house-press-strategy-480930.

32 Michael M. Grynbaum, "Biden's Low-Key Media Strategy Draws Allies' Concern," *The New York Times*, November 23, 2021, https://www.nytimes .com/2021/11/23/business/media/biden-media-strategy.html.

33 Megan Brenan, "Biden Seen as Likable, Smart; Not Strong Leader, Manager," *Gallup*, January 25, 2022, https://news.gallup.com/poll/389219/biden-seen-lik-able-smart-not-strong-leader-manager.aspx.

34 See Mike Allan and Jim VandeHei, "Biden's Epic Failures," *Axios*, January 14, 2022, https://www.axios.com/2022/01/14/biden-agenda-failure-democrats; Molly Ball and Brian Bennett, "How the Biden Administration Lost Its Way," *Time*, January 20, 2022, https://time.com/6140442/joe-biden-presidency-sec-ond-year/; Laura Santhanam, "56 Percent of Americans Think Biden's First Year Was a Failure," *PBS News Hour*, February 25, 2022, https://www.pbs.org/ newshour/politics/4-takeaways-on-americans-views-of-biden-ahead-of-state-of -the-union.

35 Amy Walter, "Stop Freaking Out Over Every 2024 Poll," *The Cook Political Report*, May 10, 2023, https://www.cookpolitical.com/analysis/national/ national-politics/stop-freaking-out-over-every-2024-poll.

36 Alex Thompson, "Old Yeller: Biden's Private Fury," *Axios*, June 10, 2023, https://www.axios.com/2023/07/10/biden-temper-us-president.

37 Kathryn Watson, "Biden Refers to Fox News Correspondent as a 'Stupid Son of a Bitch,'" *CBSNews.com*, January 25, 2021, https://www.cbsnews.com/news /biden-fox-news-peter-doocy-stupid-son-of-a-bitch/.

38 Jeff Stein, "Inside the Biden Team's Fixation on Gas Prices," *The Washington Post*, November 2, 2022, https://www.washingtonpost.com/us-policy/2022/11 /02/biden-klain-gas-prices/.

39 Kevin Liptak, "Biden Changes His Tone and Walks a Delicate Line on Inflation," *CNN*, November 11, 2021, https://www.cnn.com/2021/11/11/politics/joe -biden-inflation-messaging/index.html.

40 Aamer Madhani and Emily Swanson, "Public Approval of Biden's Approach to Economy and Gun Policy Remains Low, AP-NORC Poll Finds," *PBS.org*, May 22, 2021, https://www.pbs.org/newshour/politics/public-approval-of-bidens -approach-to-economy-and-gun-policy-remains-low-ap-norc-poll-finds.

41 Ronald Brownstein, "The House Reached a Stunning New Milestone This Year," *CNN.com*, June 21, 2022, https://www.cnn.com/2022/06/21/politics/ house-democrats-vote-unity/index.html.

42 Chris Whipple, *The Fight of His Life: Inside Joe Biden's White House* (New York: Scribner, 2023), 160.

43 Emily Brooks, "Biden Has Tense Exchange with Republicans on Social Security During State of The Union," *The Hill*, February 7, 2023, https://thehill.com /homenews/house/3848586-biden-has-tense-exchange-with-republicans-on -social-security-during-state-of-the-union/.

44 James Roosevelt, Jr., Henry Scott Wallace, June Hopkins, and Tomlin Perkins Coggeshall, "Build Back Better Is a 21st Century New Deal," *The Hill*, November 20, 2021, https://thehill.com/opinion/white-house/582443-build -back-better-is-a-21st-century-new-deal/.

45 Barbara Sprunt, "Here's What's in The American Rescue Plan," *NPR.org*, March 11, 2021, https://www.npr.org/sections/coronavirus-live-updates/2021/03/09

312 *The Low-Opportunity Presidents*

/974841565/heres-whats-in-the-american-rescue-plan-as-it-heads-toward-final
-passage.

46 Emily Cochrane, "Top Senate Official Disqualifies Minimum Wage from Stimulus Plan," *The New York Times*, February 5, 2021, https://www.nytimes.com/2021/02/25/us/politics/federal-minimum-wage.html.

47 Grace Segers, "Biden Signs $1.9 Trillion American Rescue Plan into Law," *CBSnews.com*, March 12, 2021, https://www.cbsnews.com/news/biden-signs -covid-relief-bill-american-rescue-plan-into-law/.

48 Jeff Stein, Juliet Eilperin, Michael Laris, and Tony Romm, "White House Unveils $2 Trillion Infrastructure and Climate Plan, Setting Up Giant Battle over Size and Cost of Government," *New York Times*, April 1, 2021, https://www.washingtonpost.com/us-policy/2021/03/31/biden-infrastructure-climate-plan/.

49 Tony Romm and Seung Min Kim, "Ten Senate Democrats and Republicans Say They Reached Five-year, Nearly $1 Trillion Infrastructure Deal," *Washington Post*, June 10, 2021, https://www.washingtonpost.com/us-policy/2021/06/10/senate-democrats-republicans-infrastructure/.

50 Seung Min Kim, Felicia Sonmez, and Amy B. Wang, "Biden Signs $1.2 Trillion Infrastructure Bill, Fulfilling Campaign Promise and Notching Achievement That Eluded Trump," *The Washington Post*, November 15, 2021, https://www.washingtonpost.com/politics/biden-poised-to-sign-12-trillion-infrastructure -bill-fulfilling-campaign-promise-and-notching-achievement-that-eluded-trump /2021/11/15/1b69f9a6-4638-11ec-b8d9-232f4afe4d9b_story.html.

51 Emily Cochrane, "Senate Passes $1 Trillion Infrastructure Bill, Handing Biden a Bipartisan Win," *New York Times*, August 10, 2021, https://www.nytimes.com /2021/08/10/us/politics/infrastructure-bill-passes.html.

52 Tony Romm, Seung Min Kim, and Marianna Sotomayor, "Biden Huddles with Warring Democrats as Party's Agenda Hangs in the Balance," *The Washington Post*, September 22, 2021, https://www.washingtonpost.com/us-policy/2021/09 /22/biden-democrats-infrastructure-reconciliation/.

53 Whipple, *The Fight of His Life*, 177.

54 Ibid., 178.

55 Sahil Japur, "Centrist Democrats Now Hold the Cards as Infrastructure Bill Heads to Biden's Desk," *NBCnews.com*, November 8, 2021, https://www.nbc-news.com/politics/congress/centrist-democrats-now-hold-cards-infrastructure -bill-heads-biden-s-n1283485.

56 Heather Long, "What's in the $1.2 Trillion Infrastructure Law," *The Washington Post*, November 16, 2021, https://www.washingtonpost.com/business/2021/08 /10/senate-infrastructure-bill-what-is-in-it/.

57 Jonathan Ponciano, "$1 Trillion Infrastructure Bill Would Add $256 Billion to U.S. Deficit in 10 Years, CBO Estimates," *Forbes*, November 18, 2021, https://www.forbes.com/sites/jonathanponciano/2021/08/05/1-trillion-infrastruc-ture-bill-would-add-256-billion-to-us-deficit-in-10-years-cbo-estimates/?sh =79f05aa4c638.

58 Long, "What's in the $1.2 Trillion Infrastructure Law."

59 *Congress.gov*, https://www.congress.gov/bill/116th-congress/senate-bill/3832.

60 Catie Edmondson, "Senate Overwhelmingly Passes Bill to Bolster Competitiveness with China," *The New York Times*, June 8, 2021, https://www.nytimes.com/2021/06/08/us/politics/china-bill-passes.html.

61 *Congress.gov*, https://www.congress.gov/bill/116th-congress/house-bill/7178.

62 Keith Krach, "The Bipartisan CHIPS Act — and a United U.S. — Are China's Biggest Fear," *Newsweek*, July 27, 2022, https://www.newsweek.com/bipartisan-chips-act-united-us-are-chinas-biggest-fear-opinion-1728573.

Joe Biden 313

63 Jacob Knutson, "Biden Signs $280 Billion Chip Funding Bill," *Axios*, August 9, 2022, https://www.axios.com/2022/08/09/biden-chips-bill-signing.

64 Katie Lobosco, "Here's What's in the Bipartisan Semiconductor Chip Manufacturing Package," *CNN.com*, August 9, 2022, https://www.cnn.com /2022/08/09/politics/chips-semiconductor-manufacturing-science-act/index .html.

65 Ibid.

66 Mariana Ambrose, John Jacobs, and Natalie Tham, "CHIPS and Science Act Summary: Energy, Climate, and Science Provisions," *Bipartisan Policy Center*, November 14, 2022, https://bipartisanpolicy.org/blog/chips-science-act-sum-mary/.

67 Lindsey McPherson, "How 'Build Back Better' Started, and How It's Going: A Timeline," *RolCall.com*, July 21, 2022, https://rollcall.com/2022/07/21/how -build-back-better-started-and-how-its-going-a-timeline/.

68 Todd Belt, "Build Back Smaller: What's the Best Path Forward for Democrats?" *TheHill.com*, January 27, 2022, https://thehill.com/opinion/finance/591565 -build-back-smaller-whats-the-best-path-forward-for-democrats/.

69 Joseph Zeballos-Roig, "Joe Manchin Says Negotiations on Biden's Big Bill Will Be 'Starting From Scratch' as Democrats Scramble to Save Their Economic Agenda," *BusinessInsider.com*, January 20, 2022, https://www.businessinsider .com/joe-manchin-negotiations-bidens-big-economic-bill-starting-from-scratch -2022-1.

70 Lindsey McPherson, "Biden Makes $1.75T Sales Pitch to House Democrats," *RollCall.com*, October 28, 2021, https://rollcall.com/2021/10/28/white-house -releases-1-75t-framework-for-budget-package/.

71 McPherson, "How Build Back Better."

72 Lindsey McPherson, "House Passes Budget Package after Cost Concerns Abate," *RollCall.com*, November 19, 2021, https://rollcall.com/2021/11/19/ house-vote-reconciliation-build-back-better-bill/.

73 Lindsey McPherson, "Manchin Repeats Call for 'Strategic Pause' in Big Spending Package," *RollCall.com*, December 7, 2021, https://rollcall.com/2021 /12/07/manchin-repeats-call-for-strategic-pause-in-big-spending-package/.

74 Ibid.

75 Steve Clemons, "White House Incivility is What 'Lost' Joe Manchin," *TheHill .com*, December 20, 2021, https://thehill.com/opinion/white-house/586538 -white-house-incivility-is-what-lost-joe-manchin/.

76 Alexander Bolton, "Manchin Says He Will Not Vote for Build Back Better: 'This is a No,'" *TheHill.com*, December 19, 2021, https://thehill.com/homenews/sen-ate/586450-manchin-says-he-will-not-vote-for-build-back-better-this-is-a-no/.

77 Jeff Stein and Tyler Pager, "How the White House Lost Joe Manchin, and Its Plan to Transform America," *The Washington Post*, June 2, 2022, https://www .washingtonpost.com/us-policy/2022/06/05/biden-manchin-white-house/.

78 Ibid.

79 Jen Psaki, "Statement from Press Secretary Jen Psaki," *WhiteHouse.gov*, December 19, 2021, https://www.whitehouse.gov/briefing-room/statements -releases/2021/12/19/statement-from-press-secretary-jen-psaki-4/.

80 Paul M. Krawzak, "Resurrected Budget Package No Slam Dunk as Negotiations Heat Up," *RollCall.com*, June 6, 2022, https://rollcall.com/2022/06/06/resur-rected-budget-package-no-slam-dunk-as-negotiations-heat-up/.

81 Emily Cochrane, "Sinema Agrees to Climate and Tax Deal, Clearing the Way for Votes," *The New York Times*, August 4, 2022, https://www.nytimes.com /2022/08/04/us/politics/sinema-inflation-reduction-act.html.

314 *The Low-Opportunity Presidents*

82 Anna Kaufman, "What Is the Inflation Reduction Act? Everything to Know about One of Biden's Big Laws," *USAToday.com*, May 25, 2023, https://www.usatoday.com/story/money/2023/05/25/guide-to-the-inflation-reduction-act/70249464007/.

83 Cory Turner, "The Expanded Child Tax Credit Briefly Slashed Child Poverty. Here's What Else It Did," *NPR.com*, January 27, 2022, https://www.npr.org/2022/01/27/1075299510/the-expanded-child-tax-credit-briefly-slashed-child-poverty-heres-what-else-it-d.

84 Abha Bhattarai, "5 Ways the Inflation Reduction Act Could Save You Money," *The Washington Post*, August 16, 2022, https://www.washingtonpost.com/business/2022/08/16/inflation-reduction-act-save-money/.

85 Alexander Burns, "If Biden's Plan Is Like a 'New Deal,' Why Don't Voters Care?" *New York Times*, April 21, 2022, https://www.nytimes.com/2022/04/21/us/politics/biden-pandemic-relief-democrats.html.

86 Barbara Sprunt, "Here's What the New Hate Crimes Law Aims to Do as Attacks on Asian Americans Rise," *NPR.com*, May 20, 2021, https://www.npr.org/2021/05/20/998599775/biden-to-sign-the-covid-19-hate-crimes-bill-as-anti-asian-american-attacks-rise.

87 Alexandra Hutzler, "Biden Signs Bipartisan Gun Safety Package into Law," *ABCNews.com*, June 25, 2022, https://abcnews.go.com/US/biden-signs-bipartisan-gun-safety-package-law/story?id=85692952.

88 Michael D. Shear, "Biden Signs Bill to Help Veterans Who Were Exposed to Toxic Burn Pits," *New York Times*, August 10, 2022, https://www.nytimes.com/2022/08/10/us/politics/biden-burn-pits.html.

89 Barbara Sprunt and Deirdre Walsh, "Far-right Members Threaten a 'Reckoning' over McCarthy's Debt Limit Deal," *NPR*, May 30, 2023, https://www.npr.org/2023/05/30/1178878967/mccarthy-house-conservatives-debt-ceiling-deal-vote.

90 Franklin Foer, *The Last Politician: Inside Joe Biden's White House and the Struggle for America's Future* (New York: Penguin, 2023).

91 Tyler Pager, "Shalanda Young Emerges as Quietly Essential Figure in Debt Deal," *The Washington Post*, May 30, 2023, https://www.washingtonpost.com/politics/2023/05/30/shalanda-young-debt-limit-talks/.

Part IV

Conclusion

16 Opportunity, Challenges, and Skill
Comparing the Presidents

Historians, political scientists, and even the general public are often called upon to rank the greatness of presidents.[1] These rankings are an interesting intellectual exercise but may also reflect the biases and policy preferences of those doing the rankings.[2] We argue that it is best to judge presidents not by what we wish they would have done, but against their own promises and goals. Therefore, we document each president's objectives early in each chapter prior to assessing their skill in achieving those goals.

Moreover, a central theme of this book is that each president is dealt a different hand to play: different circumstances and societal demands heavily impact a president's ability to accomplish his agenda. The opportunities and constraints facing Donald Trump and Joe Biden were vastly different than those facing their predecessors. But the high standards the public sets for the performance of presidents remain consistent. A review of landmark enactments dramatically underscores the extent to which some presidents have had far greater opportunities than others to contribute to fundamental changes in domestic policy. Moreover, some presidents have capitalized on their opportunities, while others have played their hands rather poorly. A comparison of presidents reveals that they have varied considerably in their leadership styles, strategies, and the skill with which they approach the job.

What do these findings say about the future of the presidency? Many historians and political scientists believe presidents who served in the mid-twentieth century generally produced stronger performances than more recent presidents. What does that judgment hold for twenty-first-century presidents? This chapter looks at these questions and at what strategies might work most effectively for future presidents and what roles those presidents might best fulfill.

DOI: 10.4324/9781003426684-20

318　*Conclusion*

Landmark Enactments

Landmark enactments provide important insights into both presidential leadership and the role of Congress (see Table 16.1). In fact, a look at the distribution of landmark enactments since 1932 demonstrates that the circumstances engulfing any one presidency do indeed have a big impact on policy outcomes. From 1933 to 1935, the extraordinary circumstances confronting President Franklin Roosevelt (along with his skills) produced seven landmark enactments. Some 30 years later, during the unusual period of John Kennedy's martyrdom in 1964, Lyndon Johnson oversaw the passage of three landmark pieces of legislation, and three landmark bills were passed during his peak opportunity in 1965. Two of the three landmark bills passed on Ronald Reagan's watch occurred during his first year in 1981. Similarly, two of three of George W. Bush's major enactments came during his extended period of high opportunity. Obama was able to secure a stimulus bill shortly after coming to office, and Trump got his tax cuts passed in the same period. Biden was able to get two major pieces of legislation passed in his first year. In total, 24 of the 41 landmark enactments passed after 1932 occurred during the brief periods in which presidents were experiencing distinctly high opportunity levels. For presidents, it pays to answer when opportunity calls.

Skills and strategies also matter. Specific strategy choices were evident in several of the high-opportunity situations. These include Roosevelt's third-year shift, coalition-building strategies such as the use of broad omnibus bills to maximize support (most recent presidents), particularized deal-making with key members of Congress (George W. Bush and Obama), and delegation to other principal negotiators when the president's good-will with intransigent legislators had been exhausted (Biden).

This being said, strong presidential leadership and high opportunities are not the only sources of landmark legislation. During periods in which presidents enjoy high opportunities, those same opportunities are likely to be affecting the work of Congress, much like the impact of an activist public mood or a surge in the number of new legislators committed to policy change. For example, as the "First Hundred Days" session was drawing to a close in 1933, FDR would have liked to see the Banking Act delayed until 1934—he personally opposed its provision for deposit insurance. Yet he ultimately accepted the insurance provision, as he agreed to sign the legislation once it passed in 1933. Perhaps more remarkably, in 1935 Congress passed the Wagner Act with its basic guarantees of union organizing rights even as Roosevelt was debating whether he should indicate support for the measure. (For examples of other instances in which members of Congress performed significant policymaking roles, including several points at which presidents were enjoying high opportunity levels, see Table 16.1.)

Opportunity, Challenges, and Skill   319

Table 16.1 Landmark Policy Enactments, 1933–2023

Legislation	Policy-Making Process
ROOSEVELT	
Agricultural Adjustment Act (1933) (modified in 1936)	Presidential coalition building by use of multiple components
Banking Act (1933)	Strong roles by legislative specialists; deposit insurance accepted reluctantly the by president.
Establishment, Securities and Exchange Commission (1934)	Presidential proposal; shared roles among strong public support
Establishment, Federal Communications Commission (1934)	Presidential proposal; legislative modification of final provisions
National Housing Act (1934)	Presidential proposal; strong public support; legislative specialists modified some provisions
Social Security Act (1935)	Strong presidential leadership; southern Democrats reduced some provisions
Establishment, National Labor Relations Board. Wagner Act (1935)	No direct presidential role; legislatively driven measure
Fair Labor Standards Act (1938)	Presidential support; considerable legislative leadership
G.I. Bill of Rights (1944)	Presidential promotion; congressional development of specific provisions
TRUMAN	
Employment Act (1946)	Presidential support; executive interest group and legislative bargaining
Taft-Hartley Act (1947)	Passed over Truman veto
Housing Act (1950)	Presidential initiative; considerable legislative involvement
EISENHOWER	
Civil Rights Act (1957)	Limited presidential leadership; primarily a legislative compromise
JOHNSON	
Civil Rights Act (1964)	Strong presidential support; key roles played by Senate party leaders
Economic Opportunity Act (1964)	Dominant presidential role
Tax cut (1964)	Strong presidential roles in 1963 and 1964; bargaining with revenue committee chairs
Federal Aid to Education (1965)	President-led bargaining with interest groups and a new policy design

(Continued)

320 *Conclusion*

Table 16.1 (Continued)

Legislation	Policy-Making Process
Medicare and Medicaid (1965)	Presidential support building, 1962–1965; program expansion by House Ways and Means Committee; presidential intervention in the Senate to avoid derailment
Voting Rights Act (1965)	Strong presidential address; easy passage in response to exposure of continuing violations
Open Housing Act (1968)	Shared presidential and congressional roles
REAGAN	
Economic Recovery Tax Act (1981)	Very effective presidential fast start and "going public" strategies; extensive legislative bargaining
Spending reductions (OBRA 1981)	Same as above
Tax Reform Act (1986)	Initial presidential proposal; significant legislative contributions in committee compromises and coalition building
GEORGE H. W. BUSH	
Deficit Reduction (1990)	Top-level negotiation; Congress dominant in final stages
CLINTON	
Deficit reduction package (1993)	Narrow presidential success with a partisan coalition; major legislative modification of final provisions
Welfare reform (1996)	Initial advocacy by president; major congressional initiative during 1995–1996; some modifications after presidential vetoes
Telecommunications reform (1996)	Limited advocacy by president; extensive legislative maneuvering among key interest groups
Balanced budget agreement (1997)	Result of top-level negotiation
GEORGE W. BUSH	
Tax Cuts (EGTRRA, 2001)	Very effective use of presidential fast start and some "going public" strategies; interest group pressure on key senators
No Child Left Behind (2002)	Use of key Democratic legislators to forge coalition; significant presidential role

(*Continued*)

Opportunity, Challenges, and Skill 321

Table 16.1 (Continued)

Legislation	Policy-Making Process
Establishment, Department of Homeland Security (2002)	Major presidential address; unified Congress; strong public support in wake of 9/11 attacks; Congress dominant in final stages
Prescription Drugs (MMA, 2003)	Presidential pressure on small groups of legislators; secured through "midnight" passage
OBAMA	
Economic Stimulus (ARRA, 2009)	Fast start; presidential lobbying of key senators
Healthcare Reform (PPACA, 2010)	Significant bargaining; Congressional use of budget reconciliation strategy; presidential lobbying of a few key members of Congress
Wall Street Reform and Consumer Protection Act (Dodd-Frank, 2010)	Executive bargaining with Congress; public support in wake of industry malfeasance
TRUMP	
Tax Cuts and Jobs Act (2017)	Some public pronouncements, Congressional-leadership-driven
Pandemic Response and Relief Bills (2020)	Congressionally led; some administrative bargaining
BIDEN	
American Rescue Plan (2021)	Fast start; use of budget reconciliation strategy
Infrastructure Investment and Jobs Act (2021)	Bipartisan leadership; presidential bargaining with Democratic holdouts
CHIPS and Science Act (2022)	Ripe issue; use of pandemic effects to stimulate congressional action
Inflation Reduction Act (2022)	Extensive negotiation with key senators; delegation of negotiations to Congressional leaders; use of budget reconciliation strategy

A second path to landmark legislation also underscores the importance of Congress. When presidents have not been in influential positions, the primary responsibility for landmark legislation often has shifted to Capitol Hill. This occurred quite notably with the Taft-Hartley Act in 1947, environmental legislation in the 1970s, deficit reduction in 1990, and welfare reform in 1996. George H. W. Bush contributed to the 1990 legislation by initially agreeing to top-level negotiations and then abandoning his opposition to a tax increase, and Clinton helped to give welfare reform greater prominence with his campaign pledge in 1992

322   *Conclusion*

to "end welfare as we know it." Yet in each case, the legislative role was predominant in the maneuvering that produced the final legislation. Similarly, during the presidencies of Barack Obama and Joe Biden, creative parliamentary maneuvering was needed in order to ensure passage of major legislation.

Within Congress, the size of a president's majority (if there is one) is important to the president's ability to achieve passage of landmark bills. Just how much "skill" did LBJ have to exercise to get his huge majority to support his proposals? Conceivably, Johnson could have lost dozens of votes from his own party and still won passage of legislation. By contrast, the extreme polarization that faced Biden meant that he needed to account for every legislator, then key in on the few who could get his policies over the top to passage.

An electoral mandate (as soft a concept as that may be) also can be influential. Ronald Reagan was able to claim a mandate on a few key issues in 1981, which clearly helped him persuade some members of Congress to support his proposals. Conversely, George W. Bush and Donald Trump entered the presidency under a cloud of illegitimacy, having lost the popular vote. This circumstance forced Bush to strong-arm certain senators to get his tax cuts passed—a move that cost his party control of the Senate when Jim Jeffords of Vermont defected from the Republican Party.

Other conclusions about the president and landmark legislation emerge from the patterns of enactments. For example, fundamental changes in policy are somewhat more likely to occur in the first year for a new president and during the first term of two-term presidents. Two landmark enactments were passed during Roosevelt's first year, six during Johnson's (he had two "first years," in 1964 and 1965), two during Reagan's, one during Bill Clinton's, one during Barack Obama's, one during Trump's, and two during Biden's. Similar to Johnson, George W. Bush enjoyed a prolonged period of opportunity during the aftermath of the 9/11 terrorist attacks, and three of his four landmark enactments occurred during that time. As for success in the second term, only 6 of the 41 landmark measures listed in Table 16.1, about 15 percent, were enacted after a president's first four years in office.

Exploring united rather than divided party control of Congress shows the presidency takes on greater importance for "landmark legislation" than for the broader category of "major legislation" used in David Mayhew's analysis (see Chapter 1). One of the central reasons why a divided government can produce major legislation was evident in 1996 when both the Republican-controlled Congress and President Clinton concluded that compromises to achieve some new policy commitments prior to the fall elections were mutually beneficial. Although landmark welfare legislation also was achieved in 1996, landmark legislation has been more difficult to

Opportunity, Challenges, and Skill   323

pass under conditions of divided government. Among the landmark cases, only about a third (13 of 41) were passed with divided government even though government was divided roughly half the time.

Finally, the frequent observation in this book that both a president's opportunity level and political skills can make a difference in achieving landmark legislation is just as important in thinking about the moderate- and low-opportunity presidents as in thinking about the high-opportunity presidents, whose political skills also varied. Given their more limited opportunity levels, it should not be surprising that the achievements of the moderate- and low-opportunity presidents were fewer than those of the high-opportunity presidents. Where enactments did occur during their time in office, special attention should be paid to the ways they may have played at least a significant supporting role in the legislative dynamics, which sometimes are dominated by congressional leaders.

Comparing Leadership Styles

Presidents' leadership styles stem from their diverse personal character- istics, career paths, perceptions of the failings of their predecessors, and often distinctive views of the presidents they seek to emulate. Their read- ings of their level of opportunity also may have an impact, as well as their party affiliation (for a summary of predominant leadership styles and strat- egies, see Table 16.2).

In fact, leadership orientations differ by party. Democratic presidents have tended to be activists. Roosevelt epitomized this role, and both Harry Truman and John Kennedy often sought to emulate FDR's style. Jimmy Carter, Bill Clinton, Barack Obama, and Joe Biden showed similar ten- dencies, at least in the early stages of their administrations. The circum- stances facing Obama made assertions of FDR-type activism possible. The Republicans displayed greater variation, which is to be expected from a party associated with the "conservative" value of government restraint. Reagan took an activist view of his leadership in his first year, but in some respects he was a hands-off managerial president who gazed approvingly at the White House portrait of Calvin Coolidge, a president who believed in leaving things alone as much as possible. Richard Nixon, too, believed in strong presidential leadership and in some ways was more assertive in leadership style than Reagan. Dwight Eisenhower and George H. W. Bush had more limited views, and, of the two, Eisenhower was more concerned with the importance of behind-the-scenes leadership. George W. Bush was primarily interested in showing leadership in the domains of education and foreign policy, preferring to delegate responsibility for a broad swath of domestic policy to his powerful vice president, Dick Cheney. Trump brought tremendous energy to the presidency, but his actions and attention to government policy were often chaotic.

Table 16.2 Presidential Leadership Styles and Strategies, 1933–2023

General Orientation	Approach to Decision-Making	Public Leadership	Congressional Leadership	Administrative Strategies
ROOSEVELT				
Pursue a strong role on all leadership dimensions	Undertake an aggressive search for policy ideas from many sources Operate a president-centered process	Develop an optimistic persona Use fireside chats to reassure and build support for general legislative agenda Use press conferences to shape issues and set agenda	Undertake a strong agenda-setting role Build coalitions with broad proposals Vigorously pursue fast-start and third-year shift strategies	Emphasize experimentation Shape policies extensively
TRUMAN				
Speak for the nation Act decisively	Try to do "the right thing" Pay limited attention to opinion polls	Make periodic use of strong addresses Do not worry about personal image	State a broad agenda Use the veto power aggressively Shape positions to "run against Congress" in 1948	Be willing to take strong action Desegregate armed services by executive order
EISENHOWER				
Defend the dignity of the office Use potential influence cautiously	Develop proposals in a deliberative manner Seek middle-of-the-road positions	Develop a friendly, optimistic persons Use public appeals in a selective, focused manner	Pursue a limited agenda Seek support through conciliation	Prune some New Deal programs

Table 16.2 (Continued)

General Orientation	Approach to Decision-Making	Public Leadership	Congressional Leadership	Administrative Strategies
KENNEDY				
Seek heroic leadership role	Adopt strong staff roles Take pragmatic positions Occasionally take bold action	Develop personal popularity Use policy appeals cautiously Use the bully pulpit to promote individual actions	Use normal methods but not too forcefully	Periodically take strong action
JOHNSON				
Be an active leader, like FDR Create a consensus by achieving "something for everyone"	Push very aggressively to develop legislative proposals Test political feasibility carefully	Try to impress the public with facts and bold new plans Manipulate the media	Use legislative knowledge to help steer legislation	Do not worry about implementation while passing legislation
NIXON				
Be an activist and bold planner, like Wilson	Use staff to shield oneself from conflict Seek some broad proposals Delegate many domestic policy roles Emphasize public relations values and reelection prospects in making decisions	Avoid press conferences and use skills with major addresses Appeal to "Middle America" and isolate opponents	Do the typical things the first two years and then withdraw Seek centrist coalitions	Use administrative role aggressively for reelection purposes Bring surveillance roles into White House operations

(Continued)

Table 16.2 (Continued)

General Orientation	Approach to Decision-Making	Public Leadership	Congressional Leadership	Administrative Strategies
CARTER				
Create a presidency that reflects the best aspects of average Americans	Avoid a Nixon-like delegation system, get deeply involved in policy details Seek comprehensive approaches in the public interest Pay limited attention to political feasibility	Avoid "imperial presidency" symbols Talk simply to and with the American public Do not spend a lot of time on public relations efforts and techniques	Push a broad initial agenda Do not spend a lot of time playing to the egos of legislators Gradually develop a more focused approach	Emphasize efforts to promote efficiency and "good government"
REAGAN				
Adopt early on an assertive role to achieve a longer-run reduction in the role of the federal government	Delegate extensively and only deal with broad issues Avoid losing battles Retreat quietly to the center when expedient	Build a friendly, optimistic persona Emphasize speeches and not press conferences Pursue themes for media consumption carefully	Use a fast-start and strong agenda control in 1981; pursue limited involvement after 1981	Push policy change through control of appointments
G. H. W. BUSH				
Use presidential power only when clearly necessary	Organize a comprehensive process Do not push for new initiatives Use only a few advisors on key decisions	Seek to show competence and enjoyment of job with frequent press conferences Take on public addresses very reluctantly	Propose a limited agenda Attempt initial conciliatory role Veto extensively	Pursue administrative roles for reelection purposes, 1991–1992

Table 16.2 (Continued)

General Orientation	Approach to Decision-Making	Public Leadership	Congressional Leadership	Administrative Strategies
CLINTON				
Use presidential power to pursue a broad range of policy responses	Explore options in considerable detail Use fluid decision-making process Seek distinctive policy proposals Follow polls with great care	Talk to the American public often, especially 1993–1994 Use major addresses extensively	Devote considerable time to legislation Pursue partisan support, 1993–1994; then centrist coalitions, 1995–1996	Undertake government reorganization, 1993–1994 Seek policy influence and visibility, 1995–1996
G. W. BUSH				
Restore dignity to the White House Use presidential power to develop the "ownership society"	Delegate all but a few issue domains, but ultimately be the "decider" Advisors must be on board with larger goals	Develop a "folksy" persona Use keywords to trigger support from various segments of the public Use friendly media	Use a fast-start for tax cuts Challenge members of Congress who are not on board with proposals After 9/11 withdraw to foreign policy	Delegate Use signing statements extensively to shape impact of legislation
OBAMA				
Avoid another Great Depression Be prepared to negotiate Stress openness and transparency	Be at the center of decision-making without using multiple advocacy Stress fairness	Limit public expectations Allow access to narrowcast media Tightly control access	Use a fast-start for stimulus Respect separation of powers, but focus on a few legislators to overcome gridlock Use executive branch officials, including VP, in negotiations	Get the policy enacted first, wait until later to refine it Use technology to promote support for enacted policies Use executive authority when Congress fails to act

(Continued)

Table 16.2 (Continued)

General Orientation	Approach to Decision-Making	Public Leadership	Congressional Leadership	Administrative Strategies
TRUMP				
Disrupt the normal order of governance Make better deals	Hire the "best people" Stress loyalty Govern toward the base of the party Use decisions as reward and punishment	Direct appeals through social media Harness outrage Use controversial statements to focus press attention	Delegation of negotiations to Congressional leaders and a few administration officials Public pressure rather than deal-making	Overturn predecessor's achievements through executive order Administrative proclamations through social media Use of "acting" department heads to insure loyalty
BIDEN				
Restore competency and the normal order of governance Leverage personal relationships in negotiations	Stress diversity in appointments and staffing Strong Chief of Staff role Take time to gather data and deliberate over decisions	Use "Consoler-in-Chief" role to show empathy Broad proclamations in the pursuit of unity Switch to attacks on opposition when all else has failed	Fast start Extensive bargaining Delegation to Congressional leadership when presidential good-will exhausted	Overturn predecessor's executive orders Return to normal administrative processes Appoint judges with diverse backgrounds for future policy adjudication

Opportunity, Challenges, and Skill 329

In decision-making processes, Democratic presidents have generally been more interested in finding new policies to promote; Republican presidents have tended to focus on staff processes. Among the Democrats, Roosevelt and Johnson were especially eager to find new ideas, reflecting in part their desire to maximize high opportunities. Among the Republicans, Nixon put in place energetic operations for analyzing and proposing domestic policies, while Reagan, especially after 1981, was content to conduct only a moderately aggressive search for new ideas. Both Bushes made some efforts to unearth new policy initiatives, but they stand out among presidents of both parties for their distinctively limited pursuits of new domestic policy.

Most presidents of both parties have engaged in extensive assessments of political feasibility in their decision-making processes, even those in strong positions vis-à-vis Congress. Roosevelt, Johnson, and Reagan all consulted extensively with members of Congress. More than any of their predecessors, Obama and Biden found it necessary to isolate the key votes that could be found to move their legislation through a hyper-partisan Congress. Carter and Trump were arguably the least interested in assessments of likely congressional reactions to their policy proposals. When presidents paid little attention to Congress, such as Truman on civil rights in 1948, they were often posturing rather than seeking to gain passage of legislation.

Differences in the use of public opinion polls in decision-making owe more to the evolution of polling itself as a decision-making tool than to a pattern of party differences.[3] Roosevelt showed an immediate interest when polls emerged in the mid-1930s, yet his successor, Truman, was reluctant to use them. Eisenhower showed more interest than Truman. The use of polls increased with the introduction of new technologies in the 1960s. The White House became a veritable warehouse for stocking the latest public opinion data. President Nixon, according to one aide, studied "all kinds of polls all the time."[4]

Jimmy Carter was not immune to the trend; Pat Caddell was the first pollster to have office space in the White House. Reagan met about once a month with pollster Richard Wirthlin, and George H. W. Bush's extensive use of polls during the Gulf War was partially mirrored by his attention to factors shaping his own popularity. Clinton gave more access to pollsters in his White House operations than any other president. Moreover, he utilized overnight polling extensively in planning his reelection strategies in 1995–1996. George W. Bush was less interested in polls than his successor, especially when his attention shifted to foreign policy after the 9/11 terrorist attacks. Obama was acutely attuned to the ramifications of his actions in the public view, especially as they became filtered by an increasingly partisan press corps. Trump would publicly discuss his position in the polls (particularly when they favored him) and denigrate other politicians for their poor showings in polls.

330   *Conclusion*

It is more difficult to determine the degree to which presidents have allowed public opinion data to have a direct influence on their decisions. Clinton and his aides argued that polls are used to help presidents shape their presentation of policies to the voter.[5] For example, Clinton used polls to help him find the right slogans to sell his proposed *Health Security Act* to the electorate.[6] It is difficult to imagine any president being immune to information that suggests which policy choices are likely to be popular with the voters.

Public leadership strategies and levels of success have varied widely among the presidents of each party. Of the Democrats, Roosevelt possessed a remarkable array of skills and displayed an adroit use of strategies. Kennedy adapted very well to the television era, developed a highly effective persona, and delivered some well-received addresses. Truman was something of an anomaly in that he was ineffective in maintaining his popularity and lacked eloquence. But he was able to define his positions forcefully (e.g., his ringing denunciation of the Taft-Hartley Act) and in ways that helped to rally his core constituencies. Carter was probably the least-skilled Democratic president as he seemed uninterested in improving his largely ineffective speaking style. Clinton, like Carter, suffered early in his presidency from a poor portrayal by the press. Obama used his formidable rhetorical skills to his advantage when giving speeches with the aid of his teleprompter. But when forced to comment off the cuff, Obama often seemed detached and professorial. Biden's gregariousness, warmth, and empathy were on display on occasions, but at other times he could come off as terse and scolding.

Republican performances were equally varied. Reagan had the best media strategy with his use of the theme for the day and the development of his "nice guy" and "outsider" personas. His domestic selling effort was well orchestrated in 1981, but then it weakened considerably. Eisenhower was highly successful in developing an attractive persona, in maintaining his popularity, and in his occasional efforts to support his legislative program. George H. W. Bush stands in interesting contrast to Eisenhower in that they both had a limited agenda. George H. W. Bush was fairly successful the first two and a half years of his administration in maintaining his popularity, but he could not adapt to changing political circumstances. Perhaps the most telling difference between George H. W. Bush and Eisenhower is that Ike placed more importance on his public roles and sought professional coaching to improve. George H. W. Bush was reduced to mocking his own lack of public speaking skills while avoiding obvious possibilities for major addresses. His son suffered the same problems with public speaking but developed a folksy persona to cover for it. Nixon made some quite successful major addresses—a fact perhaps little recognized—but they often were in the area of foreign policy. His failings were dramatic; his relationship with the press during his first term became

Opportunity, Challenges, and Skill   331

increasingly embittered, often at his own instigation. Trump's combative public demeanor ingratiated him to his base but did little to expand his appeal.

Party-based differences emerge when legislative leadership roles are examined more closely. For example, Democrats were more likely to engage in a fast-start strategy, reflecting in part their more robust agendas and their greater opportunities, especially in 1933 (FDR) and 1964–1965 (LBJ). Obama dealt with his moderate level of opportunity by pushing a fast-start approach for one issue—the economic stimulus. Democrats with less promising circumstances, such as Carter, Clinton, and Biden, also tried to exert legislative leadership, with only Biden achieving significant results. Kennedy proceeded somewhat differently. He made a moderate first-year effort to push for passage of federal aid to education and Medicare but focused primarily on second-tier issues such as aid to depressed areas.

With the exception of Reagan, Republican presidents approached their first years differently. Reagan proceeded much like a Democrat as he moved quickly in 1981. Nixon ultimately did produce his Family Assistance Plan (FAP), a proposal with the potential for landmark legislation, but only after he was criticized for his limited agenda. Eisenhower and George H. W. Bush proceeded with more limited first-year agendas because they preferred to study possible proposals. George W. Bush used a fast-start strategy primarily for his tax cuts prior to 9/11. Each had more success with Congress in their second year than in their first. Trump moved quickly to achieve tax cuts, but his chaotic focus for the rest of his first year provided little guidance to allies in Congress.

In their overall involvement with Congress, Democratic presidents varied considerably, and no Republican president stood out for especially high levels of interaction. Democrats Franklin Roosevelt and Lyndon Johnson spent the most time dealing with Congress. Roosevelt often devoted several hours a day to this task, and Johnson was constantly on the telephone and saw many legislators in person. Their time commitments reflected their opportunities, but also their interest in and enjoyment of legislative relations. Efforts by other Democratic presidents were more limited. Truman and Kennedy spent only a moderate amount of time greasing the wheels on Capitol Hill, and Carter was grudging in allocating his time for legislative matters. Clinton, by contrast, spent considerable time talking to legislators in 1993 and in top-level negotiations in 1995–1996. Obama's interaction with Congress was middling among the Democrats, preferring to use surrogates so that his involvement would not be a lightning rod for his adversaries. Biden took an active role in attempting to leverage his long-term relationships with members of Congress, but when bargaining failed, he turned to surrogates to complete the deals.

A look at the use of administrative strategies to pursue "good government" reveals an interesting partisan division. The seemingly plausible

332 *Conclusion*

expectation that Republican presidents would be more interested in government efficiency is not borne out by their actions. Rather, Democrats have at times been more interested than Republicans in improving government operations, perhaps reflecting Democrats' greater interest in having an efficient bureaucracy in order to enhance programmatic goals. Among the Democrats, Truman took a strong interest in the Hoover Commission reforms, Carter was uniquely interested in efficiency issues, and Clinton promoted his vice president's efforts to streamline federal operations by "reinventing government." Roosevelt's strategies for building government were closely tied to his strategies for control of government, believing that greater White House control meant greater efficiency. Obama believed that openness and transparency in decision-making—and particularly the implementation of the American Recovery and Reinvestment Act—would ensure efficiencies and generate greater public support for his subsequent agenda. Kennedy was quite skeptical of and disinterested in the federal bureaucracy.

Among the Republicans, Nixon developed the most extensive set of proposals seeking to modernize the federal government. In the wake of his reelection victory in 1972, his reorganization strategy became an obvious bid for greater presidential control as he asked for the resignations of cabinet members and envisioned a major cabinet restructuring. Nevertheless, he did display a more general interest in structural issues (such as modernization of the post office) than any of the other Republicans. Eisenhower sought to place a lid on future expansion of government agencies rather than engage in large-scale reform. Despite his extensive involvement in the federal bureaucracy and an early speech to top federal officials stressing their importance, George H. W. Bush (and later, his son) manifested little interest in "good government" issues. Donald Trump openly provoked executive branch employees and promoted a conspiracy that the "deep state" was determined to see him fail.

In the use of administrative strategies for policy purposes, a reasonable hypothesis is that presidents who have difficulty achieving policy goals through Congress would be especially active in the administrative arena. For example, Truman circumvented Congress by issuing executive orders to desegregate the military, and Nixon took steps in 1971 to establish wage and price controls. Both George W. Bush and Barack Obama took a number of administrative steps to avoid Congress. Presidents with high opportunities also found administrative strategies extremely important at times. The exception was Johnson, who spent relatively little time worrying about administrative relationships. Roosevelt, by contrast, regarded administrative strategies as an integral part of his effort to implement the New Deal. In other words, the "alphabet soup" of New Deal agencies was cooked up by a president who regarded administrative leadership as crucial to his ability to shape policy development. Reagan stands between

Opportunity, Challenges, and Skill   333

Roosevelt and Johnson. He viewed the appointment of men and women who were committed to his desire for less regulation as an important way to change policy. He had, however, far less interest in the specifics of policy than Roosevelt. George W. Bush was similar in this regard, looking to replace administrators who were unsympathetic to his agenda—such as a number of U.S. attorneys who were dismissed in 2006. Both Biden and Trump have used judicial appointments as insulation for legal tests to their policies, and both were highly active in using executive orders to reverse the actions of their predecessor.

In short, presidents have shown marked variation in their views of what the president should do, in the strategies they choose, and in their skills in handling key roles. Those differences are one of the keys to comparative assessments of overall performance.

Comparative Assessments

In the head-to-head comparisons of performance presented in this section, the presidents are grouped into the same three categories used to structure this book: high-opportunity, moderate-opportunity, and low-opportunity. These assessments pay particular attention to the ways in which skills and strategies have helped presidents to meet challenges, use opportunities, and create broad policy legacies in line with their promises.

The High-Opportunity Presidents: Roosevelt, Johnson, Reagan, and George W. Bush

Of the high-opportunity presidents, Franklin Roosevelt was the best positioned to chalk up significant achievements, but his challenges were significant. Roosevelt's major challenge in dealing with Congress and seeking passage of his preferred legislation was to identify policy solutions that could command legislative support amid the vast array of possibilities being discussed. Lyndon Johnson's opportunity level also was high, including an unusually large number of promising issues, but he faced formidable challenges. For Johnson, his first challenge was to achieve passage of significant amounts of domestic legislation that had been stalled or that only recently had begun to move toward passage in Congress. Ronald Reagan's opportunity level was similar to Roosevelt's as it included a repudiation of the opposing party rather than a Johnson-like continuation of the dominant party's position. But his economic challenges and the balance of power in Congress created difficulties in addressing the economic problems of stagflation and unemployment while seeking to fulfill his promise to deliver a smaller federal government. The presidency of George W. Bush shows an intensely "dynamic" opportunity structure. George W. Bush came into office under a cloud of illegitimacy and facing an economy that was neither

334   *Conclusion*

poor enough nor good enough to provide ample opportunity. The existence of a budget surplus provided opportunity for his tax cuts, but little else. Then, with the terrorist attacks of 9/11, Congress and the public rallied behind the president, seeking his leadership. A short-lived increase in trust in government and a public mood for government activism ensued, catapulting George W. Bush's opportunity level to significant heights.

Of these four high-opportunity presidents, Roosevelt's legacy was the largest. He helped craft a series of regulatory policies and a Social Security system that, a half-century later, remain the mainstays of domestic policy. Johnson's legacy consists of landmark legislation on critical issues such as civil rights, Medicare, and federal aid to education. Reagan's main legacy is in the form of the tax and spending cuts passed in 1981. Unlike FDR and Johnson, Reagan sought primarily to reduce the scope of domestic policy commitments rather than develop new approaches. His actions thus served to prevent the enactment of new programs in the face of mounting deficits rather than to achieve a retrenchment in federal commitments. George W. Bush's first-year landmark achievement was a tax-cut package that ballooned subsequent deficits and hindered the expansion of government programs in subsequent years. His education and Medicare reforms affected hundreds of millions of Americans, the results of which were costly and inconclusive. The creation of the Department of Homeland Security bridged domestic and foreign policy, bringing diverse agencies together under one roof in the hopes of increased efficiencies in a policy area where success often remains hidden from public view.

In developing new proposals, both Roosevelt and Johnson employed aggressive strategies that were implemented by energetic aides. Reagan and Bush mounted intensive efforts in their first years, but those efforts then declined markedly. In Reagan's case, they declined with his opportunity, but in Bush's case, his efforts in the domestic sphere declined as his opportunity increased. In public leadership, Roosevelt and Reagan displayed exceptional skills and built effective personas, George W. Bush was loved by supporters and reviled by opponents, and Johnson suffered from a public perception that he was a politician who simply could not be trusted. While Roosevelt, Reagan, and Bush were highly effective in promoting a sense of optimism in difficult times, Johnson was uniquely unsuited for a bully pulpit role as urban problems mounted during his presidency. As for "going public" to build support for new legislation, Reagan made the most sustained effort in 1981. Roosevelt was effective in his ongoing fireside chats, George W. Bush made targeted use of the "going public" strategy to achieve his early tax cuts, and Johnson correctly concluded that his primary task was to forge legislative coalitions on issues that often already commanded widespread support. Finally, in the ability of these presidents to sustain personal support, Reagan was the most successful with a consistently well-planned media strategy, spikes in George W. Bush's popularity were the result of external factors rather than a comprehensive plan, and Johnson was by far the least successful. Although poll findings are not available, Roosevelt in all likelihood would have fared very well in sustaining popular support.

On the legislative front, each of these presidents was successful with a fast start strategy. Roosevelt and Johnson had broader agendas, but Reagan's and Bush's performances were at least as well executed, although narrowly focused on tax cuts. Reagan and Bush delegated more of their legislative roles than either Roosevelt or Johnson, but did so effectively. Unlike FDR and Johnson, however, Reagan retreated after his first year, leaving legislative leaders to bear the fallout from efforts to reduce the soaring deficit. George W. Bush finalized a couple of landmark pieces of legislation after 9/11 but mostly ignored the domestic policy arena and Congress afterward. Both Roosevelt and Johnson were far more active than Reagan or George W. Bush and used many more strategies. Because Johnson was highly conscious of potential comparisons with Roosevelt's legislative performance, he may well have pushed harder to find all possible areas for enacting new legislation and to achieve greater scope in his proposals. Roosevelt was somewhat more apt than other presidents to seek centrist coalitions and pay greater attention to implementation issues.

In the administrative arena, Roosevelt surpassed both Johnson and Reagan in involvement and effective leadership. He also used the broadest range of strategies as he fostered experimentation and shaped policy without precise legislative specification. Reagan, who had the second-highest level of involvement, shaped regulatory policy through control of budgets and personnel selection. But, just as in the legislative arena, his interest waned as his first term progressed. George W. Bush vastly increased the use of signing statements to influence policy implementation and deferred to his vice president for selecting a majority of administrators. Johnson made the least use of administrative strategies; he chose to focus primarily on the passage of new legislation.

Each president's skills and strategies shaped his ability to confront challenges and utilize opportunities. Roosevelt's activism and pursuit of multiple strategies helped him promote and facilitate extensive change. Johnson's legislative skills allowed him to effectively promote the Great Society agenda, but he was less successful in adapting to changing political circumstances, even though he continued to press for new legislation. Reagan made the most of his opportunities in 1981, and he also could claim credit for effectively creating those opportunities with his election campaign. During his remaining seven years in office, however, he was something of an underachiever. He gave little encouragement to staff aides to develop new proposals that would have tested the level of possible change, and he was rather passive in dealing with Congress. George W. Bush's success in passing his tax legislation came at the price of the loss of

336 *Conclusion*

the Senate, hampering his ability to get much done until the 9/11 attacks, after which he showed little interest in domestic policy.

Of these four presidents, Roosevelt was the most skilled and most effective leader. He was at least as skilled as either Johnson or Reagan on each leadership-style dimension and used an unusually broad range of strategies and tactics. Johnson, Reagan, and George W. Bush demonstrated mixed skills. Johnson was a highly capable legislator, Reagan was uniquely gifted in the public dimensions of his leadership roles, and George W. Bush overcame the shadow of illegitimacy upon attaining office by forcing his tax cut through Congress. Johnson, however, had glaring problems in dealing with the public, and Reagan used a limited range of political strategies and exerted considerably less overall effort than either FDR or Johnson. George W. Bush found his public voice in the wake of the 9/11 attacks but then used it to fuel his foreign policy goals at the expense of his domestic agenda.

The Moderate-Opportunity Presidents: Truman, Eisenhower, Kennedy, Obama, and Trump

Of the presidents who faced moderate opportunity levels during their terms in office, Harry Truman, Dwight Eisenhower, John Kennedy, and Barack Obama stand out as relatively strong and successful performers. They all significantly surpassed the less skillful efforts of Donald Trump. Truman and Obama found themselves in more difficult situations than Eisenhower, Kennedy, or Trump: both Truman and Obama faced imposing domestic challenges and the limitations incurred by presidents who preceded them in office.

Truman's legacy lay in his promotion of civil rights and use of administrative strategies to desegregate the armed forces. Truman did not have especially impressive public or legislative leadership skills, but he did have a keen sense of political strategies. He was especially skillful in engineering his election bid in 1948. Given his circumstances, Truman performed quite respectably.

Eisenhower had in some respects the most promising opportunities of these four presidents. A military hero, he was twice elected by a wide margin and enjoyed an unusually high level of popularity. Yet, he also confronted constraints. He had to deal with a divided majority Republican coalition in Congress during his first two years and thereafter faced Democratic majorities. During his years in the White House, Eisenhower sought to prune aspects of New Deal legislation, strengthen economic capacities, and respond to calls for action on race relations.

Eisenhower displayed solid political skills. He worked actively with Congress, kept a close eye on some administrative issues, and demonstrated effective public leadership in not only maintaining his popularity

Opportunity, Challenges, and Skill   337

but also using selective, focused public appeals on legislative issues. His legacy has stemmed primarily from his legitimization of aspects of the New Deal such as Social Security and from his successful promotion of infrastructure programs such as the interstate highway system. While a president with stronger policy commitments might have accomplished more, Eisenhower nevertheless produced a solid performance.

Despite his high personal popularity, Kennedy faced distinct constraints during his abruptly shortened tenure in office—among them, his narrow election victory in 1960 and a divided Democratic coalition in Congress, accompanied by strong southern conservative strength in key committee positions. Kennedy had many proposals on his agenda but found it difficult to create supportive coalitions. When conditions changed by 1963, creating a greater opportunity for civil rights legislation, he displayed forceful presidential leadership.

Kennedy also displayed solid political skills. He was perhaps a bit too cautious with Congress, but maintained at least an average level of activity. His public leadership included developing an effective persona and contributing to the emerging era of activism with his use of the bully pulpit. Although Kennedy did not leave a major policy legacy, he deserves credit for launching a broad set of initiatives in 1963, especially his civil rights measures and an assertive tax-cut plan. He thus joins Truman and Eisenhower in the solid performer category.

Like Truman, Obama faced difficult prospects for success. The tax cuts of his predecessor had ballooned the deficit, bank bailouts had soured the public on governmental action, and a potential depression was looming. For Obama, his main obstacle in Congress wasn't the size of the opposition coalition but rather its cohesiveness. Obama found it difficult at times to win even a single Republican vote on his legislation. During the second half of his first term, polarization had reached such a level in Congress that no Democratic Senator rated to the right of the leftmost Republican, making forging coalitions to overcome Republican filibuster threats nearly impossible. Still, the economic stimulus package saved the economy from deteriorating into a full-blown depression (although millions of Americans remained unemployed during the torturously slow recovery). Obama was able to pass health care reform—achieving what both Truman and Clinton could not. Obama was a willing negotiator, prepared to strike deals with many members of Congress, but often finding no takers. When faced with senatorial holds on his nominations, Obama made recess appointments. Similarly, he used executive actions when Congress was hamstrung by gridlock. Taken together, the skill with which Obama pushed his domestic agenda exceeded that of Ike or Kennedy, falling just short of Truman.

Donald Trump came to office on a tide of anti-establishment sentiment, and he enjoyed majorities in Congress for his first two years. However, he brought in no new members on his coattails, and his legitimacy was

338   *Conclusion*

undercut by having lost the popular vote by nearly three million votes. Trump worked quickly to pass his tax cuts, but his shifting and chaotic leadership combined with his politics of personal grievance provided little direction to Congress. The pandemic forced him to acquiesce to a recovery bill, the details of which were ironed out by Congressional leaders and some administration officials, with little involvement from the president himself. Trump failed to deliver on major promises, such as repealing and replacing Obamacare and the construction of a wall on the nation's southern border. Trump also failed to uphold his promise to protect and defend the Constitution on January 6, 2021. Donald Trump falls last among the moderate-opportunity presidents in terms of performance.

The Low-Opportunity Presidents: Nixon, Carter, George H. W. Bush, Clinton, and Biden

Richard Nixon, run out of office by scandal, was ultimately an unsuccessful president on other counts as well. In political skills, he had a clearer sense of potential strategies and their relationship to his reelection needs than either Carter or George H. W. Bush, and he was more successful than both in his use of public addresses. On domestic issues, his staff system quite effectively generated policy proposals. His leadership of Congress was, at most, average, but his desire for government action in a variety of areas contributed to a climate that fostered big changes in domestic policy. Nixon also used administrative strategies to meet a variety of policy goals such as his new economic policy of August 1971. But only moderate policy legacies such as revenue sharing could be traced to his actions.

Yet Nixon also had enormous failings. The biggest, perhaps, was his rhetoric of divisiveness, contributing to an intensification of political antagonisms. Although second terms are not generally productive, the first year of Nixon's second term, 1973, held the promise of action in areas such as health care reform. Hopes were dashed, however, when the nation's capital became preoccupied with the Watergate scandal. Ultimately, Nixon contributed to growing cynicism about national politics and the emergence of congressional measures to contain the presidency, which worked to the disadvantage of his successors. President Bill Clinton was correct in emphasizing at Nixon's funeral in 1994 that evaluations of Nixon must be more than about Watergate. Yet in the end, one cannot escape recognizing this flawed president's negative impact on the presidency and the political system.[7]

Of the presidents with limited opportunities, Jimmy Carter and George H. W. Bush share several characteristics. In part, they were both unlucky to have run for reelection during difficult economic times and faced opponents who were highly effective campaigners. Moreover, they did not

Opportunity, Challenges, and Skill 339

immediately receive wide recognition for all of their policy achievements, and they possessed distinct limitations in aspects of their leadership skills.

Carter faced greater challenges than the other presidents in this category but had a somewhat greater opportunity. His challenges arose in the areas of energy and fiscal policy during an era of stagflation. His opportunities took the form of some fairly promising issues on the agenda in 1977 and the substantial Democratic majorities in Congress. Yet that coalition was divided, and there were few politically feasible solutions for some of the problems he sought to address. The president from Georgia contributed to his own difficulties with his deficient leadership skills. He managed to improve his legislative leadership throughout his four years in office, but he was never very effective with his public leadership. Indeed, he was unable to reassure the public that his administration was effectively addressing problems. The unfortunate consequence for Carter was that the public remained largely unaware of his accomplishments, which included several environmental initiatives and the beginnings of the deregulation trend in governance.

George H. W. Bush faced few challenges until the economic slump of 1991, but he also had quite limited opportunities. An "understudy" of President Reagan, George H. W. Bush had been elected in a campaign that did little to help develop promising issues. Once in office, he faced Democratic majorities on Capitol Hill and a government saddled with a large deficit. Bush undertook a "reluctant guardian" role with limited skill and was never an adroit public leader. He assisted in the passage of important measures such as the Clean Air Act in 1990. Even though Congress ultimately passed a landmark deficit-reduction package in 1990, George H. W. Bush was most noted for the extent to which he lost control of the process and thus had little influence on the final measure. Because of that lack of control, as well as the limited impact the measure had on the deficit in the wake of the 1991–1992 recession, Bush found it difficult to achieve credit for this achievement. Finally, in his underuse of administrative strategies, Bush never fully exploited opportunities for influence.

George H. W. Bush's difficulties in orchestrating his reelection bid also stemmed from his limited political skills. The contrast with Truman is especially striking. Early on, Truman developed a strategy for dealing with Congress, used his administrative powers aggressively, and campaigned with conviction to rally his coalition. George H. W. Bush, by contrast, developed his strategies too late, and persistent public doubts about his real convictions on issues contributed to his difficulties (e.g., reneging on his "read my lips, no new taxes" pledge). Bush thus joins Carter as an example of a less successful president who held office with modest opportunities.

In comparative terms, Clinton had a sense of political strategy that rivaled those of all but a few of his predecessors, and he could on occasion engage in effective public leadership roles. His early staff processes showed

340   *Conclusion*

signs of a learning curve because his second term began far more smoothly. More actively involved with Congress than many presidents, Clinton showed considerable skill in outmaneuvering Republicans in 1995–1996 on balanced budget negotiations. More generally, his legacy includes the transformation from budget deficit to surplus and a strong economy. As for building coalitions, Clinton's effort to steer the Democratic Party in more moderate directions had longer-term electoral benefits.

Yet, despite these achievements, Clinton's performance was in some ways disappointing, in part because of the significant flaws that accompanied his political skills. Republicans found Clinton an appealing target on their way to resounding victories in the 1994 midterm elections. More fundamentally, Clinton's tendency to shade the truth in defending his actions and those of his administration had an unfortunate impact on the electorate's perceptions of his credibility, and likely cost his vice president the chance to succeed him. This mixed legacy puts Clinton in the middle of the pack of the low-opportunity presidents.

Joe Biden came to office under a time of extraordinarily limited opportunity. The pandemic was raging, and the nation was sharply divided. His predecessor initially refused to leave office, casting an air of illegitimacy over his presidency. While his party had control of Congress, it was only with the narrowest of margins. Moreover, time on the Congressional calendar during his first year was limited by the second impeachment trial of Donald Trump as well as the January 6th investigation in the House of Representatives. Still, Biden was able to shepherd four major pieces of legislation through Congress in his first two years in office. Considering his limited opportunities, it is remarkable that Biden was able to achieve what he did. Biden showed flexibility in bargaining with Congress when he could and deferred to others when it was needed. Biden was also active administratively, although not all of his orders would withstand tests in the courts. We rate him as the highest achiever in the low-opportunity category of presidents.

Conclusion

Who, then, were the most "effective" or "skilled" of the post-1932 presidents? Given their levels of opportunity, Truman and Biden, whose level of political opportunity was rather limited, are the overachievers of the group, with FDR, a high-opportunity president, also ranking very high on the list. Underachievers Reagan, Carter, both Bushes, and Trump were presidents who seemed to squander opportunities. See Table 16.3 for a comparative profile of the modern presidents.

The higher rankings of the mid-twentieth-century presidents raise a key issue: are present-day presidents hampered by new forces in demonstrating

Opportunity, Challenges, and Skill 341

Table 16.3 Presidential Rankings on the Skill/Opportunity Scale

High-Opportunity Presidents	*Moderate-Opportunity Presidents*	*Low-Opportunity Presidents*
1. Roosevelt	1. Truman	1. Biden
2. Johnson	2. Obama	2. Nixon
3. G. W. Bush	3. Eisenhower	3. Clinton
4. Reagan	4. Kennedy	4. G. H. W. Bush
	5. Trump	5. Carter

their skills and taking advantage of opportunities? Presidents serving since 1973 have indeed been affected by a series of limiting influences, including greater public skepticism about government, greater capacities for independent action in Congress, the proliferation of interest groups, economic problems, more fragile electoral coalitions, a far more adversarial press, and increasing ideological polarization among members of Congress and the public.[8]

The role of the press and the media environment are especially important. Had Franklin Roosevelt had to deal with the modern-day press, for example, his confinement to a wheelchair would have complicated his creation of an energetic public persona—the press simply would not have allowed a presidential handicap to go unnoticed. Today, even the smallest details of presidents' physical examinations receive complete coverage and analysis. This scrutiny caused Donald Trump to use doctors who would provide a glowing assessment of his health. Likewise, Kennedy's womanizing would not have remained a secret but would have been subjected to constant media coverage, as would his serious health problems. Thus, the mid-twentieth-century presidents would have found their jobs more difficult in more recent years. Yet it must be noted that Reagan's performance indicates that effective media strategies and public leadership are possible, although the current era of the internet and mass media fragmentation might make his strategies less effective.

These observations aside, the mid-twentieth-century presidents were an unusually talented group. Roosevelt would stand out as a remarkable person in any era, Truman possessed uncommon political skills along with a distinctive desire to "do the right thing," and Eisenhower drew on a broader range of experiences than many realized. Kennedy suffered from youthful inexperience, but possessed an impressive range of political skills.

Any effort to rate the presidents is fraught with difficulty, especially for recent presidents who face greater constraints. Presidents Roosevelt, Truman, and Eisenhower, on the basis of their foreign and domestic policy performances, have consistently ranked above those presidents serving in more recent years. Historian Arthur Schlesinger Jr. used a 1997 survey

342   *Conclusion*

of presidential scholars to categorize Roosevelt as great; Truman as near great; Eisenhower, Kennedy, and Johnson as high average; Clinton, Bush, Reagan, and Carter as average; and Nixon as a failure. Comparable results were achieved in a larger survey.[9] Similarly, in a grouping devised by political scientists Lance LeLoup and Steven Shull, the four presidents who rated high on both their selling skills and their managerial skills were Roosevelt, Kennedy, Truman, and Eisenhower.[10] Faber and Faber's ranking of presidents in 2012 achieved results similar to others, with Obama ranking in the upper third of presidents, Clinton in the middle, and George W. Bush classified as a failure.[11] Rankings of Obama and Trump have divided starkly along partisan lines, with each party loving their own and hating the other.[12] Thus, while the job of president may have gotten tougher, to some degree, the voters may have elevated less-talented individuals to the Oval Office.

Looking Ahead

The future prospects for domestic policy leadership will depend on the roles played by Congress and presidents in that leadership. The landmark legislation passed since 1932 underscores the importance of those roles, and Congress may well become more important in the future. This section draws several lessons from the nation's policy making since 1932 to suggest possible sources of effective leadership and more promising strategies.

The Views from the Opposite Ends of Pennsylvania Avenue

Congress has sometimes shown an impressive capacity for shaping domestic policies. On some issues, Congress may more accurately reflect public opinion than a president. This is perhaps unduly influenced by a president's singular ideology or the input of only a few carefully chosen advisers. In fact, Congress should be able to address major policy issues without the president having to act as the dominant player, as the framers of the Constitution envisioned.

Dependence on Congress, however, can create problems. Procedural arrangements and strong committee chairs may thwart or skew action. In the early post–World War II era, for example, the southern Democrats who chaired congressional committees routinely obstructed civil rights and other legislation. More recently, stronger partisanship has reduced opportunities for compromise, and senatorial holds have threatened appointments to important executive branch positions. Additionally, despite "earmark reform," legislators tend to pursue short-run, pork-laden policy outcomes due to the nature of their constituencies and their reelection concerns. In short, left to their own instincts, legislators may find it hard to take any policy steps that reflect majority views in the electorate and a broad perspective on the country's needs. Effective presidential leadership on domestic policy is still needed.

The Search for Effective Presidents

Effective presidents are not easy to find. It is hard to detect the personal characteristics that will lead to successful presidential leadership.[13] Thus, when evaluating candidates, political parties must search for those ambitious enough to seek the office and shrewd enough to realize the range of strategic choices they are offered. But parties must simultaneously avoid office seekers who possess aspects of those characteristics but also have unhealthy personality traits that could spark unwise and dangerous presidential actions.

Three lessons can be drawn from history about leadership style. First, officeholders must fit the circumstances of their time in office. Franklin Roosevelt, with his energy and enthusiasm, was well equipped to lead the nation out of the Depression of the 1930s, but may not have fared well in getting his voice to cut across the fragmented hyper-partisan media landscape of the twenty-first century. A politician with Trump's bombastic and narcissistic persona would have been widely dismissed in the 1950s. Biden's empathy and relishing of the role of "Consoler-In-Chief" was good medicine for a nation suffering from a pandemic.

The second lesson is that effective officeholders must possess a wide range of skills. This lesson emerges from a review of the relatively more successful presidents: Roosevelt, Truman, Eisenhower, Kennedy, Obama, Biden, and to an extent, Clinton. Eisenhower is perhaps the best example of a president who possessed good, if not superb, skills in all areas of skill. Johnson and Reagan possessed impressive skills in one or more dimensions that worked to their advantage, but they also possessed limitations—Johnson suffered rhetorical failures and Reagan had difficulty with management and policy evaluations.

The third lesson is that while skills in all leadership areas are essential, those in the area of public leadership are especially important. These skills can contribute to policy development as well as to the ability of a president to sustain the public support necessary to function effectively in general and to shape specific policies. Roosevelt, Eisenhower, Kennedy, Reagan, Clinton, and Obama demonstrated the advantages of effective public leadership; Johnson, Carter, and George H. W. Bush dramatized the problems that can arise from weak skills. George W. Bush showed that strong public leadership skills in foreign policy do not automatically translate to domestic policy gains without the president's attention.

Where should the nation turn to find officeholders with the necessary qualities? Career paths provide some insights but no decisive patterns. The lack of pronounced patterns stems from two factors. First, personal

344 *Conclusion*

characteristics can make a major difference in the leadership styles of persons who have held similar offices. Key aspects of the leadership exerted by Johnson and Nixon, for example, flowed from distinctive aspects of their personalities and not how many years they had occupied various public offices. Second, the various learning experiences gained during a given career reduce potential career path differences. Of those presidents who had served in Congress, Lyndon Johnson learned to build coalitions as majority leader and Biden was adept at cutting deals and maintaining relationships. Truman, Kennedy, Nixon, George H. W. Bush, and Obama learned from their roles on Congressional committees, but they did not gain a broader perspective on legislative leadership. Johnson demonstrated the difficulties a legislator can encounter when having to deal with the national press rather than a friendlier state press, but Kennedy, who also served in Congress, was adroit at media relations.

The five governors who became president underscore the diversity of learning experiences that are gained in that role. Presidents Roosevelt (who served as governor of New York), Reagan (governor of California), and George W. Bush (governor of Texas) offer some support for Larry Sabato's conclusion that a governorship (although lacking a foreign policy dimension) is preferable to Congress as a training ground for presidents.[14] While they entered their governorships with some skills, Roosevelt, Reagan, and Bush learned aspects of public and legislative leadership in settings (large states) similar to that in Washington. Carter and Clinton, who served in much smaller states (Georgia and Arkansas) and dealt with part-time, one-party legislatures, had quite different learning experiences.

Yet, there are some relationships between career experiences and leadership style. First, administrative experiences are useful, especially if they have been extensive. Both Roosevelt (as governor) and Eisenhower (as Allied commander) had such experiences, whereas George H. W. Bush, who had filled many administrative roles during his brief time in various public offices, displayed no more than average administrative interests or skills as president. Second, presidents who once served as legislators, other than Johnson and Biden, have not been particularly noted for their legislative leadership skills. Perhaps legislators tend to develop a high degree of respect for congressional independence and thus are reluctant to employ strong-arm tactics. On balance, then, there seems little basis for assuming that a president who emerges from Congress will be above average in legislative leadership. Third, governors often have broader experience with public leadership than legislators and thus may be more likely to be effective presidents. They need to be quick studies when they arrive in Washington, but their range of experiences in the areas of administrative strategies, personnel selection, and legislative and public leadership—at least for those coming from larger states—more closely resembles presidential responsibilities than the experience gained by members of Congress. This is not to

Opportunity, Challenges, and Skill   345

say, however, that knowledge of how Washington works is not important for any presidential contender. Novices, including governors, often make avoidable mistakes because they lack that knowledge.

Strategic Choices

Modern presidents will continue to choose from a variety of strategies and tactics in their domestic policy making. Past performances suggest that it is possible for a president to use a fast-start strategy, but this strategy is more successful when a candidate is able to develop specific themes in an election campaign and then win by a considerable margin. First-year victories are achieved most easily when they involve policy initiatives carried over from the preceding administration and when at least aspects of existing policy ideas are included in the initial proposals. Both the public and political analysts should not place too much emphasis on the fast-start strategy, however. Despite all of the rhetoric about the presidential "honeymoon" and the "First Hundred Days," successful presidents will perceive new opportunities later in their first or second term as they arise.

Top-level negotiation is likely to be another popular strategy. Despite the problems that Bush encountered in 1990 and Obama in 2003–2004, this is a vehicle for avoiding the difficulties inherent in having to deal with multiple committees in Congress. Interest groups and rank-and-file members of Congress are not fond of this strategy, but it has considerable potential when large, complicated issues such as Social Security, Medicare, and health care are on the table. These issues will undoubtedly become more pressing in the future as the nation faces potential shortfalls in entitlement funding.

Presidents will continue to adopt and refine specific public leadership and administrative strategies. For example, they may on occasion "go public" prior to a major vote. Another important public leadership tool is the bully pulpit, whose importance in seeking to shape private behavior rather than simply seeking support for programs is somewhat under-recognized. As the Kennedy performance revealed, the bully pulpit also may help intensify general levels of public interest in political action. But this sort of moral suasion can also fail if the public is not confident in government performance, as evidenced by Carter's often unsuccessful pleas for energy conservation. Some have argued that the way to restore trust in government is for presidents to pay greater attention to implementation as a sort of managerial presidency.[15]

Presidents will increasingly adopt centrist strategies. Helping the "center to hold" on specific issues is likely to be a key strategy because of the ideological polarization that has emerged in Congress in recent years. More generally, presidents may act to posture themselves in the center, much as President Clinton did in 1995–1996. While seeking to define that center,

346 *Conclusion*

presidents may, like Franklin Roosevelt in 1935, also try to forge a coalition that will create a different center on major policy issues. Centrist roles will continue to be important vehicles for policy change as long as the president is not seen as a lightning rod by members of the other party.

Finally, we expect the trend toward administrative governance to continue. As opportunities for Congressional action are reduced by hyperpolarization, presidents will continue to look for ways to use executive authority to implement policy change (as Biden attempted with the issue of student loan forgiveness). Future evaluations of presidential effectiveness will need to increasingly focus on lasting presidential action in this realm, rather than merely the back-and-forth executive action reversals of the Trump and Biden years.

What, then, are the prospects for policy change? Regardless of the strategies they choose, future presidents will face formidable challenges. The job has become tougher, and budgetary pressures will surely intensify. Yet important strategies will still be available, and a president's strategic choices can make a difference. For those citizens desiring changes in domestic policy, it will be important not only to participate in the selection of presidents but also to engage in a "bottom-up strategy" of generating pressures that will both help and push presidents toward promoting new policy positions. Often, successes come only after initial failures and partial responses. The perfect need not be the enemy of the good, and as Obama insisted, securing some policies that can be later modified may be preferable to doing nothing. Indeed, in the future just as in the past, fundamental policy change will arise from actions already taken by members of Congress, innovative federal officials, state governments, specialists working on new policy approaches, and interest groups. While often messy and uncoordinated, these avenues do give citizens an opportunity to have their voices heard in the policymaking process. Presidents can fulfill crucial roles in this process as they exercise their leadership skills and make their strategic choices, but—like Roosevelt—often most effectively as facilitators rather than directors of policy change.

Notes

1 There are many examples, some notable ones include the C-SPAN Presidential Historians Survey (https://www.c-span.org/presidentsurvey2021/), The Siena College Presidential Experts Poll (https://scri.siena.edu/2022/06/22/american-presidents-greatest-and-worst/), and for a survey of political scientists, see Brandon Rottinghaus and Justin Vaughn, "Presidential Greatness & Political Science: Assessing the 2014 APSA Presidents & Executive Politics Section Presidential Greatness Survey," *PS: Political Science & Politics* 50, no. 3 (2017): 824–830. Surveys of the public on this topic have been conducted by Gallup, Quinnipiac, Morning Consult, Public Policy Polling, and others.

Opportunity, Challenges, and Skill 347

2 See Brandon Rottinghaus, Gregory Eady, and Justin Vaughn, "Presidential Greatness in a Polarized Era: Results from the Latest Presidential Greatness Survey," *PS: Political Science & Politics* 53, no. 3 (2020): 413–420; and Amnon Cavari, "Evaluating the President on Your Priorities: Issue Priorities, Policy Performance, and Presidential Approval, 1981–2016," *Presidential Studies Quarterly* 49, no. 4 (December 2019): 798–826.

3 John G. Geer, *From Tea Leaves to Public Opinion: A Theory of Democratic Leadership* (New York: Columbia University Press, 1996), 82–86.

4 Quoted in Samuel Kernell, *Going Public*, 3rd ed. (Washington, DC: CQ Press, 1997), 35.

5 Dick Morris, *Behind the Oval Office: Winning the Presidency in the Nineties* (New York: Random House, 1997).

6 Theda Skocpol, *Boomerang: Clinton's Health Security Effort and the Turn against Government in U.S. Politics* (New York: Norton, 1996), 116–118.

7 Michael A. Genovese, *The Watergate Crisis* (Westport, CT: Greenwood Press, 1999).

8 Michael A. Genovese, *The Presidential Dilemma: Leadership in the American System*, 3rd ed. (New Brunswick, NJ: Transaction, 2011).

9 Arthur M. Schlesinger Jr., "Rating the Presidents," *Political Science Quarterly* 112 (Summer 1997): 189; and Robert Murray and Tim Blessing, "The Presidential Performance Study: A Progress Report," *Journal of History* 70 (December 1983): 540–541.

10 Lance T. LeLoup and Steven A. Shull, *Congress and the President: The Policy Connection* (Belmont, CA: Wadsworth Publishing, 1993), 78.

11 Charles F. Faber and Richard B. Faber, *The American Presidents Ranked by Performance, 1789–2012* (Jefferson, NC: McFarland & Co., 2012).

12 Rottinghaus, Eady, and Vaughn, "Presidential Greatness in a Polarized Era."

13 For a widely read interpretation of these issues, see James David Barber, *The Presidential Character: Predicting Performance in the White House*, 4th ed. (Englewood Cliffs, NJ: Prentice Hall, 1992).

14 For an elaboration of the arguments in favor of recruiting governors rather than legislators, see Larry Sabato, *Goodbye to Good-time Charlie: The American Governorship Transformed* (Washington, DC: CQ Press, 1983), ch. 6.

15 Elaine C. Kamarck, *Why Presidents Fail and How They Can Succeed Again* (Washington, DC: Brookings, 2016).

Index

Adams, Sherman 133, 137, 140, 141
administrative strategies 5; Biden, Joe 299–300; Bush, George H. W. 263–264; Bush, George W. 97–98; Clinton, Bill 281–282; Eisenhower, Dwight David 138–139; Johnson, Lyndon B. 55; Kennedy, John F. 157–158; Nixon, Richard 223–225; Obama, Barack 178; Reagan, Ronald 75–76; Roosevelt, Franklin Delano 34–37; Truman, Harry S. 119–121; Trump, Donald 196–197
advisory process 5; Biden, Joe 298–299; Bush, George H. W. 261–263; Bush, George W. 96–97; Clinton, Bill 280–281; Eisenhower, Dwight David 136–138; Johnson, Lyndon B. 54–55; Kennedy, John F. 156; Nixon, Richard 222–223; Obama, Barack 177; Reagan, Ronald 74–75; Roosevelt, Franklin Delano 33–34; Truman, Harry S. 118–119
advisory structure 195
Affordable Care Act 185, 306
"agenda gap" 266
"Age of Limits" 221
Agnew, Spiro 225
Agricultural Adjustment Act (1933) 38, 43
Agricultural Adjustment Agency (AAA) 38, 41
agricultural economy 31
agricultural policy, decade-long deadlock on 38
Aid to Families with Dependent Children (AFDC) program 41, 84, 228, 289
Alabama National Guard 62

Alaskan National Wildlife Refuge (ANWR) 104
Albert, Carl 59
Allied Expeditionary Force 132
Ambrose, Stephen 132, 147, 222
America COMPETES Act 305
"America First" approach 194
American Civil Liberties Union 258
American Families Plan 302, 305
American Jobs Plan 302, 303, 305
American Medical Association (AMA) 61, 126, 229
American Recovery and Reinvestment Act (ARRA, 2009) 180–181, 185, 332
American Rescue Plan Act (2021) 302–303
American Revolution 72
Americans with Disabilities Act (ADA) 259, 266, 268–269, 271
AmeriCorps 286
Anderson, John 71
Anderson, Patrick 119
Area Redevelopment Act 166
Armey, Dick 288
Arnold, Joseph L. 42
ARRA see American Recovery and Reinvestment Act (ARRA)
Ash, Arthur L. 223
Ashcroft, John 97
Atomic Energy Act (1954) 142–143
Atomic Energy Commission (AEC) 143
Aviation and Transportation Security Act 102

Baker, Howard 71, 75, 79
Baker, James 75, 77, 81, 261, 262
balanced budget agreement 290

350   *Index*

bank failures 31
Banking Act 43, 318
Barr, Joseph 227
Barr, William 196–197
Baucus, Max 268
"Beer Diplomacy" 174
Bell, David 156
Benson, Ezra Taft 137, 139–140
Bentsen, Lloyd 280, 284
Biden, Joe 8, 15, 20, 173, 177, 182, 202, 294, 317, 318, 321, 322, 330, 331, 343, 346; assessment 307–308; career path 295–296; challenges and opportunities 297–298; and Congress 307; leadership style 298–302; legislative enactments 302–307; low-opportunity presidents 338–340; manner of man 296; personal characteristics 294–297; policy views 297
Bipartisan Safer Communities Act 307
Blough, Roger 157
Boehner, John 13, 184
Boettke, Peter J. 76
Boggs, J. Caleb 295
Bond, Jon 64
Bork, Robert 86
bottom-up strategy 346
Bouvier, Jacqueline Lee 151
Bowie, Robert 133
Bowles, Erskine 281
Brady, Nicholas 261, 266
Brock III, William 225
Brodie, Fawn 220
Brown, Edmund "Pat" 218
Brown, Scott 182
Brownell, Herbert 136–138, 140, 144, 147
Brown-Jackson, Ketanji 308
Brown v. Board of Education 145
BTU tax 285
Buchanan, Pat 263
budget deficits 14–15
Build Back Better agenda 302, 303, 305, 308
Bundy, McGeorge 156
Burger, Warren 223
Burns, Arthur 137, 222
Burns, James MacGregor 30
Bush, George H. W. 2, 15, 20, 71, 256, 279, 282, 286, 321, 322, 329–333, 343, 344; assessment 271–272;
career path 257–258; challenges and opportunities 260–261; and Congress 270–271; leadership style 261–266; legislative enactments 266–271; low-opportunity presidents 338–340; manner of man 258–259; personal characteristics 256–260; policy views 259–260
Bush, George W. 4, 8, 14–16, 90–91, 170, 175, 184, 194, 318, 321, 322, 329–333, 343, 344; assessment 105–106; career path 92–93; challenges and opportunities 95; and Congress 103–105; high-opportunity presidents 333–336; leadership style 95–99; legislative enactments 99–105; manner of man 93–94; personal characteristics 91–95; policy views 94–95
Bush, Prescott 256
"Bush tax cuts" 101
Byrd, Harry 59, 61
Byrd, Harry, Jr. 159

Caddell, Pat 329
Califano, Joseph 51, 241, 242, 250
Campagne, Anthony 240
campaign finance reform 288
Campbell, Colin 75
Cannon, Lou 71
capital gains tax 259, 265
Card, Andrew 97
CARES Act 302
Carswell, G. Harrold 224
Carter, Jimmy 2, 4, 5, 17, 24n52, 71, 73, 81, 86, 232, 237, 257, 271, 277, 284, 287, 323, 329–333, 343–345; assessment 252–253; career path 237–238; challenges and opportunities 239–240; and Congress 251–252; leadership style 240–245; legislative enactments 245–252; low-opportunity presidents 338–340; manner of man 238; personal characteristics 237–239; policy views 239
Carter, Rosalynn 241
Carter Glass (D-VA) 39
Cassidy, Bill 303
Castro, Fidel 154
Cavazos, Lauro 261
Central Intelligence Agency 245

CETA *see* Comprehensive Employment Training Act (CETA)
challenges and opportunities 8; Biden, Joe 297–298; Bush, George H. W. 260–261; Bush, George W. 95; Carter, Jimmy 239–240; Clinton, Bill 278–280; declining opportunities 16; economic conditions and budget deficits 14–15; Eisenhower, Dwight David 135–136; foreign policy influences 15; Johnson, Lyndon B. 52–53; Kennedy, John F. 154–155; legislative setting 10, 13; Nixon, Richard 220–221; Obama, Barack 175–176; promising issues 14; public mood 8–9, 9; public support 10, **11–12**; Reagan, Ronald 73–74; Roosevelt, Franklin Delano 30–33; second term 15; Truman, Harry S. 116–118; Trump, Donald 193–194
Cheney, Dick 93, 96, 97, 100, 105, 177, 323
Chervinsky, Lindsay 299
child tax credit 306
CHIPS and Science Act (2022) 304–305
Christians 174
Churchill, Winston 155
Civilian Conservation Corps 35, 286
civil rights 119–120, 144–145, 158, 164–165, 230, 270; administrative action on 120; progress on 128; and race 134
Civil Rights Act 58–65, 145, 259, 268
civil rights bill 60
civil rights groups 145
civil rights legislation 83–84
Civil Service Commission 120
civil service reform 243
Civil War 32
Clay, Lucius 136
Clean Air Act 161, 248, 264, 267, 339
Clean Air Act Amendments 230, 266, 270, 271
Clean Water Act 248
Clear Skies initiative 104
Cleveland, Grover 31–32, 239
Clifford, Clark 118–119, 121, 122, 125, 156
Clinton, Bill 2, 9, 13, 14, 20, 98, 101, 103, 117, 126, 182, 256, 274, 321, 322, 329–332, 341, 343, 345; assessment 291–292; career path 275–276; challenges and opportunities 278–280; and Congress 290–291; first-year successes and failures 284–286; leadership style 280–284; legislative enactments 284–291; low-opportunity presidents 338–340; manner of man 276–278; mounting difficulties (1994) 286–288; 1995-1996 288–290; 1997 balanced budget agreement 290; personal characteristics 274–278; policy views 278
Clinton, Hillary Rodham 7, 173, 190, 193, 201, 281, 287, 295
Clinton, Roger 275
coattails 10, 13
Cohen, Wilbur 162
Cohn, Gary 199
Cold War 260
Collins, Susan 180, 303
Committee on Economic Security (CES) 41
Community Action Programs 58, 63
compassionate conservatism 99, 103
Comprehensive Employment Training Act (CETA) 81, 249
comprehensive policy approach 245
Congress 2, 3, 5, 6, 32, 37, 341–342; Biden, Joe and 307; Bush, George H. W. and 270–271; Bush, George W. and 103–105; Carter, Jimmy and 251–252; Clinton, Bill and 290–291; conservative members of 59; Democratic strength in 53; Eisenhower, Dwight David and 145–146; Johnson, Lyndon B. and 64; Kennedy, John F. and 165; Nixon, Richard and 230–231; Obama, Barack and 183–185; power relationships in 3; presidential relationships with 6; Reagan, Ronald and 84–85; Roosevelt, Franklin Delano and 43; strategies dealing with 43; Truman, Harry S. and 127; Trump, Donald and 202
Congressional Budget Office (CBO) 103, 250, 269
congressional leadership 6–8, 13; Biden, Joe 301–302; Bush, George H. W. 265–266; Bush, George

352 *Index*

W. 99; Clinton, Bill 283–284; Eisenhower, Dwight David 140–141; Johnson, Lyndon B. 57; Kennedy, John F. 159–160; Nixon, Richard 225–226; Obama, Barack 179–180; Reagan, Ronald 77–78; Truman, Harry S. 122; Trump, Donald 198–199
congressional relations 283
Congressional Responsibility Act 288
Connelly, Matthew 118
Connor, Eugene "Bull" 164
conservatism 253n10
Consumer Product Safety Commission 230
Continental Can Company 136
"Contract with America" 288
Coolidge, Calvin 32, 323
Corker, Rob 199
Coronavirus Aid, Relief, and Economic Security Act (CARES) 200
Coronavirus Preparedness and Response Supplemental Appropriations Act 200
cost of living adjustments (COLAs) 82, 83, 229
COVID-19 Hate Crimes Act 307
COVID-19 pandemic 8, 9, 294, 297, 300, 301, 304, 308; response and relief 200
Craft, Kelly 201
Craig, Barbara 243
credibility gap 56
creeping socialism 134
crime legislation 227
"crisis of confidence" 247
Cruikshank, Nelson 61
Cuban missile crisis (1962) 150, 154, 157
Curtis, Carl 144

DACA program *see* Deferred Action for Childhood Arrivals (DACA) program
Daley, Richard M. 172
Darman, Richard 262, 269
Dawson, Donald 118
Deaver, Michael 74, 77
"debt ceiling showdown" 184
decision-making approach 3, 5; Biden, Joe 298–299; Bush, George H. W. 261–263; Bush, George W. 96–97;

Clinton, Bill 280–281; Eisenhower, Dwight David 136–138; Johnson, Lyndon B. 54–55; Kennedy, John F. 156; Nixon, Richard 222–223; Obama, Barack 177; public opinion polls in 329; Reagan, Ronald 74–75; Roosevelt, Franklin Delano 33–34; Truman, Harry S. 118–119; Trump, Donald 195
Defense of Marriage Act 174
Deferred Action for Childhood Arrivals (DACA) program 184, 203–204
"deficit hawks" 73
deficit-reduction package 81, 83, 291
Democratic Convention (2004) 114, 172
Democratic Leadership Council 278
Democratic National Committee 231
Democratic National Convention 173, 256
Democratic Party 28, 35, 116, 133, 134, 161, 276, 278, 297
Democrats 1, 79, 80, 98, 101, 102, 144, 155, 170, 175, 180, 200, 202, 226, 229, 232, 238, 274, 290, 298, 302–303, 307, 329–332, 342; permanent dominance 138
Dent, Harry 222
Department of Homeland Security (DHS) 102
Depression 28, 32, 37, 40, 154, 343
"detente" 221
Dewey, Thomas 127
Diem, Ngo Dinh 154
Dillon, Douglas 156, 162
Dirksen, Everett 60, 64, 159
Disraeli, Benjamin 222
Distinguished Service Medal 132
"Dodd-Frank" 183
Dodge, Joseph 137
Dole, Robert 71, 285, 290
domestic agenda 1
domestic issues 133
domestic policy 77, 137, 140, 231, 262, 279, 334, 341, 342
domestic spending 74
The Donald J. Trump Foundation 191
Donovan, Robert 135
"Don't Ask Don't Tell" rule 183, 185
Douglas, Helen Gahagan 218
Douglas, Paul 161

DREAM Act 178
Drew, Elizabeth 281
Duberstein, Kenneth 77
Dukakis, Michael 258
Duke, David 270

"earmark reform" 342
economic conditions 14–15
economic crisis (2008) 91, 176, 177
economic deregulation 249–250, 252
economic growth 31, 52, 53
Economic Growth and Tax Relief
  Reconciliation Act (2001) 99–101
Economic Opportunity Act
  (1964) 58–59
economic planning 122–124
economic recession (1991-1992) 279
Economic Recovery Tax Act 78
Economy Act (1933) 37, 37–38
Edelman, Peter 292
Edwards III, George 6, 43, 283
effective presidents, search for
  343–345
Ehrlichman, John 219, 222, 225
Eisenhower, Dwight 2, 4, 20, 54,
  69, 115, 117, 128, 131, 152, 158,
  159, 198, 218, 220, 329–332,
  341–344; assessment 146–147;
  career path 132–133; challenges
  and opportunities 135–136; and
  Congress 145–146; leadership style
  136–141; legislative enactments
  141–146; manner of man 133–134;
  moderate-opportunity presidents
  336–338; personal characteristics
  131–135; policy views 134–135
Eizenstat, Stuart 242
election campaigns 2, 7
electoral politics 304
Ellsberg, Daniel 231
Elsey, George 118, 128
Emergency Banking Act 39
Emmanuel, Rahm 175, 181
Employment Act (1946) 123
employment-related policies and
  environment 160–161
energy bill 246
energy legislation 104
energy policies 240, 245–247
environmental and consumer
  protection policies 229–230
environmental legislation 321

environmental policies 247–248
Environmental Protection Agency 225
Equal Employment Opportunities
  Commission 230
expectation–resource gap 1

Fair Employment Board 120
Fair Employment Practices
  Committee 120
Fair Labor Standards Act 40
faith-based initiative legislation 99,
  101, 103
Fallows, James 238
Families First Coronavirus Response
  Act 200
Family and Medical Leave Act 285,
  290, 291
Family Assistance Plan (FAP) 222,
  228, 331
federal aid to education program
  61–62, 65, 160
Federal Communications Commission
  (FCC) 42
Federal Deposit Insurance
  Corporation 39
Federal Emergency Relief
  Administration (FERA) 35
Federal Employment Practices
  Commission (FEPC) 44, 120, 138,
  263, 264
Federal Housing Administration
  (FHA) 163
federalism initiatives 84
Federal Reserve Board 39
federal tax system 81–82
Federal Trade Commission 157,
  253n10
Feldman, Mike 156
financial institutions, regulation of
  38–40, 44
Finch, Robert 221
"First Hundred Days" session 37, 37,
  39, 40, 318, 345
First Step Act 200–201
Fishel, Jeff 241
Fitzwater, Marlin 264
Fleisher, Richard 64
Ford, Gerald 21, 71, 231–232, 238,
  239, 247, 248
foreign policy 31, 155, 223, 266, 279,
  330; challenges 118; demands of 15
Francis, Les 243

354 *Index*

Franken, Al 180
Freeman, Orville 156
Friedersdorf, Max 77
Frohnmayer, John 263
Fulbright, William 117, 275
"full speed ahead" approach 4

"Gang of Eight" 184
Gardner, John 62
Garment, Leonard 222
Garner, John 115
Garn-St. Germain Depository
  Institutions Act (1982) 250
"gas guzzler" tax 246
Geithner, Timothy 183
general revenue sharing 227–228
Gergen, David 283
GI Bill of Rights (1944) 42
Giglio, James 152
Gingrich, Newt 13, 16, 277, 288
"go it alone" strategy 196
Goldberg, Arthur 157
Goldwater, Barry 70, 218
Gonzales, Alberto 97
"good government" reform 156
Goodwin, Richard 156
Gore, Albert 5, 14, 90, 93, 125, 281
Gosnell, Harold 114
Gramm-Rudman Act 269
Grant, Ulysses S. 131
Great Depression 174, 185
Great Recession 170, 175, 185
Great Society programs 52, 53, 56, 58,
  64, 72
Green, Fitzhugh 257
Greene, John 223
Greenspan, Alan 100, 291
Greenstein, Fred 4, 72, 131
gross domestic product (GDP) 85,
  86, 180
gross national product (GNP) 117
Gulf War 260, 265, 329

Hagerty, James 139
Hague, Gabriel 137
Haldeman, H. R. "Bob" 219, 222,
  223, 225, 226, 228, 230
Halleck, Charles 140
Hargrove, Erwin 252
Harlow, Bryce 220, 225
Harris, Richard 264
Hart, Gary 102

Harvard Crimson 28
Hastert, Dennis 102, 103
"Hastert Rule" 13
Haynesworth, Clement 224
Health, Education, and Welfare
  (HEW) 221, 222
health care: costs of 251; entitlement
  programs 288–289; reforms 182,
  287; welfare, Social Security and
  228–229, 250–251
health care reforms 279
health maintenance organizations
  (HMOs) 229
health policy 126–127
Health Security Act 287, 288, 292
Heller, Walter 58, 156, 162
Highway Beautification Act 63
Hill, Anita 264
Hill-Burton Act 126
Holmes, Oliver Wendell 30
Home Affordable Modification
  Program 185
Homeland Security Act (2002)
  102–103
Hoover, Herbert 28, 29, 32, 50, 138
Hoover Commission reforms 332
hostage crisis 240
House Bill 306
House of Representatives 1
housing desegregation policies 158
housing policy 126, 163–164
Hughes, Karen 93, 97
Hull, Cordell 33–34
Humphrey, George 137, 142
Humphrey, Hubert 60, 121
hyper-partisanship 16, 205

Ickes, Harold 34
Immigration and Nationality Act
  (1965) 66
Immigration Reform and Control Act
  (1986) 85
"imperial presidency" 2, 237, 240
"inclusive coalition" 43
individual retirement accounts
  (IRAs) 249
inflation 298, 301
Inflation Reduction Act (2022)
  305–307
infrastructure bill 305–306
Infrastructure Investment and Jobs Act
  (2021) 303–304

integrative complexity 178
Internal Revenue Service 231
interpersonal relationships 94
Interstate Commerce Commission 249
interstate highway system 143–144
IRAs *see* individual retirement accounts (IRAs)
Islamic State 194

Jacobs, Jill 295
Jayapal, Pramila 303
Jean-Pierre, Karine 301
Jeffords, Jim 99, 100, 322
Job Corps program 58
Jobs and Growth Tax Relief Reconciliation Act (2003) 101
Johnson, Lyndon B. 8, 10, 15, 16, 24n50, 49, 140–141, 144, 145, 152, 155, 220, 318, 322, 329, 331–333, 342–344; assessment 65–66; career path 50–51; challenges and opportunities 52–53; Civil Rights Act 59–60; and Congress 64; Economic Opportunity Act (1964) 58–59; 91th Congress (1965-1967) 60–63; environmental measures and Model Cities 62–63; federal aid to education 61–62; high-opportunity presidents 333–336; leadership style 54–57; legislative enactments 57–64; manner of man 51–52; Medicare 61; 92th Congress 63–64; personal characteristics 49–52; policy views 52; Tax-Cut Legislation 59; Voting Rights Act 62
Joint Congressional Committee on Atomic Energy (JCCAE) 143
Joint Training Partnership Act (JTPA) 81
Jordan, Hamilton 241, 244
juvenile justice system 93

Kefauver, Estes 152
Kempton, Murray 131
Kennedy, Edward 251, 258
Kennedy, John F. 2, 3, 8, 13, 20, 24n50, 51, 52, 56, 58, 59, 135, 139, 150–151, 218, 229, 258, 277, 280, 286, 318, 323, 330–332, 341–345; assessment 165–166; career path 151–152; challenges and opportunities 154–155; and Congress 165; leadership style 155–160; legislative enactments 160–165; manner of man 152–153; moderate-opportunity presidents 336–338; personal characteristics 151–154; policy views 153–154; *Profiles in Courage* 153
Kennedy, Joseph P. 40, 151
Kennedy, Robert 164
Kennedy, Ted 101, 103, 175, 180, 182
Kerbel, Matthew 6
Kerner Commission on Civil Disorders 54
Keyes, Alan 172
Keynes, John Maynard 32
Khrushchev, Nikita 154, 218
King, Martin Luther, Jr. 62, 64, 84, 164
Kingdon, John 14
Kirkpatrick, Jeane 74
Klain, Ron 298–299, 301
Knowland, William 140
Knutson, Harold 125
Kolb, Charles 259, 265
Korean War 119, 135, 142
Kristol, William 288
Krock, Arthur 121
K-12 education system 95, 101, 186
Kucinich, Dennis 182
Kushner, Jared 195, 201

labor policies 40
LaGuardia, Fiorello 34
landmark deficit-reduction legislation 269–270
landmark enactments 318, **319– 320**, 322
landmark housing legislation 126
landmark legislation 322, 323, 342
Larson, Arthur 134, 136
leadership styles 2–4; administrative strategies 5; advisory processes and decision-making approaches 5; Biden, Joe 298–302; Bush, George H. W. 261–266; Bush, George W. 95–99; Carter, Jimmy 240–245; Clinton, Bill 280–284; comparison of 323, **324–328**, 329–333; congressional leadership 6–8; differences in 3; Eisenhower, Dwight David 136–141; Johnson, Lyndon B. 54–57; Kennedy, John F.

155–160; Nixon, Richard 221–226; Obama, Barack 176–180; public leadership 6; Reagan, Ronald 74–78; Roosevelt, Franklin Delano 33–34; Truman, Harry S. 118–122; Trump, Donald 194–199

legislative enactments: Biden, Joe 302–307; Bush, George H. W. 266–271; Carter, Jimmy 245–252; Clinton, Bill 284–291; Eisenhower, Dwight David 141–146; Johnson, Lyndon B. 57–64; Kennedy, John F. 160–165; Nixon, Richard 226–231; Obama, Barack 180–185; Reagan, Ronald 78–83; Roosevelt, Franklin Delano **37**, 37–38; Truman, Harry S. 122–127; Trump, Donald 199–202

legislative leadership 57

legislative setting 10, 13

LeLoup, Lance 342

liberalism 30, 253n10

Lieberman, Joe 102

Lighthizer, Robert 201

Lilly Ledbetter Fair Pay Act 175, 180, 184–185

Lincoln, A. 30, 150, 206

Lippmann, Walter 29, 41

Lodge, Henry Cabot 151–152

Long, Russell 246, 250

Lott, Trent 100, 290

Lujan, Manuel, Jr. 261

MacArthur, Douglas 132, 136, 140

MacGregor, Clark 225

Magaziner, Ira 287

"managed competition" 287

Manchin, Joe 15, 299, 301, 305, 306

Mansfield, Mike 155, 295

Marshall, Burke 165

Marshall, Thurgood 128, 263

Marshall Plan (1949) 118

Martin, Joseph 140

Martin, William McChesney 156

Mayhew, David 10–11, 284, 322

McCain, John 170, 173, 198

McCarthy, Eugene 49, 66

McCarthy, Joseph 117, 135, 139

McCarthy, Kevin 298, 301, 307

McClure, Fred 265

McConnell, Mitch 175, 177, 186, 202, 298, 303

"The McConnell Whisperer" 296

McCormack, John 13, 155

McCoy, Donald R. 115

McLarty, Mack 281, 285

McNamara, Robert 156

McPherson, Henry 54

Meadows, Mark 200

Meany, George 249

Medicaid 84, 181, 182, 228, 288, 289

Medicare 61, 65, 82–83, 85, 95, 99, 154, 159, 160, 269, 285, 288–290, 301; reforms 104, 334

Medicare Modernization Act (Medicare Part D) (2003) 103

Meese, Edwin 74

Mellon, Andrew 125

Mervin, David 270

Milkis, Sidney 264

Mills, Wilbur 61

Miroff, Bruce 29, 45

Mississippi Council of Federated Organizations 166

Mitchell, George 267

Model Cities legislation 60, 63

"Modern Republicanism" 138

Moley, Raymond 36

Mondale, Walter 71, 258

Moore, Frank 244

Morgenthau, Henry 34

Morris, Dick 281, 282, 290

Mosbacher, Robert 261

Moses, Robert 166

"motor voter" bill 286

Moyers, Bill 54

Moynihan, Daniel Patrick 222

Muir, William 77

"multiplier" effect 33

Murphy, Charles 118

Murphy, Emily 299

Muskie, Edmund 62, 230–232

Muslims 194

NAFTA *see* North American Free Trade Agreement (NAFTA)

National Association for the Advancement of Colored People (NAACP) 120, 121, 128

National Cancer Institute 229

National Education Association 242

National Endowment for the Arts (NEA) 263

National Energy Policy Development group 105
National Environmental Protection Act (1969) 229
National Housing Act (1934) 42
National Industrial Recovery Act (NIRA) 40, 41, 43
National Labor Relations Act 40, 43
National Labor Relations Board (NLRB) 44, 75, 124, 125
National Partnership for Reinventing Government 281
National Performance Review 281
National Social Welfare Assembly 162
National Youth Administration 34, 50
NATO see North Atlantic Treaty Organization (NATO)
Nelson, Ben 180, 182
Neustadt, Richard 3–4, 159
New Deal 118, 119, 127, 302, 307, 332; agenda 57; domestic policy 43–45; legislation 336; programs 133, 135, 136, 147
"New Democrat" 282, 286
"New Frontier" 154
New York Stock Exchange 39
Niles, David 118
9/11 terrorist attacks 8, 9, 16, 91, 95, 96, 98, 102, 104, 105, 183, 329, 334
NIRA see National Industrial Recovery Act (NIRA)
Nixon, Richard 8, 20, 21, 24n50, 70, 106, 137, 140, 143, 152, 217, 238, 247, 257, 283, 329, 330, 331, 332, 344; assessment 232–234; career path 218–219; challenges and opportunities 220–221; and Congress 230–231; leadership style 221–226; legislative enactments 226–231; low-opportunity presidents 338–340; manner of man 219–220; personal characteristics 217–220; policy views 220; Watergate and the Ford interregnum 231–232
NLRB see National Labor Relations Board (NLRB)
No Child Left Behind policy 101, 186
Noonan, Peggy 71
Norris, George 42

North American Free Trade Agreement (NAFTA) 201, 283, 284, 287
North Atlantic Treaty Organization (NATO) 118, 133

Obama, Barack 1, 2, 5, 8, 9, 14, 20, 117, 170–171, 191–193, 294, 295, 318, 321–323, 329–332, 341–346; assessment 185–186; career path 172–173; challenges and opportunities 175–176; and Congress 183–185; leadership style 176–180; legislative enactments 180–185; manner of man 173–174; moderate-opportunity presidents 336–338; personal characteristics 171–174; policy views 174
Obamacare 194, 198, 199, 202, 229
O'Brien, David 243
O'Brien, Lawrence 156, 159
Occupational Safety and Health Administration 229–230
Occupy Movement 179
O'Donnell, Kenneth 156
Office of Economic Opportunity (OEO) 223
Office of Management and Budget (OMB) 223, 233, 262
Office of Planning and Evaluation (OPE) 74
Office of Public Liaison 246
Omnibus Budget Reconciliation Act (OBRA) 78, 79, 269
Omnibus Crime Control Act (1970) 227
Omnibus Tax Act 142
O'Neill, Paul 97, 98
O'Neill, Thomas "Tip" 73, 78, 82, 83
O'Neill, Tip 244, 247
Open Housing Act (1968) 65
"Operation Warp Speed" initiative 204
optimism 71, 145
Organization of Petroleum Exporting Countries (OPEC) 240
Organized Crime Control Act (1970) 227
Orzag, Peter 181
ownership society 94, 99, 101

PACT Act 307
Palin, Sarah 173

358　*Index*

Palmer, Alice 172
Panetta, Leon 283, 287
Paper, Lewis 165
Paris Climate Accord 186, 300
Paris peace accord 234
party-based differences 331
"patient education" approach 141
Patient Protection and Affordable Care Act (PPACA, 2010) 181–182
Patients and Communities Act 201
"pay as you go" (PAYGO) provisions 269
Paycheck Protection Program 200, 303
PAYGO rule (2010) 200
PCCR *see* Presidential Commission on Civil Rights (PCCR)
Peace Corps 159, 286
Peek, George 35
Pell, Claiborne 159
Perkins, Frances 29, 34
Perot, Ross 256
Persian Gulf War (1990-1991) 15
Persons, Wilton 137
Pertschuk, Michael 253n10
Peterson, Mark 64, 145–146, 230, 231
"Philadelphia Plan" 224
"Plumbers" 231
policy challenges 8
policy czars 177
policy legacy 165
political opportunity 8
politics of transgression 205
Porter, Rob 195
Portman, Rob 303
post-Watergate reforms 239
Powell, Adam Clayton 160
Powell, Colin 96–97
presidential campaigns 90, 154, 278
Presidential Commission on Civil Rights (PCCR) 120, 121
presidential commissions 54
presidential leadership 3, 4, 6, 87, 343; Franklin Delano Roosevelt (1901-1909) 27, 28
Presidential Power 3
presidential rankings, on skill/opportunity scale 341, **341**
presidents: categorizing and comparing 16, **17–20**, 20–21; challenges and opportunities 8–16; limitations of skills 22n29; public role of 6
price controls 122–124

Professional Air Traffic Controllers Organization 75
Profiles in Courage (Kennedy) 153
property tax protest 253n10
Psaki, Jen 301, 306
Public Company Accounting Oversight Board 104
public frustration 8
public hostility 39
public leadership 6, 43; Biden, Joe 300–301; Bush, George H. W. 264–265; Bush, George W. 98; Clinton, Bill 282–283; Eisenhower, Dwight David 139–140; Johnson, Lyndon B. 55–57; Kennedy, John F. 158–159; Nixon, Richard 225; Obama, Barack 178–179; Reagan, Ronald 76–77; strategies 331; Truman, Harry S. 121–122; Trump, Donald 197–198
public mood 8–9, 9
public policy 3
public role, of president 6
public speaking 56
public support 10, **11–12**, 60
public trust 9, 9
Public Works Administration 35

"Quadriad" 156
Quayle, Dan 264
Quirk, Paul 270

Rayburn, Sam 13, 50, 113, 140–141, 155, 159
Reagan, Jack 69
Reagan, Ronald 2, 6, 10, 13, 16, 24n50, 69, 94, 106, 238, 253n10, 259, 261, 262, 264–266, 271, 280, 318, 322, 323, 329–331, 343, 344; assessment 85–87; career path 70–71; challenges and opportunities 73–74; and Congress 84–85; high-opportunity presidents 333–336; leadership style 74–78; legislative enactments 78–83; manner of man 71–72; 1981 (big year) 78–80; personal characteristics 69–73; policy responses (1982-1989) 80–83; policy views 72–73; regulatory policy changes 83–85
recession, responses to 80–81
reconciliation bill 303
Reeves, Richard 153

Index   359

Regan, Donald 74, 75
Reich, Robert 280, 290
Reischauer, Robert 269, 271
Renshon, Stanley 278
Republican Party 64, 70, 103, 133–135, 137, 138, 170, 173, 203, 220, 270, 322
Republicans 7, 10, 14, 32, 50, 60, 79, 83, 95, 98–105, 116, 117, 119, 123–125, 127, 136, 142, 162, 170, 175, 178–184, 186, 194, 200, 203, 220, 226, 274, 278, 285, 287, 288, 290, 291, 297–303, 307, 308, 329, 332, 340
Reserve Officers' Training Corps (ROTC) 276
Revolutionary War 5
Ribicoff, Abraham 161
Rice, Condoleezza 97
Richards, Ann 93, 256
Richardson, Elliot 219
Richardson, Elmo 145
Rockefeller, Nelson 228
Roe v. Wade 224, 243, 298
Rogers, Will 30–31
Romasco, Alberto 43
Romney, Mitt 303
Roosevelt, Eleanor 34, 113
Roosevelt, Franklin 2–4, 10, 16, 27, 50, 52, 64, 74, 113–116, 127, 144, 155, 159, 252, 280, 318, 323, 329–333, 341–346; administrative strategies 34–37; advisory process and decision-making approach 33–34; assessment 43–45; career path 28–29; and Congress 43; congressional leadership 36–37; the court 33; economic problems and solutions 32–33; four immediate challenges 31–32; high-opportunity presidents 333–336; leadership style 33–34; legislative enactments 37, 37–38; manner of man 29–30; personal characteristics 27–30; policy views 30; public leadership 35–36; regulation of financial institutions 38–40; relief, welfare, and Social Security 40–43
Roosevelt, Theodore 2, 221, 261
Ross, Charles 118
Rostenkowski, Daniel 265, 267
ROTC see Reserve Officers' Training Corps

Rove, Karl 93, 97
Rozell, Mark 244
Rubin, Robert 290
Rudman, Warren 102
Rumsfeld, Donald 223
Rush, Bobby 172
Russell, Richard 50, 60
Ryan, Jack 172

Saddam Hussein 260
Sanders, Bernie 193–194
Sanders, Elizabeth 246
Sandy Hook massacre 178
Schlesinger, Arthur, Jr. 8, 30, 36, 155, 156, 239, 341
Schlesinger, James 241
Schumer, Chuck 301, 304, 306
Scott, Hugh 227
"Second New Deal" 115–116
second term 15
Securities Act (1933) 39
Securities and Exchange Commission (SEC) 39, 92, 151
Securities Exchange Act 39
self-deprecation 71
Senate bill 102, 104
Senate Budget Committee 100
Senate Finance Committee 163
Shalala, Donna 280
Sheehy, Gail 259
short-term political purposes 5
Shull, Steven 342
Shultz, Moynihan 222
Sidey, Hugh 258
Sinclair, Barbara 271
Sinema, Kirsten 305, 306
skepticism 131
Skinner, Samuel 262, 263
Snowe, Olympia 180
Social Security Act 41, 44
Social Security Administration 127, 144, 250
Social Security programs 73–75, 82–83, 85, 94, 95, 144, 233, 288, 301, 337; changes in 126–127; health and 126; health policy and 126–127; public's fondness for 127; reforms 91, 118, 126; welfare and health 161–162, 228–229, 250–251
Sorensen, Theodore 156
Soviet Union 143, 154, 221
Specter, Arlen 175, 180

360   *Index*

Sputnik 136
State of the Union 58, 81, 102, 141, 262, 283, 290, 301
State Unemployment Relief Act 28
Steelman, John 119, 122
Stevenson, Adlai 135, 152
Stockman, David 73, 78–80, 82
strategic choices 2
Stuckey, Mary 76, 159
Sullivan, Louis 261
Summerfield, Arthur 137
Sununu, John 97, 261–262, 265
Supplementary Security Income (SSI) 228
Supreme Court 33, 40, 95, 119, 134, 135, 138, 140, 144, 202, 224, 263, 270, 298, 300

Taft, Robert 124, 125, 133, 140–142
Taft-Hartley Act 50, 124–125, 128, 141, 321
Taiwan Semiconductor Manufacturing Company 305
Task Force on National Health Reform 287
tax-cut legislation 59, 80
tax cuts 94, 99–101, 141–142, 174, 175, 183, 184, 199–200, 285, 331, 334–338; measures 72–73, 79
Tax Cuts and Jobs Act (TCJA) (2017) 199–200
Tax Equity and Fiscal Responsibility Act 81
tax policies 125, 162–163
tax reform 162, 227
Tax Reform Act (1986) 81
tax/taxation: and budgetary issues, Dwight David Eisenhower 140–142; jobs, and minimum wage 248–249
Taylor, Zachary 131
TEA Party movement 170, 175, 176, 178–180, 184, 185
Tennessee Valley Authority (TVA) 42, 134, 147
terrorism 194
Thomas, Clarence 263, 270
Thornburgh, Richard 268
"a thousand points of light," voluntarism initiative 265
Thurmond, Strom 222
Timmons, William 225, 226

Toomey, Pat 199
Tower, John 265
Trans-Pacific Partnership (TPP) 201, 203
Transportation Security Administration (TSA) 102
Troubled Asset Relief Program (TARP) 183, 185
Truman, Harry 8, 17, 43, 54, 113, 136, 142, 143, 280, 323, 332, 341–344; assessment 127–128; career path 114; challenges and opportunities 116–118; and Congress 127; leadership style 118–122; legislative enactments 122–127; manner of man 115; moderate-opportunity presidents 336–338; personal characteristics 113–116; policy views 115–116
Truman Doctrine (1947) 117
Trump, Donald 1, 4–6, 20, 186, 190, 294–297, 299, 300, 302, 317, 322, 323, 329–332, 340–343, 346; administrative governance 203–205; assessment 205–206; career path 191–192; challenges and opportunities 193–194; and Congress 202; impeachments 202–203; leadership style 194–199; legislative enactments 199–202; manner of man 192; moderate-opportunity presidents 336–338; personal characteristics 190–193; policy views 192–193; *Trump: The Art of the* Deal 198
The Trump Organization 190
Trump: The Art of the Deal (Trump) 198
"trusee" leadership 4
Tugwell, Rexford 35
TVA *see* Tennessee Valley Authority (TVA)

Udall, Morris 248
Ullman, Al 250
"Ultra-MAGA" Republicans 300
uncertainty 3
uncivil war 298
unemployment 31, 80, 160
United States Innovation and Competition Act (USICA) 304, 305
Uslaner, Eric 240

Vance, Cyrus 241
Veneman, John 221
veterans' benefits, Franklin Delano Roosevelt **37**, 37–38
Veterans' Emergency Housing Act (1946) 126
Vietnam War 15, 56, 65, 221, 232, 274, 276, 277
Volcker, Paul 183
"Volcker Rule" 183
Volunteers in Service to America (VISTA) 58
"voodoo economics" 259
Voting Rights Act 60, 62, 65, 84, 230

Wagner, Robert 40
Wagner Act 44, 318
Walker, Herbert 257
Wallace, Henry 34, 114
Wall Street Journal 79
Wall Street Reform and Consumer Protection Act (Dodd-Frank, 2010) 182–183
Wards Cove Packing Co. v. Antonio 270
War on Poverty program 52, 58–59, 64, 65
Warshaw, Shirley Anne 262
Washington, George 5
Washington community 4
Watergate 220, 221, 223, 231–232, 234, 243, 338
Watson, Jack 243
Watt, James 74, 83
Watts riots 53
Welch, Laura 92
welfare: reforms 288; relief and Social Security 40–43; Social Security and health 161–162, 228–229, 250–251
Wexler, Anne 245
White, Walter 44

White, William 120
White House 6, 7, 9, 329; Biden, Joe 298–299; Bush, George H. W. 259; Bush, George W. 90, 93; Carter, Jimmy 237, 238, 240, 241; Clinton, Bill 274, 277–278, 287, 290, 291; Eisenhower, Dwight David 141, 143; Johnson, Lyndon B. 52, 55, 57; Kennedy, John F. 156, 158, 160, 164; Nixon, Richard 221, 226, 232; Obama, Barack 174; Reagan, Ronald 69, 76, 77; Roosevelt, Franklin Delano 29–30, 37; Truman, Harry S. 113–115, 124, 126; Trump, Donald 190, 195, 202, 205
Whitewater 283, 288
Whitman, Todd 104–105
Wills, Garry 29, 34
Wilson, Joan Hoff 217
Wilson, Joe 179
Wilson, Woodrow 31–32, 221, 237
"windows of opportunity" 14
Wirthlin, Richard 329
Witte, John 147, 227
Wofford, Harris 165
Works Progress Administration (WPA) 35
World Health Organization 300
World War I 28, 114, 123, 132
World War II 13, 32, 42, 45, 123, 124, 132, 155, 218, 239, 256
Wright, Jeremiah 174
Wyman, Jane 70

Young, Todd 304

"zero-sum game" 240
"zero-tolerance" immigration policy 204
Zients, Jeff 298

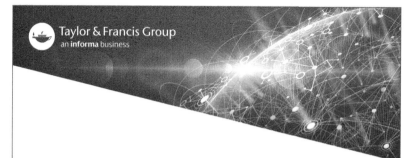